THE HUNT FOR HITLER'S WARSHIP

THE HUNT FOR HITLER'S WARSHIP

PATRICK BISHOP

REGNERY
HISTORY

Regnery History™ is a trademark of Salem Communications Holding Corporation; Regnery® is a registered trademark of Salem Communications Holding Corporation

First Regnery paperback edition published 2015: ISBN 978-1-62157-290-9
First Regnery edition published in hardcover, 2013: ISBN 978-1-62157-003-5

Cataloging-in-Publication data on file with the Library of Congress

Published in the United States by
Regnery History
An imprint of Regnery Publishing
A Division of Salem Media Group
300 New Jersey Ave NW
Washington, DC 20001
www.RegneryHistory.com

Originally published in 2012 by Harper*Press*
        An imprint of HarperCollins*Publishers*
        77–85 Fulham Palace Road
        Hammersmith, London W6 8JB

Manufactured in the United States of America

10 9 8 7 6 5 4 3 2 1

Books are available in quantity for promotional or premium use. For information on discounts and terms, please visit our website: www.Regnery.com.

Distributed to the trade by
Perseus Distribution
250 West 57th Street
New York, NY 10107

To Tony and Mary

CONTENTS

Maps and Illustrations ix

Ranks of the Kriegsmarine xx

Prologue xxi

CHAPTER 1   The Belly of the Beast 1

CHAPTER 2   Wilhelmshaven, Saturday, April 1, 1939 9

CHAPTER 3   Swordfish 19

CHAPTER 4   Trondheim 43

CHAPTER 5   "A Wonderful Chance" 67

CHAPTER 6   "A Somewhat Desperate Venture" 89

CHAPTER 7   Smoke and Fog. 107

CHAPTER 8   Provoking Nemesis 125

CHAPTER 9   "A Heart-Shaking" Decision. 147

CHAPTER 10   A Ha'Porth of Tar. 163

CHAPTER 11   The Iron Castle. 191

CHAPTER 12   Enter the Lion. 207

CHAPTER 13   Madmen 227

CHAPTER 14 The Great Adventure 255

CHAPTER 15 A "Bloody Great Bang" 269

CHAPTER 16 North Cape 291

CHAPTER 17 Tungsten 311

CHAPTER 18 The Third Man 335

CHAPTER 19 "My God Mac, They've Had It Today" 361

Epilogue 391

Acknowledgments 397

Notes 399

Index 413

MAPS AND ILLUSTRATIONS

Northern Waters . . . . x–xi

The Northern Front. xii

Trondheim Area. xiii

Battleship *Tirpitz* . . . . xiv–xv

Tirpitz Armament . . . . xvi–xvii

X-Craft . . . . xviii–xix

Loire Estuary and St Nazaire 93

Convoy PQ.17 157

Operation Source. 286

The Battle of North Cape 307

The Final Attack. 376

Interpretation Report S.A. 2923. 378

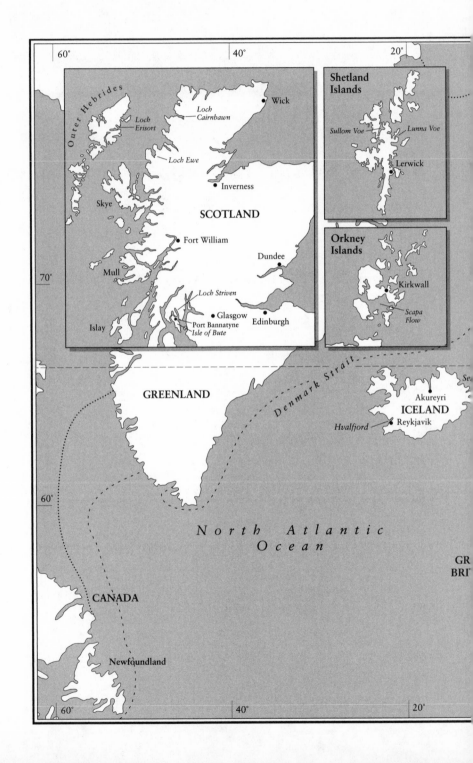

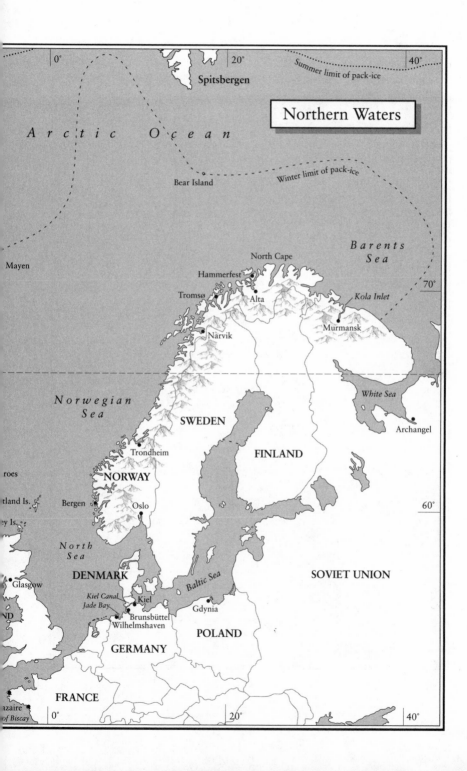

0°   20°   Summer limit of pack-ice   40°

Spitsbergen

Northern Waters

A r c t i c   O c e a n

Bear Island   Winter limit of pack-ice

B a r e n t s
S e a

Mayen   North Cape

Hammerfest
Tromsø   Alta   Kola Inlet   70°

Narvik   Murmansk

N o r w e g i a n
S e a   White Sea

SWEDEN
Trondheim   FINLAND   Archangel

roes
NORWAY

tland Is.
y Is.   Bergen   Oslo   60°

N o r t h
S e a

DENMARK   *Baltic Sea*   SOVIET UNION

Glasgow
Kiel Canal   Kiel
Jade Bay   Gdynia
ND
Brunsbüttel
Wilhelmshaven   POLAND

GERMANY

FRANCE   0°   20°   40°
azaire
of Biscay

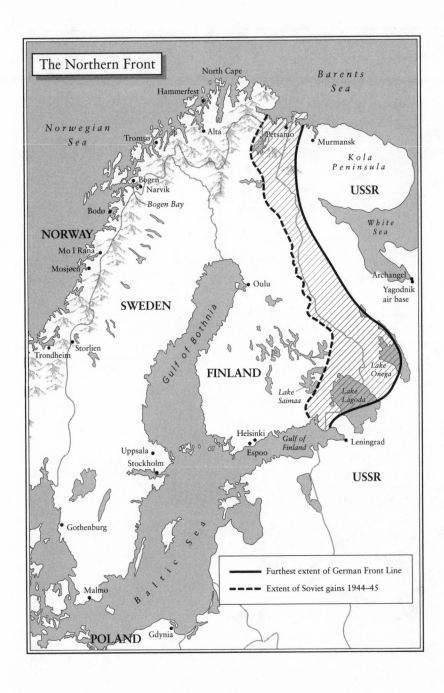

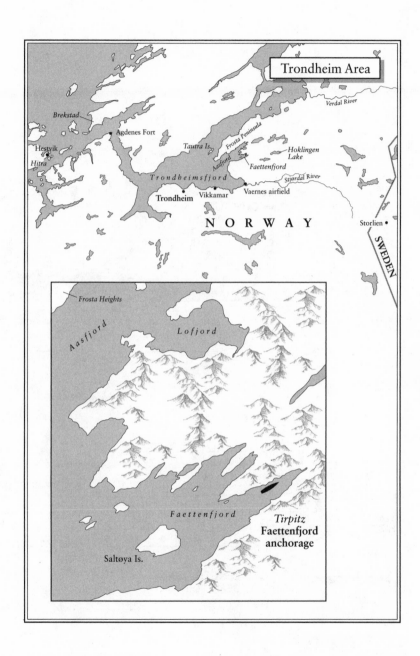

Trondheim Area

Verdal River

Brekstad

Agdenes Fort

Tautra Is.

Frosta Peninsula

Hoklingen Lake

Aasfjord

Faettenfjord

Hestvik

Hitra

Trondheimsfjord

Stjørdal River

Vikkamar

Vaernes airfield

Trondheim

N O R W A Y

Storlien •

SWEDEN

Frosta Heights

Aasfjord

Lofjord

Faettenfjord

Tirpitz
Faettenfjord
anchorage

Saltøya Is.

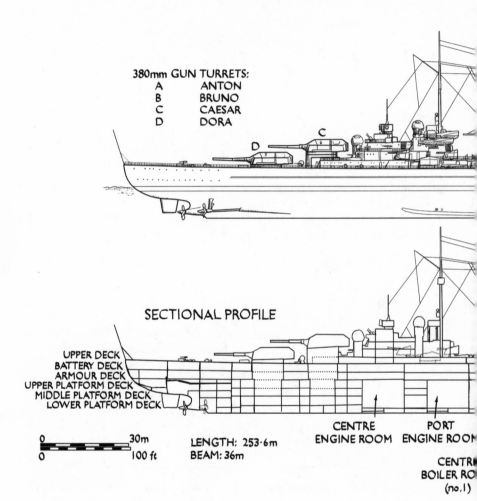

380mm GUN TURRETS:
A   ANTON
B   BRUNO
C   CAESAR
D   DORA

SECTIONAL PROFILE

UPPER DECK
BATTERY DECK
ARMOUR DECK
UPPER PLATFORM DECK
MIDDLE PLATFORM DECK
LOWER PLATFORM DECK

0   30m
0   100 ft

LENGTH: 253·6m
BEAM: 36m

CENTRE
ENGINE ROOM

PORT
ENGINE ROOM

CENTR
BOILER RO
(no.1)

BATTLESHIP *TIRPITZ*

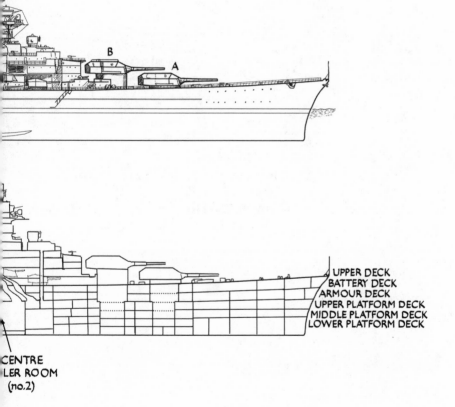

B

A

UPPER DECK
BATTERY DECK
ARMOUR DECK
UPPER PLATFORM DECK
MIDDLE PLATFORM DECK
LOWER PLATFORM DECK

CENTRE
LER ROOM
(no.2)

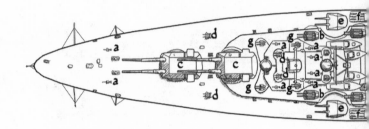

a 20 mm/L65 MG C/30 Single
b 105 mm/L65 SK-C/37
c 380 mm/L48.5 SK-C/34
d 20 mm/L65 MG C/38 Quadruple

TIRPITZ ARMAMENT
MARCH 1943

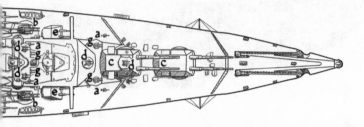

e   150 mm/L55 SK-C/28 End Turret
f   G7a T1 (Torpedo Launcher)
g   37 mm/L83 SK-C/30
h   150 mm/L55 SK-C/28 Middle Turret

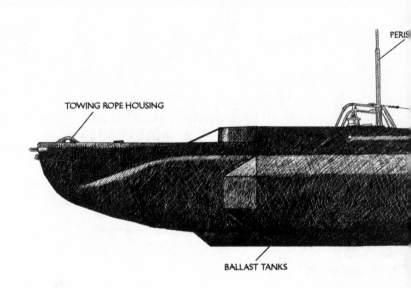

TOWING ROPE HOUSING

PERIS

BALLAST TANKS

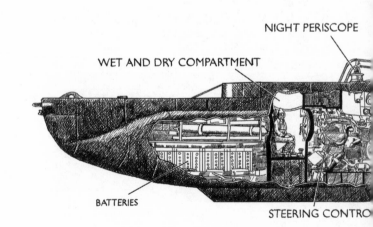

NIGHT PERISCOPE

WET AND DRY COMPARTMENT

BATTERIES

STEERING CONTRO

X-CRAFT

CHARGE

PROPELLOR

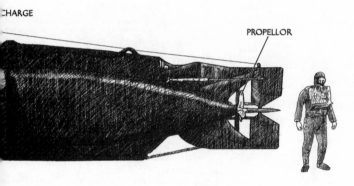

SCOPE

HYDROPLANE AND MAIN MOTOR CONTROLS

AFTER HATCH   DIESEL ENGINE

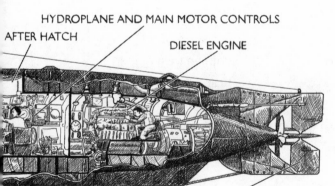

RUDDER AND HYDROPLANES

RANKS OF THE KRIEGSMARINE

Seamen

Matrose	Ordinary Seaman
Matrosen-Gefreiter	Able Seaman
Matrosen-Obergefreiter	Leading Seaman
Matrosen-Hauptgefreiter	Senior Leading Seaman

Warrant Officers

Bootsmann	Boatswain
Oberbootsmann	Chief Boatswain
Stabsoberbootsmann	Senior Chief Boatswain

Officers

Fähnrich zur See	Midshipman
Oberfähnrich zur See	Sub-Lieutenant
Leutnant zur See	Lieutenant (Junior)
Oberleutnant zur See	Lieutenant (Senior)
Kapitänleutnant	Lieutenant Commander
Korvettenkapitän	Commander
Fregattenkapitän	Captain (Junior)
Kapitän zur See	Captain (Senior)
Konteradmiral	Rear Admiral
Vizeadmiral	Vice Admiral
Generaladmiral	No equivalent
Grossadmiral	Admiral of the Fleet

PROLOGUE

The shortest memorandum in Winston Churchill's vast wartime output of queries, instructions, and exhortations is three words long. On Monday, December 14, 1942, he wrote to the First Sea Lord, Sir Dudley Pound, demanding: "Where is TIRPITZ?" The reply was reassuring. She was stuck safely in a Norwegian fjord near Trondheim undergoing repairs. Far from getting ready for a potentially devastating sortie, the crew was busy decorating the messes in preparation for Christmas.

The terse tone of the memo reveals a tremor of alarm. Churchill's manner, both real and contrived, radiated unflappability, even in the face of towering danger. Yet throughout her life this one battleship, the last of Hitler's fleet, could disturb his calm, nagging at his thoughts when it might be imagined he had bigger concerns to worry about. His wish to see it sunk, or at least disabled, bordered on the obsessive. The archives contain a stream of calls for action addressed to admirals and air marshals. A note from Churchill's office dated January 22, 1942, reports that "the Prime Minister rang up the First Sea Lord and instructed him to see tonight the Chief of the Air Staff and concert means for making an attack on the TIRPITZ." It goes on to record his opinion "that the crippling of this ship would alter the entire face of the naval war and that the loss of 100 machines or 500 airmen would be well compensated for."

In the cruel ledger of war, this, at the time, would have counted as a bargain. The destruction of no other enemy asset would absorb so many resources and so much time and energy. As long as *Tirpitz* was afloat she cast a shadow over British naval planning, mesmerizing the Home Fleet and forcing its most powerful ships to keep a constant watch against a breakout into the Atlantic, where, in the anxious eyes of those watching her, she might cut Britain's transatlantic lifeline.

Fear of her destructive power inspired a heroic feat of arms, the blowing up of the St Nazaire dock in March 1942, thus depriving the battleship of a haven should it ever make it into the Atlantic. It also triggered the shaming decision a few months later to abandon Convoy PQ.17 to its fate when it was thought that *Tirpitz* was at sea.

The effort to deal with her was unrelenting. Between October 1940 and November 1944 she was the target of twenty-four major air and sea operations. They ranged from heavy bombers' conventional attacks to human torpedoes' and midget submarines' innovative operations that even in wartime seemed risky to the point of being suicidal. Churchill's prodding produced other schemes, even more hazardous and fanciful, that mercifully were never implemented.

Whether the prize was worth the cost is open to question. Churchill's determination, though, ensured that it would be paid in full. The actions that followed produced one of the great dramas of the war, testing the limits of human courage and folly. This is that story.

CHAPTER 1

THE BELLY
OF THE BEAST

A t 8:30 a.m. on the morning of November 12, 1944, the gun crews and lookouts on the decks of the battleship *Tirpitz* stood at their action stations staring intently into the eastern sky. It was a crisp, clear day. The sunlight sparkled on the waters of the Norwegian fjord in which they lay anchored, close to a small, humped island smudged with the first snow of winter. A few minutes before there had been a clamor of bells and blaring loudspeakers as an air raid warning was announced.

Below deck in the gunnery fire control section a young midshipman called Alfred Zuba was reading a book on German history when the alarm was sounded. He put it aside and waited for information about the approaching aircraft to start crackling in the earphones clamped to his head. The first report placed the raiders less than twenty miles away to the southeast, flying at an estimated 9,000 feet. The details changed fast. The aircraft were closing rapidly. Like everyone on board, he knew what they were—Lancaster bombers, carrying big new bombs that exploded with the destructive power of an earthquake. Nonetheless, he felt confident. *Tirpitz* had dealt with a similar attack a fortnight before, and there was a squadron of fighter aircraft nearby tō protect her. As yet, though, there was no sign that they were flying to the rescue. When the raiders were nearly thirteen miles away, the ship opened fire on the attackers. The first salvo erupted from "Anton" and "Bruno," the forward turrets each housing two 15-inch guns hurling shells that weighed almost a ton each and whose force made *Tirpitz* vibrate like a tuning fork.

Above decks, men were shouting and pointing excitedly at a cluster of small dots, black and ominous against the sky's innocent blue. The heavy anti-aircraft guns and their light flak opened up and the stink of burned powder filled the air.

Then, over the industrial thud of artillery and the clatter of cascading shell cases, a different noise was heard. A deep, elemental thunderclap rolled over the decks and echoed through the passageways and stairwells. It was followed by another. It seemed to Zuba that the great craft was "staggering." She was being "shaken by giant fists."

In an instant the atmosphere of quiet efficiency inside the steel walls of his battle station was swept away, and everywhere was "disorder, confusion, mess, chaos—the bedlam of near and distant noises." The deck below him began to tilt, and he had to cling to a bulkhead to stop himself from falling. He called the central flak control station but got only silence. Nearby, Oberleutnant[1] Ludwig Mettegang, a twenty-three-year-old communications officer, was scrambling up the sloping floor to reach the emergency telephone that connected with the bridge. This line was still working. Mettegang demanded information and instructions, shouting to be heard over the din of explosions and the shriek of tortured metal. The thirty men around him, crouching in the gathering darkness as the lights flickered and died, watched and listened. They were on the lowest deck of the ship. To reach the outside world meant climbing through four levels up a succession of ladders. Mettegang turned to them with some dismaying news. The orders from the bridge were that they were to stay at their posts. Then came "new terrific hits, new gigantic shakings." Mettegang was shouting, "Get out! Now!"

Zuba described how he "tore the phones from my head. I took my gas mask and rushed to the emergency exit. Fifteen, twenty men were standing there. Everybody wants to go up, wants to get out—out to life, to escape from death! But there is only room for one at a time ... so we are standing there and waiting for our turn."

As he shuffled forward he could feel the "bottom burning under our feet." Then it was his turn, and he was "clambering through, along the pitch-dark narrow hold" that led to the gun deck. As he reached the next hatchway the ship made another sickening lurch. He slid down the linoleum-covered floor, slippery with oil and water, away from the exit. Water was tumbling into the compartment, "black and oily," reaching up to his chest. He felt "death take hold of me with iron hands." He yelled for a lifebelt, but no one could help. He scrambled on the slick linoleum as "more and more water comes streaming in, holds me tight and does not let me go." He could feel the shock of more explosions shaking the ship. At last he "found a handhold and pulled myself up. A comrade stretched out his hand to me so I could reach a ventilator [pipe]." The respite was short. The ship slumped again. The pipe that had been upright was now horizontal, and he was hanging above the water swirling below. The weight of his sodden clothes was dragging him down and he could "literally feel the strength draining out of my fingers." Zuba had decided that in "a few minutes then it will be over" when the ship shifted again. His dangling feet found another pipe, and he was standing upright once more. Someone was shouting that everyone should go back through the emergency exit. He could see the opening but to reach it he would have to leap six feet over the inky, freezing water. He braced to jump, knowing that, if he fell short, "death was waiting underneath … my knees were trembling." In this fatal moment an absurd concern floated into his mind. Somewhere along the way he had lost his cap. He pushed the thought aside and jumped. Then he was hauling himself through the hatchway. There was a thud as another man landed behind him, missed his footing and slipped, leaving him hanging there with the water lapping at his feet. Zuba went back to help him. He recognized him, a seaman called Hegendorf. The ordeal was only beginning but Hegendorf had already had enough. "He was crying 'Let me go, I must die.' 'Don't talk nonsense,' I answered. I pulled him out through the hatchway. He was very heavy. Then we closed the exit to stop the water."

They climbed through the bowels of the ship, collecting other survivors on the way, until they reached a mess room. A young sub-lieutenant, Willi Völsing, the senior officer in the gunnery fire control section, took charge. He told Zuba and the others to stay put while he took a party off to search for a way out. They sat down to wait. At least they were out of the water and had air to breathe. Someone found a battery lamp which gave a little light. There was silence. They "tried to be calm. Nobody wanted to show what they were thinking about." The one exception was Hegendorf who was a "bundle of nerves." Zuba tried to calm him down. He took no notice, only stopping when Völsing returned and warned him that he would shoot him if he did not shut up.

Völsing took Zuba aside "and said to me in a low voice, 'It's no use. We can't get out. We've been searching everywhere.'" For the benefit of the others though, the sub-lieutenant put on a brave face, announcing loudly, "We'll find some way out. I won't abandon this fight." Now Zuba took over the search. He and his team found their way into the A Deck radio room where there were more survivors whom he led back to join the others. During their search they had found another lamp and some dry clothes. Zuba stripped off his uniform and put on white underpants, green trousers, and a blue mechanic's jacket, which made him look "like a comic actor." They had also found bread, coffee, cognac, sweets, and a large box of cigarettes.

For a while their fear lifted and their spirits rose. "Suddenly someone said, 'Good Lord, today is my birthday.' We all congratulated him." It seemed to Zuba, though, that many were thinking "let us hope your birthday is not your death day as well." The "birthday boy was allowed to take the first big swig. Then it was the turn of the others."

They sat, warmed by the cognac, chewing coffee beans. One of the wireless operators, "a regular brick, calmness itself," gave an optimistic assessment of their situation. He was sure that everything was being done to save them—they would have to be patient until the cutting gear arrived. The ship was 118 feet wide and the water she lay in was shallow. Now that she had keeled over, "there is always going to be a bit sticking out of the water."

Soon afterwards the wireless operator's prediction seemed about to come true. Zuba heard "a knocking somewhere—bang, bang, bang." Someone seized a fire extinguisher and began knocking back, but the noises got weaker and faded away. Their spirits slumped again. They sat in the cold metal box, each alone with his thoughts. Zuba worried how his mother would take the news of his death. His brother had been killed a year and three days before on the Eastern Front. What would the effect be on his fiancée Ruth who, when he had told her that he was being posted to *Tirpitz*, "was glad because she thought that being on a battle-ship was safer"?

Someone blurted out, "'If I get out of here I will get married at once.' Now they all start saying what they intend to do if they get out." While the others gabbled, though, hope was ebbing from Zuba. He could hear the rush of water. Then one of the radio operators noticed it too. He began asking "again and again, 'is the water rising?'" The others told him to shut up. They sat sunken in silence. Then, over the sinister gurgling, they heard men calling out.

They shouted back together, "where are you?" A chorus of voices came back but the reply was indistinct. The yelling continued. Finally they understood what they were saying. Their unseen comrades were trapped in Switch Room 3. Zuba and his companions shouted back that they were in the forward mess, but there was no answering call. They sank back into silence.

Then, someone thought they heard other voices and a sharp hissing noise. It sounded, he said, like gas from an oxyacetylene torch. To Zuba, though, it seemed more likely to be the rustle of invading water. Others, though, seized on this rope end of hope. A leading seaman took the fire extinguisher and smashed through the compartment wall nearest to where the noise was coming from, only to be faced with a slab of thick steel. Zuba could hear the hissing more clearly now. It was stopping and starting. He began to think that "it could come from cutting apparatus ... again there is hissing, crackling and banging."

They started yelling again, "shouting 'hurry up, the water is rising.'" Their room was still dry but they could see the compartment below them filling up. Zuba felt they were "in a running race with death." The torch noises were getting closer, though. Someone "puts his hand on the steel wall. It is quite warm. 'Hurry!' we shout."

Then, a molten red spot appeared on the wall, followed by a shower of sparks. They shouted with joy "like little boys" as the glowing line crept along the wall. They were "staring at it, drinking in every centimeter of its growth," when "suddenly the hissing stopped. We heard voices moving away. There was a deathly silence around us."

The captives shouted in dismay. They screamed and banged on the cold steel walls of their prison, but "there is no answer, only the echo of our desperate shouting." In the darkness below they could make out a "mirror of black gleaming water" rising towards them.

Just as despair settled over him, Zuba heard more banging and sparks sprayed from the wall. A molten spot reappeared and slowly traced a glowing rectangle. There was a clang of falling metal and faces appeared in the hole. Their saviors looked "as if they had come from another world." The hole was only sixteen inches wide. Each man had to be pushed and pulled through it. They emerged into another space with a ladder leading upwards. When Zuba reached the top he saw a square in the metal above him and, through it, the sky. It was evening. The stars "were twinkling, a sight I will never forget." He climbed up and out into the freezing night, "standing free and saved and sucking … air into my lungs."

He was standing on a vast expanse of red-leaded metal. It took him a moment to realize it was the hull of the ship. As he was led away a soldier told him why the rescue had been broken off. Working in the cramped space between the hull and the lower deck, the welders had started to pass out from lack of oxygen. The twenty survivors were put on a launch and taken off to another ship, where they were fed and bathed and clothed. Zuba was anxious to know the fate of the men he was with when the ship began to topple. Leutnant Mettegang was still missing, believed trapped with twenty-four men. The next day, when Zuba asked again for news, he was told that they were dead. According to the story that went around, the rescue team had been able to hear the trapped men but not to reach them. They had been singing "Deutschland, Deutschland, Über Alles" before they suffocated.[2]

CHAPTER 2

WILHELMSHAVEN, SATURDAY, APRIL 1, 1939

Adolf Hitler descended from a Mercedes limousine and strode along the dockside beneath the slipway supporting the gigantic hull. His face wore an expression of childish delight as he looked up at the soaring flank of his new battleship, then turned to salute the crowds packed in thousands in orderly squares alongside. They had been brought in from all over Germany's ever-expanding territories to provide the numbers needed for a theatrical display of might, and they played their part enthusiastically—cheering, waving swastika pennants, and pressing forward for a glimpse of the leader as he strode past.

He skipped up the steps to a high platform raised before the bow. It was a bright, sunny day, but a cold wind whipping in from Jade Bay snapped at the flags and bunting and rattled the still-bare branches of the trees. Surrounding him on the platform was a cluster of admirals and generals. Among them, wearing a cloche hat and a fur stole, stood a lone woman. Frau Ilse von Hassell was there to name the ship in honor of her father, Admiral Alfred von Tirpitz, the architect of the Imperial German navy. She was a reluctant participant. Her husband Ulrich, a diplomat, had watched the ascent of the Nazis with dismay. The head of the modern German fleet, Admiral Erich Raeder, had first asked Tirpitz's seventy-eight-year-old widow Marie to perform the ceremony, but she claimed to be too old and infirm to attend. He turned next to Ilse and her younger sister Margot but they too declined. Ilse recalled that he then "sent a second appeal, urgently demanding my presence. It was practically an order. I need not explain ... what such an order meant in those times in Germany."[1]

The Führer and the admiral's daughter stood in the blustery wind for a minute or so in uncomfortable silence. Eventually he looked down at the sea of joyful, upturned faces and, "in a sort of monotone," murmured "I have sent trains to all parts of Germany, of Austria, of Czecho-slovakia. It is the best propaganda." An official called her forward to the microphone. In a clear voice she declared: "By order of the Führer and Supreme Commander of the Wehrmacht, I christen you with the name 'Tirpitz.'" The bottle swung and smashed. A large, hand-lettered sign reading TIRPITZ in Gothic script was lowered over the side. Then the hull began to move slowly, gathering speed as it went stern-first down Slipway Number 2, hitting the basin in a maelstrom of churning water. Only the steel vanes welded onto the sides and sticking out like elephants' ears prevented a collision with the far jetty. The cheers of the crowd mingled with "Deutschland Über Alles" blaring from loudspeakers as the notables descended the steps and were driven to the town hall square for the next event.

The day was charged with nervous expectation. The world was watching Wilhelmshaven. Europe was sliding toward war, and Hitler's words might give a sign of how fast or slow the catastrophe would be in coming. The omens were not good. The previous day Britain had abandoned its policy of appeasement. The decision had been forced by Hitler's demand that Poland hand over the free city of Danzig, pried from Germany by the Treaty of Versailles. Prime Minister Neville Chamberlain, who had stood by timidly as the Reich swallowed Austria and Czechoslovakia, at last made a stand, telling the House of Commons that Britain and France would lend Poland "all the support in their power" if Germany attacked.

The about-face triggered a Wagnerian rage. Hitler had hoped he would not have to go to war against the British. Admiral Canaris, the head of German Military Intelligence who was with him when the news came through, watched as he pounded his fists on a marble table, his face contorted with anger, shouting that he would "cook them a stew they'll choke on."[2] Around noon, Hitler began the speech everyone was waiting for. Wilhelmshaven's main square had been decked out with flags and banners, Nuremberg-style. Reporters in the press area noticed something they had not seen before at such events. Hitler was standing behind a curved glass screen, apparently designed to protect him from an assassin's bullet.

His speech was long and disjointed, now soft, now hard, swinging between cajolery and bluster. Its main theme, though, was Britain, or "England" as Germans chose to call it. The change of heart in London amounted to a declaration of enmity. Instead of staying on the sidelines as Hitler had hoped, Britain, its army and above all its navy would now have to be counted in the forces arrayed against his plans for European domination.

He started by reopening an old wound. He reminded the crowd that during the last war the British had "systematically" encircled Germany, imposing a "hunger blockade" that had resulted in hundreds of thousands of deaths. Now, by blocking her efforts to reclaim her historic territories, she was seeking to do so again. Germany, he warned, was "not going to put up in the long run with a policy of intimidation or ... of encirclement."

The warning was reinforced by a threat aimed at the British navy— which had enforced the wartime blockade. Only four years before, Britain and Germany had made a naval pact that limited the size of the German fleet. It had been based, he said, "on the fervent desire we all possess never to go to war with England." He went on, "If this wish no longer exists in England, then the practical condition for this agreement is removed." The German people would be "quite content to put up with this. We are so sure of ourselves because we are so strong and we are strong because we are united."[3]

The speech ended in a volley of "sieg heils" ("Hail Victory!"). Hitler was driven away to board a launch which sped out into the sparkling waters of Jade Bay, carrying him to the battle cruiser *Scharnhorst*, which had gone into service less than three months before and seemed to embody all the power and vigor of the new order. There he met Erich Raeder, carrying the baton which marked his promotion that day to the rank of Grossadmiral—the highest pinnacle of the naval hierarchy.

At 2:30 p.m. they sat down to eat, flanked by admirals and generals past and present. The exaltation that flooded through Hitler during great public performances had subsided and he appeared subdued. "He arrived, saluted, sat down, spoke to his neighbours and disappeared as he had arrived," wrote Ulrich von Hassell[4] in his diary. "He said not a word to any of the old officers, nor did he even look them in the eye."[5]

After lunch Hitler was ferried to another ship, the *Robert Ley*, a large liner that took party loyalists on holiday cruises. He stayed on board throughout Sunday, while the ship tacked back and forth in the waters off Wilhelmshaven, escorted by *Scharnhorst* and a pair of destroyers. To amuse the Führer, Raeder at one point ordered the battle cruiser to steer directly at the liner, only swerving away at the last minute.[6]

These carefree activities seemed calculated to demonstrate Hitler's lack of concern at the new international developments. Whether he understood their full import for the navy he was reviewing was open to question. Naval matters played a subordinate role in Hitler's military calculations; an attitude he did not bother to disguise. He was a soldier not a sailor. Throughout the time at Wilhelmshaven he had worn a brown greatcoat and tunic, the color of the Flanders mud he had fought in bravely which stood out against the navy blue and gold braid of the attendant admirals. He came from landlocked Austria and was often seasick on his occasional voyages aboard the state yacht *Grille*.

Grossadmiral Raeder, though, was disturbed by the turn that events had taken. The son of a devoutly Christian teacher, he had been born sixty-three years before in Hamburg and entered the Naval College at Kiel at eighteen. The Dreadnought era was approaching when great battleships, bristling with guns and laden with armor plating, were the peak of naval power and prestige. He fought the British at Dogger Bank and Jutland and remained in the navy, serving the Weimar Republic loyally. In 1928 he was appointed Commander in Chief of the Kriegsmarine, the German navy.

Raeder kept his distance from Hitler until he came to power. His first impression of him was favorable. Hitler seemed to him "an outstanding personality with a real claim to leadership."[7] He had gained the Führer's confidence and, once the strategic decisions had been taken, had been given a free hand and a generous budget to build up the navy. Hitler had been presented with two choices for his navy. The first proposed a cheap, light, flexible force, centered on submarines and the small but powerfully armed long-range cruisers that the British had nicknamed "pocket battleships." This plan had no pretensions to challenging Britain as a naval power but carried great potential to harm her. The second was to build a big fleet of modern surface ships that would establish Germany as a world maritime force. He had chosen the grandiose option, with Raeder's approval. The result was "Plan Z," which Hitler had finally agreed to only two months before. It envisaged a fleet with ten battleships at its core and four aircraft carriers to provide the air power that was becoming a vital adjunct of naval operations. Supporting them would be fifteen pocket battleships, over a hundred cruisers and destroyers, and an underwater strength of more than 250 U-boats.

A force of this size would take up to ten years to build. The plan had been designed on the assumption, reinforced by Hitler's frequent assurances, that a war with Britain was still well over the horizon. Only four years before, the two countries had signed the Anglo-German Naval Agreement, which Hitler mentioned in his speech. Germany agreed to limit its surface ship-building program to 35 percent of the British fleet and its submarines to 45 percent of the Royal Navy's tonnage, with a clause allowing it to rise to parity in special circumstances. The deal was negotiated in a friendly atmosphere. Historically, both sides had felt respect for one another. When the commander of the British Fleet at Jutland, Lord Jellicoe, died in November 1935, Raeder ordered all German warships to fly their flags at half-mast.

A confrontation with the Royal Navy had seemed a distant prospect when Plan Z was being worked out. Now, with Chamberlain's guarantee to the Poles, it loomed suddenly and alarmingly into view. Raeder's exalted title scarcely reflected the might of his fleet. As he waved his landlubber leader off at the end of his Wilhelmshaven jaunt, he knew very well that he had limited assets with which to face the coming crisis.

The German fleet that spring had only two big ships in service—the battle cruisers *Scharnhorst* and *Gneisenau*, both weighing 32,000 tons. (All displacements are given as standard: minus the weight of fuel, water, and stores that would be carried on voyage.) There was a heavy cruiser, the 14,000-ton *Admiral Hipper*, which would be joined in the coming year by two ships of the same class, the *Blücher* and the *Prinz Eugen*.

Three pocket battleships were in commission, the *Deutschland, Admiral Graf Spee,* and *Admiral Scheer.* Despite weighing only 12,000 tons, they packed heavy firepower in their six 11-inch guns. Of the four planned aircraft carriers, only one, the *Graf Zeppelin,* had been retired, but years of work remained. As for submarines, about fifty would be ready for operations by the summer's end.

In numerical terms, this was a tiny force compared with the Royal Navy. It could muster twelve battleships with five more on the way, four battle cruisers, six aircraft carriers with another six under construction, and twenty-four heavy cruisers. Numbers were only equal below the waves.

But strength was not measured in numbers alone. The qualitative difference between the two fleets went a long way towards correcting the quantitative imbalance. The core of the German fleet was modern, whereas many of the British ships dated back to the previous war and only some of them had been updated. The new ships in the pipeline were inferior to their German counterparts. Britain, it would often be lamented in the years to come, had played the game squarely when it came to honoring the limitations agreements it had made in the interwar years. The Germans, on the other hand, had systematically and ruthlessly cheated.

All of Germany's large ships were bigger than they were supposed to be. The *Scharnhorst* and *Gneisenau* were actually 6,000 tons heavier than officially claimed. The extra weight came from the thick armor plating which reduced the danger from the British battle cruisers' heavier guns. They were also faster than claimed and could muster thirty-one knots, which gave them the edge over their counterparts if forced to run.

It was in the top class—the battleships—that German superiority was most marked. Since *Tirpitz* and her sister ship *Bismarck* were retired in 1936, the German Embassy in London had lied to the Foreign Office about their specifications on Raeder's instructions. Instead of being

35,000 tons—the upper limit decided upon in the Anglo-German Naval Agreement—they would both weigh in at 42,500 tons. The British, by contrast, stuck to the rules. As a result the battleships of the *King George V* (KGV) class under construction were nearly 12 percent lighter than their German counterparts.

It was not merely a question of size. When finished, *Tirpitz* and *Bismarck* would best the Royal Navy's new ships in every department. They each mounted eight 15-inch guns against the 14-inch main armament of the *King George V*. They were faster and could travel much greater distances without refueling. They were also immensely well protected, with thick layers of steel armor encasing decks and hull, turrets, engine rooms, and magazines. Their enemies often said that the Germans had declared their battleships "unsinkable." The claim does not seem to have been made officially. The builders revealed after the war that the Kriegsmarine often intervened during the building of *Tirpitz* and *Bismarck* to "raise their levels of unsinkability."[8] The result was that, in the case of *Tirpitz*, 40 percent of her overall weight was made up of armor plating. The belief grew that *Tirpitz* and *Bismarck* could survive any torpedo, shell, or bomb that the British ships or aircraft could hurl at them—and it was not unfounded. The British navy had been starved of funds in the postwar years and little effort had been made to develop new weaponry. Torpedoes and shells carried feeble charges and lacked penetrative power. The greatest failure to keep pace with technological developments lay in the area of naval aviation. The Admiralty was only now regaining control of the Fleet Air Arm from the RAF, whose equipment programs had given priority to fighters and bombers. The navy was entering the war equipped with biplanes that looked like survivors from the previous conflict.

Even with his long-term plan in tatters and *Tirpitz* and *Bismarck* still far from completion, Raeder could still cause Britain great harm. The Royal Navy suffered from a crucial strategic disadvantage. Britain depended for survival on its seaborne trade. The navy had the duty of protecting a web of routes that stretched to all corners of the globe. Germany, as a continental power, was far less reliant on overseas supplies. If it came to war, its navy's responsibility was clearer and narrower. Its function was not to protect but to attack, ravaging the sea lanes that linked Britain to the rest of the world.

As the countdown to hostilities accelerated, it was the powerful German warships rather than the U-boat fleet that the Admiralty most feared. "Nothing would paralyse our supply system and seaborne trade so successfully," wrote the First Sea Lord Sir Dudley Pound just before the outbreak, "as attack by surface raiders." It was to their detection, pursuit, and destruction that the Home Fleet turned as the long overture finished and the curtain went up on the war.

CHAPTER 3

SWORDFISH

Caked with the salt of the northern seas, her flanks streaked with rust, HMS *Suffolk* slid gracefully towards the Icelandic haven of Hvalfjord. The heavy cruiser had been patrolling the Denmark Strait between Greenland and Iceland and her crew were looking forward to a quiet evening in harbor. Then a signal arrived warning them that their respite might be a short one. *Bismarck*, the ship they had been watching for, had been sighted at the Norwegian port of Bergen.

Upon arrival in Hvalfjord, *Suffolk* went off directly to refuel. The company were eating supper when another signal arrived. They were to return immediately to the Denmark Strait. The following morning, Friday, May 23, 1941, they met up with their sister ship *Norfolk* in the harbor at Isafjordur on the northwest coast of Iceland and headed off to take up their patrolling positions. The Strait was the most distant of the possible routes German warships could take from their own ports to the Atlantic. It was 300 miles long and 180 miles wide at its narrowest point, but even at this time of year it was still choked with pack ice which stretched eighty miles eastward from the Greenland coast.

The cruisers spent the day crisscrossing the sleeve of green water, flecked with floes, but saw nothing. Then, early that evening, the voice of Captain Robert Ellis sounded over the loudspeaker. He broadcast news that was both exciting and alarming. *Bismarck* had left Bergen. Her destination was unknown, but there was a strong chance she was heading their way. The ship's officers did not allow the revelation to disturb their sangfroid. They gathered, as usual, in the wardroom for a drink before dinner. The captain had just walked in to join them when a horn blared, calling all hands to their action stations. The officers slammed down their sherries and pink gins and dashed to their posts. "It was the enemy!" Lieutenant Commander Charles Collett recorded afterwards, "[and] they were only six miles away, slinking along the edge of the ice in a snowstorm."[1]

The moment that Winston Churchill and the Admiralty had been waiting for had arrived. *Bismarck* was at sea. Simultaneously, a great threat and a great opportunity had materialized. Sinking her would count as a magnificent naval victory. It would also provide some longed-for good news after a succession of setbacks, failures, and disappointments. The relief of surviving the Battle of Britain had given way to the bleak realization that the nation was isolated and faced immense difficulties ahead. The country was now engaged in another struggle for existence, which Churchill christened the Battle of the Atlantic. Having failed to bring Britain to terms by the threat of invasion, Germany had switched its strategy and was trying to starve her into submission by cutting off the lifelines that connected her with the rest of the world. Churchill said later that "amid the torrent of violent events one anxiety reigned supreme … dominating all our power to carry on the war, or even keep ourselves alive, lay mastery of the ocean routes and the free approach and entry to our ports."

It was the navy's principal duty to defend these routes but the task was overwhelming. It no longer had the resources of the French fleet, a large part of which lay at the bottom of Mers-el-Kebir harbor, sunk by British guns. America gave all the help it could, but it had yet to enter the war. Early engagements in the battle for Norway and on the high seas had failed to neutralize the threat from the German navy. Instead, in the spring of 1941, the Kriegsmarine was setting the pace in the struggle.

The main battleground was the vital sea lanes of the North Atlantic. In March and April 1941, nearly half a million tons of Allied shipping had been sent to the bottom. Most of it was sunk by U-boats, whose effectiveness a complacent Admiralty had badly underestimated in the interwar years. Until now the surface raiders that Admiral Pound had feared would "paralyse" the sea lanes had played a secondary part in the campaign. That seemed about to change. A foray by the battle cruisers *Scharnhorst* and *Gneisenau* in February and March had resulted in the destruction or capture of twenty-two ships totaling 115,600 tons. Now it was *Bismarck*'s turn and the transatlantic convoys, already ravaged by land-based bombers' bombardment and prowling U-boats' ambush, would be at the mercy of the most powerful German warship yet put to sea.

When the news of the sighting came through, Churchill was embarked on a weekend at Chequers with his wife Clementine, his daughter Sarah, her husband the comedian Vic Oliver, and the devoted Major General Hastings "Pug" Ismay, Churchill's Chief of Staff as Minister of Defence. Churchill had also invited W. Averell Harriman, President Roosevelt's special representative. Before dinner that Friday night the Prime Minister was pondering a stream of unwelcome reports from Crete. British resistance to the German invasion was faltering. After a poor start, the Germans were recovering. Paratroopers had seized the

vital airfield at Maleme and reinforcements were flying in. Luftwaffe
fighters and artillery units had begun to arrive that day. *Bismarck*'s detection raised hopes that some better tidings might be on the way. Churchill
waited up for the latest developments until 3:00 a.m. but eventually gave
up and went to bed.

The *Bismarck*'s breakout had been expected for days. An initial report
from Captain Henry Denham, the busy British naval attaché in neutral
Sweden, confirmed that the battleship had left the Baltic and the report
was soon reinforced by RAF sightings on reconnaissance flights and the
Bletchley Park code breakers' decryption of German naval signals.

The question was which way the *Bismarck* would come. There were
two possibilities. She could aim for the Denmark Strait or she could take
the shorter route and dart at the gap between the Faroe Islands and
Iceland. Commander of the Home Fleet Sir John Tovey had dispatched
Norfolk and *Suffolk* under the command of Rear Admiral William Wake-
Walker to deal with the first possibility. He simultaneously detached a
squadron under Vice Admiral Lancelot Holland, consisting of the battle
cruiser *Hood*, the battleship *Prince of Wales*, and six destroyers, to plug
the Faroes-Shetlands gap.

At first sight, this force was formidable. *Hood* was the biggest ship in
the British fleet. *Prince of Wales* was brand new—so new that she had
yet to complete preparations and still had workers from Vickers-
Armstrongs on board when she sailed. On the evening of May 22, Tovey
himself left Scapa Flow aboard his flagship *King George V*, and together
with the aircraft carrier *Victorious*, led the Home Fleet westward.

With the resources at his disposal, Tovey had every chance of intercepting *Bismarck* and bringing her to action. It was a thrilling prospect.
Great sea actions were rare, yet they were the unspoken end of all naval
training and preparation. From early adolescence, naval cadets were
steeped in stories about the legendary battles of Trafalgar and Gravelines,
against the Spanish Armada. Below decks, the pride in tradition, though

more subdued, was equally present. An epic battle offered those who fought in it the chance of distinction and those who directed it the prospect of greatness. Tovey knew that if he sank the *Bismarck* his place in the Royal Navy's history was assured. He knew, too, that his peers were harsh judges and that failure would bring ignominy.

The odds of an interception were in his favor. Even so, there was still a good chance that the *Bismarck* would reach the Atlantic unscathed. It had happened before. In February, *Scharnhorst* and *Gneisenau* had evaded the Home Fleet to squeeze through the Faroes-Iceland gap to begin their Atlantic raid. If *Bismarck* repeated the feat, a ripe cluster of targets awaited her. There were eleven convoys plying the Atlantic, some of them perilously close to *Bismarck*'s likely point of arrival in the ocean's northern reaches.

It was important for Hitler's long-term war plans that the battleship make it through. He was about to turn his armies eastward against the Soviet Union and he needed a cowed and docile Europe at his back. The war at sea presented the best chance of bringing his last enemy in the west to heel. The original operation, code-named Rheinübung, or Rhine Exercise, had been correspondingly ambitious. Admiral Raeder's plan had been to combine his four biggest ships in a powerful task force that could, temporarily at least, cause a suspension of the convoys, cutting off Britain's maritime life-support system. *Bismarck* and *Tirpitz* would sail from Germany and meet up with *Gneisenau* and *Scharnhorst*, now lying at Brest on the French Atlantic coast. One by one, though, his force had been whittled away. A lucky torpedo dropped from a RAF Coastal Command Beaufort had done *Gneisenau* enough damage to put her out of action for six months. Then the boilers powering *Scharnhorst*'s steam turbines needed replacing. The battleships would have to operate on their own. For each it would be their first maneuver.

One more blow was about to fall. *Tirpitz*'s progress from launch to commissioning had been slower than her sister's. She had finally gone into service on February 25 that year. Spring sea trials in the Baltic had revealed that she had numerous small mechanical difficulties. Raeder decided that he dared not risk her on a long and testing venture. The decision dismayed the crew and their new commander, Kapitän zur See Karl Topp. A fortnight before the Rhine Exercise was to start, Hitler paid a visit to the battleships as they lay at Gotenhafen, as the Germans called the Polish Baltic port of Gdynia. Topp begged him during the visit to overrule Raeder. Hitler refused. When *Bismarck* left Gotenhafen just before noon on May18, she had with her only a single big ship consort— the 14,000-ton heavy cruiser *Prinz Eugen* that, although new, had limited firepower and a short range.

The operation was led by Admiral Günther Lütjens, the commander of the German fleet. His reputation stood high. It was he who had led *Gneisenau* and *Scharnhorst* during their late winter rampage. Lütjens's down-turned mouth and hard eyes seldom broke into a smile. He looked what he was—cold, proud, and utterly confident of his abilities, rarely feeling the necessity to explain critical decisions to those above or below him. His abilities were tied to a strict sense of duty. He could be relied on to follow the spirit of his orders even when he doubted their wisdom. Lütjens was quite aware of the dangers ahead. His ship outclassed any vessel in the British fleet. But the task force he was commanding had shrunk to a fraction of its original strength. It seemed to him probable— even inevitable—that it would eventually be overwhelmed by sheer weight of numbers. Before the start of Rheinübung he had called on a friend at Raeder's Berlin headquarters to say goodbye. "I'll never come back," he told him in a matter-of-fact voice.[2]

The mood aboard *Bismarck*, though, was buoyant. The ship thrummed with excitement and anticipation as she headed out towards the Norwegian Sea. At noon, over the loudspeakers, the ship's commander Kapitän Ernst Lindemann at last told the 2,221 officers and men on board where they were going. "The day we have longed for so eagerly has at last arrived," he said. "The moment when we can lead our proud ship against the enemy. Our objective is commerce raiding in the Atlantic imperiling England's existence." He signed off with "the hunter's toast, good hunting and a good bag!" There was nothing about their methods that would be sporting, however. The orders Lindemann had received stated that "the work of destruction is not to be delayed by life-saving activities."[3]

Two days later, Lütjens's task force was two hundred miles off the Norwegian coast. Just after noon, ignoring the preferences of the headquarters staff who favored the Faroes-Iceland passage, he decided he would take the long way around to the Atlantic. He ordered course to be set for the Denmark Strait, hoping that the fog, snow, and rain that were gathering in the west would cloak his movements.

At 7:11 p.m. on May 23, as the task force steamed along at a brisk twenty-seven knots—with Iceland's black peaks to port and the antiseptic blue of Greenland's pack ice to starboard—lookouts picked up an ominous shape among the shifting banks of fog. It was the *Suffolk*. The flimsy hope of concealment was gone and, whether it came soon or late, the crew realized that a battle was now all but inevitable.

Suffolk's lookouts had also sighted their enemy. Their first reaction was alarm. *Bismarck* and *Prinz Eugen* were only six miles away and the battleship's guns would make short work of the *Suffolk*. It seemed to Charles Collett that "at that short range [she] could have blown us out of the water." But surprisingly, nothing happened. Lütjens gave the commander of *Prinz Eugen*, Kapitän Helmuth Brinkmann, permission to fire, but the target was too indistinct. *Suffolk* was able to turn away rapidly into the mist and wire the momentous news. When the word reached Tovey, he ordered the Home Fleet to alter course to the northwest to bring them to an intercepting point south of the Denmark Strait. Aboard the *Hood*, Holland had also picked up the sighting report. He, too, changed course and steamed at full speed on a line that he hoped would bring his ship and the *Prince of Wales* across the path of the raiders as they emerged from the Strait at about 5:30 a.m. on May 24.

Throughout the night, *Suffolk* and *Norfolk* kept a high-speed tail on *Bismarck* and *Prinz Eugen*, helped by the *Suffolk's* new Type 284 long-range search radar. It was a delicate business, requiring them to keep close enough to stay in radar range but beyond the reach of German shells. At one point the 15-inch guns of *Bismarck* flamed out of the murk sending five salvoes in the direction of *Norfolk*, but they fell wide and she suffered only minor damage. The cruisers lost the scent for a frantic ninety minutes but then, Collett recorded, they were "rewarded in the early morning by seeing, mere smudges on the horizon, the *Hood* and the *Prince of Wales* to the eastward and the German ships, by now also specks on the horizon (as we had opened our distance as it became lighter) to the southward." The sight of the British ships was "a great relief … it meant that our main job was completed successfully and that there was little likelihood of the German ships turning round and engaging us—always a distinct possibility whilst we were shadowing." Collett, in his air defense role, had a station on the upper works with all-around vision. It gave him a grandstand view of what happened next.

As dawn came on May 24, *Prinz Eugen* and *Bismarck* emerged at high speed from the southern end of the Denmark Strait. *Hood* and *Prince of Wales* were closing with them from the east at an angle. At 5:35 a.m., a lookout in the crow's nest of the *Prince of Wales* saw smoke on the northwest horizon and yelled down the voice pipe to the bridge that the enemy was in sight. Seven minutes earlier the *Prinz Eugen* had already spotted distant ships off her port bow. The two forces plunged toward each other on a converging course and at 5:52 a.m., at a range of over thirteen miles, *Hood*, in the lead, opened fire with four shells from her 15-inch guns. Holland gave the order to engage the left-hand ship. He had picked the wrong one. It was *Prinz Eugen*, a much less dangerous adversary than *Bismarck*. Captain John Leach in *Prince of Wales* did not make the same mistake and engaged *Bismarck*. The *Hood*'s salvoes missed their target. *Prince of Wales*'s 14-inch guns scored three hits on *Bismarck*, the last bursting through the hull below the water line and doing considerable damage.

Lütjens, on *Bismarck*, held his fire. Then, at 5:55 a.m., he ordered both ships to aim at *Hood*. At least one shell hit her, starting a fire. *Hood* and *Prince of Wales* now turned to port to bring their main aft guns to bear. As they did so a salvo from *Bismarck* crashed around *Hood* amidships. One shell appeared to hit just behind the mainmast. Collett, watching from *Suffolk*, saw "a terrific sheet of scarlet flame suddenly reach up high into the heavens … and then die down to be followed by billowing clouds of thick black smoke." He knew at once that a magazine had gone up and that "this must be an end to her."[4]

So it was. On board *Prince of Wales* a young midshipman, G. P. Allen, was at his station in the Upper Plot, the chart room just below the bridge. His duties including recording events in the ship's log as they were called down on the voice pipe from above by the navigator. He remembered later how "the *Hood* was only a few cable lengths away on our port bow when at 06.02 I heard '*Hood* hit,' at 06.04 I heard '*Hood* on fire' and at 06.05 '*Hood* sunk.'"[5] As Allen, whose nineteenth birthday was that day, struggled to absorb the information, a shell impacted a few yards over his head. It smashed into the bridge and killed two of his fellow midshipmen. The Upper Plot was connected to the bridge by a funnel through which the captain could peer down to check the ship's progress on the chart stretched out below. The shell had blown the top off the funnel and "blood began to drip steadily onto the chart table. We caught the drips in a half-empty jug of cocoa." The *Prince of Wales* was by now in no fit state to fight back. She had been hit seven times by the German ships. Two of her ten 14-inch guns were out of action—not because of the damage wrought by the German ships but because they were still not properly installed when the order came to sail. Captain Leach "very wisely" in Allen's view decided that he risked losing his ship without any chance of damaging the enemy. He turned her away, made smoke, and ran for safety.

The loss of the *Hood* was heard with disbelief among the rest of the fleet. One minute it had been on the surface firing its guns. The next it had disappeared along with all but three of its 1,419-strong crew. The "mighty *Hood*" as she was known to the Royal Navy was the symbol of Britain's maritime power, whose appearance in the great ports of the world on flag-flying visits sent a message that—despite the challenges from rising powers—the navy still ruled the waves.

The catastrophe sent a shudder through the surrounding ships. Patrick Mullins, an ambitious and well-read young ordinary seaman with the Home Fleet on board *Repulse*, wrote later that it was "difficult to comprehend the effect that the sudden loss of this great, glamorous and handsome ship had [on us]. Suspension of belief was the first reaction, followed by awe and then by the realization that now it was up to us ... suddenly our side did not look nearly so strong."[6]

Tovey, aboard *King George V*, heard the news in a stark signal sent from the *Norfolk* stating simply, "*Hood* has blown up." Soon it reached the Admiralty who passed it on to Chequers. "Pug" Ismay was woken by the sound of voices and got out of bed "to see the Prime Minister's back disappearing down the corridor." Averell Harriman's bedroom door was open and Ismay went in. He was told that Churchill had arrived a few minutes before "in a yellow sweater, covering a short nightshirt, his pink legs exposed," muttering "'Hell of a battle. The *Hood* is sunk, hell of a battle.'"[7]

The news should not have come as such a great surprise. *Hood* was bound to come off worst in a contest with a strongly armored opponent whose guns could comfortably outreach her own. She was a battle cruiser, not a battleship, and at the age of twenty-one a relatively elderly one. Her 42,100-ton displacement made her the biggest ship in the navy.

But at the time she was designed, the existing technology did not allow her to carry eight 15-inch guns as well as heavy armor. Subsequent refits had failed to add adequate protection. Her deck armor was an inch thick in places and only three inches thick over the magazines where the shells and charges were stored. *Bismarck*'s deck was plated all over with between 4.2 and 4.7 inches of Krupp steel. *Hood* was highly vulnerable to *Bismarck*'s shells, especially if they were fired at a high trajectory. It was recognized that "plunging fire," as it was called, would slice easily through her armor decking. Holland had known this better than anyone. Yet he had chosen to gamble at intercepting his adversary sideways-on, laying his ship open to the battleship's broadsides rather than getting ahead of the German force and confronting it head-on—which would have reduced his ship's size as a target.

The battle, though, had not been altogether one-sided. The three shells that *Prince of Wales* managed to land on *Bismarck* knocked out one of her electrical plants, flooding a boiler room and rupturing fuel tanks. She could now only manage a maximum speed of twenty-eight knots, trailing an iridescent banner of spilled oil in her wake. In this state a prolonged raiding expedition was out of the question.

Lütjens was faced with two choices. He could turn round and go home, having scored a memorable victory, and await further chances for glory. Or he could hold course and seek the safety of the French coast to recuperate. It was a desperate dilemma. If he carried on, he knew that his ships were in a race against the avenging forces of the British fleet, and the chances of interception were high. Turning back was equally perilous since the navy would be alerted and waiting. So, too, would the air force, whose bombers were within easy reach of his homeward routes. He chose to press on, aiming to run for St Nazaire at the mouth of the Loire, where there was a dry dock big enough to carry out repairs.

The Brittany ports were still nearly two thousand miles away, and two enemy naval forces were converging on the German ships. Trailing doggedly in their wakes as they pressed on southward were the *Suffolk*, *Norfolk*, and *Prince of Wales*. By now, Tovey and the Home Fleet were hurrying southwest on a course which he hoped would place his ships in a position to cut off Lütjens's retreat at about 9:00 a.m. the following day.

Bismarck ploughed on through worsening weather. Her bows were 3 degrees down in the water, the result of a hit in the foredeck from a shell fired by the *Prince of Wales*. The *Prinz Eugen*, though, was unscathed. As long as she was tied to *Bismarck* her chances of remaining so diminished. On the afternoon of May 24, Lütjens decided to set her free. He signaled her commander, Kapitän zur See Helmuth Brinkmann, his intention to take advantage of the next squall to turn westward in the hope of shaking off *Suffolk* and *Norfolk*. The *Prinz Eugen* was to carry on the Atlantic raiding mission alone. *Bismarck* briefly turned on her pursuers to buy time for her consort while she got away.

That evening she was butting westward through heavy weather when Tovey decided to throw the aircraft aboard the carrier *Victorious* into the hunt. At 10:00 p.m. a small force of Swordfish torpedo bombers and Fulmar fighter reconnaissance aircraft flew off into a storm-swept night. Despite the conditions they tracked down the *Bismarck* 120 miles ahead. One Swordfish got off a torpedo that struck the hull. The point of impact was at the thickest part of the armored belt and the damage was slight. The explosion, however, shook loose the collision mats sealing the earlier damage, causing renewed flooding and pushing the battleship further down at the bows.

As Sunday, May 25 dawned, the *Bismarck*'s luck turned. Frantic work by the crew had restored some speed. Her pursuers, though, had been forced to slow down. On entering the broad waters of the North Atlantic, *Suffolk* and *Norfolk* began to zigzag to shake off any waiting U-boats. By 3:00 a.m. they had lost radar contact with their quarry. Without the tracking reports of the heavy cruisers to assist him, the great prize might slip from Tovey's grasp. It was an appalling prospect.

He had been asleep in his sea cabin on *King George V*, about a hundred miles to the south and east of where *Bismarck* was last sighted, when Tovey was shaken awake with the bad news. He climbed up through two decks to the plotting office for a staff conference. His ships were now widely dispersed, and half of them were running low on fuel. The weather was bad and promised to worsen, cutting down the chances that either the aircraft aboard *Victorious* or the long-range reconnaissance planes based on the coast would spot the *Bismarck*.

In the absence of real information about her condition, there were two eventualities to consider. *Bismarck* might be undamaged, in which case she would be heading west to carry out her raiding mission, or she might be in trouble and heading east towards a French port. He decided to concentrate his forces on searching to the west. In the meantime, more ships were approaching from the south which could help comb the east.

Force H, an ad hoc fleet which operated out of Gibraltar under Vice Admiral Sir James Somerville's command, had been ordered north to join the hunt. At its core were Somerville's flagship, the aging battle cruiser *Renown*; the heavy cruiser *Dorsetshire*; and the light cruiser *Sheffield*. Most importantly for what was to come, the fleet included an aircraft carrier, the *Ark Royal*, which had twenty Swordfish torpedo bombers aboard and whose crew had seen much action in the Mediterranean.

For a while it seemed that the pursuers had regained the scent. Lütjens, unaware that he had shaken off the pursuit, radioed a situation signal to the Naval Group Command West headquarters in Paris. It was picked up by HF/DF receivers at British shore stations, and it gave an indication of the *Bismarck*'s whereabouts, although it would take time for the code to be broken. She was somewhere to Tovey's east, but more than that was impossible to say. Tovey and his staff took the view that she was heading for home and hurried back on his own track away from his quarry.

As the morning advanced, the level of desperation rose. The damp, showery weather over Buckinghamshire matched the gray mood inside Chequers. To Churchill, *Bismarck*'s disappearance was an avoidable disaster. She should have been finished off when the chance arose in the Denmark Strait. His anger fell on Admiral Wake-Walker and Captain Leach of the *Prince of Wales*, who in Churchill's opinion should have carried on engaging *Bismarck* even if doing so invited disaster. He returned to London around noon and made frequent, scowling appearances in the Admiralty's Operational Control Centre throughout the rest of the day, greatly intensifying the staff's anxieties as they struggled to make sense of the situation.[8]

For the rest of the day, *Bismarck*'s chances improved with each passing hour. An increase in German naval and air force radio traffic along the Brittany coast eventually persuaded the Admiralty that the battleship was heading to Brest or St Nazaire and orders were issued to change course, but hours of steaming time had been lost, and one by one the British ships broke off the search and left to refuel.[9] *Bismarck*'s precise course was not known. Reconnaissance flights by RAF Coastal Command had turned up nothing and the weather was worsening, with thick clouds and low visibility.

By mid-morning on Monday, May 26, *Bismarck* was only a day from safety. The mood on board was lightening. They might not have reaped the glory promised by Kapitän Lindemann at the start of the voyage, but they would be content with the survival which seemed imminent. Even so, the ship's anti-aircraft crews did not slacken their concentration. At 10:30 a.m. they caught a glimpse of a large twin-engined aircraft through a hole in the blanket of cloud overhead. The alarm was sounded, and the thud of outgoing flak could be heard over the rising wind.

The airplane was a PBY Catalina long-range reconnaissance seaplane. It was operated by Coastal Command's 209 Squadron and had taken off on a search mission from the base at Loch Erne in Northern Ireland at 3:45 that morning. It was an Anglo-American effort. Flying Officer Dennis Briggs was accompanied by Ensign Leonard B. Smith of the U.S. Navy who had volunteered to go with a consignment of Catalinas, supplied under the Lend-Lease agreement, to train British crews. His mission stretched the boundaries of his duties but was in keeping with President Roosevelt's determination to offer Churchill all assistance short of formally entering the war.

Smith had seen the ship through a patch of clear sky from ten miles away, and he and Briggs had neared it through the murk, hoping to track it from a safe distance. Instead they had emerged directly overhead, providing the anti-aircraft gunners with a few seconds of point-blank firing time. Bullets and shells punched through wings and fuselage, and one shell punctured the floor of the pilots' cabin. But then they were smothered once again in cloud and radioed back the sensational news. *Bismarck* had been found and from now on she would be tracked by shadowing aircraft.

There was still hope for the German crew. They were 790 miles northwest of Brest at the time of the sighting, and they did not need to reach port to find relative safety. The U-boats and the Focke-Wulf Condor bombers operating from the Brittany coast were daunting deterrents to the British pursuers. By now most of the heavy ships had departed in search of fuel, leaving only *King George V* and *Rodney*, and they were far away—too far to make an interception if *Bismarck* maintained her speed.

That left Somerville's Force H, which was approaching *Bismarck* from the south. The *Ark Royal* was less than a hundred miles from the battleship at the time of the Catalina sighting. Her Swordfish had been searching in the same area and soon sighted their quarry. There was no question of engaging. Somerville's flagship, *Renown*, was an old-fashioned battle cruiser and no match for the *Bismarck*, even in her damaged state. Nor were the cruisers *Dorsetshire* and *Sheffield*. At noon, Somerville detached *Sheffield* to pick up *Bismarck*'s trail with instructions to follow her at a safe distance.

He calculated that the best chance lay in an aerial attack that would slow her down and allow Tovey to catch up. "Slim" Somerville was a popular commander, who sometimes took exercise before breakfast by rowing a skiff round his ships. His Fleet Air Arm crews thought he had a better understanding of the uses of aircraft than most admirals. He had learned to fly himself and sometimes flew as a passenger on training flights "just for fun."[10]

Perhaps his Swordfish, flimsy and insubstantial though they seemed against the power of the elements and the might of their opponent, might complete the job themselves. "With any luck we may be able to finish her before the Home Fleet arrives," he said in a message to the crews.

At 2:50 p.m., fifteen Swordfish from 818 and 820 Squadrons took off to attempt an attack. The weather all day had been atrocious. Even the *Ark Royal*, which reared sixty feet above the waves in calm seas, had green water coursing over her bow. The crews stepped out onto the bucking deck and groped their way to their aircraft. "The after end of the flight deck … was pitching something like fifty feet up and down," recalled Sub-Lieutenant Charles Friend, an observer. "The take offs were awesome in the extreme. The aircraft, as their throttles were opened, instead of charging forward on a level deck were at one moment breasting a slippery slope and the next plunging downhill towards the huge seas ahead and below."

Lieutenant Commander James Stewart-Moore, who flew as an observer, led the force. He was eager and confident as he prepared to take off. He admired Somerville and was anxious to do him proud as "he took good care of us and we did our best for him."[11] The mission seemed "fairly straightforward." One of the Swordfish in his flight was equipped with radar which would aid the hunt. At the pre-operational briefing he was assured that there were no British ships in the search area, which was "a great help as it meant we did not have to identify the ships before we started our attack."

Despite the howling Force 8 gale, all the aircraft got off safely. The radar-equipped machine led the way. It was operated by the observer, Sub-Lieutenant N. C. Cooper. There was no wireless communication between aircraft, and crews relied on hand signals. "After a while I saw Cooper waving to me," Stewart-Moore recalled. Cooper indicated that the set had picked up something twenty miles away to starboard. This was puzzling. The position did not seem to correspond with the last known course of the *Bismarck*. Nonetheless, as Stewart-Moore had been told there were no British ships in the area, "it had to be German." As they swooped down through the clouds to torpedo-dropping height, keeping close together, "everything looked promising."

But as soon as they were clear of the clouds, his pilot, Lieutenant Hugh de Graff Hunter, "called to me down the voice pipe, 'It's the *Shef-field*.'" Instead of the *Bismarck*, they had come across the cruiser that Somerville had detached to shadow her. Hunter waggled his wings furiously to alert the other aircraft but it was too late. One by one, they dropped their "kippers," as they called their torpedoes, while their commander "watched from above, horrified and praying for a miracle."

To his enormous relief, "the miracle department was paying attention to incoming prayers and the miracle was provided at once. Without any apparent reason, all the torpedoes except one or two, blew up within half a minute of striking the water."

Back on board *Ark Royal* they were met with "profuse apologies" for the intelligence snafu. Plans were already in place for another strike. Stewart-Moore was anxious to alert his superiors about the premature detonation of the torpedoes. They were the standard 18-inch-diameter model, but equipped with an innovative Duplex magnetic firing pistol. When these were fitted, the torpedoes were set to run just below the target ship. The sudden change in the magnetic field surrounding the torpedo, caused by its steel hull, activated the pistol. The ship then caught the full force of the subsequent blast. In the old-fashioned pistols, the torpedo instead activated upon collision with its target. The disadvantage of the older system was that much of the explosion's force was vented uselessly into the atmosphere.

Stewart-Moore guessed that the Duplex mechanisms had been disoriented by the heavy swell, causing them to go off early. The contact pistols stood a much better chance in the rough seas. He found it very hard, however, to get anyone to listen to him. Eventually Somerville, a torpedo specialist in his early days, ordered the detonators to be changed for the next attack himself.

Six sub-flights of Swordfish, fifteen aircraft in all, were lined up for another attempt before night fell. The attack was led by Lieutenant Commander Tim Coode, of 818 Squadron. His wingman was a twenty-one-year-old Scotsman, Sub-Lieutenant John "Jock" Moffat. He felt the full weight of the expectations pressing down on him and his comrades. "It was all on us now," he remembered. "It was a question of salvaging our reputations. There was serious concern that we didn't make a mess of this again. By now we were under no illusions about how important this was to the Navy and to Churchill and we felt under enormous pressure to pull it off."[12]

As the Swordfish were brought up from the hangars below, the weather worsened steadily. On the flight deck "the wind hit you like a hammer, threatening to knock you down ... the deck crews were really struggling with the aircraft, spray was coming over the side and the waves were breaking over the front of the flight deck." The 22,000-ton *Ark Royal* was bucking and sliding as he took off. "I felt that I was being thrown into the air rather than lifting off," he wrote. "I was struggling to control the aircraft while the wheels were still on the deck, watching for a sideways gust that might push me into the bridge, praying that we would clear the tops of the mountainous waves."

They were helped on their way by the Deck Control Officer, Lieutenant Commander Pat Stringer, who, at well over six feet tall, had to be anchored with a harness to a stanchion to avoid being blown overboard. Stringer had an instinctive understanding of the ship's position in relation to the sea. "He would signal to start the take off when he sensed that the ship was at the bottom of a big wave so that even if I thought that I was taking off downhill, the bows would swing up at the last moment and I would be flying above the big Atlantic swell rather than into it."

Eventually all the aircraft were airborne and after forming up together headed off. Moffat tucked in behind Coode and within a few minutes they had found—and correctly identified—*Sheffield*. The signal lamp winking from the deck told them that *Bismarck* was only twelve miles ahead. They were flying low, at 500 feet, and Coode ordered them to climb to 6,000 feet. They broke through a thick blanket of cloud into clear, freezing air. Moffat's first concern was the ice forming on the leading edges of his wings and main struts. It was quickly overtaken by alarm at the black smoke from exploding shells mushrooming all around them. "We knew then that *Bismarck* was nearby and we assumed she had found us on her radar." Coode signaled them to form a line astern, and they dived through the cloud. Almost immediately they lost sight of each other. When Moffat broke out of the cloud at 300 , he found he was alone.

In the pre-operational briefing, the pilots had been given a detailed plan of attack. It followed the standard Fleet Air Arm method for firing torpedoes at ships at sea. The first three flights were to come in on the port beam from differing bearings. The second wave would do the same on the starboard side. The intention was to force the anti-aircraft gunners to divide their attentions between two targets and to bracket the ship with torpedoes, severely restricting its ability to steer out of their path.

Any chance of this happening had now vanished. There were no other aircraft in sight. Moffat glanced around. There, about two miles away to the east, was the *Bismarck*. "Even at this distance the brute seemed enormous to me," he recalled. He turned to his right towards her. Almost immediately "there was a red glow in the clouds ahead of me about a hundred yards away as anti-aircraft shells exploded." Then the gunners were aiming just ahead of him and their fire threw up "walls of water" in his path. Two shells erupted next to and below the Swordfish, knocking it 90 degrees off course. Moffat dropped to fifty feet, just above the height where he might catch a wave and cartwheel into the sea.

This seemed to be below the angle at which the flak guns could operate but, in their place, cannon and machine guns were pumping out red tracer bullets that flowed towards Moffat and his two-man crew "in a torrent." As he raced towards the target he felt that "every gun on the ship was aiming at me." He could not believe that he was flying straight into the hail of fire. "Every instinct was screaming at me to duck, turn away, do anything." But he suppressed his fear and pressed grimly on as the target grew larger and larger.

His training taught him to assess the speed of the ship under attack and fire ahead, using a simple marked rod mounted horizontally along the top of the cockpit to calculate the correct distance to lay off. With *Bismarck* looming ahead of him, Moffat felt he could not miss. "I thought, I'm still flying. If I can get rid of this torpedo and get the hell out of here, we might survive." He was about to press the release button on the throttle when he heard his observer, Sub-Lieutenant John "Dusty" Miller, shouting "Not yet, John, not yet!" Moffat looked back to see Miller's "backside in the air ... there he was hanging over the side and his head [was] down underneath the aeroplane and he was shouting 'not yet!'" Moffat realized what was going on. "It dawned on me that if I dropped that torpedo and it struck the top of a wave it could go anywhere but where it's supposed to." Miller was waiting for a trough. Then "he shouted 'let her go!' and the next [moment he] was saying 'John, we've got a runner.'"

Relieved of the torpedo's ton weight, the Swordfish leapt upwards and it was all Moffat could do to wrestle it down below the gunfire streaming overhead. It would have taken ninety seconds to follow the track of the torpedo to the target. Hanging around meant certain death. Moffat put the Swordfish into a "ski turn. I gave the engine full lick and I stood on my left rudder and I shuddered round flat." It was a maneuver that only the slow-moving Swordfish could pull off and it kept them down beneath the lowest elevation of the guns. He headed away at maximum speed, keeping low until he judged it was safe to climb into the cover of the clouds. He had no idea of whether his torpedo had found its target or not.

There was one last hazard to face. When he reached *Ark Royal* the deck was still heaving. As he finally touched down "there was nothing more welcoming than the thump of the wheels on the deck and the clatter of the hook catching on the arrestor wire." Clambering down from the cockpit, he felt light-headed from adrenaline and fatigue. He told the debriefing officers the little he could, then headed below for a special meal that he was too tense to eat.

The mood among the crews was subdued. Everyone had been disoriented by the cloud and the attacks had all taken place in ones and twos. Only two, possibly three, torpedoes had been seen to hit the target. That was not a cause for celebration. *Bismarck*'s thick armor meant that even a direct hit amidships would not necessarily prove fatal, as the attacks from *Victorious* had shown. Moffat thought he might have been responsible for one recorded strike. A pilot who followed him in saw a torpedo exploding two-thirds of the way down the port side.

Visibility was too poor for another attempt that night, but the pilots would be sent off again the following morning. Someone gloomily remarked that "the Light Brigade had only been asked to do it once." Then a stream of information started to arrive that lifted their spirits. *Sheffield* signaled that the *Bismarck* had slowed down. Then came the astonishing news that she had turned around and was heading straight toward the battleship *King George V*, which was approaching from the north. A little later, two Swordfish returned to *Ark Royal* from a long reconnaissance to report that *Bismarck* had lost speed and had steamed round in two full circles. HMS *Zulu*, which by now had arrived on the scene, confirmed the news: *Bismarck* had been stopped, less than five hundred miles from the French coast.

Moffat learned later that it was probably his torpedo that had stopped her. It had exploded at the battleship's stern, jamming her rudders at 12 degrees and making steering impossible. With that, *Bismarck*'s fate was sealed. Throughout the night she was subjected to repeated torpedo attacks from fast destroyers which had now caught up. In the morning, *King George V* and *Rodney* arrived and closed in for the kill. The end was never in doubt but it still took forty-five minutes of pounding from the two British battleships and the heavy cruiser *Dorsetshire* before the *Bismarck*'s big guns stopped firing. By then Lütjens was dead, probably killed when a shell from *King George V* hit the bridge. *Dorsetshire* administered the coup de grâce. An able seaman on board, A. E. Franklin, watched two 21-inch torpedoes leave the cruiser's tubes then saw "a tremendous explosion … the fish having truly planted themselves in the bowels of the *Bismarck* far below the water line amidships." *Dorsetshire* closed in to 1,000 yards to deliver another torpedo, which struck squarely on the port side.

John Moffat was flying overhead when she went down. He saw a sight "that … remained etched in my mind ever since. This enormous vessel, over 800 feet long, her gun turrets smashed, her bridge and upper works like a jagged ruin, slowly, frighteningly toppled over, smashing down into the sea and her great hull was revealed, the plates and bilge keels glistening dark red as the oily sea covered her. Still leaping from her were men and sailors. There were hundreds more in the sea; some desperately struggling for their lives, others already inert, tossed by the waves as they floated face down." Moffat was pierced by the knowledge that "there was nothing that I could do to save even a single one." *Bismarck* finally sank, stern first, at 10:39 a.m., four hundred miles west of Brest, an hour and fifty minutes after the battle was joined.

Only 118 of the 2,224 men on board were saved. Most were taken aboard the *Dorsetshire*. Franklin recorded that with "the battle finished, the humanitarian instinct rises above the feeling of revenge and destruction … ropes come from nowhere. Willing hands rush to haul on board the survivors."[13] But then came a warning that an enemy submarine was in the area. The rescue work broke off and *Dorsetshire* and the destroyer *Maori*, which was also standing by, made for safety, leaving hundreds of men bobbing in the oil-stained sea to await death.

The relief in London was immense. Churchill's desperation for a victory had caused him to issue some unfortunate instructions. The night before the end Tovey had signaled that he might have to break off the chase. *King George V*'s fuel bunkers were draining fast and if they ran dry his flagship would be dead in the water, at the mercy of any prowling U-boat. Churchill's response, passed on by Pound, was that "*Bismarck* must be sunk at all costs and if to do this it is necessary for the *King George V* to remain on scene then she must do so, even if it subsequently means towing *King George V*." Tovey was to describe this later as "the stupidest and most ill-considered signal ever made,"[14] and the exchange deepened the mistrust developing between the two men.

Churchill broke the news to the nation in dramatic style. He was on his feet in Church House, where the House of Commons conducted its business while the Palace of Westminster was repaired from bomb damage, describing the battle raging in the Atlantic, when there was a commotion and a messenger handed him a piece of paper. He sat down, scanned it and got up again. "I have just received news that the *Bismarck* is sunk," he announced and the assembly erupted in a roar of applause.

There was much to celebrate. *Hood* had been avenged and a serious threat to Britain's war effort neutralized. While the nation savored the victory, satisfaction in the Cabinet and the Admiralty was tempered by the understanding that it had been a close call, revealing many weaknesses in the navy's armory.

It had taken six battleships and battle cruisers, two aircraft carriers, thirteen cruisers, and twenty-one destroyers to bring the *Bismarck* down. Most of the torpedoes of the Fleet Air Arm's obsolescent aircraft had bounced off her, and in the end it was a lucky strike that doomed her. Of the 2,876 shells fired by the fleet, only 200–300 hit the target. Even when utterly at the mercy of her pursuers, *Bismarck* had proved extremely hard to kill. What, then, would it take to seal the fate of her surviving sister, *Tirpitz*?

CHAPTER 4

TRONDHEIM

light Lieutenant A. F. P. Fane was turning his Spitfire for home after a frustrating reconnaissance flight over the eastern end of Trondheimsfjord in central Norway when he glimpsed a large shape in the confused pattern of gray seas, dishcloth clouds and white-capped hills below. "I saw something like a ship hidden in the shadow of the far end," he recorded in a neat, penciled hand in his diary. It was so large that he thought he was mistaken and it "must be an island." He went down for a closer look. "By God it's a ship—it's *the* ship," he wrote. He "rolled onto my side to have a good look and remember saying out loud, 'my God I believe I've found it!' I couldn't believe my eyes or my luck."[1]

Fane's delight at his coup wore off as he struggled to reach home. The cloud pressed down to 600 feet and he was flying into "a hell of a wind from the south." Twenty minutes after he should have landed he was "getting really worried." There was still no sign of land and he was down to his last twenty gallons of fuel—less than half an hour's flying time. Then a gap appeared in the cloud and he recognized Scapa Flow. He turned south and scraped down at Skitten, a satellite field near Wick. A little later he was back at base telling his flight commander Tony Hill that "I'd thought I'd found the old Rowboat but could not believe it." He "hopped about on one foot then the other waiting for photos to be developed. When film was ready tore in to look at negatives." He was still worried that "maybe I'd missed the b—— thing. NO! there it was— no doubt now, it was the TURPITZ [sic] all right."

Fane, a dashing thirty-year-old who was a Grand Prix racing driver before the war, had been sent with C Flight of No. 1 Photographic Reconnaissance Unit (PRU) to Wick on the north Scottish coast on January 21, 1942, with the specific job of searching for Tirpitz. Now, only two days later, he had found her, tucked into Faettenfjord, a finger of deep water forty miles from the open sea.

Churchill received the news with great excitement. He immediately ordered the Chiefs of Staff to draw up plans for Tirpitz to be bombed. "The destruction or even the crippling of this ship is the greatest event at sea at the present time," he told them. "No other target is comparable to it." A successful attack would mean that "the entire naval situation throughout the world would be altered," freeing the Royal Navy to assert itself in the Pacific against Japan, which had now entered the war. He concluded: "The whole strategy of the war turns at this period on this ship, which is holding four times the number of British capital ships paralysed, to say nothing of the two new American battleships retained in the Atlantic. I regard the matter as of the highest urgency and importance."[2]

The dramatic tone of the memo made it apparent that the removal of Bismarck had done nothing to diminish Churchill's concern about Hitler's remaining battleship. During the second half of 1941, the PRU had kept a continuous watch on Tirpitz, flying regular reconnaissance missions over Kiel—her homeport for the period. Failure to spot her during one of her frequent excursions on sea trials generated a flurry of alarm. Even when safely in view, she still exercised a peculiar menace. At the beginning of August, Churchill set off on board HMS *Prince of Wales* for his first wartime conference with President Roosevelt at Placentia Bay, Newfoundland. A surveillance flight had located *Tirpitz* at Kiel on August 6, much too far away to pose any threat, yet speculation persisted that she might attempt an ambush. Colonel Ian Jacob, an astute staff officer on board *Prince of Wales*, noted in his diary that "the Prime Minister did not seem to worry in the least, and he is secretly hoping the *Tirpitz* will come out and have a dart at him."[3]

As the summer turned to autumn, worry about the battleship's whereabouts and intentions continued to distract the navy, tying up, as the Prime Minister noted in his memo to the Chiefs, a disproportionate number of capital ships as well as part of the American naval task force which from September 1941 was based in Iceland to assist the Home Fleet. The Admiralty believed that three battleships were needed on standby to overwhelm *Tirpitz* were she to break out. Churchill thought the caution overdone, complaining to Pound that this was an "excessive provision" and "incomparably more lavish than anything we have been able to indulge in so far in this war."[4]

He was nonetheless impressed with the influence *Tirpitz* was able to assert. This attitude led to what can be counted as *Tirpitz*'s first indirect success of the war—a result that was achieved without her having to leave port. During the 1930s Churchill had paid little attention to the maritime threat posed by Japan, despite the fact that it was in the process of building a powerful fleet. He continued to underestimate the danger until early 1941 when he first admitted, in a letter to Roosevelt, "the weight of the Japanese Navy, if thrown against us, would confront us with situations beyond the scope of our naval reserves." As the year advanced and this dire prospect grew more likely, he considered moving a battleship of the most modern *King George V* [KGV] class to the East to deter Japan. The hope was that it would exercise the same mesmeric effect on the Japanese navy as *Tirpitz* did on the Home Fleet. "*Tirpitz* is doing to us exactly what a 'KGV' in the Indian Ocean would do to the Japanese Navy," he wrote to Pound on August 29, 1941. "It exercises a vague, general fear and menaces all points at once. It appears and disappears, causing immediate reactions and perturbations on the other side."[5]

By October he had settled on sending the *Prince of Wales*, and in the War Cabinet discussion of October 17 he again cited the "example of the battleship *Tirpitz* which ... compelled us to keep on guard a force three times her weight in addition [to the] United States forces patrolling the Atlantic."[6]

Prince of Wales was duly dispatched to Singapore on October 23, over the strong objections of the Admiralty, which feared that *Tirpitz* might attempt a breakout at any minute. She sailed first to Ceylon where she met up with the aging battle cruiser *Repulse*. On December 2 they arrived in Singapore. Their deterrence mission was long obsolete. Five days afterward the Japanese attacked Pearl Harbor and launched an invasion fleet towards Malaya. *Prince of Wales* and *Repulse* set out to intercept it. On December 10, both ships were sunk within an hour of each other by Japanese torpedo bombers, a disaster that plunged the nation into gloom, temporarily extinguishing the hope aroused by the arrival of the United States into the war.

Though Churchill and the admirals were not to know it, *Tirpitz* represented no threat at all during the second half of 1941. Having lost *Bismarck*, Raeder was taking all care of his single greatest resource; the tests and trials to establish her sea- and battle-worthiness that filled the rest of the year were rigorous even by peacetime standards. While the Home Fleet steeled itself for the battleship's appearance, she was engaged in a leisurely preparation program cruising back and forth between Baltic ports.

The fate of her sister ship *Bismarck* seems to have had surprisingly little effect on the morale of the ship's company. Onboard routine and the spirit of the ship were described in great detail by the administration officer, Korvettenkapitän Kurt Voigt, in his letters home to his wife Erika (or "Klösel" as he affectionately called her). He was a member of the Prussian professional middle class who had joined the navy in 1917 and carried on as a career officer in the interwar years. Voigt comes across in his correspondence as a decent man, a loving husband and father, and a considerate boss. He was now in early middle age, considerably older than the rest of the crew. He nonetheless showed a boyish pride in his association with a famous vessel. Like everyone, the first thing that struck him about *Tirpitz* was its immensity, after which the First World War era battleship *Schlesien* seemed "a ludicrous trawler."[7]

He arrived on board at the end of September, as the ship stood off the Aaland Islands, the Baltic archipelago at the mouth of the Gulf of Bothnia. *Tirpitz* was the core of a force that included the pocket battleship *Admiral Scheer* and four light cruisers. Since June, Germany had been at war with the Soviet Union and the fleet was assembled to deter Russian warships from venturing out from Kronstadt. The Soviet ships stayed put, and there is no sense at all of impending action in Voigt's accounts of onboard life. Instead his letters are taken up with marveling at the comfort and modernity of his surroundings. "My room is considerably bigger than what I'm used to," he wrote on October 7 after *Tirpitz* had returned to Gdynia. "[There's] a chair with leather-type upholstery for visitors, a comfortable writing chair, a square table, lace curtains on the portholes and the sides, all in cream." He also had a telephone "that communicates with all officers and other stations. There's an entire phone book for this little city."

The latter was an exaggeration, but *Tirpitz* certainly had the facilities of a fair-sized village or small town. There was a hairdressing salon with five barbers, a bakery, a cinema well-stocked with newish films, and a printing press that churned out regular editions of the onboard newspaper *Der Scheinwerfer* (*The Searchlight*). Officers took their meals in a mess that was like "a large and imposing restaurant with ceiling lighting." The food was plentiful and pretty good. His first meal on board was "excellent"—lentil soup followed by roast meat. During the Baltic autumn there were luxuries to supplement the staples of meat, tinned fish, and potatoes, and "now and again we get beautiful apples, tomatoes and grapes."

There was also plenty to drink. At his first meeting with Kapitän Karl Topp, he was offered sparkling wine, then whisky. He had encountered him before and found him "not much changed except a bit grayer." Topp was extremely welcoming. "He was friendly and spent a lot of time talking to me," he reported to Erika on October 1. The following day he comments again on his friendliness and proudly observes, "he treats me with respect ... something the others remarked on."

Voigt's evident admiration for his captain appears to have been shared by most of the men on board. Karl Topp was forty-five years old when he took formal command of *Tirpitz* on January 25, 1941. He was born in Vörde in Prussian Westphalia, the son of a clergyman, and joined the Imperial navy when he was nineteen, serving in submarines during the First World War. At its close he was the first officer of a U-boat in the Mediterranean that succeeded, through sinking ships and laying mines, in forcing the temporary closure of the port of Marseilles. His captain was Martin Niemöller, then a fierce nationalist, who went on to become a Lutheran pastor and anti-Nazi theologian.

Topp was one of the lucky ones who managed to stay on in the service during the harsh and chaotic Weimar years. He combined virtuoso seamanship with technical knowledge and specialized in military shipbuilding. He was stocky with a broad, meaty face and bright blue eyes. His manner was calm and methodical. He radiated authority, leavened with humour and consideration for his men. The weather was bitter on February 25, 1941, the day *Tirpitz* was officially commissioned. One of the engine room officers, Georg Schlegel, remembered that "we all went to the top deck and it was snowing and very cold. The Commander kept it short so that we didn't have to stand in the snow so long. The flag was hoisted and that was that."[8] Touches like that generated affection as well as respect among the ship's company, who had given him the nickname "Charlie."

Topp commanded a crew of 2,608, made up of 108 officers and 2,500 men. Most of them were young and inexperienced. Among them, though, was a core of sailors who had experienced the full trauma of war at sea. They were survivors of the heavy cruiser *Blücher*, the newest ship in the Kriegsmarine which had been sunk by shore-based gun and torpedo batteries as she sailed into Oslofjord during the invasion of Norway in April 1940—an event as shocking and unexpected as the loss of *Hood* was to be for the British. *Tirpitz* seemed immune from such a catastrophe. Everyone on board took comfort from the ship's armadillo hide of steel armor and the huge guns encased in turrets, named Anton, Bruno, Caesar, and Dora. "The many, very heavy guns give a sense of absolute safety," wrote Voigt to Erika in Berlin. The sheer size seemed to promise security, as reflected in the metaphors of impregnability that crop up again and again in his correspondence. The ship was a "fortress," a "slab of granite."

Tirpitz, though, was an offensive, not a defensive, weapon. In the aftermath of the *Bismarck* disaster, there was uncertainty as to how she should now be used. The loss had jolted Hitler into action. Admiral Raeder noted that the Führer abandoned laissez-faire and now became "much more critical and more inclined to insist on his own views than before."[9]

The battleground for which *Tirpitz* had originally been intended no longer seemed attractive. America's full entry into the war in December 1941 made the Atlantic a much more dangerous place for surface ships. The *Scharnhorst* and the *Gneisenau* were still in the area, lying up at Brest, where they were harassed by Bomber Command and afflicted by mechanical problems that delayed their return to operational health. *Tirpitz* was still not at battle readiness and, even if she were, would face a dangerous voyage to a French Atlantic port and be exposed to RAF attack once she got there. If a raiding force did venture out, its operations would be circumscribed by a dire shortage of oil. All in all, Atlantic operations by large ships seemed to offer more danger than they did reward.[10]

Hitler's thoughts turned instead to Norway, which Germany had held since the spring of 1940. He regarded its possession as a strategic necessity. Norway commanded the Reich's northern approaches. It was also vital for the transportation of essential iron ore supplies from Sweden. During 1941, he grew increasingly worried that Germany might be about to lose it. Hitler harbored a persistent suspicion—which sometimes seemed to shade into an obsession—that Britain planned to invade Norway. A series of increasingly daring raids by British and Norwegian commandos on the Lofoten Islands, Spitsbergen and Bear Island, and Vaagsøy on the mainland raised the possibility that a landing in Norway might be imminent. The prospect of losing Narvik was particularly alarming. It was the only ice-free port in the area, through which Swedish ore could be shipped to German war factories year-round.

On November 13, Hitler met Raeder at the Wolfschanze, a headquarters in East Prussia from which he oversaw the war on the Eastern Front. It was decided to transfer *Tirpitz* from the Baltic to Trondheim. Hitler was now of the opinion that "every ship which is not stationed in Norway is in the wrong place."[11] *Scharnhorst* and *Gneisenau* would be moved north when the circumstances allowed.

Raeder doubted there was any real danger of a British attack on Norway. It was another example of Hitler's exasperating belief in instinct over logical assessment. The move, however, had his approval. He too had come to believe that the Atlantic was too dangerous for extended raiding operations. Northern waters offered a more advantageous battle-ground for his big ships. From Norwegian ports they could sally forth against the Arctic convoys which, in response to Stalin's appeals to Churchill and Roosevelt, were ferrying substantial war supplies round the North Cape to the Russian ports of Murmansk and Archangel. The first had sailed from Iceland on August 21, six more followed by the end of the year, and many more were expected in 1942.

Hitler's goal of strangling Britain had diminished in importance. The great struggle now was with the Soviet Union, and *Tirpitz* could make an important contribution to the war on the Eastern Front. The holds of the cargo ships plying the Atlantic and Arctic oceans were crammed with tanks, aircraft, lorries, engines, guns, and ammunition, shoring up Soviet resistance to the German onslaught. It was far more efficient to destroy them on the high seas than on the battlefield, and each ship sent to the bottom by the navy saved many Wehrmacht and Luftwaffe lives.

The mere presence of *Tirpitz* and the other big units in northern waters would also add greatly to the Royal Navy's already crushing bur-den of duty. The convoys needed heavy protection and a substantial force of capital ships, destroyers, minesweepers, anti-aircraft vessels, and submarines would have to shield them as they came and went. Even if the German ships never left port, they would act as a "fleet in being," forcing the enemy to maintain a countervailing force in the area and tying up valuable units that could be put to much-needed use elsewhere.

Raeder summarized his intentions in his sailing orders. *Tirpitz*'s new home was to be Trondheim, halfway down Norway's western coast.

From there she was to "protect our position in the Norwegian and Arctic areas by threatening the flank of enemy operations against the northern Norwegian areas and by attacking White Sea convoys ... to tie down enemy forces in the Atlantic so they cannot operate in the Mediterranean, the Indian Ocean or the Pacific."[12] *Tirpitz* would get support from the pocket battleship *Admiral Scheer* and the heavy cruiser *Prinz Eugen*, which would soon be on their way from Germany.

Tirpitz left Gdynia on the Polish Baltic coast on the afternoon of January 12, 1942. At 7:00 a.m. the following morning she arrived at Holtenau at the eastern end of the Kiel Canal, which linked the Baltic to the North Sea. There she unloaded stores and equipment in order to lighten the load and ease the passage through the waterway. On board, excitement was mounting. After nearly a year of training exercises the preparations seemed to be over and operations about to begin. "Nobody knew anything," remembered Adalbert Brünner, a young midshipman who had joined the ship the previous autumn. "Everybody hoped we were off on a *Gneisenau* or *Bismarck* type of operation." The crew wondered whether "we were on our way to the Atlantic ... the ship was humming with rumors."[13] It seemed barely possible that her broad beam would be able to squeeze through the canal. Water from the wash overflowed the banks and it appeared to Brünner as they passed under the high bridge at Rendsburg, halfway along the route, that "one could almost shake hands with the pedestrians."

That evening *Tirpitz* arrived at Brunsbüttel on the mouth of the Elbe at the canal's western end, where she took on fuel and reloaded the cargo previously taken off. The following day she steamed out into the North Sea. It was there that the crew finally heard of their destination. They were going to Norway not the Atlantic. The news did nothing to deflate spirits. Either way they would soon be in action. To some, the move seemed predestined. By a curious chance, the ship's symbol was the curved prow of a Viking longship.

It was deep midwinter, and the weather was on their side. Before setting off, Navy Group North reassured Topp that the forecast was bad for central England and Scotland, "with poor take-off conditions."[14] His ship stood a good chance of getting to Trondheim without being spotted by reconnaissance aircraft. On January 15, *Tirpitz* was on her way. The seas were so rough that the escorting destroyers were unable to keep pace and had to follow in the battleship's wake as it sliced through the waves close to its top speed of just over thirty knots.[15] Then, on the morning of January 16, those on deck caught their first sight of the Norwegian coast. "It was hung with cloud, sombre, covered with snow," remembered Brünner. "It was a strange sight for all of us, scattered houses which didn't look as if they were connected up by roads—it seemed like the quintessence of loneliness."[16]

In the afternoon they turned to starboard and passed between the low headlands at the entrance to Trondheimsfjord, which plunged for eighty miles east and north into the Norwegian mainland. Their final destination was a narrow finger of water at the southeastern end— Faettenfjord. It was only about three-quarters of a mile across at its widest, with a small island, Saltøya, planted at the entrance, and it took great skill to bring *Tirpitz* in. Topp managed the feat easily. "The commander simply made fast there without any pilot ships or tugs," said Georg Schlegel. "He was the best. He could really drive that ship."[17]

In Faettenfjord a berth had already been prepared with two massive concrete capstans sunk into the rocks on the northern side of the fjord as mooring points. The crew was immediately set to work stretching gray camouflage nets over the length and breadth of the ship, which they covered with fir branches cut from the forest that covered the hill above. Soon *Tirpitz* was cloaked in a dusting of snow and its outlines melted into the monochrome landscape of hill and water.

The anchorage had been well chosen. *Tirpitz* was tucked into the tail of the inlet. The hills standing 400 to 600 feet above plunged straight into the water, making a natural mooring deep enough to take the ship's nearly thirty-four-foot draught. There was another ridge on the southern shore, about 700 feet high. Any attacking aircraft would have to approach from the western seaward side, making the task of the defenders much easier. Clusters of anti-aircraft batteries mounting sixteen 105-mm, forty-four 20-mm, and eight 37-mm guns—sited to give an all-around field of fire—protected the ship. Within a few days more flak batteries were placed on the slopes above it, along with chemical smoke generators that could pump out a thick, protective cloud within minutes. Soon afterward the ship was fully protected by attack from the water by steel anti-submarine and anti-torpedo nets, hung at right angles a hundred yards from the stern, which faced backwards toward the mouth of Faettenfjord.

Topp and his superiors were certain that the British would soon learn about the new whereabouts of the *Tirpitz* and immediately attack her. Thanks to Fane's reconnaissance flight of January 23, the battleship had indeed been found. The Admiralty and Air Ministry now sought to find a plan that would satisfy the Prime Minister's impatient demand that *Tirpitz* be sunk without further ado. In his instructions, Churchill had raised the possibility of an attack by carrier-borne torpedo planes. That would mean sailing a carrier close enough to put their aircraft within range of the target. To do so would expose the carrier and its escorts to great risk from the Lufwaffe's Ju88 and Ju87 bombers and dive-bombers and Heinkel 111 torpedo planes that had begun arriving in the region in response to Hitler's new focus on Norway. Even if the Fleet Air Arm's Swordfish and Albacore biplanes made it to Faettenfjord, the narrowness of the anchorage made it extremely unlikely they would be able to hit the target.

It was left to Bomber Command to come up with something. *Tirpitz* lay at the extreme limit of the target range of even the four-engine bombers that had now come into service. To reach the target and return safely home they would have to take off from bases in Scotland. The operation that ensued was given the name "Oiled." It was undertaken in a spirit of hope rather than expectation. The RAF had long been aware that it lacked the means to pose a deadly threat to large German warships. Since the second day of the war it had been trying to sink them, with very little success. *Tirpitz* herself had been the object of five operations while lying at Wilhelmshaven and Kiel. The results were negligible, even when large numbers of aircraft were involved. On the night of June 20–21, 1941, a force of 115 Wellingtons, Hampdens, Whitleys, Stirlings, and Halifaxes set off for Kiel to "identify and bomb the *Tirpitz*." Not one aircraft succeeded in doing so.[18]

At this stage navigational aids were still primitive, and it was a considerable achievement to find the target. Even then, the chances of hitting it were small. Bombsights were simple and hopelessly inaccurate. To limit the risk from flak, aircraft had to drop their bombs from heights of 10,000 feet or more. To hit a target as tiny as the deck of a warship from this range was a considerable feat. When bombs did strike they were unlikely to cause fatal damage. Once again, postwar economies had held back research and development and RAF aircraft went into the new conflict with much the same ordnance as they had carried in 1918. The biggest bomb that the twin-engined Whitley, Hampden, and Blenheim bombers in service at the start of the war could carry weighed 500 pounds, of which only a third was explosive charge. Bomber crews sometimes endured the heartbreak and frustration of struggling through flak and fighters to strike their target, only to be let down by their weapons. Such was the experience of the fifteen Halifaxes of 35 and 76 Squadrons which broke through fierce fighter opposition to hit *Scharnhorst* where she lay at La Pallice on the French Atlantic coast on July 24, 1941. Three armor-piercing bombs passed through the ship without exploding. Another two bombs did detonate but the damage was repairable and *Scharnhorst* was ready for action again in four months. If the quality of the crews' weapons had matched their skill and courage, she should have been sent to the bottom.

The nine Halifaxes and seven Stirlings from 15 and 149 Squadrons which took off in the early hours of January 30 from Lossiemouth on the northeast coast of Scotland to attack *Tirpitz* were almost certainly destined to fail. So they did. The weather was terrible. Only two aircraft managed to find Trondheim and they dropped their bombs over some unidentified shipping without effect. One Stirling was shot down. Churchill's incessant prodding meant it unlikely that the failure would deter further attempts. On February 22 Bomber Command got a forceful and ruthless new commander, Sir Arthur Harris, who was anxious to impress. There would be two more attempts by the RAF to sink *Tirpitz* in Faettenfjord before the start of the summer.

The ship was now under regular surveillance. A picture taken by a PRU overflight on February 15 shows it lying at its usual berth, the long, finely tapered bow flaring out into a broad 118-foot beam. It looks safe and secure inside its protective netting, with a cluster of small maintenance and supply craft huddled around it feeding its needs, and a sheet of snow on its upper surfaces. The photographic intelligence was soon supplemented by reports from Norwegian agents in the area.

The agents were operating in an extremely risky environment. By now the German occupation had come down hard over Trondheim and the surrounding area. The army had garrisoned the town. Navy control boats plied the length of Trondheimsfjord checking fishing boats and cargo vessels while bigger ships stood sentry at the entrance. In their wake came the Gestapo, led by Obersturmbannführer Gerhard Flesch, who arrived in October 1941. He took over the local prison as his headquarters and set up a concentration camp at Falstad, near Levanger, northeast of Trondheim.

Trondheim was historically and economically important. Norwegian kings were still crowned there in the Gothic cathedral of Nidaros whose triple spires poke elegantly above the merchant houses and leafy squares of the old town. The banks of the Nidelva river, which snakes around the center, were lined with slipways, small canning factories and ware-houses, painted yellow and red and topped with steep-pitched, corru-gated-iron roofs. The smells of the sea—drying nets, fish, salt, tar, and diesel oil—hung pleasantly over the town.

A small minority of Norwegians had welcomed the Germans' arrival. The Norwegian Nazi Party, led by Vikdun Quisling, had a pres-ence in the area. Over time they planted their supporters in influential jobs in schools, hospitals, and local administration. They forced the Protestant bishop out of the cathedral, installing a collaborator in his place.

With his arrival, congregations dwindled. It was the young who seemed to feel the German presence most, especially the students at the Institute of Technology, an imposing granite pile, which had been train-ing architects and engineers since 1910. The Gestapo was quick to sup-press displays of patriotism. Gestures of defiance, though, hardly posed a threat. Their main concern was the presence of enemy agents who could pass on intelligence about German dispositions and movements, particularly about the activities of *Tirpitz* which now lay only fifteen miles to the east of the town.

British intelligence agencies had already set about trying to establish a network of agents under the Germans' noses, in Trondheim and other key points along the Norwegian coastline. Their activities were to pro-vide a continuous stream of human intelligence, gathered by direct observation. It would prove to be extremely valuable. Despite the aerial reconnaissance and the watch kept by British submarines at the sea entrance to Trondheimsfjord, bad weather meant that there were fre-quent holes in the surveillance. Agents could fill the gaps. *Tirpitz* had only one route to the sea—westward along the fjord. This took it right past the 50,000 inhabitants of Trondheim, which lay on the southern shore. There were further settlements strung along either side of the fjord. Reliable agents equipped with radios would be able to alert the Admiralty to any significant comings or goings.

About the time of the battleship's arrival, Bjørn Rørholt, a twenty-two-year-old Royal Norwegian Navy lieutenant, exiled in London after escaping the Gestapo, was called to Admiralty Headquarters in London. Rørholt came from a patriotic military background. His father Arnold was an early member of the resistance and had been taken hostage after Bjørn had fled Norway. Bjørn had studied radio communications at the Institute of Technology in Trondheim and joined the Norwegian Military Academy at the outbreak of the war. He was taken prisoner during the invasion fighting but was released in the autumn of 1940 and returned to his studies at the Institute.

A clandestine radio service was already in operation by then. The British Secret Intelligence Service (SIS) had helped set up two stations for broadcasting information back to London. One, code-named Sky-lark-A, was in Oslo. The other, Skylark-B, was in Trondheim, under the direction of Erik Welle-Strand who was also based at the Institute. The students formed a pool of potential spies and saboteurs. Their natural patriotism was sharpened by resentment at the German presence which, despite the theoretical kinship the invaders felt for their fellow Aryans, was clumsy and arrogant. When black-bordered notices appeared around the town announcing the first executions of resistant fighters, indignation curdled into hatred.

Skylark-B sent back important information on troop and naval movements. It took a year for the Gestapo to track the transmitter down. Rørholt had just finished a transmission when the secret police arrived. He said later he escaped "after an unintentional shooting match with the Germans … most of the others were captured. Since I had escaped the Germans blamed me for most of what had been done."[19] He made his way to neutral Sweden and then on to Britain where he joined the

Norwegian navy. There he had teamed up with Polish officers and technicians working on miniature radio transmitters in a workshop near London. Now the Admiralty was asking him to go back to Norway. His task was to set up another, more comprehensive, radio network to spy on *Tirpitz*. Even though he was well-known to the Gestapo and his father was a hostage in their hands, he agreed.

He had one night to spend in London before flying to Shetland where the exiled Norwegian resistance had a base. He drew some money from a bank in the city and had a lavish dinner at the Savoy. Two days later, on January 20, with a lieutenant named John Turner, he flew to Lerwick on attachment to Naval Intelligence. They put up at the Queens Hotel and spent days discussing the details of the operation. Rørholt was to travel by sea to Trondheim, carrying a number of transmitters powerful enough to send a signal to Naval Intelligence headquarters. He was to identify potential agents in useful locations who would then make regular reports of enemy activity in their areas, particularly anything related to *Tirpitz*.

Rørholt was taken to Norway by a seaman called Leif Larsen. Larsen was thirty-six years old, quiet and modest, a brilliant sailor, and a natural and inspirational leader. He had learned his craft as master of a small passenger ship that plied the southern Norwegian coast and had an intimate knowledge of its confused contours of islands and inlets. He escaped from Norway in February 1941 aboard a fishing boat, the *Motig 1*, and joined an outfit set up by the Special Operations Executive, the Norwegian Naval Independent Unit. It operated a ferry service using disguised fishing vessels carrying agents and saboteurs to and from the Norwegian coast and became famous as the "Shetland Bus."

There was a six-day wait before the weather allowed them to sail. Rørholt used the time to dye his blond hair black. It was not much of a disguise, as the suspiciously raven locks clashed with his blue Scandinavian eyes. They set off on Saturday, January 26, 1942, on the cutter *Feie* with the aim of landing Rørholt south of Trondheim. The improvement in the weather had been minimal. It was freezing cold and heavy seas battered the boat. Water had leaked into the fuel tanks by the halfway mark, causing the engine to cut out repeatedly. At one point Larsen had to hoist canvas to make any progress while he carried out repairs. With the engine back in service they butted on. The motor cut out again. When he went to raise the sails they refused to budge. The rigging was solid with frozen spray. After more work on the engine it eventually spluttered into action and they finally reached the shore, numb, exhausted, and seasick after thirty-six hours on the water.

They anchored in the lee of an island to wait for daylight. There some friendly fishermen discovered them and warned them that the Germans had set up a new control point on the route they had been planning to take. They changed their plans and diverted to an island farther south that was home to one of the *Feie*'s crewmen. His father had a boat there, which was well known in local waters. They could put Rørholt aboard and with luck he would be able to slip through the German control.

The new route would take them past another island where Larsen had previously landed an agent, who had been equipped with a transmitter. He was anxious to hear how he was getting on. They soon found the agent but he had bad news. He had failed to make any contact with Britain. He had come to the conclusion that the radio was faulty and had been trying to arrange a voyage back to Shetland.

Rørholt cast his expert eye over the set it but could not find the fault. He decided to try one of his own radios. Again, he failed to get a response on any of the agreed frequencies. The three of them came to the same dismaying conclusion. The radios were useless. They would have to go back.

There was no improvement in conditions on the voyage home. They struggled through heavy seas, nauseated from the motion of the ship and frozen stiff by the wind and flying spray. The engine misbehaved constantly. They were blown off course and instead of making for Lerwick, Larsen decided it was easier to head for the haven of Lunna Voe. On January 30, the *Feie* made harbor in a snowstorm.

The failure had at least taught some lessons. The transmitters were too unwieldy and unreliable to justify the risks entailed in operating them. Rørholt remembered the miniaturized set he had seen his Polish colleagues experimenting with in London. "It had slightly less power than the others but it had an ingenious antenna arrangement which made up for it and it fitted in a briefcase of normal dimensions," he said. "However I had not been able to take that set as it was a prototype. Now I decided that I was definitely going to get that set and some others if possible. That was why my only concern when we reached Lunna was to get to London as quickly as possible."

There were some bureaucratic difficulties in his way. Arriving in London, he was once again refused the use of the Polish transmitters. According to the subsequent legend, Rørholt decided simply to steal some of them. He returned to Shetland and on February 11 set off for Norway. Larsen was at the helm once more. This time he had a more reliable craft, the *Arthur*, which he had liberated to escape back to Shetland after a previous escapade. Rørholt was now "Rolf Christiansen." There were two other agents making the trip, including Odd Sørli, who would play a major role in the *Tirpitz* story. The crossing was rough but uneventful. On February 13, he arrived in the Trondheim area to begin his vital mission.

The dangers he faced were considerable. Ranged against him and the men he hoped to recruit was a strong force of professionals unconstrained by moral scruples, led by Gerhard Flesch. Flesch did not look or sound like the conventional image of a secret policeman. He had warm eyes and a mouth that in photographs seems always to be smiling. He was born in the city of Posen (Poznań in Polish) in 1909, when it was still part of the German empire. He joined the Nazi Party in 1933 while a law student. He had joined the Gestapo by 1936 and had the job of monitoring Germany's religious sects. He was part of the organization that operated in the Sudetenland and later in Bohemia and Moravia following their occupation. After the invasion of Poland in September 1939 he returned to his hometown where he was leader of an Einsatz-kommando that started the work of exterminating the 3,000 or so Jews who still lived in the city.

Flesch had help from local collaborators. The most enthusiastic was Henry Rinnan. Rinnan belonged to the category of misfits and socio-paths, found throughout the occupied territories, for whom the arrival of the Nazis was liberation. He was born into a poor family in Levanger, north of Trondheim, on May 14, 1915, the oldest of seven children. He was short—five feet three inches—and dark-haired in a land of large, healthy blonds, which marked him out for ridicule and teasing. His early life was a story of disappointment and disgrace. He got a job working at his uncle's petrol station but was sacked for stealing. He was twenty-one at the time, and married. To make restitution he was forced to sell all the household goods he had acquired on hire purchase. When the war began he tried to join the Finnish forces resisting the Soviet invasion but was turned down on the grounds of his puny physique. He served as a lorry driver in the Norwegian army, ferrying weapons around Trondheim in April 1940. Two months later he was working as a car salesman.

The Germans had arrived in town, and his employer gave a party to which he invited some of them. The invaders seemed friendly enough and Rinnan responded warmly. Three days later he was summoned to the Hotel Phoenix in Trondheim where he met a Gestapo official called Gerhard Stubs. By the time he left, he had become an agent and received his first reward—a hundred-krone note. As the Gestapo's first local employee, he was agent 001 and had the alias "Lola." The attention revived his withered self-esteem. He bought a new suit with the money. There was little work for him, though, until the arrival of Flesch, who gave him the task of infiltrating communities in the districts surrounding the town. He had another Norwegian to assist him, a former Trondheim policeman called Ivan Grande, and together they built up a network of informers and *agents provocateurs*.

The open atmosphere of a town where everybody knew and largely trusted everyone else had been corrupted and Rørholt and his companions were heading for a Trondheim that was tainted with fear and suspicion. They arrived by passenger steamer after being dropped off on an outlying island. He later recounted how, when disembarking, a German soldier offered to carry his suitcase. The weight of it surprised him. Inside were three miniaturized transmitters, which Rørholt now set about distributing. There was one man whom Rørholt was sure he could trust. Birger Grønn was the manager of the dockyard. He had learned where *Tirpitz* was anchored from one of his engineers who lived near Faettenfjord. While cycling to work along the road that ran along the southern shore, he had been amazed to see the battleship looming out of the morning gloom.

Grønn set out to investigate. Posing as an innocent passerby he took note of the piers being built on either side of the water and the flak batteries installed on the hill beneath which the ship was anchored. To increase the hazards, the Germans had also strung steel hawsers from the ridge to the high ground on the southern side. He sketched the detail in a notebook and returned to Trondheim.

Rørholt already knew Grønn from his student days at the Institute. As soon as he arrived in Trondheim he went to see him, taking a taxi to his house in a suburb in the hills above the town. They discussed the best vantage points for the three transmitters. Ideally, one should be on hand near Faettenfjord, one in Trondheim, and one at the mouth of Trondheimsfjord, through which *Tirpitz* would have to pass on its way to the open sea. Grønn told him of a man who might be willing to cover the latter location.

Magne Hassel lived at Agdenes, near the old fortress that commanded the seaward approaches to the city. Grønn knew Hassel's brother Arne, who was one of his welders at the port. Before Rørholt's arrival he had telephoned Hassel to gauge his willingness to cooperate, and Hassel had agreed to the assignment. The problem for Rørholt was how to get a transmitter to him. The headland at Agdenes was in a closed military area.

Rørholt soon established a useful cover. He arranged a job as an insurance salesman with the firm of Tobias Lund. He equipped himself with brochures, packed them in a cardboard suitcase, hid the transmitter underneath, and set off for Agdenes. After talking his way through the checkpoint, he was taken to see the commander, a naval officer. He was friendly and swallowed Rørholt's story that he was in the area to visit clients but had only just arrived from Oslo and had not had time to get clearance from the German authorities at Trondheim. He even expressed interest in a policy himself. Rørholt was unsure whether or not he was joking. He replied with a straight face that his firm did not insure the lives of German officers because "the risk is too great." The commander laughed and sent him on his way with a sailor escort.

He found Hassel's green-painted mill house looking out over the mouth of the fjord and left the sailor at the gate. Hassel had been warned of the visit by his brother and was waiting. He was ready to help but explained that he did not know Morse code. Rørholt gave him a card with a simple code. One signal meant that *Tirpitz* had put to sea. Another, that it had returned. A third gave warning that other major ships had left the fjord. They hid the transmitter under the floorboards. Over the next thirteen months Hassel would diligently record *Tirpitz's* comings and goings, providing invaluable real-time intelligence that the

Admiralty could match against information gleaned from signal intercepts and Enigma decrypts.

Rørholt, meanwhile, was given a lift back to Trondheim on a naval motorboat thanks to the courteous fort commander. He stayed on in Trondheim recruiting several more volunteers. They would be required to transmit more detailed data than the simple reports that Hassel would provide. To do that, they needed training. Rørholt made arrangements for them to meet up with the Shetland Bus network, and they were taken by fishing boat to England to undergo short courses in wireless telegraphy.

British intelligence was going to need all the help it could get in Norway. On the night of February 11, the move to shift the main elements of the German surface fleet northward took a dramatic step forward, when *Scharnhorst* and *Gneisenau*, with the heavy cruiser *Prinz Eugen*, nosed out of Brest and headed for home ports. Vizeadmiral Otto Ciliax, who had replaced Lütjens as Commander of Battleships after his death, commanded the force. With the fate of *Bismarck* in mind, Hitler had forbidden it to return to Germany via the Atlantic. Instead it was to take the direct route through the Channel—an intelligently calculated risk. The nearest British battleships were at Scapa Flow and the Luftwaffe had air bases the length of the northern European coastline that could provide cover. British intelligence had anticipated the move but had not expected that the ships would dare to negotiate the narrows of the Strait of Dover in daylight. It was twelve hours before the German fleet was spotted, crossing the Bay of Seine. The combined efforts of navy torpedo boats, Fleet Air Arm and RAF torpedo planes, fighters and bombers, and the army's shore batteries failed to stop the escapers. Night had fallen and they were off the Dutch coast before they suffered a setback. Mines damaged both *Scharnhorst* and *Gneisenau*, but they were still able to make their way to Wilhelmshaven, from which they arrived at the mouth of the Elbe at 7:00 a.m. on February 13.

The Channel Dash was regarded at home and abroad as a humiliation for the British navy. From the Kriegsmarine's perspective, though, it represented "a tactical victory but a strategic retreat," as the German Naval Staff admitted in their summary of the outcome.[20] There were no German capital ships left in French Atlantic ports to menace the convoys. That was now left to the U-boats, which continued through the spring and summer to savage the Atlantic convoys.

The big units of the German fleet would be concentrating henceforth on a different target. A week after reaching Germany, Ciliax took *Prinz Eugen*, accompanied by the pocket battleship *Admiral Scheer* and the destroyers *Hermann Schoemann*, *Friedrich Ihn*, and *Z-25*, and headed for Trondheim. Enigma intercepts told the Admiralty of their departure, and four submarines were waiting for them outside Trondheimsfjord. HMS *Trident* managed to hit *Prinz Eugen*'s rudder with a torpedo but she was still able to make it to Aasfjord, just west of Faettenfjord, by midnight on February 23. Rørholt watched them arrive. "We have got the two babies. They are safe and sound with their other playmates," he signaled.

Their presence in Norway made the Atlantic a safer place, but it greatly increased the dangers to the Arctic convoys. A powerful squadron, led by *Tirpitz*, was now concentrated at the eastern end of Trondheimsfjord. It could not be long before it ventured out.

CHAPTER 5

"A WONDERFUL CHANCE"

I n the first two months of 1942, nine Allied convoys crossed the Arctic Ocean, going to and from Russia. The voyage tested the seamanship and character of the crews to the limit. In the freezing heart of winter, the sea lapping the polar ice cap was the grimmest place on earth. They traveled in darkness, relieved by only a few hours of wan twilight in the middle of the day, through fog-smothered and snow-swept waters seething with submerged growlers and jagged floes that could rip through the hull of a merchantman like a can opener. Sudden storms whipped placid seas into cliffs of angry water, seventy feet high, tearing the formation apart and scattering ships far and wide. Strange happenings compounded the feeling that they were sailing to the end of the world. Cold air settling on warmer water created wraiths of mist that made the sea appear to be boiling. On a clear night the Northern

Lights flickered mystically in the black, star-dusted canopy above, filling those who looked up at it with awe and apprehension.[1]

The narrowness of the waters east of Bear Island meant that ships could not turn into the waves and meet heavy seas bow-on as they did in the Atlantic. Instead, they were rocked from side to side, rolling as much as 30 degrees to port and starboard. Temperatures could plunge to sixty below, sheathing the upper deck with ice which the crew attacked with axes and steam hoses to prevent the added weight tipping the ship over. Able Seaman Bill Smith, who made the voyage aboard the anti-submarine sloop HMS *Magpie*, recalled how eyebrows, eyelashes, and nasal hair froze solid, "like needles." Men came off watch with their faces covered in blood from rubbing their noses without thinking.[2]

These were not waters into which sailors ventured happily and the First Sea Lord, Sir Dudley Pound, and the Home Fleet commander, Sir John Tovey, had opposed the Arctic convoys. They argued instead that supplies to the Soviet Union should be sent via the Persian Gulf which, though longer and slower, would cost fewer ships and lives.

Churchill overruled them. His motives were political as well as practical. As the summer of 1941 faded, German armies prepared to close on Moscow, and Stalin needed swift and solid proof that Britain and America were genuine allies. The first convoy sailed on August 21, 1941, opening a pipeline that, with some significant interruptions, gushed tanks, aircraft, and stores to the—largely ungrateful—Soviets until the last days of the war.

There were frequent differences between Churchill and some of the admirals. On the whole his relations with Pound were good—a result, said critics, of the First Sea Lord's emollient and accommodating attitude—and his opposition to the convoys was soon forgotten. The clash with Tovey, however, merely deepened Churchill's irritation with the Commander in Chief of the Home Fleet. Even as an adolescent at Dartmouth, "Jack" Tovey had been marked for the top, and he had a stubborn faith in himself and his judgment. He was also deeply religious and if he had to choose between the will of his Maker and the dictates of the Prime Minister, God was always going to trump Churchill.

Tovey's robust integrity had caused problems with Pound in the aftermath of the *Bismarck* episode. With the Prime Minister's encouragement, the First Sea Lord had proposed disciplining senior officers for their alleged timidity during the battle of the Denmark Strait. He started moves to bring court-martial proceedings against the commander of the *Prince of Wales*, Captain John Leach, and Rear Admiral William Wake-Walker, who took command of the force after Admiral Holland went down in the *Hood*. It was Wake-Walker who ordered *Prince of Wales* to break off the action against *Bismarck* on the grounds that she was bound to come off worse. Tovey agreed with the decision. He let it be known that if proceedings were brought, he would resign and appoint himself "prisoner's friend" at the service of the accused, and Pound was forced to drop proceedings.

Churchill interpreted this behavior as evidence of excessive cautiousness rather than moral fortitude. Even though he had—after some initial dithering—put Tovey in charge of the Home Fleet, he came to regard him as lacking in offensive spirit, the military quality that he prized above all others. By the beginning of 1942, he was complaining to Pound about Tovey's "negative, un-enterprising and narrow-minded" attitude.[3] Tovey, for his part, had a professional's contempt for Churchill's continuous interventions, which often seemed wildly at odds with reality. After an early meeting he wrote to his friend Vice Admiral Sir Andrew Cunningham expressing surprise at the Prime Minister's "astonishing statements about naval warfare both at home and abroad."[4] Cunningham shared his view, confiding in a letter to an aunt that Churchill was "a bad strategist but doesn't know it and nobody has the courage to stand up to him."[5]

Churchill had served two terms as First Lord of the Admiralty, first in 1914–15 and then from September 1939 until his arrival at Downing

Street in May 1940. Like Hitler, he had an extraordinary capacity for absorbing facts, and few matters, great or small, escaped his attention. There was no phony war at sea and the first weeks of the naval conflict were fraught with drama and incident. Churchill nonetheless found time on November 21, 1939, when the new cruiser HMS *Belfast* had had her back broken by a German mine in the home waters of the Firth of Forth, to dictate a memo on the question of whether having a cockney accent should be an impediment to advancing in the service (he held that it should not). His experience, and his image of himself as a born warrior, persuaded him that his judgment was at least equal to that of the admirals. There were enough occasions when he was demonstrably right and they were wrong to confirm him in this view.

Churchill's intention to keep the Arctic convoys sailing at regular intervals throughout the year presented Tovey with a continuing logistical migraine. He did not have the ships to provide a strong escorting force as well as mount an effective guard on the northern passages to the Atlantic. The lengthening hours of daylight made the voyage increasingly hazardous. In the first few months of 1942, the convoys had got off lightly. Only one destroyer and one merchantman had been sunk, and several convoys had passed undetected. The concealing robe of darkness, however, was slipping away. The same was not true of the polar ice cap, which would take several more months to retreat, forcing the convoys to pass through narrow waters patrolled by U-boats and within easy reach of the newly arrived Luftwaffe reinforcements on land. Tovey voiced his fears, but Churchill was adamant that the risks were acceptable and the convoys would sail.

Tovey could take some comfort in the thought that a great opportunity had arisen from the new situation. *Tirpitz* was now in Norway, with the pocket battleship *Admiral Scheer* to support her. Another convoy was due to set sail at the beginning of March. Surely they would venture out to attack it, providing him with the chance to bring off an extraordinary coup? He had already sent *Bismarck* to the bottom. Now he was well placed to sink her sister. It was a thrilling prospect and he was eager to seize it. So was Churchill. The Prime Minister's fascination with *Tirpitz* was unabated. On January 27, he had taken the trouble to complain to Alexander about the waste of time involved in signalmen, cipher staff, and typists referring to the ship as "Admiral von Tirpitz" in every signal when "surely TIRPITZ is good enough for the beast."[6] Now there was a chance that the beast might come out to fight. On March 3, he once again emphasized *Tirpitz's* great significance in the strategic picture, telling the War Cabinet Defence Committee that she was "the most important vessel in the naval situation today" and that "her elimination would profoundly affect the course of the war."[7]

By then, a new convoy, PQ.12, was already at sea. It had set sail on March 1, bound for Murmansk with seventeen vessels from Iceland. At the same time, Convoy QP.8, made up of fifteen ships that had made the same journey earlier, set off from Murmansk for home. The lurking presence of the Trondheim squadron meant that, for the first time, the movement in both directions would be covered by the main body of the Home Fleet. PQ.12 would have a close escort comprised of a cruiser, *Kenya*; two destroyers, *Oribi* and *Offa*; and several Norwegian whaling vessels converted to hunt submarines. A larger force consisting of the battleship *Duke of York*, the battle cruiser *Renown*, and six destroyers, commanded by Vice Admiral Alban Curteis, had put to sea from Iceland on March 3 to cover from a distance. Tovey, on board *King George V*, followed two days later from Scapa Flow, together with the cruiser *Berwick* and six destroyers. To provide air cover and to attack any German shipping, the 29,500-ton carrier HMS *Victorious* sailed with them. She was fast and modern and could accommodate thirty-six aircraft. It was a lavish use of the Home Fleet's stretched resources. Altogether, the thirty-two merchantmen in the outward and inward convoys would be protected by forty-two escorts.

Around noon on March 5, 1942, one of the Luftwaffe long-range Focke-Wulf Condors that scoured the northern sea routes for enemy convoys saw ships sailing eastwards near Jan Mayen Island, a barren lump of rock in the middle of the Norwegian Sea about 350 nautical miles northeast of Iceland. The news was passed on to the headquarters of Naval Group North, at Kiel. Its commander, Generaladmiral Rolf Carls, eagerly signaled the naval staff in Berlin for permission to attack.

Raeder, with Hitler's blessing, gave permission. Here, at last, was a chance for *Tirpitz* to do something to justify its existence. The Kriegsmarine's big ships soaked up enormous amounts of materiel and manpower that were much needed elsewhere yet had made little difference so far to the war at sea. It was becoming clear from the battle in the Atlantic that submarines and airplanes were far more effective than surface vessels at the business of ravaging allied seaborne commerce. By now U-boats had destroyed more than five and a half million tons of Allied merchant shipping. Enemy aircraft had accounted for nearly two million tons. Warship raiders, however, had managed only to sink seventy-three ships totalling a paltry 363,146 tons. Submarines and aircraft had also proved a deadlier enemy to the Royal Navy's big ships than their opposite numbers in the Kriegsmarine's surface fleet. Of the eight battleships, battle cruisers, and aircraft carriers lost to enemy action in the war to date, only two had been sunk by gunfire.

Raeder, though, was cautious. The prize of destroying the convoy was not worth the risk of the loss of his battleship. Vizeadmiral Ciliax, in command of the operation, was told to avoid confronting enemy forces unless it was absolutely necessary to complete the destruction of PQ.12. Even then, he was to engage only if he was confident that he was facing an equal or inferior force.

There was plenty of time for an interception and nothing to be gained by an early appearance that would give the enemy time to react. It was not until the following morning that *Tirpitz* slipped her moorings at Faettenfjord and set off westward into Trondheimsfjord. Darting ahead were the slim shapes of the destroyers *Hermann Schoemann*, *Friedrich Ihn*, and *Z-25*. Snapping in the wind, high on the mast, flew the flag of Otto Ciliax, flushed with success from the Channel Dash and as anxious as Tovey for another triumph.

That afternoon *Tirpitz* passed the Agdenes fortress and steered round the Brekstad headland and out into the open sea. Norwegian agents onshore seem either to have missed her passing or their reports did not reach London in time, for the first sighting was made by one of the British submarines, now on regular picket duty off the entrance to Trondheimsfjord. Lieutenant Dick Raikes was patrolling in *Seawolf*, trying to stay hidden on a "horribly flat sea" from the German aircraft that appeared frequently overhead, when, just before 6:00 p.m., the submarine's hydrophones picked up the ominous churning of big propellers. He stayed on the surface long enough to glimpse the foretop and funnel of a large warship which he immediately took to be *Tirpitz*. He dived and set off towards her but "never got within ten miles of her." It was just as well that he did not, he reflected later, for the destroyers and the escorting aircraft circling the squadron would have made short work of *Seawolf*.[8]

He broke off the chase to report the news to London. Nerves everywhere—in the Admiralty, in Downing Street, and on all the ships at sea—were already strained in expectation. The Condor's signal had been picked up and decoded. Just after midnight, Raikes's confirmation that *Tirpitz* had been unable to resist the temptation presented by PQ.12 was in Tovey's hands aboard *King George V*, and he paused to consider his options.

Tirpitz was at sea, but what about her companions? *Prinz Eugen* was still out of the picture, thanks to the damage done by a torpedo from HMS *Trident* on the journey to Trondheimsfjord, but where was the *Admiral Scheer*? The answer was that she was still at anchor, immobilized by the caution of Raeder, who was worried that she was too slow to take part in the operation. Tovey continued to worry about a big ship break-out into the Atlantic. There was a danger that one enemy ship might engage the convoy, diverting the attention away from the other while it raced for the North Atlantic. He considered dividing his force to cover both possibilities but an intervention from the Admiralty stopped this line of thought. They were sharply aware of the threat posed by the Luftwaffe squadrons now based in the area. The navy's losses from air attack in Norway, Dunkirk, and Crete had taught them a painful lesson. Tovey was told to keep his fleet concentrated under the protective air umbrella that the Fulmar fighters provided aboard *Victorious*.

Fleet Air Squadrons 817 and 832 made up the striking force that would be thrown at German shipping. They were equipped with Fairey Albacore torpedo planes, the replacement for the Swordfish. The RAF's interwar control of naval aviation had meant that the navy had inherited a service that was dismally lacking in aircraft and weapons capable of taking on ships. For the first years of the war the men of the Fleet Air Arm were stuck with inadequate and ill-equipped airplanes, which they flew with extraordinary élan and determination despite being pro-foundly aware of their shortcomings.

Sub-Lieutenant Charles Friend had just arrived on 832 Squadron, his latest posting in an incident-packed war that had included taking part in the air attacks on *Bismarck*. He was a reservist, a "hostilities only" volunteer. Like many young men of the time he was fascinated by flying, and in 1939 had given up his job as a lab assistant at the Paint Research Station in Teddington, Middlesex, to join the Fleet Air Arm. Friend was a grammar school boy, intelligent and lively. He brought a healthy dose of civilian skepticism with him into the enclosed world of the profes-sional navy. On the whole, though, he found his new life congenial. "I had been made aware of the military virtues of obedience and loyalty in my family and school life as most of us had at the time," he wrote later.

"The loss of complete independence in service life at all levels was compensated for by an abiding sense of belonging to an organization with a purpose."[9] In the early spring of 1942, he was just twenty-one but had already seen enough action to furnish several military careers. As well as the *Bismarck* operation, he had watched the sinking of the French fleet at Mers-el-Kebir, hunted submarines in the Atlantic, and been aboard the carrier *Ark Royal* when a U-boat sunk her in the Mediterranean in November 1941.

Friend was an observer, and most of his flying had been done in Swordfishes. He found the Albacore "like a first class version of the Swordfish. It was an improvement on the dear old Stringbag because it had a more powerful engine and it was more aerodynamically efficient." Unlike the "Stringbag" it had an enclosed and heated cockpit, which represented an enormous improvement to the lives of the crew, particularly in the savage conditions of the Arctic. It also had an automatic life raft ejection system which triggered in the event of the aircraft ditching. One innovation was particularly welcome. The installation of a "P Tube" meant they could relieve themselves in comfort. In the Swordfish, the crew had to make do by filling the empty containers of aluminum dust markers or flame floats, used to determine wind direction and tide speed, before flinging them overboard. It was important to choose the right side, "because over the wrong one, the slipstream opened them and showered the contents back into the cockpit."

The Albacore already bore an air of obsolescence. It was a biplane, and its fixed undercarriage hung below, dragging through the air and slowing it down. Even with the extra horsepower offered by its new 1,065-horsepower Bristol Taurus II fourteen-cylinder radial engine, it could still only manage a top speed of 150 knots (172 mph) in straight and level flight. Its usual speed was a mere 90 knots (103 mph), which made the observer's job of navigating easier but severely limited its searching capabilities especially when the wind was against it.

Some pilots felt the controls were heavier than those of the Swordfish and it was harder to take evasive action after dropping a torpedo.[10]

There were other antiquated touches. The pilot's seat was just ahead of the upper main plane, and a long fuel tank separated him from the observer. Communication took place via a Gosport speaking tube—a simple length of flexible pipe. Pilots often forgot to connect them. According to Friend, to gain the attention of the man at the controls of a Swordfish, "one simply reached over and banged his head." In Albacores, though, "we all carried a long garden cane to reach forward past the tank to tap him on the shoulder." Detailed messages were written down and passed forward in an empty Very signal cartridge stuck on the end of the stick.

Contact among aircraft and back to the ship took place by radio and Morse code and was used only to report a sighting of the enemy or in extreme emergencies. The Aldis lamp was still a useful tool to signal from air to deck or to other aircraft. When flying in formation they "resorted to making Morse with a swung forearm—'zogging' it was called." As protection the Albacore had one fixed forward-firing .303-inch machine gun in the starboard wing, which the pilot operated. The rear cockpit was fitted with twin Vickers K guns operated by a third member of the crew, which delivered more firepower than the Swordfish's single Lewis gun.

Compared with the Luftwaffe's sleek Condors and Heinkels, compared with the Japanese Mitsubishi torpedo and bomber aircraft, the "Applecore" was slow and feebly armed. Thus equipped, the Fleet Air Arm could hope to achieve little. Given the quality of its aircraft, it had performed remarkably well. So far, the FAA actions had sunk three Italian battleships and six destroyers, as well as a German light cruiser, largely thanks to the skill and boldness of the crews. These qualities were about to be tested again as the British fleet and the *Tirpitz* squadron headed towards what all involved believed would be an epic encounter.

By the evening of March 6, *Tirpitz* was steaming northeastward up the Norwegian coast at a steady twenty-three knots through heavy seas before turning due north at midnight. At ten the next morning an attempt was made to send two of the battleship's four Arado seaplanes off to try and locate the convoy. The Arado 196 was a robust, fast, and well-armed monoplane designed for reconnaissance. It carried a pilot and an observer who also operated the guns. It was equipped with two floats and got airborne by being fired off the deck by a thirty-four-yard-long catapult that could be extended telescopically over the side. Its main shortcoming was that on returning it had to land on the water as near as it could to the ship's side, where a crane could lift it back aboard. In anything other than calm conditions, this was a difficult and dangerous maneuver.

Arados had folding wings and were usually housed below decks. The *Tirpitz* aircraft, though, were parked on deck. It was appallingly cold and snow gusted over the heaving, iron-gray seas. When the crews inspected their airplanes they found the wings were coated in ice. Flying was impossible. There would be no aerial reconnaissance that day. Ciliax did the next best thing and detached the three destroyers to head off north-north-west, while he took *Tirpitz* on a northwesterly heading, judging that one or the other force would sail across the route the convoy would take.

Tovey had been moving steadily in the opposite direction, with the intention of putting a defensive shield of warships between the expected German line of approach and the convoy. Like Ciliax, he was operating blind. The weather brought no advantages to either side. The Albacores aboard *Victorious* had iced up, just like the *Tirpitz*'s Arados. There was no way of tracking the enemy from the air, and no other technological aids to decision-making to fill the information gap. Radar only stretched to the horizon. The great boon of Ultra had its limitations. The Kriegs-marine used an Enigma encrypting machine which had a different key system than that used by the army and air force. The code breakers at Bletchley Park found naval intercepts more difficult to decipher. It was sometimes twelve hours between a message being picked up and the decrypted content arriving at the Admiralty's Operational Intelligence Centre (OIC), and so far there was nothing to reveal Ciliax's intentions.

As the forenoon of March 7 wore on, both admirals were sifting their options in a manner that would have been familiar to a fighting captain of Nelson's era. Into their calculations went the state of the sea and the weather, the speed and capabilities of the enemy force and, not least, their own assessment of the character and propensities of their opponent. Tovey's intention was not only to protect PQ.12 but to lure *Tirpitz* and her companions into a battle which he hoped would end in her destruction. Ciliax was content with doing the maximum damage to the convoy.

The day was likened later to a gigantic game of blind man's buff, as both commanders groped through the great wastes of empty water, swept by frequent squalls and blizzards. Through the middle hours of the day both forces held their headings, waiting for a development that would propel them on a more promising course. While they did so, the returning Convoy QP.8, traveling westward, and the outgoing ships of PQ.12 crossed through each other's lines in a snowstorm.

Though they did not know it, the hunters and the hunted were close to brushing each other. Z-25, the destroyer Ciliax had sent off earlier in the day to find PQ.12, had passed only ten miles from the home-bound QP.8 but in the snow and gloom had failed to see its smoke. As the afternoon wore on, visibility improved and the weather quieted. Another destroyer, the *Friedrich Ihn*, saw a smudge of smoke on the horizon and hurried off to investigate. The smoke was trailing from the funnel of the slow-moving Russian cargo ship *Izhora*, a straggler from QP.8. She was pathetically easy meat. At about 4:30 p.m. a torpedo from the destroyer hit her squarely on the port side. A photograph taken from the decks of the attacker shows a fierce fire burning amidships and black and gray smoke swirling above and behind. In the next one the bow has already disappeared beneath the surface of the sea which is now flat calm. *Tirpitz* hurried to join the destroyers as the *Izhora* went down, but the job was done and there was no need for her to fire her guns. Before the stricken merchantman disappeared, her radio operator managed to get off a distress signal which was picked up by the Home Fleet.

Tovey now had a rough idea of the enemy's position. It was supplemented by wireless bearings of an unidentified ship which might have been the *Tirpitz* and which led him to take the main body of the fleet off eastward toward Bear Island in pursuit. In case this proved to be a false scent and the battleship had turned for home, he detached six destroyers to hunt along a line stretching from the last position of the *Izhora* to Trondheim. Tovey kept up his search to the east until midnight and then turned south so that he could stay in touch with his destroyers and place *Victorious* in a position where her aircraft could set off on an aerial reconnaissance in the morning.

Ciliax was still intent on attacking PQ.12. By the evening of March 7, his destroyers were running low on oil. There was no accompanying tanker to allow them to refuel at sea. Ciliax ordered *Friedrich Ihn* back to Narvik to replenish and rejoin him as soon as possible. The other two destroyers tried twice to refuel from *Tirpitz's* bunkers but it was impossible to hook up the hoses in the heavy swell. They were sent back to Tromsø to fill up.

The following morning, March 8, he carried on the hunt with *Tirpitz* alone. He ordered Topp to turn due north toward Bear Island, calculating this would put him ahead of the advancing convoy. Once there, they turned again, heading southwest on a zigzag course which Ciliax believed would bring him onto a collision course with his prey. He was sure his instinct was right, and the crew members were called to action stations. But as the tension mounted and Topp and his men steeled themselves for their first battle, the convoy was steaming safely eighty miles to the north.

PQ.12 had been warned of the ambush. An Enigma intercept had reached the OIC which gave notice of Ciliax's move toward Bear Island and the news was passed on in enough time for the convoy to steer away from danger, moving north along the edge of the Arctic pack ice.[11] It was yet another example of the blessings of Ultra. Had the intercept not been made, the merchantmen might well have sailed into Tirpitz's guns while Tovey's fleet was still two hundred miles away. By now Tovey had concluded that Tirpitz had eluded him and was on her way back to port. He intended to take the fleet back westward to Iceland to replenish his destroyers. The new intelligence reached him in the late afternoon and at 5:30 p.m. he turned his ships round and headed northeast again in the direction of Bear Island.

Ciliax had spent a frustrating amount of time steaming along his chosen line of interception. At 8:00 p.m. he finally decided to give up the hunt and return south to Norway. He signaled his intentions back to Kiel. The message was duly intercepted and passed to the Bletchley Park decrypters who worked frantically to crack it in time for it to be put to maximum use. By the early hours of March 9, the information that the German fleet was on its way reached Tovey. At 2:40 a.m. he ordered the fleet around and steered southeast as fast as his ships were able in an attempt to cut off Ciliax and his force before they reached safety.

It was too late to catch them and bring them to battle. The aircraft aboard Victorious, however, provided a strike force that could land a significant blow. By skill or luck, some of the Albacores' torpedoes might find their target, slowing Tirpitz enough for the Home Fleet to catch her and presenting Tovey with the chance to crown his earlier triumph against Bismarck.

As the minutes passed the prospects of success seemed to grow. An Ultra signal reached Tovey from London giving further, invaluable details. An intercepted message from Naval Group North in Kiel gave the position, off the Lofoten Islands, where *Tirpitz* was going to rendezvous with its replenished destroyers at 7:00 a.m. At 3:16 a.m. the information was passed to Captain Henry Bovell, the commander of *Victorious*, with the order "report proposals."[12] Charles Friend was in the Operations Room when the new information arrived. "[It] said in effect that *Tirpitz* would be in a stated position just off Vestfjord which leads up to Narvik," he wrote. He remembered that it also gave the battleship's speed and course. The precision prompted him to think "that to have such prior knowledge Admiral Tovey must have had a spy on board *Tirpitz*."[13] It was only some time after the war ended that those who had fought in it finally learned of the existence of Ultra.

It was still too dark to fly but Bovell assured Tovey that operations would begin at first light. He signalled back: "Propose fly off searching force of six aircraft at 0630 ... fly off striking force of 12 as soon as ranged about 0730." The Albacore crews were woken at 5:30 a.m. Seventy minutes later, three aircraft each from 817 and 832 Squadrons left the carrier to comb the waters to the southeast. By now *Tirpitz* had been reunited with one of its destroyers, the *Friedrich Ihn*, returned from refueling at Narvik, and was west of the Lofotens steaming hard for home. Over the horizon, the Home Fleet sailed only 115 miles to the west-north-west.

The Albacores climbed through patchy clouds and gusting snow into a lightening sky. At 8:03 a.m. Sub-Lieutenant Tommy Miller, piloting the lead Albacore, spotted *Tirpitz* plowing through the leaden seas. The trim hull of the *Friedrich Ihn*, tiny in comparison, skimmed along beside it, a mile or so to the west.

He radioed back the news. The twelve Albacores of the strike force were waiting for the signal to go. Before they flew off Tovey left them in no doubt of the hopes that they carried with them. "A wonderful chance which may achieve most valuable results," he signaled. "God be with you."

For a few minutes after Miller's aircraft had made contact, the battle-ship sailed blindly on. The mood on board *Tirpitz* was subdued. After years of preparations and months of anticipation the ship's first foray had been desperately disappointing. For all the expenditure of energy and adrenaline, for all the massive consumption of scarce fuel oil, the expedition had resulted only in the sinking of a single merchant ship. At the moment the Albacores arrived, Ciliax was having breakfast in his quarters and Topp was resting in the lookout room. The ship was in the temporary charge of the navigating officer, Korvettenkapitän Gerhard Bidlingmaier, who was writing up his log when he heard a shout of "aircraft astern!" and ran to the bridge.

He ordered the ship to full speed and the Arados into the air. All over *Tirpitz*, alarm bells clanged and men ran to their action stations. Ciliax abandoned his breakfast and Topp his rest and they rushed to the bridge. It was clear that a torpedo attack was imminent. Ciliax took the decision to stay on the same heading until the Arados were airborne, then change course and run for the shelter of Vestfjord which lay behind the Lofotens and led into the haven of Narvik.

Only one Arado managed to take off. It turned toward the pursuers, dodging in and out of the drifting cloud cover, apparently directed towards the followers by *Tirpitz*'s radar. One of the Albacore's gunners opened fire but it had no serious effect. The Arado was more successful. One Albacore was hit and the observer, Sub-Lieutenant A. G. Dunworth, wounded in the thighs. Despite the attentions of the Arado, the pursuers stuck with the battleship, and at 8:30 a.m. radioed back her change of course toward the narrow entrance of the Moskenes Strait that opened into Vestfjord.

The strike force, formed into four sub-flights of three aircraft each, was now heading straight for *Tirpitz*. It was led by Lieutenant Com-mander Bill Lucas of 832 Squadron. Lucas was the most senior pilot in the force. He was not, however, the most experienced. He had arrived on the squadron only a few weeks before to replace Lieutenant Commander Peter Plugge who had disappeared with his crew in atrocious weather off the Norwegian coast on a futile search for the *Prinz Eugen* as it sailed for Trondheim. According to Charles Friend, Lucas was an "unknown quantity." In contrast, his subordinate in the operation, Lieutenant Commander Peter Sugden of 817 Squadron, had been flying operationally for two years and had won the Distinguished Flying Cross.

At 8:40 a.m. Lucas sighted the target in the distance, cutting strongly through the corrugated seas, and the Albacores fell in behind. It seemed to Friend that it was taking an eternity to reach it. They were "flying upwind against a thirty-five knot wind and ninety knots air speed, to a target which was steaming directly downwind at twenty-five knots. Our closing speed was therefore thirty knots—about the speed at which one carelessly drives in a built up area."

On spotting the target, Lucas had taken them up to 3,500 feet, hoping the scattered cloud would mask their approach. Friend found that, as they climbed, ice began to form on the wings. "The huge ship seemed to be there for hours as we crawled towards her," he recalled, "although it was only ten minutes from sighting to attack."

The sub-flight led by Lucas was approaching *Tirpitz* on the port side. The other three were to starboard. The recommended drill for a squadron-strength, twelve-aircraft torpedo attack on a ship was for the force to overhaul the target and then turn back onto it. Two sub-flights were to attack on the port quarter and two on the starboard, dropping their torpedoes in a fan-shaped pattern from a height of fifty to a hundred feet across her bows. This would cover a 90-degree arc, making it difficult for a big ship to take evasive action and greatly increasing the chances of a hit. The method had its dangers. The quarter attack exposed the aircraft to the ship's guns, which were presented with an ideal opportunity—as the pilots approached, flying straight and level, low and slow—to drop their torpedoes at an optimum range of between 800 and 1,000 yards.

Lucas, however, decided against the textbook approach. They were only catching up at a rate of a mile every two minutes and the danger of icing up was increasing. He gave the order for each sub-flight to attack in its own time, choosing its own trajectory. The concentration of force mustered by a coordinated attack was now lost. If a torpedo did hit *Tirpitz* it would be more by luck than design.

Lucas led his sub-flight in first. As he got closer there was a break in the cloud which he thought would expose their position. He decided on an immediate attack from the side rather than a head-on approach. At 9:18 a.m. the three Albacores dropped almost to sea level and released their torpedoes. According to Friend the others watched the attack with "astonishment … the subflight was led down immediately on *Tirpitz*'s port beam leaving the other three [sub-flights] badly placed should she turn to port which she forthwith did."[14] Lucas claimed, no doubt sincerely, that he had released his torpedoes from 1,000 yards, the outer limit if there was to be any chance of success. Friend's account says it was closer to a mile.

From the bridge, Topp could see the torpedoes hit the water and head toward his ship at forty knots. Without hesitation he shouted to the helmsman to wrench the ship hard to port. His instruction was countermanded immediately by Ciliax, standing alongside him, who ordered the helmsman to steer to starboard. There was a moment of silence. Topp spoke quietly but firmly. "I am in command of this ship, sir, not you," he told his chief, and repeated his order. The helmsman obeyed. A photograph, crisscrossed by the rigging of the wings of the Albacore from which it was taken, shows the ship turning with a tightness that seems extraordinary given its size, making a near semi-circle in the water.[15] The torpedoes from Lucas's flight cruised harmlessly astern, with the nearest one passing 150 yards away. The second 817 sub-flight now crossed over to the port side and launched another broadside attack.

All the *Tirpitz's* many guns were blazing in unison, supported by those of the *Friedrich Ihn*, but the pilots stuck to their course, releasing their torpedoes at 1,000 yards. Once again, they missed. The two remaining 817 Squadron flights under Sugden had anticipated the first evasive action and their pilots cut the corner of the turn to port to place themselves ahead. But *Tirpitz* now changed course again and swung sharply to starboard, taking her back on an easterly tack. Instead of a frontal attack they were forced to come at her from behind.

The 817 Squadron crews were heading into a blizzard of shells and bullets. Film taken from deck level shows two low-flying Albacores desperately clawing for height as gunfire whips up ramparts of spray in the sea right behind them. A close-quarters attack was suicidal. "With shots from her coming all around us I dropped my torpedo at almost extreme range," admitted an 817 pilot, Lieutenant Commander John Stenning, later.[16] One Albacore of 832 Squadron and another of 817 Squadron were hit just as they released their torpedoes and tumbled into the sea. There was no chance of rescue by the fleeing battleship and all six on board were killed or drowned.

Despite the furious defense they encountered, the attackers came remarkably close to scoring a hit. According to the *Tirpitz* log, three of the torpedoes went wide, but a fourth passed ten yards from the stern. A near miss, however, counted for nothing. The determination and sacrifice was in vain. No damage had been done to the target. The only German casualties of the attack were three men wounded by machine-gun fire from the Albacores.

As the torpedo planes dwindled into the distance, relief swept the ship. The decks jingled with shell cases. In the brief action, *Tirpitz's* sixteen large-caliber 105-mm flak guns, the size of field artillery, had fired off 345 rounds. The 37-mm light flak guns had got through 897 rounds and the 20-mm guns 3,372. The ship's eight gigantic guns had also been fired in anger for the first time, loosing two broadsides against their flimsy attackers. Ciliax made amends to Topp for his intervention. "Well done, captain," he said in front of the rest of the officers on the bridge. "You fought your ship magnificently." Exercising his prerogative as fleet commander he made an immediate award to Topp of the Iron Cross, taking off his own and pinning it on the captain.[17]

The surviving aircraft arrived back on the carrier at 11:00 a.m. to a cold reception. "The processes of debriefing and dissection of the fiasco ended in the surviving crews being mustered on the quarterdeck of *Victorious* to be addressed by senior officers in a very recriminatory way," Charles Friend remembered. "We received for our efforts and the loss of six men what can only be described in the naval slang of the time as a 'severe bottle.'" Friend considered his superiors' disappointment as "natural." But he judged that "their humanity seemed to have left them at that time."[18]

Lucas was criticized by Bovell for launching his attack prematurely. He went on to conclude that "all aircraft were deceived by *Tirpitz*'s large size and dropped their torpedoes at too great a range."[19] A fairer criticism would have been of the system that placed Lucas in charge, even though he had received no training for such an operation and had never flown in action with his men before that day. In the judgment of the official historian of the war at sea, "to be called on to carry out so critical an operation in such circumstances was a very severe, even unfair test."[20]

It was, as Tovey had said, a wonderful chance. But God was not on his side that day and the opportunity had been lost. For a few hours *Tirpitz* had been uniquely vulnerable, in open sea, with only her own guns and those of a single destroyer to defend her. There was some consolation in the safe arrival of PQ.12 at Murmansk on March 12. But weighed in the scales of war, Tovey regarded the sinking of *Tirpitz* as "of incomparably greater importance ... than the safety of any convoy." To him the battleship remained a mortal menace, whose removal was worth gamble and risk.[21] The moment had passed and there was no knowing when it would come again. As *Tirpitz* slipped into the safety of the sheltered anchorage at Bogen, near Narvik, the Home Fleet, with *Victorious*, headed disconsolately back to Scapa Flow.

The game was not quite over. The Bogen Bay anchorage provided only a temporary haven. If she lingered, *Tirpitz* could find herself bottled up by a blockading force stationed at the exit where the narrow Vestfjord met the sea, and vulnerable to air attack. Group Headquarters in Kiel ordered her back to Trondheim. She left at eleven o'clock on the night of March 12, accompanied by five destroyers. They had been due to sail early on March 13, but Topp, chastened perhaps by the near miss of the torpedo, superstitiously brought the departure forward.

They picked their way through the inner leads and raced south through foggy seas, keeping a watch for mines. Those on board did not know it, but there were other dangers lurking. Once again Ultra had given warning of the movement. A flotilla of eight destroyers from Scapa Flow arrived off the coast between Bodø and Trondheim at 1:30 a.m. and steered north into the path of the oncoming *Tirpitz*. By 3:30 a.m., they had to turn away, so as to be clear of the coast when dawn came up and exposed them to Luftwaffe attack.[22]

Tirpitz steamed southward, hugging the coast through fog and snow, passing close to four waiting submarines deployed tactically at points along the way where she had to leave the shelter of the leads for the open sea. By 9:00 p.m. on March 13, she was back in her anchorage in Faetten-fjord. The thick weather persisted. It was not until six days later that a reconnaissance flight confirmed that *Tirpitz* had returned home.

The failure to nail *Tirpitz* was badly received in Downing Street. On March 13, Churchill sent Pound a message asking him to "kindly let me have a report on the air attack on TIRPITZ, explaining how it was that 12 of our machines managed to get no hits as compared with the extraordinary efficiency of the Japanese attack on PRINCE OF WALES and REPULSE."[23] The underlying explanation, as he knew well, was that the Japanese had the airplanes and weapons to wage successful war at sea. The FAA was paying the price of its neglect. Its aircraft were outmoded and outclassed and, in the rapid expansion now going on, training had been rushed and units diluted with untested new arrivals. The debacle hastened efforts to repair these weaknesses so that the next time the FAA met the *Tirpitz* the results would be different. In the meantime, Churchill could take satisfaction from an operation that was very much to his taste.

CHAPTER 6

"A SOMEWHAT DESPERATE VENTURE"

T*irpitz* and all the Kriegsmarine's other large units were now grouped in northern waters, but at the Admiralty the fear persisted that at some point they would return to the Atlantic. If they did, the expectation was that they would then make their base in France. The journey home for refit and repair after a raiding expedition would be extremely hazardous. It would make more sense to operate from ports on the Bay of Biscay, and in particular St Nazaire.

St Nazaire lies five miles along the northern bank of the mouth of the Loire where it meets the Atlantic Ocean. During World War II it housed a complex of reinforced concrete pens from which German U-boats sallied out against Allied shipping. It was also home to the world's biggest dry dock, built between 1928 and 1932 for the construction of the great French luxury liner SS *Normandie*. The dock was the only one on the Atlantic coast large enough to handle a big battleship. It was where Admiral Lütjens had been heading when the *Bismarck* was damaged and was the obvious place from which *Tirpitz* could lunge at the transatlantic convoys.

Hitler by now had no intention of risking *Tirpitz* on a long-range mission. Raeder agreed with him. Her performance against PQ.12 was disappointing. Nonetheless, she was providing a great service tying up a large portion of the Home Fleet which otherwise might be operating to greater effect in the Mediterranean or Far East. U-boats were sinking large amounts of transatlantic Allied shipping every day anyway without any help from the surface fleet—1.2 million tons were lost in the first three months of 1942.

In these circumstances, the U-boat pens at St Nazaire would appear a more vital target than the dry dock. The port had already been subjected to air attack. In the spring of 1941, as the crisis of the Battle of Britain faded and the Battle of the Atlantic intensified, Churchill had demanded a maximum effort from the RAF against the two enemy weapons that were wreaking most of the destruction. His words were repeated in the directive handed to Bomber Command: "We must take the offensive against the U-boat and the Focke-Wulf (Condor) wherever we can and whenever we can."[1] St Nazaire was listed as a target. It was not until the next year that regular raids were launched. The bombing was inaccurate and ineffective and operations were restricted by Churchill's instruction that aircraft were to attack only when visibility was good enough to minimize the risk to French civilians. A chance had been missed. By March 1942, nine out of fourteen planned submarine pens were finished. Shielded from bombs by massive layers of reinforced concrete, there was no hope of destroying them from the air. A land attack would take enormous resources and involve considerable losses.

The pens, then, were too tough a target, whichever way they were approached. The *Normandie* dock, however—even in the changed circumstances of early 1942—still appeared a worthwhile proposition. The Admiralty had not interpreted the shift of all Hitler's big ships northward, a shift that was completed with the *Scharnhorst* and *Gneisenau*'s dash through the Channel, as meaning that the Kriegsmarine's surface ships would no longer venture south.

Fear of the *Tirpitz*'s destructive capabilities remained as intense as ever. As long as the facilities at St Nazaire were intact, the possibility existed that a raiding force with *Tirpitz* at its heart would launch into the North Atlantic, laying waste to the convoys and diverting most of the Home Fleet into the effort to hunt it down. The destruction of the *Normandie* dock would shut down that possibility for ever.

In January 1942, following a conversation with Churchill, Sir Dudley Pound asked the Admiralty's Plans Division to examine the possibilities. They in turn asked the newly appointed Chief of the Combined Operations Headquarters, Lord Louis Mountbatten, to devise a solution. Combined Ops was an inter-service organization tasked with devising disruptive raids that would harass and unnerve Axis forces. It could call on the troops of the Special Service Brigade's Commandos, set up after the fall of France by Churchill to "develop a reign of terror down the enemy coast." But it had no real resources of its own and was dependent on the cooperation of the other services, which was by no means automatically forthcoming.

Over the next weeks, Mountbatten and his team drew up a plan of outrageous boldness. It depended on speed, surprise, and devastating force and was just the sort of operation that delighted Churchill, appealing to his romantic weakness for the dash of pre-industrial-era soldiering. If successful, its psychological as well as material results would have been very welcome. With the Soviet Union and the United States as allies, Britain was no longer alone. On land and sea, though, the war was not going well. As Commander Robert Ryder, who would lead the naval force in the attack, observed, "some feat of arms that would hearten the country in such a dark hour" was an added good reason for the great risks involved.[2]

The *Normandie* dock was 1,148 feet long and 164 feet wide with lock gates—known as *caissons*—at each end. It ran at a slant with one end opening into an inner port basin, the Bassin de Penhoët. The other connected to the river. The *caissons* were made of hollow steel sections and were thirty-five feet thick.

The basic plan was to sail an old destroyer, the *Campbeltown*, accompanied by eighteen shallow-hulled launches, up the Loire estuary to St Nazaire and drive her at full speed through the lock gates. Next, 277 commandos, split into eighteen teams, would set about destroying the dock machinery. Then, time-delayed fuses would detonate the four and a half tons of Amatol high explosive packed into the *Campbeltown*, destroying the dock.

The commandos at the heart of the operation were all volunteers, dedicated, skillful, and aggressive. In the six weeks they had to prepare, the teams trained with an intensity that reflected the hardening professionalism and determination of the British war effort, carrying out practice runs in the port facilities at Cardiff and Southampton. In Southampton they had the advantage of familiarizing themselves with the *King George V* Dry Dock, which was an almost exact replica of the one they were going to attack.

The force was led by Lieutenant Colonel Charles "Charlie" Newman of 2 Commando, which provided most of the troops. Newman was an amiable and good-natured thirty-seven-year-old who was married with four children and a fifth on the way. He had been a successful civil engineer before the war as well as a Territorial Army officer. Much of the rest of his spare time was spent playing rugby, golf, and the piano. He smoked a pipe and reminded one of his young volunteers of a "benign elephant ... due to the downward curve of his prominent broken nose," the result of his time as an amateur boxer.[3]

A week before the operation was due to begin, Newman returned from a meeting with the Chief of Combined Operations and addressed his commandos frankly. One of his men recalled him telling them that Mountbatten was confident that they would "get in and do the job." He made it clear, though, that "we cannot hold much hope of you getting out again." Newman also passed on Mountbatten's offer that "any man could volunteer out of the forthcoming operation should he wish to do so. Charlie though was wasting his time … Everyone stayed put, satisfied in their work and of course laboring under that strange illusion—their own immortality."[4]

The flotilla set off from Falmouth on the afternoon of March 26, escorted by two destroyers. The *Campbeltown* was in her second incarnation. In her previous life she had been USS *Buchanan* of the United States Navy and had been transferred to Britain as part of the Destroyers for Bases Agreement earlier in the war. She was captained by Lieutenant Commander Stephen "Sam" Beattie, a thirty-three-year-old Welshman

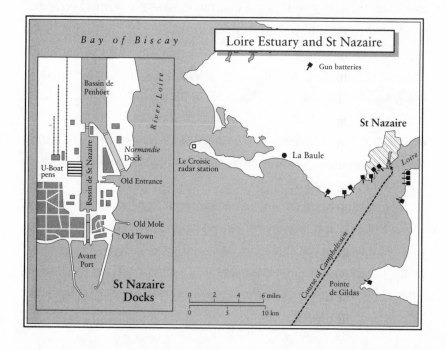

who was to win the Victoria Cross for his part in the raid. The rest of the flotilla was made up of sixteen wooden-hulled motor launches, one small MGB (motor gunboat), and one MTB (motor torpedo boat) to provide covering fire and to evacuate the survivors of the raiding party.

The raid was to open spectacularly with the *Campbeltown* driving at full speed into the southern *caisson*, lodging herself firmly in the middle of the structure to cause maximum devastation when the twenty-four Mk VII depth charges she was carrying, each weighing 400 pounds, exploded. They were packed into a steel tank and concreted over and fitted with long-delay fuses timed to detonate after eight hours.

Then it was the turn of the commandos. The teams were divided into three groups, one on the *Campbeltown* and the other two on the launches. They were to storm ashore and set about their demolition tasks. Each team was divided into two, with one half laying their charges while the others held off the defenders with guns and grenades.

The force on board *Campbeltown* had the mission of wrecking the machines that operated the *Normandie* dock—the pump house and winding sheds that filled and emptied the basin. They were also tasked with destroying the northern *caisson*. The other two groups were to be landed to the west at the Old Mole and the Old Entrance to smash up bridges and locks. In the unlikely event of the operation going perfectly to plan, they would then seal off the area to allow an orderly evacuation on the motorboats. Finally, the flotilla's MTB was to fire torpedoes at the lock leading to the main dock, the Bassin de St Nazaire, on which the submarine pens lay.

The mission bordered on the suicidal, as all who took part in it knew. Major Bill Copland, Newman's second in command and a forty-four-year-old veteran of the First World War, was leading the group embarked on the *Campbeltown*. He spelled out the likely consequences in a farewell letter to his wife Ethel. "My dearest," he wrote. "I have to write this letter although God knows I hope you never receive it—which you only will if I don't come back. We sail in a day or two on a somewhat desperate venture, but one of high purpose. If we succeed, and only the worst of ill-luck will stop us, then we shall have struck a great blow for the cause of freedom. Remember too that if I do get blotted out I shall probably die in good company, for never did a finer crowd set out on a doughtier task."[5]

The force sailed southwest, across the English Channel, then south round the Brittany Peninsula and into the Bay of Biscay, taking a meandering route and keeping well out to sea to disguise their ultimate destination. The *Campbeltown* had been given a quick cosmetic refit to try and alter her lines to something resembling a German warship, reducing her four funnels to two. All in the flotilla flew Kriegsmarine ensigns, weathered and tattered for authenticity.

The assumption was that sooner or later they would be spotted by an enemy vessel or airplane and on the morning of the March 27 they were. They were 160 miles southwest of St Nazaire and just turning back towards the coast when they sighted a U-boat that was making its way back to port. One of the destroyers gave chase and dropped depth charges but the submarine got away. Its radio message reporting the encounter led the German naval command onshore to conclude that the British force was on passage to Gibraltar or on a mine-laying mission.

The expedition's luck had held, but the hazards were only just beginning. Even with surprise on its side the risk of catastrophe was high. Gun emplacements operated by German naval troops heavily protected the area around St Nazaire. To reach St Nazaire they had first to sail past the heavy seaward defenses set up at the mouth of the Loire. There were forty-three guns ranging from 75 mm artillery pieces to hefty 240 mm howitzers mounted on railway trucks. Closer to the port they would face flak batteries equipped with 40 mm, 37 mm, and 20 mm cannon. The port itself was defended by a thousand men and studded with pillboxes and strong points, while harbor defense boats patrolled the waters outside. The whole area could be lit up at night by searchlights sweeping the docks and waterways. If the men charged with the defense of St Nazaire failed in their duty there were another 5,000 German troops based in the town to fall back on.

The purpose of all these precautions was not, however, solely to protect the *Normandie* dock. In the minds of the Germans, the most important potential target were the submarine pens which lay on the west side of the Bassin de St Nazaire, surrounded by flak batteries and searchlights.

Moored inside the pens were the craft of the 7th Submarine Flotilla. More U-boats were on the way and the facilities were being extended to accommodate the 6th Flotilla, which was in the process of transferring from the Baltic. The day before the raid, the officer commanding the U-Boat fleet, Vizeadmiral Karl Dönitz, had inspected the defenses together with the commander of the 7th Flotilla, Kapitänleutnant Herbert Sohler. He asked him what he would do if the "English" attacked. Sohler replied that it was "out of the question" as they would never be able to reach the harbor.[6]

On the evening of March 27, the attacking force turned to make its last approach and headed towards the mouth of the Loire. The destroyer escorts slid away and the raiders were on their own. They were led by the MGB with Colonel Newman and Commander Ryder on board. Immediately behind came *Campbeltown* with the other motor launches arrayed in two columns on either side with a tail of three bringing up the rear. Most were wooden-built Fairmile "Bs." They were 112 feet long and nearly twenty feet wide, and their two 600-horsepower engines could push them through the water at twenty knots. Extra guns had been fitted for the operation. They had two 20mm Oerlikon cannons mounted fore and aft with two .303 machine guns on the bridge.

As the little fleet progressed, those on board could hear the rumble of explosions. A bombing raid was included in the plan, timed for just before midnight. It was a diversionary effort with thirty-five Whitleys and twenty-seven Wellingtons taking part. According to Ryder, "it was hoped that under the general confusion caused by this air raid, directed right on the waterfront, our landing would be comparatively unopposed." However, in keeping with Churchill's concerns about French civilian casualties, the crews were under instruction to bomb only if they could see their targets. The blanket of cloud made identification impossible. Only four aircraft dropped their bombs and the main result of the raid was to sharpen the Germans' reflexes and arouse their suspicions.

"In effect, the raid raised the alarm," wrote Ryder later. "Every gun was manned; patrols, fire parties and others had fallen in, and the gun control and look out system [was] thoroughly on the alert … thus the surface attackers reaped every disadvantage in having their attack heavily opposed by an enemy fully prepared."[7]

The very feebleness of the attack had made the defenders suspicious. Kapitän Karl-Conrad Mecke, who commanded the naval flak brigade responsible for the close defense of the port, noticed that the bombs were seemingly dropping at random and warned everyone to be on their guard against a possible assault by parachute troops or an attack from the sea.

By now the raiders were past the radar station at Le Croisic and inside the estuary. Just after 12:30 a.m. they passed a grim monument to disaster. The hull of the SS *Lancastria* loomed out of the water, lying where she had been sunk in June 1940, with a loss of four thousand lives evacuating the last British troops from France. Sam Beattie handled the *Campbeltown* deftly, taking advantage of the spring tide to steer her through the shallow waters on the western side of the approach, avoiding the central channel.

The modified destroyer drew only eleven feet of water. Twice its hull scraped against the muddy estuary bottom but she slithered on. At 12:45 a.m. they swept past the 75mm guns on the Pointe de Gildas without challenge. Looking back from his gunboat at the head of the column, Ryder found it "difficult to imagine there could be any successful deception. Each craft, with her silvery bow wave, stood out clear and bright." It was too good to last. "This is a queer do," remarked Lieutenant Tom Boyd, a twenty-seven-year-old commanding one of the launches, to his coxswain. "It'll be a bloody sight queerer soon," came the reply.[8]

Once a searchlight flashed across the water, passed them, and went out. Then, just before 1:20 a.m., a lookout noticed the shapes gliding through the darkness and radioed the harbor commander's headquarters with the news that a flotilla of unidentified vessels was heading upriver. The report was dismissed at first. When the sighting reached the cautious Mecke, however, he put all units on alert. All along the banks of the river searchlight batteries flicked on. The Kriegsmarine ensigns streaming from the masts of the destroyers and motor launches caused some hesitation. There were a few warning bursts. Sliding along in his launch tucked in on the starboard side of *Campbeltown*, Lieutenant Commander Billie Stephens was beguiled by the sight of tracer. "It was a beautiful bright red color and as it sailed towards us I couldn't imagine that if it hit us it was going to harm us ... very shortly afterwards I was disillusioned."[9]

Twice they were challenged from the shore. Standing next to Ryder in the MGB leading the flotilla was Leading Signalman F. C. Pike, who was trained in German Morse. He signaled back "wait" then gave the call sign of a German motor torpedo boat obtained from naval intelligence, followed by the message: "Two craft damaged by enemy action. Request permission to proceed to harbor without delay." The lights went off, the firing stopped and the flotilla carried on. Then, at 1:28 a.m., when the force was less than a mile from the harbor, the Germans realized their mistake.

"All at once the searchlights came on us again and the guns commenced to open fire in real earnest," recalled Stephens. "Things were getting pretty hot. *Campbeltown* was hit again and again and anything which missed her stern was passing mighty close to us." The British gunners were giving as good as they got. They were "magnificent and continued to fire quickly and with accuracy and when one was killed or wounded, another stepped up, took his place and continued."

Campbeltown was closing rapidly on the lock. Beattie ordered the White Ensign to be run up and went full steam ahead for the gates. The incoming fire was devastating. The helmsman was killed at the wheel. His place was taken by the quartermaster and he too soon fell dead. Another stepped forward, the expedition's explosives expert Lieutenant Nigel Tibbets, who had just set the timers for the detonation of the three tons of TNT that lay concreted into the hold. The MGB leading the charge veered aside as planned, leaving *Campbeltown* a clear run. The view ahead, though, was obscured by an explosion, sparked by an incoming round which hit the main gun, killing the crew and a number of commandos sheltering on the foredeck.

Then the smoke cleared and Beattie could see the *caisson* ahead of him only a few hundred yards away. The *Campbeltown* was crashing along at a boiler-bursting twenty knots. Her bows ripped through the heavy steel net rigged up to protect the gates from torpedoes. Then, in a cacophony of screeching metal, she buried herself in the southern lock gates. The commandos leapt down while Beattie gave the order to evacuate and prepared to scuttle the ship so that it settled on the harbor bed, blocking the lock gates. Even if the explosives failed to ignite, it would still render the dock unusable for a long time to come. With the destroyer wedged tight into the *caisson*, the MTB was free to fire its time-delayed torpedoes at the lock gates that led into the Bassin de St Nazaire. They hit their target and sank to the bottom.

The commandos on board the destroyer now set about their tasks. One group under Lieutenant Johnny Roderick jumped down from the starboard side. They silenced a gun emplacement and a bunker and moved on to their objective, a complex of underground fuel tanks to the south of the dock. Charges were laid but the fuel failed to ignite. They pulled back to provide flank protection for the other teams in the area.

Captain Donald Roy, a proud Highlander who had dressed in a kilt for battle, led his group off the port side of *Campbeltown*. Their job was to attack the guns on top of the pump house, which lay alongside the *Normandie* dock. The pump house, which emptied the dock of water after a ship sailed in, was the second most vital objective after the *caissons*. When Roy's group reached the guns, though, the defenders had fled, and they retreated a few hundred yards south to the Old Entrance bridge. Their task was to hold the bridge until the demolition teams working in the dock finished their work and had retreated over it to the Old Mole, sticking out into the river on the southwest side of the port. From there, according to the plan, they would be picked up by the motor launches to run the gauntlet back to the sea. Then the bridge would be blown.

Now it was the turn of Lieutenant Stuart Chant's demolition team to move into the pump house. He had been wounded in the legs in the fight on the way in, and so had his number two, Lance-Sergeant Bill Chamberlain. They hobbled to the entrance and blew the door. Leaving Chamberlain on guard, Chant led his other three sergeants down the steps. Thanks to their endless practices, they were able quickly to plant their charges around the machinery before retreating to a safe distance. A few minutes later the pump house erupted with a colossal bang. They picked their way through the swirling smoke and dust to check the damage. The pump house was a wreck. The floor had collapsed, and two of the electric motors powering the impeller pumps lay toppled in the basement. To complete the destruction they set fire to the oil pooling in the debris and retreated towards the Old Entrance bridge.

By now, another team led by Lieutenant Chris Smalley had left the ship and made its way to the winding shed operating the dock gates, which lay along a small canal that ran from the *caisson*. It was undefended and they had no difficulty blowing it up. Other groups were making their way to the northern end of the dock to deal with the other *caisson* and its winding gear. They ran into fierce fire from a gun emplacement which they eventually cleared with hand grenades. When the team placing the charges on the *caisson* reached the lock gates, they came under even more heavy fire. Despite the bullets sparking off the machinery and ricocheting from the concrete of the dock, they succeeded in placing their charges in the water in front of the *caisson* where it plunged into the Bassin de Penhoët. It was impossible, though, to lift the access cover that would allow them to lower explosives into the hollow interior of the *caisson*, thereby guaranteeing its demolition. As the fire grew hotter they were forced to blow up the existing charges and retreat. Another team successfully destroyed the winding shed and the force withdrew south to try and reach the Old Mole to be taken off.

Colonel Newman had gotten ashore safely and was trying to direct the operation from the German Dockyard HQ. The attack on the dock had achieved almost all its objectives. But elsewhere there was chaos and failure—and everywhere there was death.

The attack on the *Normandie* dock was to have been supplemented by a commando landing on and around the Old Mole. The motor launches were supposed to put ashore demolition and protection teams which would lay waste to the facilities at the southern end of the port. Of the six boats that attempted to do so, only one succeeded. As Billie Stephens led the force towards the objective it seemed that, although his launch had "been hit a number of times, [we] were still quite seaworthy and whilst we had some wounded, they were none of them serious." But then "our luck turned and they got us twice at point-blank range with something very large ... the results were sudden and disastrous." Both engines and the steering had gone and the impact of the shells swung the boat hard to port, which brought it up sharply alongside the Old

Mole. A few of the commandos managed to scramble ashore. So did Stephens' signalman, but he was killed before a line could reach him to make the launch fast. Instead it bounced back from the wall of the Mole and into a curtain of point-blank fire from a 20mm gun ashore. "The damage was simply frightful," said Stephens. "There was virtually no engine room left and some incendiaries must have hit our tanks because we were blazing fiercely."

He gave the order to abandon ship and they lowered the Carley Float life rafts. The murderous gunfire had died away, "it being only too obvious to the enemy that we had already 'had it.'" There was not enough room for everyone and Stephens decided to swim. He had sensibly packed a hipflask. "After a very long pull at my flask I slid over the bows on a line and into the water and my God it was cold." He set off, "quite slowly and casually" at first because the shore was only sixty or seventy yards distant. Then he felt the current carrying him away and had to kick off the flying boots he was wearing to struggle against it. "I had to fight to stop myself panicking," he wrote. "Slowly I began to make headway. Time seemed interminable, but I suppose I had only been in the water seven or eight minutes when I reached a small slipway and having arrived at it I just lay there half in and out of the water and quite exhausted." With the others, he tried to join up with the party ashore but it was hopeless. They were stranded and weaponless and at 2:30 a.m. they were all taken prisoner.

At the back of the flotilla the story was the same. Philip Dark was first lieutenant aboard ML 306, in the rear of the port column. It was carrying three officers, ten ratings, and fifteen commandos. By the time they reached their objective, Dark had been wounded, and as they drew near the Old Mole "it was apparent that there was no way that we could get alongside as there was a [Motor Launch] burning on either side."[10] They reluctantly decided to withdraw, as there was no chance of landing the troops.

The dockyard was now illuminated by a ghastly chiaroscuro of dancing flames, gusting smoke, and glittering tracer. Flaming boats glowed on the water and the screams of burning and drowning men mixed with the thud of heavy machine guns. To stay meant certain death or injury. They "proceeded down the Loire at 18 knots." Occasionally the boat would be bathed in the stark white of a searchlight, or a round from one of the shore batteries would plunge in the water nearby. Just before dawn, they sighted three enemy destroyers. They tried to creep away but were "immediately illuminated" by a searchlight on the last ship. Almost as it caught them it went out, extinguished by a burst of Bren gun fire from Sergeant Tom Durrant, one of the commandos aboard. In the firefight that ensued, the destroyer tried to ram the launch. The captain, Lieutenant Ian Henderson, brought the wheel over to lessen the impact but it was still enough to throw several men in the water. One managed to climb back on board but his foot had been half-severed by a propeller. The destroyer now opened up with its 4-inch guns "which rapidly reduced us to a shambles. The coxswain was killed by a shell bursting in the wheel house. Another landed in the bridge, killing Ian and knocking me into a corner." By the end only Tom Durrant was left, firing doggedly back despite his wounds, until he too stopped.

The destroyer took the survivors off. Dark was impressed with the crew's courtesy and compassion. There was no doctor aboard but Dark had studied medicine before the war, so the Germans helped him to do what he could to patch up his shipmates before starting on the German wounded. Durrant was "conscious but bespattered with shrapnel. He suffered but bore up incredibly." He died of his wounds ashore. Dark later remembered the time as "a sordid, rather ghastly dream of blood everywhere and torn flesh soaking blankets and bunks and human beings no longer real people."

Later, though, there was a moment of satisfaction. Dark was in the middle of a conversation with a German doctor who had come on board who was "expressing the sentiment of how mad our raid had been [when] there was an almighty explosion [and] the ship shuddered from stem to stern." It was 10:15 a.m. and the *Campbeltown* had gone up. A brother officer who was on deck at the time told him that "nothing was left of the ship or dock gates. Huge concrete slabs were thrown into the air like so much chaff." The prisoners, huddled under guard ashore, heard and felt it too. It was some compensation. Gratitude at having survived when so many others were dead was starting to be replaced by the depressing realization that they would be spending the rest of the war in captivity.

The explosion set the seal on the success of the mission. The *Normandie* basin was destroyed and would not be repaired until after the war. The operation had cost many lives. Of the 611 men who took part, 105 sailors and 64 commandos were killed. Panicking Germans had also gunned down townspeople and forced laborers. The courage and determination of the raiders was reflected in the number of medals awarded to the living and the dead. Five of the participants won the Victoria Cross, including Tom Durrant.

The dead were among the most spirited, intelligent, and skillful warriors of their generation. In the minds of the planners, though, the losses had been proportionate given the perceived importance of the objectives and the success in achieving them. As a comparison, three months later, on the night of June 25–26, Bomber Command lost 48 aircraft and 208 highly trained airmen in a single raid on Bremen, which destroyed many houses but had little lasting effect on the shipyards and aircraft factories.

The St Nazaire raid demonstrated imagination and cunning, great intelligence in the way that difficulties were foreseen and overcome, patience and thoroughness in the preparations, and ruthless determination to see the plan through. The question was whether the target was worth it. As far as the Germans were concerned, the *Normandie* dock was of secondary value. Their chief concern was the submarine pens, and on the morning of March 28 they stood unscathed.

In Britain, the raid was celebrated as a triumph. It provided a feast of propaganda at a time when good news was still rare. The target that had inspired the operation, though, remained untouched, and seemed untouchable. Tucked snugly inside Faettenfjord, *Tirpitz* was immune to attack by conventional submarines or torpedo planes. It was time for a new approach.

CHAPTER 7

SMOKE AND FOG

With the move to Trondheim, the hope that the RAF might be able to inflict significant damage on *Tirpitz* seemed to have receded further. It did not, though, stop it from trying. In February 1942, the Air Ministry came up with a proposal to overcome the fact that Trondheim was beyond the range of their available bombers. The plan was to take Beaufort aircraft from Coastal Command's 217 Squadron and modify them, stripping out all but the most essential equipment. They would then take off from RAF Wick in northeast Scotland, fly to Trondheim, and attack Faettenfjord. After that they would either continue to neutral Sweden, where the crews would take to their parachutes leaving the aircraft to crash, or turn around and head out to sea. When their fuel ran out they would bale out. Naval vessels, so the theory ran, would be standing by to rescue them. Work was well advanced on modifying the aircraft before this mad idea was abandoned.

The new four-engined Halifax and Lancaster planes that began to arrive at Bomber Command squadrons in 1942 did have the legs to get to Trondheim and back. There were serious doubts, though, about their ability to hit such a small target as the deck of a battleship. Another problem was the limitations of the bombs then available. Despite their names, the 500-lb. semi-armor-piercing (SAP) and 2,000-lb. armor-piercing (AP) bombs had had little success in penetrating the well-armored craft of the modern German fleet. Any that landed on *Tirpitz* were likely to bounce off. According to naval intelligence, she had two armored decks. The upper was 2 inches thick. The lower was 3.2 inches thick and 4.3 over the magazines and engine rooms. The side armor was calculated at 12.6 inches. These figures are not far from the truth. The side plating was in fact 13 inches, the upper deck 2 inches and the main deck 3.7–4.9 inches. Even at the lower assessment, the bombs were almost certain to fail.

In the spring of 1942, Bomber Command took delivery of a new bomb, which it was hoped, might bring results. The Mark XIX spherical contact mine was a modified anti-shipping weapon. Its horns were removed, its casing toughened to withstand the impact of being dropped from a great height, and the explosive charge boosted from 100 lb. of Amatol to 770 lb. It was given the unconvincing name "roly-poly." The aim was not to hit the ship but to drop the mine so that it rolled underneath the hull. It was detonated by a Mark XIV hydrostatic pistol, activated by water pressure. It was estimated that, if delivered accurately and set to go off at the right depth, it would rip a giant hole in what was supposed to be *Tirpitz*'s most vulnerable point—her bottom.

Delivering the weapon on target, though, posed a number of problems. The mine was aerodynamically awkward. It was round and weighed 1,000 lb. Initial tests revealed that it was hopelessly inaccurate when dropped at normal bombing heights. After further experimentation it was decided that to have any chance of being effective the crews would have to bomb at no higher than 600 feet.

That was asking a great deal. The Faettenfjord anchorage was narrow and sheltered on three sides by hills. Flak emplacements on the slopes reinforced the ship's own strong anti-aircraft defenses. To drop their mines, pilots would have to hold their Halifaxes straight and level for the final approach. It was a prospect to test the strongest nerves. "Such an operation would be quite possible with a helicopter," judged Don Bennett, one of the pilots tasked with carrying it out. "But to do it in four-engined bombers was, to say the least, a little difficult."[1]

Air Marshall Sir Arthur Harris, the new chief of Bomber Command, believed a daylight operation would have no chance of success and result in heavy losses. They would have to attack at night. On March 13, the chief of the air staff, Air Chief Marshall Portal, told Churchill that Bomber Command would make an attempt at the next full moon, using the new mines to "do serious underwater damage."

The task was given to 10, 35, and 76 Squadrons, based at Leeming and Linton-on-Ouse in North Yorkshire and Middleton St George in County Durham. The operational order with their instructions described their target as "one of the most powerful war vessels afloat … its presence in these waters apart from the constant menace to our convoys [has] a widespread influence on the strategical situation at sea." Its destruction or crippling "would have a profound effect on the whole course of the war, the importance of which cannot be overstated."

A total of thirty-two aircraft were to take part. They would launch from Lossiemouth, Kinloss, and Tain on the northeast coast of Scotland. The ten Halifaxes from 10 Squadron and ten of the twelve from 35 Squadron would each carry four mines and ninety 4-lb. incendiary bombs. The other two 35 Squadron bombers would be loaded with 50-lb. incendiaries. The ten airplanes from 76 Squadron would each take one 4,000-lb. High Capacity blast bomb, and four 500-lb. or 250-lb. general-purpose bombs to inflict damage on the superstructure. The 10 Squadron crews were to try to drop their mines in sticks at intervals of 100 feet, and those of 35 Squadron at 200 feet. The large incendiaries would be dropped 50 feet apart. The distance from northern Scotland was 1,300 miles. Every aircraft would carry 1,872 gallons of fuel and the trip was expected to take eight to eight and a half hours in total.

The attack required great skill, precision, and nerve. The danger from the anti-aircraft guns was augmented by the threat from the nearby airdrome at Vaernes, only eight miles south of Faettenfjord. There were thought to be about sixty fighters there, Me 110s and, more worryingly, Me 109s for whom the heavily laden bombers would be easy prey. The attackers were unlikely to have surprise on their side. The German radar chains would pick up any aircraft approaching from seaward flying higher than 1,500 feet. To divert the defenders' attention, a parallel raid was ordered. Two of the new Lancasters from 5 Group were scheduled to bomb Vaernes airdrome before the main attack went in.

Despite the trickiness of the operation, preparations were minimal. Sergeant Ian Hewitt, a navigator on 35 Squadron who would fly in S-Sugar on the raid, remembered carrying out only "two or three practice bombing exercises" on the ranges near their Linton base, "diving down from 2,000 to 250 feet and dropping a practice bomb."[2]

In the days before the scheduled operation, Spitfires from Number 1 PRU flew repeated sorties over the area. Local agents had reported the battleship's arrival back in Faettenfjord on March 13 but bad weather prevented a reconnaissance flight until five days later.

The pilots were from the unit's C Flight, based at Wick, and A. F. P. Fane, who had been the first to spot *Tirpitz* when it arrived in Trondheim in January, was among them. Fane was a veteran now, who had notched up fifteen trips to Norway by the time the big raid was scheduled. The duties of the PRU were tough. The weather conditions were frequently dreadful. Pilots had to contend with dense clouds that concealed the hills and peaks of the Norwegian coast and fjords. The conditions at their home base were hardly better. The round trip took about four and a half hours. Exhausted pilots often spent the last part of their mission desperately searching for a gap in the clouds through which they could spot a landmark that could guide them home. Often the Orkneys provided the fix. If they missed them, which was all too easy to do, there was nothing ahead except thousands of miles of ocean.

Sometimes pilots and aircraft just disappeared. On March 18 Fane wrote that one of his comrades, Flight Sergeant Tommy Tomlinson, "took off for Bergen and did not return. Weather here bloody ... land and sea search made around these parts but nothing seen."[3] It was not just the weather that posed a threat. On March 5, Fane noted in his diary: "Sandy Gunn missing. Took off for Trondheim. No news. No plot of him coming back." Next day he recorded that "German wireless reported that 'an English fighter was shot down by AA over the Norwegian coast and the pilot was a prisoner of war.'"

Fane had his own encounter with the German defenses fifteen days later. He was flying through brilliant, clear skies over Aasfjord where *Tirpitz* and two destroyers were resting in the inlets after their outing against PQ.12. He had run in low over the ships and taken several "obliques," framed to show as much of the side view of the vessels as possible. He had "just started a second run [and] was flying bang into the sun when I suddenly saw a [Messerschmitt] 109E practically formating on me to starboard. [I] nearly jumped out of the airplane with shock." Fane reckoned that his attacker must have approached him from underneath as he "kept a reasonably good look out." He "closed throttle and turned on his tail—that shook him. He took violent avoiding action. Felt better but was soon really upset by seeing a second Me 109 which was following the first one 1000 yards behind and 500 feet above. He immediately dived to make a beam attack. That was fairly easy to cope with as I turned into him and shot underneath long before he could get his guns on."

Fane then "took a quick look around to see if there were any more about. Thank God that was all." Nonetheless he was "worried about where the first one had got to so instead of heading straight for home went into a screaming, climbing turn back into the sun. Sure enough they were both still turning back towards me but the important thing was that they were well below me." Showing remarkable coolness, Fane then "went straight toward them and inside their turn and went screaming into the sun and never saw them again."

Fane's sangfroid was all the more remarkable given than he had nothing to defend himself with. PRU aircraft were not armed. The guns had been stripped out to reduce weight and allow for the fitting of long-range tanks. The camera itself was mounted vertically on a frame inside the fuselage and behind the pilot's seat. It was bulky, with a thirty-six-inch lens, set at a slight angle. It took strips of film nine inches wide that could record an area three miles across. By overlapping the photographs and using a stereoscope, a three-dimensional image emerged. The modified Spitfires did have speed on their side. The aluminum skin of the fuselage and wings was buffed to a shine and coated with a special pale blue-green eggshell paint called "camotint." The refinements reduced drag and allowed the planes to reach 400mph.

By March 28 the Halifaxes and their crews detailed for the big raid had moved to their bases in northern Scotland and the full moon was looming. The PRU was under even more pressure than usual to bring back good photographs. "Hell of a flap on because we have not been able to cover Trondheim for seven days now owing to lousy weather," wrote Fane in his diary. His CO Tony Hill was on leave and he found himself in charge and having to deal with impatient "Group Captains, Air Commodores, Air Marshalls, Admirals and the like who seem to take it as a personal insult that the poor little Spittie can't get through fog, hail, snow, rain, cloud and mountains."

That morning Fane took it upon himself to deliver the goods. He took off at 7:30 and climbed up through the all-enveloping cloud and headed northeast. The skies cleared over Trondheim. He took some photographs of the seaplane base at Hommelvik, just to the south of Faettenfjord, and then got lost in a snowstorm. When he emerged, an anti-aircraft battery opened fire.

He "dived onto [the] ground and tore round the countryside at 0 feet, 2850 revs and +9 boost doing about 300[mph]." He picked up a landmark on the shore of Aasfjord and swung into Faettenfjord. There was *Tirpitz*. He flew in parallel to it, then "screamed round to the left and shot [over] the top of it, in a vertical bank, taking one oblique photo." Then he "dropped to the water and flew towards Trondheim." By now the anti-aircraft batteries along the shores of Faettenfjord were waiting for him and as he skimmed along he saw "flak from both banks … splashing in the water both sides." He bobbed up and down "from 100 feet to 0 feet." A speedboat was coming towards him. It "nearly upset getting out my way. I expect he thought I was going to fire at him." He thought the sight was "damn funny. I hope it had the Admiral in it."

Despite these adventures he was still on the lookout for targets. He ran into another snowstorm and emerged to see a large warship in the waters below. He turned around to photograph it. Fane was skilled at ship recognition. He knew as he pressed the shutter button that he was filming the heavy cruiser *Admiral Hipper*, which had arrived a week before from Brunsbüttel. *Admiral Scheer* and *Prinz Eugen* were already in place, lying in Lofjord, just north of *Tirpitz*. Together they made a formidable force. The urgency of the Bomber Command effort sharpened.

The attack was scheduled to start on the evening of March 30. The operation began to fall apart even before it had begun. The Lancaster raid on Vaernes airport was abandoned after one of the two aircraft taking part crashed at Woodhall Spa when taking off to join the main force in Scotland. The thirty-four Halifaxes nonetheless set off into skies thickly blanketed with cloud just after 6:00 p.m. When they reached the target area there was nothing to aim at. No one claimed to have seen *Tirpitz*. They could only guess her whereabouts from the muzzle flashes from the flak batteries and the glow of searchlights in the murk below. Only three of the aircraft dropped bombs. Four Halifaxes were shot down in the area of Trondheim. Another two crashed into the sea on the way home.

The episode only emphasized the extreme difficulty of hitting *Tirpitz* in her Faettenfjord berth. The determination to keep trying, however, was unabated. The PRU continued to fly sorties and take casualties. On April 4, Flight Sergeant Mervyn Jones, who had been given leave from his navigation course to ride the 1940 Grand National winner Bogstar, was shot down and killed. Two days later C Flight were replaced by B Flight and returned to Benson. Fane had flown thirteen reconnaissance missions. On ten of them he had managed to photograph the targets. Given the frequently atrocious weather and the strength of the local defenses, this was an outstanding record, and he had been congratulated by the Commander in Chief of Coastal Command, Sir Philip Joubert de la Ferté, who assured him he was "fully aware of the skill and daring necessary" to bring the pictures home. But Fane knew that the odds against his survival shortened inexorably the more he flew. He categorized three of the trips as "dicing"—the pilot's term for a sortie when the conditions were so bad that whether or not you returned was a matter of fate. Just over three months later his luck ran out. He was killed when his Spitfire crashed in bad weather near Great Shelford in Cambridgeshire, returning from a trip photographing Flensburg.

Between April 8 and the end of the month, the PRU mounted eighteen sorties, only failing to operate when the weather was impossible.

Such was the preoccupation with *Tirpitz's* activities that on some days they flew three separate missions. On April 16, pictures that showed her "emitting smoke" as if in preparation for a voyage caused anxiety, but she stayed put for the next few days. There was more concern on April 24 when it was reported that she was "almost free from camouflage netting," suggesting again that she was getting ready to put to sea.[4] Again it was a false alarm. The next "reccos" showed the camouflage was not only back in place but had been supplemented by more nets and rafts. Local agents reported that the ship's defenses were being steadily strengthened with additional anti-submarine and torpedo nets draped on floats in a curtain a hundred yards from the vessel. She now had an all-around anti-aircraft defense from flak and searchlight batteries set in concrete emplacements on either side of the fjord to supplement her own onboard guns, as well as smoke generators to brew up an artificial fog as thick as the natural one that had thwarted the Halifax attack of March 30–31.

Despite these hazards and obstacles, another attempt was scheduled for the end of April. It would follow the same lines as the original plan, using the same squadrons and taking off from the same north Scotland airfields. There were some refinements, however, which asked even more of the crews than had the original orders. The initial attack would be launched by 76 Squadron and twelve Lancasters from 44 and 97 Squadrons. They were to drop 4,000 lb. blast bombs on *Tirpitz* from 6,000 feet then hang around overhead seeking flak and searchlight emplacements on which to unload their four 500-pounders. There would be no shortage of targets. Intelligence estimates calculated that there were twenty-four heavy anti-aircraft artillery pieces in the immediate area and possibly twice as many light guns. This was a tall order at any time and in any place, let alone in the narrow declivity of Faettenfjord at night.

Then it was the 10 and 35 Squadrons' turn. They were to approach from the west at a new, even lower height of 150–200 feet. Each of the

twenty Halifaxes would carry four of the Mark XIX "roly-poly" spherical mines which they were expected to deposit "close to the stern and
between the ship and the shore" at 100- and 200-foot intervals.[5] The
crews were told at the briefing that "one mine directly under the stern
will damage propellers and rudders, thus making it necessary to tow the
battleship back to a major naval depot for repairs—a battleship in tow
would be a set up for our air and naval forces."[6] According to Wing
Commander Don Bennett, who led 10 Squadron on the raid, the crews
were assured that "the mines, rolled down the surface of the mountain
which was very steep, sloping under the base of the ship, could have burst
the hull from below. That was the theory of it ... All we had to do was
drop these mines between ship and shore and they would go down and
do their stuff and when they got to a certain depth they would go off."
The briefing notes for the operation say only that the mines were to be
dropped behind the stern of the ship—which faced the approaching
aircraft. Either way, it was an unlikely proposition.

The tail of Faettenfjord where *Tirpitz* lay was only 350 yards across.
The gap between the hull and the northern shore, where it plunged
almost vertically into the water, was ten yards wide. The berth, as Dudley Pound pointed out later, was the maritime equivalent of a slit trench.[7]
To slot the mines neatly into the gap would require a degree of accuracy
that was unheard of at this stage of the war. With bombs gone, the aircraft were to execute a tight turn to the north, over the 700-foot ridge
above Faettenfjord and into neighbouring Lofjord, where *Scharnhorst*,
Prinz Eugen, and *Hipper* were anchored in a small, natural harbor. These
were designated as secondary targets if the attack on the *Tirpitz* proved
impossible. Like *Tirpitz* they bristled with anti-aircraft guns which
would be trained on the skies once the raid began.

The crews were left in no doubt about the importance of the mission.
Senior naval officers made a morale-boosting visit to Kinloss and
Churchill sent a message assuring the participants "[you] will be proud

to tell your grandchildren."[8] The operation was planned for April 25, but fog along the north Scottish coast forced cancellation. It was the same story the following night. The crews relieved their anxieties with beer and horseplay. On the morning of Monday, April 27, a PRU flight reported all the warships in their usual anchorages. There was some good news from Vaernes airport. There was no sign of the thirty Me 109s that were thought to be there. Then the meteorological forecast arrived, predicting reasonable weather. The raid was on.

The bombers started taking off from the three bases just after 8:00 p.m. Around the time of their expected arrival, Coastal Command aircraft would distract the radar stations in the target area by carrying out small diversionary attacks on airdromes. For once the weather was perfect. "The night was calm, the sea was dead flat," remembered Don Bennett. The full moon glittered on the water and lit up the mountains ahead like a stage set. It was perfect bombing weather. But it was also ideal conditions for the defenders who were now preparing themselves all along the approach path.

The Germans had ample warning of the bombers' arrival. At 11:08 p.m. local time, the radar station at Kristiansund had warned of approaching four-engined aircraft, and by 11:30 p.m. *Tirpitz* was at action stations. Just before midnight the first aircraft loomed into view and the guns began to thump.

The first to arrive were the Lancasters of 44 and 97 Squadrons and the Halifaxes of 78 Squadron which approached from the south side of Trondheimsfjord and began their run-in. The route brought them close to Vaernes airdrome at 12,000 feet, where flak began to burst around them. They then dived to 7,500 feet and began the dive down Faetten-fjord into the dazzle of the searchlights and the fire blossoming at the end. The lead Lancaster managed to drop its 4,000-lb. bomb over the ship then turn sharply to port, releasing its four remaining bombs on the guns on the hillside as it went.

Down below, the men operating the smoke generators frantically fed canisters of chlorosulphonic acid into the machines, and a white cloud began to smother the outlines of the ship. The rest of the lead force followed, dropping their bombs over the rapidly disappearing form of the *Tirpitz* or aiming at the flashes from the barrels of the anti-aircraft guns pumping out shells below.

The flak was already taking its toll of the second wave. Don Bennett's Halifax was still forty miles from the target when he started to take hits from a shore battery. Bennett was an Australian with a reputation for technical brilliance and outstanding flying ability which was matched by his self-confidence and willingness to clash with his superiors if he thought he was in the right. He had broken several flying records and already distinguished himself in wartime by organizing a mass ferry service of aircraft across the Atlantic. He had reached the conclusion that the bombing campaign at the time was "a complete failure." To improve Bomber Command's dismal performance he had come up with the idea of a vanguard that would identify and mark targets for a following stream of bombers to attack. The idea was eventually adopted as Pathfinder Force, and Bennett would be its first commander and remain in charge of it for most of the war.

Given his experiences that night, he believed that he was extremely lucky to have survived to take up his post. As he approached the target, the fire started by the flak began to take hold. "I was a flamer so I was picked on all the way," he remembered.[9] He pressed on, identifying another island which had been chosen as the starting point for a "stopwatch run" which relied on exact speed, height, and timing to take the aircraft to the precise point when the four mines on board should be dropped.

When he reached Faettenfjord, though, he found "fog filling the whole of the fjord" and all he could make out of the *Tirpitz* was the masts sticking through the blanket of smoke. Braving the flak erupting through the murk, he went round for a second run, which was also "pretty hope-less."

By now the aircraft was burning fiercely and he gave the order to bale out. The others scrambled for the hatches snapping on their parachute packs as they went. Bennett's, though, was out of reach. He was "sitting in my seat in a flaming aircraft and a very hot one, ready to do what? Bail out without a parachute?" Mercifully the flight engineer, Flight Sergeant J. Colgan, turned back to hand Bennett his parachute even as the Halifax went into its final, screaming descent. As he struggled up from his seat, scrambling to clip on the pack, "the starboard wing folded up and I got out in a hurry and pulled the plug immediately. I didn't count to three seconds or anything like that and hit the deck just as it opened. If I'd counted the three seconds I wouldn't have made it." He landed in thick snow and was buried up to his neck.

The crew of another Halifax, S-Sugar from 35 Squadron, got a better look at the target as they skimmed in below the hills of the fjord. "We went down to forty feet," said Rear Gunner Ron Wilson. "The flak was coming both down at us and up at us. I was firing at cliffs and boats as we went by. Then the skipper said, here's the *Tirpitz* now, and I went be[r]serk on the guns and sprayed [her] from stem to stern."[10] Imme-diately after, the bomber was hit by flak.

"There was a great bang and the starboard engine caught fire," remembered Ian Hewitt, S-Sugar's navigator. "There was no hope of flying on to Sweden let alone returning to Scotland." They were too low to bail out. The captain, Flight Lieutenant Don MacIntyre, began to search for a stretch of water. Soon what looked like a lake gleamed out of the darkness below. As they touched down, they realized they had landed on ice. "The aircraft skidded along for about a couple of miles before coming to rest and slowly began to sink." Hewitt scrambled out of the upper hatch and onto the wing. He discovered then that one of the oddities of war was "the virtual impossibility of keeping farce out of the most dramatic situations." As he jumped off the wing he fell straight through the ice. As they fished him out, "the rest of the crew who saw the funny side of the situation before I did, began to laugh." Soaked and freezing, he set off with the others in what they hoped was the direction of the Swedish border.[11]

Despite the flak and the fog, the forty-one crews that reached the Norwegian coast had pressed home their attack with remarkable persistence. Thirty-two claimed to have dropped their bombs on *Tirpitz*, though very few of the crews admitted to having actually seen her. Three others said they had attacked other targets. One late-arriving 76 Squadron Halifax reported bombing *Prinz Eugen* and *Scheer* in Lofjord.

All the effort produced no result. *Tirpitz* was unharmed. The Mark XIX mines had failed completely. Six aircraft were brought down and fifteen airmen killed. By a stroke of luck that contradicted all the odds, eighteen of the thirty-three men shot down survived to be taken prisoner, or, like Bennett, managed to escape. He struggled from his snowdrift to see the wreck of his Halifax glowing in the distance. He could hear dogs barking and knew that German soldiers would soon be upon him. "The dogs were my main worry," he recalled. "To get away from the dogs I would have to cross a stream." There was one nearby but it was not an inviting prospect. "The water in the stream was flowing ... but the banks were eight or ten feet wide [and made of] of ice. You had to slide across the ice into the water and then get out the other side." By now he had met up with his wireless operator, Sergeant C. Forbes. They found a stretch with trees on both banks. "We slid down the ice hanging onto the tree branches and waded through the water and then on the other side, the branches in one place were where we could grab them so we dragged ourselves across the ice. That shook off the dogs."

They now headed east towards the Swedish border which lay tantalizingly close, less then fifty miles away. Sweden was neutral. If they made it they would be interned, but it was better than ending up in a

POW camp. The journey would take them over more freezing rivers and up and down snow-choked valleys. After two days they had still not reached the frontier. They were tired and hungry and desperate when they emerged from the woods to see a farmhouse on the side of a hill with lights in the window and smoke drifting from the chimney. "We were in a pretty far gone state," Bennett remembered. He was still concerned, though, that the inhabitants might turn them in to the Germans so he told Forbes to be ready to run if they got an unfriendly reception. The man who came to the door took a look at the shivering, half-starved visitors and invited them in. "He was able to speak English," said Bennett. "He'd lived in Australia and was generally wonderful. They gave us some of the very little food they had, laid us on the floor in front of a wood stove and gave us two hours sleep, the only sleep we got in three days."

After their brief rest the farmer handed them on to another local man who was to take them to the frontier, guiding them through the German patrols. They walked through the darkness and as dawn came they could see the rock cairns planted with the Norwegian and Swedish flags that marked the frontier. They spent an anxious half-hour trekking across an open snowfield. Then they were inside the border and a little later were picked up at the ski resort of Storlien.

Ian Hewitt had also managed to make it across the border. Soon after leaving their burning aircraft, the six-man crew had split up. Hewitt and the wireless operator Dave Perry set off with their pilot Don MacIntyre, a Canadian from New Brunswick, who was "used to snow." They, too, received help from Norwegians along the way who gave them food and showed them the route.

On crossing the frontier they knocked on a farmhouse door. The inhabitants "made us quite welcome, gave us a meal and rang the local police." They were then taken off to the local jail by the police who treated them courteously and hospitably.[12]

Bennett and Forbes were put in an internment camp in central Sweden. Bennett was suffering from frostbite and had lost a lot of weight. The other internees donated part of their rations, which included silver fox meat, to help him recover. Bennett's relief at his deliverance did not last long. He was determined to get back to the war. The British legation in Stockholm sent an official to see him. He was not impressed. "They'd sent up a relatively junior man," he said. A few days later, though, he had more visitors. Two women and a Swede arrived with a message that Count Bernadotte, the eminent Swedish diplomat later assassinated by Zionists, wished to see him in Stockholm, to clarify his situation. The hopes that were raised by the intervention evaporated when he arrived. According to Bennett's bad-tempered account, Bernadotte seemed strangely unhelpful. Bennett had constructed a complicated argument claiming that the laws of internment did not apply to his case. When Bernadotte disagreed, he threatened him with legal action.

Faced with Bennett's brusque determination and clear willingness to cause the maximum trouble to get his way, Bernadotte gave in. Bennett was released into the custody of the British ambassador and promptly sent a signal to London asking for an aircraft to take him home. One was soon on its way. "The ambassador was furious," said Bennett. "He'd been trying to get one for months and months, [then] some little whippersnapper of a wing commander comes along and gets one straight away." The reason for the swift response was that Bennett was urgently wanted at home to start forming the Pathfinder Force. The ambassador, though, "was not to be allowed into that secret."[13] Within thirty days of being liberated he was back in Britain. Hewitt, Perry, and MacIntyre followed soon after.

Despite the dismal results of the raid, twenty-three Halifaxes from 10, 35, and 76 Squadrons and eleven Lancasters from 44 and 97 Squadrons had taken off from Scotland again the following night. Once again the same method of attack was used. Once again the onboard defenses of *Tirpitz*, the shore batteries, and above all the smoke machines combined to thwart it. Forty-eight "roly-poly" mines were dropped. None of them did any damage. The closest one landed seventy yards from the starboard beam of the ship. The Germans recovered eight of them caught in the trees in the steep hill against which the battleship was anchored. Two Halifaxes from 35 Squadron were shot down by flak, which appeared capable of offering enough protection to the ships for there to be no real necessity for fighter cover. Three men were killed, but, again, and unusually, nine more survived to become POWs.

Bennett arrived home in a black mood. He returned to 10 Squadron to find it under the temporary command of a twenty-five-year old wing commander called James Tait, who had already established a reputation for skill, courage, and coolness. "Father said drily that he'd managed to do some useful work with the squadron while Bennett was away," said his son, Peter Tait. "Bennett was rather a prickly character. So he didn't actually take it as a joke."[14] Two and a half years later, Tait would pull off what Bennett had failed to achieve.

The operation left some lasting bitterness in Bennett's combative mind. He accused Naval Intelligence of failing the bomber crews on two crucial points. First, they had wrongly assumed that, despite the thick armor plate on its hull and deck, *Tirpitz* had a "soft belly" that would be vulnerable to the "roly-polys." "We now know that nothing would have touched the 'soft belly' of the *Tirpitz*," he said many years after the event. He also claimed that the crews had not been warned about the *Tirpitz*'s smoke generators—even though their existence was well known to the navy. They were "wrong in letting us go into an area where there was going to be this fog without telling us," he said. "And they knew, which I discovered afterwards. So we had plenty to complain about with Royal Navy planning."[15]

CHAPTER 8

PROVOKING NEMESIS

The navy looked ahead with apprehension to the summer of 1942. The failure to sink *Tirpitz* in March meant the Russian convoys would need constant protection. As the days lengthened and the nights shrank, the risks from surface ships, submarines, and aircraft multiplied. Yet there seemed no likelihood that the sailings would be suspended. The Red Army sorely needed the tanks, trucks, and aircraft in the merchantmen's holds. The cargoes also carried great political significance.

By keeping the pipeline open, Britain and America demonstrated their commitment to the Soviet Union at a time when it was paying the terrible price of fighting the Germans practically alone. In the absence of a second front in Europe, the convoys were proof of British and American willingness to accept a share of the costs of going to war with Hitler.

President Roosevelt had insisted that the sailings continue and contributed a US Navy task force of a battleship and two cruisers to help with escort duties. The reinforcements did little to calm the Admiralty's fears. On May 18, the First Sea Lord, Sir Dudley Pound, sent a worried message to the Commander in Chief of the United States Fleet, Admiral Ernest King. "The whole thing is a most unsound operation with the dice loaded against us in every direction," he wrote.[1] King was a difficult character, whose Anglophobe tendencies had been nurtured during a period when he was seconded to a British warship during the First World War. However, he agreed with Pound. So did every sailor who sailed in the convoys. Even as he argued, Pound knew that his protest was in vain.

Churchill had accepted that the necessity to appease Stalin outweighed the dangers of maintaining the shuttle. On May 17 he wrote to the Chiefs of Staff underlining that "not only Premier Stalin but President Roosevelt will object very much to our desisting from running the convoys now. The Russians are in heavy action, and will expect us to run the risk and pay the price entailed by our contribution." The USSR's attitude had nonetheless been ungracious and uncooperative. It was a constant complaint of the Allies that the Soviets seemed unwilling or unable to deploy their own navy and air force to provide cover for the convoys at their end of the route, where about a fifth of the losses occurred. Eight days before, in a letter to Stalin, Churchill had felt compelled to be "quite frank and [emphasize] the need for increasing the assistance given by the USSR naval and air forces in helping to get these convoys through safely."[2] The Soviets thawed sufficiently to allow two RAF squadrons equipped with American Catalina flying boats to operate from bases in north Russia and patrol the Norway coast.

Pound was writing at the end of a string of disasters that had struck in the Arctic since the *Tirpitz*'s sortie against PQ.12. The next two convoys to sail were the outgoing PQ.13, and QP.12 would cross with it as it returned home. Of the nineteen ships in PQ.13, five were sunk: two by aircraft, two by U-boats, and one by a destroyer. In addition, two escorting warships, the cruiser *Trinidad* and the destroyer *Eclipse*, had been damaged—the *Trinidad*, bizarrely, by its own torpedo, which turned around after its steering mechanism was disoriented by the freezing water. An enemy destroyer and a U-boat had also sunk. But if the value of the operation was judged in material terms alone, the convoy would have to be marked as a failure. Pound repeated his misgivings to the Defence Committee in early April but to no avail. He had been accused by some in the navy of being too pliant in the face of political demands. He was not so now. It was as if he sensed the disaster coming.

At Roosevelt's insistence, the next convoy, PQ.14, was larger than its predecessor. Of the twenty-four ships that sailed, sixteen turned back when they ran into heavy ice. Of those that battled on, one was sunk by a U-boat. The returning convoy, QP.10, lost four of its sixteen ships.

PQ.15 and QP.11 were made up of twenty-five and thirteen ships, respectively. They sailed at the end of April. A large force was in place to protect them, including the cruiser *Edinburgh*, the Rear Admiral Stuart Bonham-Carter's flagship. While zigzagging in front of the homecoming convoy she was hit by a torpedo fired by a U-boat and had to limp the 250 miles to Murmansk with her stern blown away, unable to steer except on her engines. German destroyers caught up with her and in the fight that followed, the *Edinburgh* was caught amidships by another torpedo and almost cut in half. Two of her destroyer escorts, *Forester* and *Foresight*, were also badly hit. Despite being barely afloat, the *Edinburgh*'s gunners succeeded in fatally damaging the destroyer *Hermann Schoemann*. It hardly compensated for the loss of the *Edinburgh*, which was eventually abandoned and sent to the bottom with a friendly torpedo. She was followed, on May 15, by another cruiser, the *Trinidad*, which a lone Junkers 88 dive-bomber attacked as she headed home from Murmansk. Again the ship was abandoned and then sunk to deny her to the enemy.

The next pair of convoys fared slightly better. PQ.16 had thirty-five ships, the largest number yet sailed. The returning QP.12 had fifteen. The homecoming journey was mercifully uneventful. The Germans reserved their energy for PQ.16. After the two convoys passed each other on May 25, the Murmansk-bound ships were subjected to almost continuous air assaults with Heinkel 111 torpedo planes taking turns with Junkers 88 dive-bombers. On one day, May 27, 108 attacks took place. Four of the merchantmen were sunk. Two others, and a Polish-manned destroyer, the *Garland*, were badly damaged.

Among the submarines protecting the convoy was HMS *Seawolf*, commanded by Lieutenant Commander Dick Raikes, who had raised the alarm when *Tirpitz* left Trondheim in March. During the first two days out, the seas were clogged with fog which increased the risk of collisions but at least hid the ships from the eyes of German reconnaissance aircraft. As soon as it cleared, they were joined by a Focke-Wulf long-range spotter which circled out of range of the guns. Raikes recalled later, "from then until arrival in Russia, one of these planes was always with us, 'homing' the enemy aircraft from the many airfields in Norway."[3]

The submarines were under instructions to attempt to sink any surface raiders with their torpedoes but to dive if the convoy was attacked from the air. It was soon clear that the orders were impracticable. After submerging following the first actions and finding himself miles astern of the convoy, Raikes resurfaced and signaled to the close escort commander, Captain Dickie Onslow, on board the fleet destroyer *Ashanti*, "in the event of future air attack, intend to remain on the surface." Back came the wry reply: "So do I."[4]

For the next five days everyone involved in PQ.16 lived in a state of adrenaline-soaked anxiety as each attack arrived, or nervous trepidation as they waited for the next one to develop. They were naked on the water, illuminated by a merciless sun that never fully set. "The convoy was attacked practically without a pause by high level bombers, dive bombers and torpedo-carrying bombers," Raikes remembered. The U-boats stayed away at first. Then, on the third day, just as Raikes was heading to his bunk for a rest he was "summoned back to the bridge to see a U-boat torpedo narrowly missing my stern. It was running shallow and nearly all guns in the convoy were firing at the spume to try and explode it." Raikes had on board a new sub-lieutenant who remained "commendably unmoved by the whole experience and announced that the spume was caused not by a torpedo but by an Arctic whale. He had just said the word 'whale' when the torpedo hit a large Russian ship carrying ammunition."

The normally insouciant Raikes reported that "we were all shaken by this as the Russian ship was only about three hundred yards from us and after an instantaneous change to white heat, exploded and totally disappeared in a few seconds. It was blown into tiny smithereens and didn't even leave any traces of wreckage of the surface."

It was not long before Raikes had recovered his normal, jokey composure. "After three or four days watching the Focke-Wulf aircraft circling the convoy and knowing we were powerless to do anything about it, I told the signalman to call it up on the signal lamp. I made 'you are making me dizzy. Please go round the other way.' To my great surprise he replied 'Certainly.' And did so." The last leg was as harrowing as the rest of the trip. The exhausted survivors endured their last air attack "within a dozen miles of a Russian fighter airfield. Not a single fighter came to our assistance." It confirmed his view of his Soviet brothers-in-arms. "Bastards," he wrote.

The convoy had lost seven ships and four escorts, with many more damaged. They had managed to shoot down twenty German aircraft. Nonetheless, Raikes and every other sailor took satisfaction in the fact that the convoy had got through, "albeit to a thoroughly ungrateful ally."[5]

The sunken ships were carrying valuable war materiel—77 aircraft, 147 tanks, and 770 military vehicles were now on the bottom of the

Arctic Ocean. It amounted to a quarter of the cargo. In a single day, a few Luftwaffe aircraft had disposed of materiel that it might take an armored brigade a month to destroy, and they had done so at relatively little cost.

The danger from the air was already plain. After the experiences of PQ.15 the Commander in Chief of the Home Fleet, Sir John Tovey, had agreed with Admiral Bonham-Carter that unless the airfields from which the Luftwaffe operated in northern Norway could be knocked out or the convoys allowed the cover of darkness, the whole punishing exercise should stop. "If they must continue for political reasons, very serious and heavy losses must be expected," he wrote.[6] Like his chief, Admiral Pound, he believed that the strategic situation was "wholly favorable to the enemy."

In the Admiralty, preparations for the next convoy took place in an atmosphere of impending disaster. The official historian of the war at sea, Captain Stephen Roskill, wrote that "it was plain to all involved in the work of planning the convoys and the associated fleet movements and in the long drawn out anxieties of their execution, that we were gambling with fate to an extent that was bound, sooner or later, to provoke nemesis. All realized that a disaster was likely; but when, and on which convoy would it fall?"[7]

There was a brief lull before the tempest blew up. In early June 1942, the demands of Malta took priority over the Arctic convoys. Ships were detached from the Home Fleet to protect the "Pedestal" convoy, carrying vital supplies to the besieged island. By the end of the month they were back in Scapa Flow waiting for the Russian convoys to resume.

The next eastbound convoy was coded PQ.17 and was made up of thirty-five vessels. The homecoming QP.13, which it would cross, had thirty-six. Both were set to depart on June 27. They would be sailing in virtually continuous daylight. To compensate, they would have a formidable force to protect them, bolstered by the US Navy's Task Force 99 under the command of Rear Admiral Robert C. Giffen. It was made up of Giffen's flagship, the battleship USS *Washington*; two cruisers, the *Wichita* and the *Tuscaloosa*; and some destroyers. For the first time in the war, substantial American forces had been placed under British command.

The crew of the *Wichita* included a film star. Lieutenant Douglas Fairbanks Jr. was thirty-five years old, and an established Hollywood actor with a marriage to Joan Crawford behind him. He spent some of his youth in Britain and moved easily in upper-class and royal circles. He was a friend of the Duke of Kent and had met the duke's brother, King George VI. He was equally well-connected at home. Roosevelt sent him in 1941 as a special envoy to South America.

Fairbanks was unusually politically committed for an actor of the period, particularly for a star of the American film industry where commercial concerns steered studios away from subjects that might alienate any section of the mass audience. From the outset, he had been disturbed at the rise of fascism in Europe. He was friendly with two rising talents of the Conservative Party, Anthony Eden and Duff Cooper, both of whom resigned over the government's appeasement policy. Fairbanks attributed his political awareness to "an accumulation of anger at the whole Nazi system and what it threatened, not to Britain or to my country in particular, but in terms of what it threatened to the world and to what that world had built up over two thousand years."[8]

His transatlantic sympathies convinced him that strong joint action by Britain and America was the only way to confront the menace. He propagated his pro-British views in speeches and letters to newspapers and even in his choice of roles. In 1938, at the height of the Munich crisis, his film *Gunga Din*, which grafted Kipling's famous poem by the same name onto his novel *Soldiers Three*, was screened in cinemas across Britain and America. A British critic, Paul Holt, wrote in the *Daily Express*: "I don't have a doubt that in these days of power politics and propaganda, this tale of tough and stupid British soldiery, grinning heroes with cropped hair and thick necks, is as valuable to this country as a thousand front-line bombers. Particularly when our friends the Americans have got it into their skulls that this country is soft and decadent."[9] In fact, Fairbanks's support brought him a certain amount of resentment in an America where anti-British feeling and the spirit of isolationism were strong.

He was already a reservist in the US Navy at the start of the war. When America entered it, he was sent to join the staff of Mountbatten's Combined Operations Headquarters. By the spring of 1942 he was putting into practical effect his belief in Anglo-American cooperation, as a member of the screening force that would protect PQ.17 and QP.13.

The operation represented far more than a political gesture. It was one of the most valuable convoys ever to go to sea, with an estimated worth of £200 million. On board were nearly 300 aircraft, 600 tanks, 400 lorries, and 150,000 tons of general cargo. Together it amounted to enough materiel to equip an army of 50,000 men.[10]

It was a lot to risk given the perils facing the operation. The experience of PQ.16 had shown what German airplanes could do. Hitler had kept a promise to Raeder to provide extra aircraft for Norway and by now there were 250 on hand in four bases in northern Norway to locate and bomb Allied shipping. The menace from U-boats and torpedo boats was also obvious. And now there was a fourth element of German military power on hand. At the end of March the heavy cruiser *Hipper*, a veteran of the Norway campaign and several Atlantic sorties, arrived to join *Tirpitz* in Trondheim. The pocket battleships *Scheer* and *Lützow* were already in the area as well as three destroyer flotillas. Together they would form a fleet under the command of Generaladmiral Otto Schniewind, who until then had been chief of the Kriegsmarine's naval operations. So far a surface force of this size had not been used in combination with aircraft and submarines in an attack on a convoy.

As preparations for PQ.17 continued, there was disturbing news that the situation could be about to change.

A "most immediate" signal dated June 18 arrived at the Admiralty from Captain Henry Denham, the British naval attaché, who under the terms of Swedish neutrality was allowed to operate, albeit under serious restrictions, in Stockholm. Despite these difficulties he had befriended a sympathetic officer high up in Swedish intelligence who had called him to his office to provide him with some startling information. Denham rushed back to the British Legation to draft his report, which was encoded and radioed to London at 7:00 p.m. "Following is German plan of attack on next Arctic convoy," he announced in his coded telegram. "It is hoped to obtain early reconnaissance report when eastbound convoy reaches vicinity of Jan Mayen. Bombing attacks from aircraft based in North Norway will then commence."

He went on to predict the naval movements that would follow.

> 1. Pocket battleships with six destroyers will proceed move to Altenfjord [Altafjord] ...

> 2. *Tirpitz* with *Hipper*, two destroyers and three torpedo boats will proceed to Narvik area, probably Bogenfjord. Naval forces may be expected to operate from their anchorages once convoy has reached 5 degrees east. The intention for the two groups of surface forces is to make a rendezvous on the Bear Island meridian and to make a simultaneous attack on convoy supported by U-boats and aircraft.[11]

He graded the information "A.3," indicating that the source was utterly reliable but the information was un-checkable. The chances were good that the information was solid. The German teleprinter lines to north Norway passed through Sweden, and the Swedes had cracked the codes.

Denham's stock was high. It was his report the previous year that had alerted the Admiralty to the move north by *Bismarck* and *Prinz Eugen*.

There was no question of canceling the convoy. To do so would be to confirm that, merely as the core of a "fleet in being," *Tirpitz* was able to shut down one of the Soviet Union's main supply lines and throw more grit in its already abrasive relationship with its Western allies. Preparations went ahead with mounting unease.

Despite the misgivings of Pound and his team there was nothing inevitable about the disaster that was about to occur. In certain circumstances, the sailing of Convoy PQ.17 might have been the occasion for a great victory. The escorting force should have been more than a match for the Germans.

Altogether there were forty-five surface ships in the force, more than one for each of the thirty-three merchantmen. In addition, thirteen submarines, including two supplied by the Soviets, would be mounting patrols. The fleet was split into three. The convoy would have a close escort of nineteen vessels, under Commander Jack Broome in the destroyer *Keppel*. It was made up of six destroyers, four corvettes, and two submarines, plus two anti-aircraft ships, two anti-submarine trawlers, and three minesweepers. They in turn would be covered by a cruiser squadron comprising the *London, Norfolk, Wichita,* and *Tuscaloosa*, commanded by Rear Admiral Sir Louis Hamilton, scion of an old naval family, who in line with the navy's fondness for nicknames was known widely as "Turtle." Three destroyers were in attendance.

Beyond these two groups, roaming at a distance in the waters around Jan Mayen Island and poised to launch into action as the situation dictated, was the British battle fleet under Tovey, who was flying his flag in the battleship *Duke of York*. Alongside him was Rear Admiral Giffen in the *Washington*, plus two British cruisers, the *Nigeria* and the *Cumberland*, and the aircraft carrier *Victorious*, together with fourteen destroyers.

The surface fleet would protect the convoy from heavy attack during the western leg of its journey from Iceland to Bear Island, a barren block of rock and ice about 280 nautical miles (310 statute miles) north of Norway, lying on the western edge of the Barents Sea. Captain Broome's destroyers would huddle around the merchantmen while Admiral Hamilton's cruiser squadron hovered protectively in the distance. Tovey and the Home Fleet would be following at one further remove, ready to intervene if needed. Once the convoy passed Bear Island, PQ.17 would have to rely on the close escort and accompanying submarines to defend it from surface attack.

The orders contained some elasticity. The cruisers could go beyond Bear Island—as far as latitude 25 degrees east—if a German surface force emerged to threaten the convoy. There was, however, a proviso. No confrontation was sanctioned unless the cruisers had a chance of winning the ensuing fight. In other words, they were forbidden to sail into battle if *Tirpitz* was present.

Tovey had no quarrel with this restriction. He had always been opposed to the idea of sending cruisers to escort convoys into the Barents Sea. They were highly vulnerable to attack by land-based bombers and torpedo planes and U-boats and if they were damaged it was a long, slow, and dangerous journey to Murmansk—where the repair facilities were, anyway, inadequate. This view had only been strengthened by the recent examples of the *Trinidad* and the *Edinburgh*. He had other objections, though, which he aired to Pound at the Admiralty in telephone conversations from his base in Scapa Flow. He argued that the convoy was too big for the size of the escort that had been provided. He proposed that it should be split up and sent in two sailings—a solution that would have doubled both risk and effort. Pound overruled him, as Tovey must have known he would.

His main concern, though, was an alarming detail of the plan which emerged in his phone exchanges.[12] Pound told him that if *Tirpitz* did appear, and if he thought the convoy was facing likely annihilation, he would consider ordering it to scatter. The logic was that the German attackers would find it easier to destroy a concentrated formation of ships than have to go to the inconvenience of hunting down individual vessels. The dispersed merchantmen would therefore have a better chance of survival on their own.

Tovey seems to have been genuinely shocked and surprised by this statement. It ran against the lessons of all recent experience. The examples of convoy traffic in all the oceans where the war at sea had so far been fought had been that as long as ships maintained discipline and close order, the escorts could provide some sort of effective protection for the merchantmen. Once the formation dissolved, each scattered ship was easy meat for whichever U-boat, airplane or surface vessel came across it. Tovey did not mince his words when he gave his reaction to his chief. He let it be known later that he told Pound that if the order ever were given, it would result in "sheer, bloody murder."[13]

Hindsight has made Tovey's judgment seem darkly prophetic. His own feeling, though, was that *Tirpitz* was unlikely to venture out. His reading of the German admirals' minds was that they would not risk sending their last remaining battleship into the perilous waters of the Barents Sea where she would be beyond the protection of land-based aircraft. The Germans had no aircraft carrier in their fleet. One was supposed to be under construction—the *Graf Zeppelin*. Despite Raeder's urging and Hitler's acquiescence, it was still far from completion. The German admirals thought *Tirpitz* had been lucky to escape the Swordfish attacks at the end of her March excursion. A sortie against another convoy would expose her to the same risk.

Nonetheless, if she did venture out, Tovey would be happy to see her. It would provide an opportunity for another epic battle like the one he had fought against *Bismarck*. He regarded escort duties as a departure from the real business of naval warfare, which was to close with the enemy fleet and destroy it. Tovey nurtured the hope that *Tirpitz* could be enticed into an encounter that he was sure he would win. A victory would bring enormous benefits. The risk to the convoys would now be manageable. And the large number of naval resources, now passively engaged in containing the *Tirpitz*, could be used much more effectively elsewhere.

What was needed was a deception that would persuade the Germans that they had no choice but to send their last battleship to sea. Several weeks before the convoy sailed, Tovey began to work on a subterfuge by which *Tirpitz* might be brought to battle. Sixty-one years after the event, declassified documents in the Public Record Office revealed an extraordinary intervention by the Home Fleet commander to mount a spoof operation to lure the German fleet towards the coast of Iceland where his ships would be waiting to pounce. The papers make it clear that it was Tovey himself who approached MI5 with the ruse, which was code-named "Plan Tarantula." A meeting was held at MI5 headquarters in Broadway, central London, on May 29, 1942, a month before the convoy sailed. The minutes, stamped "Most Secret" and typed on flimsy paper, state that "the object of the plan which has been conceived by C-in-C Home Fleet is primarily to assist the passage of a convoy (PQ-17) [parentheses in original document] from Iceland to Russia … it is hoped that if this plan is successful, the Home Fleet will be able to bring the German fleet to battle."[14]

Tovey's idea was to "inform the Germans that a convoy is assembling in Iceland and that another convoy is assembling in Scapa Flow and that it is believed that these two convoys may in all probability be taking troops to effect a landing on the Norwegian coast." The minutes note, "it is known that the Germans are at the present moment in an extreme state of agitation for fear lest an attack should be made by us on the Norwegian coast." The false story was to be fed to the Germans by two agents, "Land Spider" and "Mutt," who German intelligence had recruited to report on convoy movements from Iceland but who had gone over to the British side.

At that stage the two convoys were expected to sail on June 11. As the date approached, the two double agents were to start sending coded wireless reports to their controllers leaking details of the supposed invasion convoy. The plan was based on the premise that the Germans would find it impossible to ignore the threat and sail out to intercept the convoys, which the reports would say were to be protected only by light escorts. Once the Germans were at sea, the convoy would turn back toward Iceland, luring their pursuers to where the Home Fleet and its American allies would be waiting to annihilate them.

Tovey's gambit started to play out. The plan was subsequently revised and it was not Land Spider or Mutt but another agent who laid the bait. "Cobweb" was Ib Arnason Riis, a seaman born in Denmark to Icelandic parents who had been recruited by the Abwehr German military intelligence organization while demoralized and unemployed in Copenhagen in 1940. In April 1942 he was landed by submarine in Iceland with a cover story that he was a returning refugee from occupied Denmark. He was provided with a radio, a code book based on the Penguin edition of Maxim Gorky's *Leaves from My Diary* and $1,800 largely in $50 notes. His instructions were to find out everything he could about airdromes, industrial and military sites, and shipping movements, particularly anything concerning the convoys. Soon after his arrival, however, he "took the first opportunity of reporting his presence to the British authorities and readily accepted the proposal that he should work as a double agent." Under the supervision of two MI5 officers he began to make wireless transmissions to his Abwehr controllers.

The Germans declined the bait. A dummy convoy of minesweepers and colliers escorted by two light cruisers and five destroyers did sail from Scapa Flow but it provoked no reaction. The Germans had either failed to locate it, or, if they had, chosen to ignore it. It was always unlikely that Admiral Raeder would abandon the policy of caution, bordering on timidity, that had governed all *Tirpitz*'s movements, and sail into waters where the strategic balance tilted back strongly in the Allies' favour. Even if he had, it was almost certain that Hitler—who admitted that, however bold he might be in his approach to land warfare, he was a "coward at sea"—would overrule him.

Despite the wariness of the high command, the appetite for action among crews and commanders was strong. The concentration of *Tirpitz*, *Hipper*, *Scheer*, and *Lützow* so close to the convoy routes created an atmosphere of expectation. The men and those who led them chafed at inaction and were anxious to justify their existence. The reinforcements of aircraft and an increase in the submarine strength in the Arctic boosted their advantages. The arguments for a sortie were further strengthened by the allocation of 15,000 tons of scarce fuel oil for fleet operations in June.[15]

The objectives, nonetheless, remained modest. Operations would only be sanctioned if they carried a good chance of cheap and relatively risk-free success. Hitler had told Raeder that when the next convoy sailed, no move was to be made against it until the Luftwaffe had located and attacked any British aircraft carriers in the escorting force. The order virtually ruled out any chance of the *Tirpitz* or any other heavy ship attacking the convoy. By the time the Luftwaffe's task was completed, it might be too late for the big surface ships to close with their targets. Raeder hoped to increase his room for maneuver by moving his big ships to anchorages in the far north of Norway as soon as a convoy was sighted, to be in a better position to strike when it passed by. That was not to say that he was anxious for a fight. He, too, believed that a major naval set-back at this stage of the war would be disastrous and his views conditioned the attitude of Naval Group North at Kiel.

Excitement grew aboard *Tirpitz* when Generaladmiral Schniewind arrived to take up command of his fleet. On May 30, Raeder visited

Trondheim to discuss future operations. On June 14, the plan—the one that Denham in Stockholm had passed on to London—was settled. At that time, Schniewind's force was split in two. One group, clustered around the *Lützow* and the *Scheer*, under the command of Vizeadmiral Oskar Kummetz, was in Narvik with a flotilla of destroyers. *Tirpitz* and *Hipper* lay near Trondheim with two flotillas. It was decided that as soon as the convoy was known to be on its way, the Narvik force would move to Altafjord in the far north. The Trondheim group would sail for Vestfjord, which led into Narvik. The two squadrons would set sail from their new locations once the convoy passed the meridian of 5 degrees east, meeting a hundred miles north of Norway's most northerly point, the North Cape. They would attack when the convoy was in the Barents Sea, east of Bear Island, between the 20 degree and 30 degree meridians. The British fleet had never sailed that far east and the planners assumed, correctly, that they would not do so now. The German ships, submarines, and aircraft would then be in a position to destroy the merchantmen in their own time. Admiral Carls would have overall control of the operation from Naval Group North in Kiel. He in turn would be in touch with Vizeadmiral Krancke—Raeder's representative at Hitler's headquarters in Berlin. The operation carried the code name Rösselsprung—the Knight's Move. The Führer was shown the plan and approved it in principle, though the fleet would have to await his order before putting to sea. *Tirpitz* was set for its long overdue triumph.

PQ.17 left on the afternoon of June 27, 1942. The thirty-five merchant ships sailed from the anchorage of Hvalfjord, an inlet to the north of Reykjavik, in a column and when they reached the open sea arranged themselves in nine columns. They were sailing to Archangel, farther than Murmansk, which had been put out of action by heavy air raids. There was something very touching about the sight. It was impossible not to feel a stirring of pity at the ships' pathetic vulnerability. Douglas Fairbanks recorded in his diary how he watched them "waddle out to sea like so many dirty ducks. Everyone who was watching them paid a silent tribute and offered some half-thought prayer."[16]

For the next four days they steamed to the northeast at a steady nine knots. The sky was overcast and a mist often covered the flat sea. The disadvantage the convoy faced in operating in continuous daylight was counterbalanced a little by the fact that the Arctic ice cap had retreated in the summer sun, and it was now possible to sail north of Bear Island. The route was longer, but it meant that the ships were further away from the Luftwaffe's Norwegian bases. On June 30, the long-range close escort under the command of Jack Broome joined them. It was made up of six destroyers, led by his ship *Keppel*, four corvettes and two submarines as well as two anti-aircraft ships, the *Palomares* and the *Pozarica*. There were also three rescue ships to take on survivors from ships that had been sunk.

Pozarica was a 1,900-ton converted cargo ship commanded by Captain E. D. W. Lawford with a crew of about three hundred, many of them young and green. Among them was Godfrey Winn, traveling as a war correspondent for Beaverbrook Newspapers. Winn was thirty-four years old and a star Fleet Street columnist and feature writer whose sensitive persona and confiding style made him a favorite with women readers. He had been an actor and retained a rather camp manner. He was brave and determined and had just volunteered for service in the navy as an ordinary seaman when he was diverted onto PQ.17.

On the afternoon of July 1, the day after the close escort joined the convoy, he was called onto deck to see an ominous sight. A "half-glimpsed presence [was] zooming about in the fog, which turned out to be a German recco plane and which sent a shiver down our spines." It was a Blohm and Voss 138 seaplane, nicknamed the Flying Clog by the Luftwaffe for its clunky profile. The *Pozarica*'s crew christened it, and the others that followed, "Snoopy Joe." They understood, as they watched it curve "round the horizon, now reappearing, now disappearing again in the veils of mist, and always just out of range of our guns, that she was not wasting time, but was busy counting the number of ships and their escorts and wirelessing back to her base in Norway the exact composition of the convoy."[17]

So it was. The aircraft's report was relayed to *U-456*, one of a string of submarines keeping a standing patrol in expectation of the next convoy. Aircraft and submarines now started the long hunt that preceded the kill, with all the patience and efficiency of predators of the African plains.

The initial sighting produced a flurry of aerial attacks, but they were efficiently beaten off by the escort's anti-aircraft guns. On the afternoon of July 2, PQ.17 and QP.13 crossed each other northeast of Jan Mayen Island. That evening there was another unsuccessful torpedo plane attack and an enemy plane was shot down. By now the cruiser fleet under "Turtle" Hamilton was overhauling the convoy, steaming forty miles to the north of its route, hoping to keep out of sight of German reconnaissance aircraft. That evening, the elements sided with the convoy and a fog rolled in that persisted until well into the following morning.

Far to the south, though, the German fleet was on the move. *Tirpitz* and *Hipper* had left Trondheim as planned on the evening of July 2 and by the following day had reached the Lofoten Islands off Narvik. The *Scheer* had also moved from Narvik to Altafjord, leaving behind its partner, the *Lützow*, which, along with three destroyers from the *Tirpitz* group, ran aground near Narvik and played no further part in the proceedings. At 7:00 a.m. on July 3, PQ.17 turned due east toward the Barents Sea. An Admiralty update reported that the ice cap had retreated farther than earlier thought and Hamilton proposed that the convoy swing to the north to put yet more distance between it and the mainland. Broome, though, was anxious to press on and altered course only slightly. At 10:15 p.m. the convoy was thirty miles north of Bear Island and crossing into the perilous waters of the Barents Sea.

Hamilton's orders had allowed him to accompany the convoy east of Bear Island to a limit of 25 degrees if he saw fit. He decided to do so. The sailors aboard the convoy had reason to feel reasonably optimistic as they steamed through the twilight and the welcome embrace of a fog. The Luftwaffe's attentions, though, were unrelenting. Early on the morning of July 4, a single torpedo plane managed to find a hole in the low cloud and swooped through to cripple an American merchantman, the *Christopher Newport*, which had to be abandoned. This setback did nothing to dent the conviction of the escorting force that when the serious attacks began, as everyone knew they soon would, they would be able to deal with them. Hamilton had noted the date and sent Captain Hill on *Wichita* congratulations. Hill had replied, "Independence Day always requires large fireworks. I trust you will not disappoint us."

At noon that day, Hamilton was told by the Admiralty that he could keep company with the convoy past the 25 degrees east meridian if he saw fit. Tovey, however, issued a qualification to the message. He told Hamilton that "once the convoy is east of 25° East or earlier at your discretion you are to leave the Barents Sea unless assured by Admiralty that *Tirpitz* cannot be met."

The whereabouts of *Tirpitz* was now of paramount importance to the dispositions of the convoy and the ships that were there to protect it. The ships at sea had no direct information of their own apart from the evidence of their own eyes and radar. Their intelligence came primarily from the Admiralty, and they were reliant on what they were told and the interpretation that had been put on it in London.

At 6:00 p.m. on July 4, Hamilton reported back that he intended to leave the convoy at 10:00 p.m. The signal came back from the Admiralty that "further information may be available shortly. Remain with convoy pending further instructions." The implication was that there were new developments concerning the German surface fleet that would determine the cruiser squadron's next move.

A little after the exchange, the attacks anticipated earlier in the day arrived, and the Independence Day fireworks began. The convoy's radio operators had been picking up signals from U-boat and aircraft homing beacons since mid-afternoon. At 4:45 p.m. Broome ordered his ships to close in on the convoy to provide anti-aircraft support and soon afterward the first wave of Heinkel He 115 torpedo bombers, equipped with floats, arrived. On board *Pozarica*, Godfrey Winn, pressed back against the narrow passageway, watched "the surging throng, rushing upwards to Action Stations, putting on their tin hats as they went, cursing and blasting but no sign of panic." The ammunition crews supplying the ship's fourteen guns were "stripped and ready for loading an endless relay of shells onto the pulleys that would take them to the guns." They were "naked to the waist, sweating like cattle, blind." For two hours the Heinkels buzzed around, trying to penetrate the curtain of fire thrown up by the escorts. They dropped torpedoes but most were ranged too far to have any effect. Winn watched one cruise by, "its wash like that of a porpoise."

The *Pozarica* claimed no hits, but Winn saw an airplane in the water about four miles away. "A few minutes later, a sister plane landed beside it, and picked up the pilot from his rubber dinghy. We all saw the rescue quite clearly through our glasses." He thought it "pretty cool—and you couldn't help admiring the maneuver, even though regretting it meant another pilot was safe to bomb us again." The effect of the attack was "like champagne on the ship's company. They had come through their first challenge without loss of face, and many of those lads had never been to sea, let alone battle."[18]

The elation was short-lived. At 8:15 p.m., German aircraft were back. The first attack by Junkers 88 bombers was driven off, but then the Heinkels returned again. This time they split into two groups which massed to attack the convoy on the starboard bow and quarter. The convoy was lucky to have the American destroyer *Wainwright* alongside which had left Hamilton's cruiser squadron to refuel from one of the convoy's oilers.

She steamed at full speed to where the aircraft attacking on the bow were grouping, with all guns firing. One Heinkel was shot down, and none of the torpedoes that were dropped found a mark.

The second group, however, managed to break through the wall of anti-aircraft fire, and drop at least twenty torpedoes. Once a torpedo was in the water it was still possible to deflect it with machine-gun fire and several were knocked off course. Three got through, hitting a Russian tanker, the *Azerbaijan*, and two cargo ships, the *Navarino* and the *William Hooper*. The *Azerbaijan*, which had at least one woman among the crew, was, in the words of Broome, "holed but happy" and able to make nine knots, so she stayed with the convoy. Two of the Heinkels were shot down, one of them hitting the sea close to the freighter *El Capitan*. There was to be no rescue for them. The men on the freighter's deck shouted abuse at the doomed airmen as their burning airframe slid under the waves.

The rescue ships moved in to pick up survivors from the *Navarino* and *William Hooper* and convoy and escorts resumed the plod eastward. By now the men who sailed in the convoys and those who protected them were hardened to sinkings. These were to be expected and by the arithmetic of such operations, the loss of three ships was unremarkable. The convoy was now less than a thousand miles from its destination. Confidence was high. In Broome's estimation the feeling was that, "provided the ammunition lasted, PQ.17 could get anywhere."[19]

CHAPTER 9

"A HEART-SHAKING" DECISION

T he mood in London was far less confident. At about the time the attacks were going in, Pound was in the middle of a conference in the Admiralty to assess a situation that seemed to him to be increasingly loaded with danger.

His main concern was not the air attacks and the U-boat menace but the possibility that *Tirpitz* and her companions were about to enter the picture. The Admiralty's knowledge of her whereabouts had been patchy from the beginning. Between July 1 and the morning of July 4, the RAF Catalinas now operating out of north Russia had been providing thorough reconnaissance cover of the fjords and coastline of Norway. But there had been a gap in surveillance between the hours of 11:00 a.m. and 5:00 p.m., due to one of the aircraft breaking down. By the time the flights resumed, Pound was in an agony of uncertainty. The last sighting of *Scheer* and *Lützow* had been at Vestfjord when they were photographed leaving from Narvik. There was nothing to show where they had gone. The expectation was that they had moved to Altafjord, near the tip of northern Norway. As for *Tirpitz* and *Hipper*, they had last been heard of on the afternoon of July 3 when all that was known was that they had left Trondheim. In the absence of any hard facts, Pound had only suppositions and his own instincts to help him decide what to do next. It was entirely possible that during the surveillance blackout, all four heavy warships were at sea and steaming at full speed towards PQ.17.

By the time the conference started the picture had cleared a little. In his signal to Hamilton, sent just before 7:00 p.m., Pound had stated that "further information may be available shortly" and ordered him to stay with the convoy for the time being. This referred to the message Pound had just received from Bletchley Park that the German naval codes for the twenty-four-hour period ending at noon that day had been broken and the details would be at the Admiralty soon. The decryption included a signal from the Kriegsmarine's Naval Group North headquarters in Kiel revealing that *Tirpitz* and *Hipper* were expected to arrive in Altafjord that morning, that is the forenoon of July 4, and their destroyers had been ordered to top up with fuel. It was now 8:00 p.m. Anything could have happened in the meantime.

Once he received the report, Pound made some rapid calculations with dividers and chart. The squadron would probably need a few hours to turn around in Altafjord. If it then set off at an easy cruising speed of twenty-eight knots, it would be in position to intercept the convoy at about two o'clock on the morning of July 5. There was no doubt that if that happened, the German fleet would win the ensuing battle. Its guns were bigger and its ships were faster. Broome's close escort could be dealt with at long range without the destroyers' guns being able to land a single shell on their attackers. The convoy would be destroyed in minutes and if Hamilton's cruisers sailed to the rescue they, too, would be out-gunned, outranged, and outmaneuvered. If that was the case, then Pound believed he had no choice but to order the escort to turn away to avoid annihilation and for the convoy to then scatter, leaving every ship to make its own, plodding run for the nearest Russian port.

There was nothing in the decrypt, though, to suggest that a foray by the German ships into the Arctic Ocean was imminent. Pound needed expert advice. He left his office to pay a visit to the intelligence officer with responsibility for the Kriegsmarine's large units, Paymaster Commander Norman Denning. Denning was the son of a Hampshire draper who had been forced on account of his poor eyesight to make his way up the navy ranks in non-operational jobs.[1] He had promoted the use of systematic intelligence analysis in the shaping of operational decisions and had championed the cause of the Photographic Reconnaissance Unit. He now presided over the Operational Intelligence Centre, inside the squat, bombproof bunker of the Admiralty Citadel that since 1940 has disfigured the northern side of Horse Guards Parade.

Denning was a master of his craft and his opinion was worth a great deal. He recalled later how "the First Sea Lord came down to my room ... at about seven o clock in the evening, and he wanted to know what *Tirpitz* was doing. From one source and another I was able to assure [him] that as far as I was concerned *Tirpitz* was still safely in Altenfjord [*sic*]. He seemed to accept that at the time and when he left my room I was fairly convinced that he had taken it in."[2]

Denning did not spell out the reasons for his judgment, and Pound did not ask for them. His opinion was based on several factors. For one thing, the decrypted signals from Naval Group North had not warned U-boats operating in the area of the presence of friendly ships—standard practice in order to prevent them from attacking their own side. Nor had the Royal Navy submarines patrolling off the narrow inlets that led from Altafjord to the open sea reported any movement. A Norwegian agent was in place at the entrance to Altafjord. There had been no radio message from him saying that the battleships had put to sea. Lastly, there was none of the high volume of the radio signals buzzing back and forth between Naval Group North and the ships that were to be expected before a large sortie.

This was perhaps the most difficult decision Pound had had to make in his career. He was a quiet man in a service in which senior officers tended to be loud and colorful. His silence made him enigmatic. The night would deepen the mystery about Pound's character and thought processes.

The crucial conference took place at 8:00 p.m. Pound sat down with about a dozen of his officers and asked each of them in turn their opinion as to what should be done next. No formal record has survived of the meeting, but some versions relate that several present took the view that the time had not come to disperse the ships. The vice chief of the naval staff, Vice Admiral Sir Henry Moore, was said to have argued that, if the order was to be given, it should be given soon. The further east the convoy steamed the more it would be constrained by the ice cap and the less sea room it would have in which to scatter.[3]

Pound was faced with an appalling choice. The sequence of events as it had developed so far seemed to lead inexorably to a sortie by the German fleet which, without some fateful intervention, would surely result in catastrophe. Everything the Germans had done so far had conformed to the plan outlined in the intercepted orders obtained by Captain Denham the previous month. They had spoken of "simultaneous attacks by two surface groups supported by U-boats and aircraft when on the meridian of Bear Island." All the elements were in place. All logic suggested that an attack was imminent. But what if it was not? Pound knew very well that if he ordered the convoy to scatter he was sending at least some of the ships to extinction.

One account of the conference described Pound closing his eyes, and keeping them closed for so long that an officer present worried that his chief, who was known to be a sick and exhausted man, had fallen asleep. But then he opened them again. "The convoy is to disperse," he said.

Once the decision was made a volley of brief, ominous signals was fired at the fleet. The first, timed at 9:11 p.m., was marked SECRET. MOST IMMEDIATE. It directed: "Cruiser Force to withdraw Westward at high speed." The second, timed twelve minutes later, offered a sort of explanation and was rated SECRET. IMMEDIATE. "Owing to threat from surface ships convoy is to disperse and proceed to Russian ports." The third, sent at 9:36 p.m., reverted to the level of MOST IMMEDIATE. "Convoy is to scatter," it ordered.

When the orders arrived at the fleet they were met with disbelief. Jack Broome recalled that it came "out of the blue" and "shook us all to the core. We'd got no reason to believe there was anything to scatter about." His reaction was that "this could only mean one thing. That *Tirpitz* was here, she was on the horizon. Up went all our glasses focussing on various quarters of the horizon. I remember expecting someone to say, 'there she is! There's a gun flash'—something like that. But there was nothing. The waters around were empty."

Grimly and reluctantly Broome called for the flags signaling the order to scatter to be hoisted. Soon after, he noticed that on the *River Afton*, the merchantman in which the convoy's commander, Commodore John Dowding RNR, was sailing, there were no flags flying in response. Broome "thought, well there's no time to lose. She might be on us and I shot into the convoy in *Keppel*, went alongside the Commodore and switched on my loudhailer." He saw the commodore standing on the bridge wing and asked him if he had received the order to scatter. Dowding had seen it, but "he simply couldn't believe it. You see we'd just been through the air attack and we'd done jolly well. Everybody was on their toes and full of beans." Broome persuaded Dowding that the order was correct and he "finally hoisted the signal. I said, I'm sorry about this, it looks like being a bloody business and he said something like 'good-bye and good hunting.'"

The Admiralty's signal had said nothing about what the destroyers should do. It seemed to Broome, though, that if a battle with the German force was imminent, they should be alongside Hamilton's cruiser force to face it. He signaled to the other destroyers to join *Keppel*, and they set off on a direct heading westward. Every man on board the warships felt the weight of what they were doing. "There was no doubt about it," said Broome later. "They were all feeling the same as I was. Going on the opposite course to this scattering convoy, ships we were supposed to be looking after, going the other way, watching them get smaller on the horizon. That was terrible."[4] The convoy was not completely naked. Broome ordered the two anti-aircraft ships, including *Pozarica*, and the twelve anti-submarine corvettes, minesweepers, and armed trawlers to carry on.

On board the US cruiser *Wichita* there was "stunned shock," Douglas Fairbanks recalled. "We felt there must have been some error in transmitting the signal." When it became clear that there had been no mistake, the Americans blamed their allies. His shipmates "were particularly bitter, cursing the British for what they believed was running away in the face of a good battle which we had a chance of surviving. We resented leaving the defenseless merchant ships to straggle at nine and ten knots through icy water, which we knew from experience would not permit survival for more than a very limited time." The latter was a reference to the loss of two of *Wichita*'s observation pilots who had died of exposure before they could be rescued after crashing. The Americans' anger was "made more intense by the philosophic and good natured spirit in which the merchant ships received the order and saw us turn tail."[5]

Deep inside the Admiralty Citadel, Norman Denning heard the news of the order to scatter from his superior, Rear Admiral Clayton. He was now sure that *Tirpitz* had not left Altafjord. There was still a telling absence of the radio chatter from Naval Group North which would have been picked up if a big raid had been in progress. His belief was confirmed when a decrypt arrived from Bletchley of a signal from Admiral Schmundt, the officer commanding Northern Waters at Narvik. It was addressed to the *Eisteufel* (Ice Devil) submarine group waiting for the convoy in the Barents Sea and stated: "No own naval forces in the operational area." With the arrival of the new information Denning decided to take the initiative. He asked Clayton to take the evidence to Pound and try and get him to reverse the order. Clayton did so. Pound, though, was unmoved. Clayton returned to Denning and told him: "Father's made his decision and he's not going to change it now."[6]

It is hard not to sympathize with Pound's predicament and easy to imagine the immense burden of anxiety weighing down on him as he struggled to make up his mind. He was a sick man, in constant pain from an arthritic hip, which stopped him from sleeping, and suffering from a brain tumor. The tumor had been diagnosed in 1939, but Pound had tried to suppress the discovery. Everyone in the Admiralty knew, nonetheless, that he was desperately ill. Pat Trehearne, a young female clerk in the cipher office, remembers "a grey figure, descending the main staircase, having to lean on the railing for support."[7]

Pound faced a dilemma that would mean lost lives whichever way it was resolved. Churchill described it later as a "heart-shaking" decision.[8] Yet it was clear, almost from the outset, that he had made a strange choice. Stephen Roskill, the naval officer who was given the first unrestricted access to the signals traffic and related documents covering the disaster, wrote that "whilst making every allowance for the strain and anxiety felt in London, it is hard to justify such an intervention, made in such a way. If it was felt that dispersing the convoy would turn out to be the less perilous action, such a proposal, and the grounds on which it was made, could justifiably have been sent to the responsible officers for them to carry out or not as they saw fit." Roskill, who spoke to all the commanders at sea, concluded that if Tovey, Hamilton, and Broome had been in possession of the very sparse information on which Pound and his staff had been making their calculations "it is beyond doubt … the convoy and the escort would have been kept together." As it was, the three signals taken together seemed to convey that the "further information" mentioned earlier had now arrived and that the fleet was in imminent danger of attack from *Tirpitz* which made it imperative for the cruisers to cut and run.[9]

None of those things were true. As the merchantmen chugged stoically on, watching their escorts dwindle to nothing on the western horizon, *Tirpitz* and the fleet were still stuck in Altafjord. On board, crews were straining to get into action. But a flurry of mistaken information had meant that Raeder, in Berlin, still hesitated to go to Hitler for the approval to let them off the leash. On the night of July 3, while *Tirpitz* and *Hipper* were on their way to Altafjord, a reconnaissance aircraft had sighted Hamilton's cruiser squadron and reported back that it contained a battleship. Hitler had insisted that no operations were to take place if there was a battleship in the British force. Another pilot corrected the error the following day, only for it to be repeated again in a report from a shadowing U-boat. To add to the confusion, at 6:30 p.m. on July 4 another reconnaissance flight reported seeing "torpedo planes" near the cruiser squadron. They were, in fact, spotter planes from the *Wichita*, but Raeder could not discount the possibility that they had flown off an aircraft carrier—the presence of which would, again on Hitler's orders, mean an attack was ruled out.

It was not until 6:55 the following morning, when a Luftwaffe flight came across the Home Fleet 200 miles northwest of Bear Island, that he felt confident enough to commit his big ships to action. The pilot reported that the British force was steering southwest, toward home, and that the aircraft carrier *Victorious* was with it. There were now eight hundred miles of sea between Tovey and the point where the German fleet would intercept the convoy. That meant the Home Fleet was still at least thirty hours away. The dangers were minimal. Even so, when Raeder issued his orders, after first passing them to Hitler for his blessing, they were cluttered with warnings and provisos. Schniewind was advised that "a brief operation with partial success is more important than a total victory involving major expenditure of time. Report at once if overflown by enemy aircraft. Do not hesitate to break off operation if situation doubtful. On no account grant enemy success against fleet nucleus."[10]

By the time the orders arrived Schniewind had given in to his frustration and *Tirpitz* was already under way, leaving Altafjord just before noon on July 5. By 3:00 p.m. she was cruising at twenty-five knots heading east-northeast into the Barents Sea. It was not long before she was sighted. A Soviet submarine, *K-21*, spotted her off the North Cape. The captain fired his torpedoes and signaled excitedly that two had hit, but it was wishful thinking. The *Tirpitz* swept on unharmed. An hour afterward, a RAF spotter plane operating from Murmansk picked up the German battle fleet parting the waves below. Two hours later again, the British submarine *Unshaken* saw her at a distance, too far away to engage.

The main concern of Schniewind and his men was that there would be no ships left to sink by the time they arrived. The excitement of anticipated action, though, did not last long. The signals from the British spotter plane and submarine had been intercepted and reported to Kiel and Berlin. It was now the Germans' turn to overestimate the aggressive intentions of their enemy. Now that the British knew *Tirpitz* was at sea, they might decide to turn round and go after her. The risk was slight, but it was not one Raeder was prepared to take. At 9:00 p.m. he radioed Schniewind and told him that he was breaking off the operation.

The red pennant signaling a 180-degree turn was hoisted. In the early hours of July 6, the dejected crews arrived back into Altafjord.

For everyone from Schniewind down, the exercise had been another anticlimax. The Knight's Move had turned out to be a feint. It was, though, a spectacularly successful one. Without firing her guns, the German fleet had scored a remarkable physical and moral victory. All across the Barents Sea merchantmen were being hunted down while British and American warships fled in the opposite direction from the shadow of the *Tirpitz*.

The scattered merchantmen were now virtually defenseless. A welcome fog had descended just after they received the order to scatter, but it had lifted by 2:00 a.m. on July 5. "Snoopy Joe" appeared over *Pozarica*. Godfrey Winn asked one of his shipmates what he thought their chances were now. He replied, "about fifty-fifty if we are rather lucky."[11]

At breakfast time the sinkings began. The 6,645-ton *Empire Byron* was the first to go. Her master was the convoy's rear commodore, Captain John Wharton. She was carrying a cargo of the new Churchill tanks and a REME officer, Captain John Rimington, was aboard to give technical advice to the Soviets. Wharton had collapsed in an exhausted sleep in an armchair in his day room on the bridge after thirty-six hours at action stations when Kapitänleutnant Bielfeld in *U-703* launched his first two torpedoes at extreme range. They passed harmlessly ahead, unnoticed by the crew. Two more also missed. The fifth, though, struck the engine room. Wharton slept through the explosion and had to be shaken awake by his gunnery officer. Outside the crew was frantically lowering the lifeboats. There was no escape for the sailors whom the explosion trapped below, and their screams mingled with the shouts of those on deck as they struggled to get the boats into the water.

Wharton stayed on the bridge long enough to destroy all documents, then dove into the icy water. He was picked up by a raft and then put aboard one of the lifeboats. He ordered everyone to concentrate in two of the boats, one of which had an engine. Bodies were clustered face down in the sea around. As they moved away from the *Empire Byron*, the boiler exploded, ripping open the hull and the trapped men were dragged into the depths. Eighteen gunners and sailors were dead, but forty-two were now huddled in the lifeboats watching the black, glistening hull of the U-boat that had sunk them emerge from the sea and head toward them. A tall blond man, an officer they assumed, had descended from the conning tower to the submarine's deck accompanied by a rating with a machine gun. When the U-boat drew up, he demanded to know which of them was the captain. Wharton had told his men not to reveal his identity. After failing to correctly identify him the blond officer ordered Rimington, who stood out in a new white duffel coat, to climb aboard. Then they were given tins of biscuits, apple juice, and a piece of sausage and informed that the nearest landfall was 250 miles to the

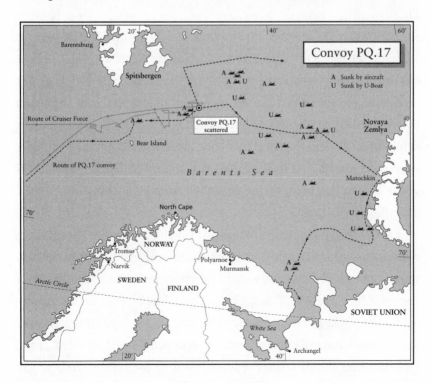

south. They handed back the engineer who had been taken below after his rescue. He told his crewmates that the U-boat commander had said he was sorry to sink the ship but it had been his duty.[12]

There were several instances of the German air force and navy showing humanity toward their victims. The forty-one survivors of the American merchantman *Carlton* assumed the worst when a Heinkel torpedo plane returning from a sortie swooped down and began to circle them. But then it put down nearby and taxied over to the lifeboats. The pilot signaled to them that he could take three passengers. Two of the seamen managed to make it aboard. The third was too heavy to haul himself onto the float. Two hours later a Dornier 24 hospital plane landed and took off ten more. Later, two more rescue aircraft took off another twelve. The last pilot warned those left that there would be no more flights. The remaining seventeen rigged a sail and steered toward Russia.

For those who survived the sinkings, another ordeal was beginning. William Kenyon, a merchant seaman, managed to get aboard a lifeboat but the drinking water soon ran out. "We were reduced to drinking our own urine," he remembered. One man went mad with thirst. They soon noticed a strange phenomenon. "When you haven't had anything to drink for a few days, you find that your tongue swells up and protrudes from your mouth and this ... is how we all looked. There were thirty-seven men in this boat, sitting with their tongues sticking out of their mouths."[13]

Of the thirty-two ships that sailed on alone into the Barents Sea, aircraft sunk thirteen and U-boats sunk ten. Altogether, only thirteen ships survived. The materiel losses were enormous. Out of the 594 tanks aboard, 430 were lost. Of the 297 aircraft, all but 87 went to the bottom. So, too, did 3,350 of the 4,246 vehicles and 99,316 tons of the 156,492 tons of food, steel plate, ammunition, and other much-needed cargo. One hundred and fifty-three seamen lost their lives. They died quickly in the initial explosions or the first contact with the icy sea, or slowly succumbed to exposure, wounds, and burns as they drifted in the perpetual, pearly light.

The German navy and air force had won a significant victory and at a tiny cost. None of their ships were lost, and only 5 of the 202 aircraft that took part in the attacks were shot down. The disaster did not bring the convoys to an immediate halt. One more, PQ.18, sailed early in September. After ten of its ships were sunk, further sailings to Russia were suspended until winter darkness increased the odds of survival.

The disaster and the cutting of the supply route inevitably caused bitterness between the Soviets and their allies. "Has the British Navy no sense of glory," taunted Stalin in a message to Churchill on August 16 while the pain of the catastrophe was still raw.[14] That was to be expected. But the episode also created suspicion and hostility between the Americans and their new comrades. This was the first time in the war that the British and American navies had worked together on a big operation and it had ended in disaster. Douglas Fairbanks recorded how back "in the officers mess at Scapa, after rather too many beakers, there was much mutual recrimination and many hard words were passed. These were finally resolved in cursing the Admiralty and their inability to judge a tactical situation from a lot of pins on a board more than a thousand miles away. It was a pusillanimous defeat and a shocking error of judgment." The same verdict was delivered by virtually everyone who had not been directly involved in the decision. "The order to scatter the convoy had been premature," wrote Tovey in his dispatch covering the episode. "Its results were disastrous."

The decision finally rested with one man. Pound had chosen to make it alone, declining to press Denning for all relevant details and neglecting to share what information he did have with his admirals at sea, who would surely have gone against the decision to scatter if they had been aware of the full intelligence picture. As Hamilton remarked, plaintively and with restraint in a letter to Tovey, "it would have been of great assistance to me had I known that the Admiralty possessed no further information on the movements of the enemy's heavy units other than I had already received." Like everyone involved in the responsibility, he was haunted by the thought that he should have acted differently. "I suppose I ought to have been a Nelson," he remarked to his flag captain. "I ought to have disregarded the Admiralty's signals."[15]

It was Pound who had the most to regret. Yet initially, at least, little blame landed on him. The First Sea Lord made no move to accept culpability, and Churchill seemed reluctant to chastise his old friend. In his account of the episode given after the war, he offered an explanation for Pound's actions, saying he would "probably not have sent such vehement orders if only our own British warships had been concerned." There were American ships to think of, too, and "the idea that our first large joint Anglo-American operation under British command should involve the destruction of the two United States cruisers as well as our own may well have disturbed [his] poise."[16] Pound himself gave a version of events that offered a crucial but unsubstantiated explanation. On August 1 he told the Cabinet that on the night of July 3–4, the day before the order to disperse was given, "the Admiralty had had information … that the TIRPITZ, having eluded our waiting submarines, would, if she continued on her course, be in a position to attack the convoy early the following morning."[17] As Stephen Roskill noted after his unrestricted search through the papers, "the existence of such precise intelligence has not been confirmed by postwar research."[18] Pound also offered the War Cabinet a tacit excuse for the urgent wording of the "scatter" order. It was phrased like that because the convoy was traveling so slowly and would need as much warning as possible. It was not intended to suggest that "it was about to be attacked at any moment."

Pound died fifteen months after the debacle. His achievements would always be overshadowed by the disaster of PQ.17. Each year for many years to come the date of July 4 would revive bitter memories among the merchant seamen seething at what they regarded as a great betrayal. There were many within the Royal Navy who accepted the charge. Vice Admiral Bill O'Brien, who served as a young officer on HMS *Offa*, one of the close escort destroyers, remarked years later: "I have never been able to rejoice with my American Friends on Independence Day, because July 4 is to me a day to hang my head in grief for all the men who lost their lives on Convoy PQ.17, and in shame at one of the bleakest episodes in Royal Navy history, when the warships deserted the merchant ships and left them to their fate for in simple terms, that is what we were obliged to do."[19]

CHAPTER 10

A HA'PORTH OF TAR

One morning in April 1942, a lorry arrived at a deserted corner of Portsmouth naval base. Canvas screens were moved aside and the truck drove in and pulled up next to Horsea Lake, a seawater basin used for diving exercises. The screens were dragged back again to hide what followed from the sight of passersby. A strange-looking torpedo-shaped craft was manhandled off the back and winched off the deck. Two men, encased in canvas and rubber suits, lowered themselves into the water, pulled themselves on board and sat astride it, one behind the other. A small launch carrying two men in naval uniform towed it out into the middle. For the next half-hour they watched closely and made notes as the men in the water struggled to get the craft to do what it was supposed to.

The vessel was a prototype of a new secret weapon. The navy called it a "chariot." It was officially known as a Mark I Human Torpedo, a name that fairly described its look and function. The tests now underway were the result of another of Churchill's interventions. A few months earlier, on January 18, 1942, he sent a memo to the Chiefs of Staff Committee asking them to "please report what is being done to emulate the exploits of the Italians in Alexandria Harbor and similar methods of this kind." It ended on an irritable note: "Is there any reason why we should be incapable of the same kind of scientific aggressive action that the Italians have shown? One would have thought we should have been in the lead."[1]

Churchill and the Admiralty had been unpleasantly surprised by a display of ingenuity from the Italian navy a month before. On December 19, 1941, three "human torpedoes" were launched from an Italian submarine at the entrance to Alexandria harbor where the British Mediterranean Fleet was anchored. They crept in while the boom was open to allow some ships to enter and clamped delayed action mines on the undersides of the battleships *Queen Elizabeth* and *Valiant*. Both were seriously damaged and knocked out of action for many months. If the enemy could do this to our battleships, Churchill wanted to know, why should we not do it to theirs?

The idea of a human torpedo had been around since the beginning of the century. In 1909 a retired British naval officer, Commander Godfrey Herbert, had designed a one-man craft that he called the "Devastator." Its prospectus advertised it as a "means for propelling against an enemy ship or other target a large quantity of high explosive, and of effecting this with great economy of material and personnel." He had presented his idea to the Admiralty before and during the First World War only for it to be turned down by, among others, Winston Churchill—then First Lord of the Admiralty and the navy's political master.[2]

In the interwar years the idea had gained credibility and champions. They included Sir Max Horton, who had commanded one of the first ocean-going British submarines, HMS *E9* at the start of the First World War. He had provided an early demonstration of the effects small submersible vessels could have on big surface ships. On September 11, 1914, *E9* met SMS *Hela*, a German light cruiser, off Heligoland and fired two torpedoes, sending her to the bottom. After a day evading vengeful Germans, he returned safely to Harwich and sailed into harbor with the Jolly Roger flying from the observation tower—a grim tradition maintained by submariners right up to the sinking of the Argentinian cruiser *Belgrano* by HMS *Conqueror* in 1982.

By the end of 1940, Horton was head of the Royal Navy's submarine service. He had already commissioned experiments to develop the original ideas and among those involved was the father of the concept, Godfrey Herbert. As well as human torpedoes, Horton was also keen to produce a "midget submarine" that could attack ships while they were in harbor. The arrival of effective defenses such as booms and heavy steel mesh anti-submarine and anti-torpedo nets meant that conventional submarines were incapable of carrying out close attacks. Midget submarines—X-Craft as they came to be called—were intended to have a much longer range than the chariot and would take more time to develop. By the beginning of February 1942, however, Horton was working on operational plans involving both craft.

The new vessels would need specialized crews. To find men with the right temperament Horton issued an appeal for "volunteers for hazardous service." The terminology was deliberately vague to disguise the nature of the duties. Those who answered were driven by boredom, ambition, or a thirst for adventure, and by April more than thirty had been selected. Among them were Lieutenant Chuck Bonnell, a Canadian, and Petty Officer Jim Warren, a former submariner, who was given the job of testing the prototype chariot in Horsea Lake.

The men watching them were also submariners, appointed by Horton to supervise the training of volunteers. Commander Geoffrey

"Slasher" Sladen had already had an outstanding war. A few months earlier he had been in command of the submarine *Trident* when it badly damaged *Prinz Eugen* with a torpedo on passage to join *Tirpitz* at Trondheim. He was six feet tall, a talented sportsman with four England rugby caps who also kept goal for his submarine's football team. He was boisterous, noisy, and impatient with anyone who showed what he regarded as a lack of zeal or efficiency.

Commander William "Tiny" Fell was a New Zealander. He was short, quiet, and courteous. His outlook, though, was just as aggressive as "Slasher" Sladen's. He had already won a Distinguished Service Cross for leading fire ship raids against German ships that gathered in French ports in the summer of 1940 for an invasion that never came.

The prototype whose trials he and Sladen were overseeing was code-named "Cassidy" and built of wood. It was supposed to replicate some of the functions of the final version. The design was based on the prewar experiments and on some features copied from an Italian human torpedo that navy divers salvaged after a failed attack in Gibraltar. When completed it would be just over twenty-two feet long and weigh, with its warhead, 3,500 lb. It was driven by a propeller and powered by a large electric battery, which could push it along at three knots for a maximum distance of eighteen miles. The man in front sat behind a cowling that shielded an illuminated instrument console with a compass. He steered to port and starboard and moved the chariot up and down by pushing and pulling at a joystick which operated the rudder and hydroplane fins mounted at the rear. The man behind was charged with navigation and cutting through nets. He also had the task of fixing the chariot's detachable warhead, clamped on the nose, to the hull of the target ship. Pumps and a compressed air system filled and emptied the ballast tank that sank the chariot below the waves or raised it to the surface. There were also two smaller tanks in which the water level could be adjusted to trim the craft to achieve the best balance and the smoothest forward progress.

Warren and Bonnell's instructions were to open the vent in the main ballast tank which stuck up like a hump between the forward and after seats, set the hydroplanes to dive, and slide thirty feet to the bottom of the harbor. They were equipped with breathing apparatuses and two bottles of oxygen. Their nostrils were clamped shut with nose clips and they inhaled through a mouthpiece gripped in their mouths. They were to communicate with the surface by tugging on a lifeline, using simple signals. "Cassidy," however, showed no signs of wanting to submerge. It was only after many pounds of lead had been loaded onto the hull that it eventually slipped under the surface and settled on the rock, mud, and seaweed of the bottom. Fell and Sladen soon realized what was causing the problem. They had already conducted an initial test suspended by a gantry in a large tank. The tank was full of freshwater and far less buoyant than the brine of Horsea Lake.

So the development of the new weapon went on, a continuous, frequently hazardous, process of trial and error. A crucial problem which had to be solved if the charioteers were to go to war was finding a breathing apparatus that met their particular needs. To reach their target undetected and dive to place their charge, they might have to travel at depths of thirty feet or more and stay underwater for up to six hours. Oxygen was the obvious breathing medium as it produced no telltale bubbles. However, thirty feet was considered to be the maximum depth at which it could be used. Beyond that the diver was liable to suffer convulsions and blackouts, ending in death.

The Admiralty's Experimental Diving Unit began work with a specialist firm of diving equipment manufacturers, Siebe Gorman, to see if the boundaries could be stretched. The unit moved its headquarters to the company's factory in Tolworth, Surrey. There, the company's scientists worked with the hazardous service volunteers to explore the limits of physical endurance. According to the firm's chairman, Sir Robert Davis, what followed "was probably the most exhaustive program of human experiments ever attempted on one aspect of diving." In all it involved more than a thousand dives to depths considered "toxic." Many of the divers suffered convulsions or passed out, yet carried on, showing "great courage in submitting themselves cheerfully to these experiments, in spite of the risk and unpleasantness of the job." They invented a mythical monster to represent the ever-present threat of toxicity, "Oxygen Pete," who lurked at the bottom of the high-pressure water chamber, waiting to snare them.[3]

One difficulty was overcome with the unwitting assistance of the German air force. The breathing apparatus's steel oxygen cylinders were found to interfere with the chariot's compass. Alloy cylinders would get around the problem, but none were being manufactured then in Britain. Then someone remembered that German bombers carried their oxygen supply in aluminum alloy bottles of almost exactly the right shape and size. "Fortunately the Royal Air Force maintained its toll of the Luftwaffe at a sufficiently high rate to meet the needs of the Human Torpedo scheme … until production of similar cylinders could be started in England," noted Sir Robert.

The charioteers were clad in rubberized cotton "diving dress" but extra clothing was also needed to withstand the extreme cold of a northern Norwegian winter without adding too much bulk. In the end they settled for silk underwear with padded kapok vests and trousers for another light layer of insulation. The quest for satisfactory gloves ended in failure, despite the efforts of guinea pigs who sat with their hands immersed in crushed ice to reproduce the right level of numbness. Most of the charioteers simply coated their fingers with a thick layer of "Peddo" grease.

Diving was a miserable business. Somehow water always managed to seep through the seals of the one-piece dry suits and they had earned the nickname "clammy death." They were also bulky and cumbersome. Getting into one was painful and needed the assistance of a "dresser."

It involved squeezing your head into a thick, tightly fitting rubber hood and forcing your hands through watertight cuffs that cut off circulation.

The volunteers were officially part of the Experimental Submarine Flotilla based at Fort Blockhouse, the Royal Navy's Portsmouth submarine base at Gosport, opposite Portsmouth. By the start of the summer, the pool of recruits had grown to twenty-four RNVR officers, mostly young sub-lieutenants and lieutenants, and thirty-one ratings, some of whom had exchanged safer berths as cooks and signalmen to answer Horton's call. Two army officers had also found their way to Portsmouth.

In June most of them transferred to the opposite end of the country. Trainees and instructors moved by train and ship to set up an operational training base at Lake Erisort, on the Outer Hebridean island of Lewis. The remoteness of the spot was suited to the tight secrecy that had been imposed on the project. It also meant there were few distractions from the continuous drills. Stornoway, the island's capital, was picturesque but sedate. It was a stronghold of the puritanical Free Church of Scotland and had more churches than pubs.

The volunteers still had to practice on "Cassidy," the faithful wooden prototype. Shortly after the group moved north, though, another experiment was carried out in Portsmouth with a new, metal-hulled model, which became known as "The Real One." The final trial, with Sladen in the forward seat, took place in front of a VIP audience that included Sir Max Horton and Admiral Ernest King, the prickly Commander in Chief of the US Fleet. The "Real One" behaved immaculately, diving, maneuvering, and surfacing to order. King was skeptical. For Sladen and his chief, though, the display seemed to prove that the experiment had produced a weapon of real value. It was soon on its way to Lewis for an intense period of further training in preparation for serious operations.

Throughout the summer the teams underwent a punishing regime designed to give them an instinctive ability to handle the craft under any conditions and difficulties. It was a wretched process, chilly and uncomfortable and fraught with continuous dangers. The occasional pleasure of drifting serenely beneath the choppy surface of the lake was outweighed by the misery of enduring, for several hours at a time, tight-fitting nose clamps while biting hard on a large steel-and-rubber oxygen mouthpiece which left the gums bruised and bloody.

The physical strains were matched by psychological pressures. It took a particular form of mental toughness to withstand the rigors of training. The divers operated in an atmosphere in which the potential for catastrophe was always present. Their survival depended on new and complicated equipment which could go wrong at any time. When accidents happened, there was often no explanation. The first fatal casualty had occurred before they left Portsmouth. Lieutenant P. C. A. Browning had been doing a routine dive in perfect conditions when one of the attendants who kept a constant watch found there was no answering tug when he pulled on the lifeline. That was not a cause for immediate concern as it was relatively easy for a diver in difficulties simply to jettison his lead-weighted boots and kick himself to the surface. After a few minutes with no sign of Browning, sound signals were broadcast underwater, ordering him to abandon the dive. There was no response. When the body was recovered by divers there was no clue as to how he had met his end.

The volunteers soon discovered that Lake Erisort brought its own peculiar dangers. A chariot could be cruising along at three knots, well trimmed, and at a comfortable depth suspended between surface and bottom, then suddenly plunge away sharply. The result was a drastic and alarming surge in pressure. The divers felt their eardrums bulge, their joints throb with pain, and their lungs flatten against their ribs.

The explanation was simple. Close to the rocky banks, streams that fed in freshwater thinned out the salt water of the lake, causing a dramatic change in buoyancy. Divers were briefed to expect it. It still required steely composure to follow the correct drill. The first step was to hang on as the chariot began a vertiginous drop of up to a hundred

Hitler arrives at Wilhelmshaven dockyard. On the right is Frau Ilse von Hassell, daughter of Admiral Alfred von Tirpitz. *(Time & Life Pictures/Getty Images)*

Karl Topp (left) and Kurt Voigt. *(Courtesy Jurgen Voigt)*

Reconnaissance photograph taken shortly after *Tirpitz* arrived in her Faettenfjord berth. *(ww2images.com)*

Human Torpedo with charioteers in training, 1942. *(ww2images.com)*

X-10 departs Loch Cairnbawn under tow. Sub-Lieutenant Page (the passage CO) is on the casing. *(The Royal Navy Submarine Museum)*

Interior of X-Craft with Sub-Lieutenant R. G. "Robbie" Robertson at the controls. *(The Royal Navy Submarine Museum)*

X-Craft crew commanders (left to right): Martin, Hudspeth, McFarlane, Place, and Cameron. *(The Royal Navy Submarine Museum)*

Leif Larsen. *(Courtesy Literary Estate of David Howarth)*

Captains Courageous: Place and Cameron after their release. *(Popperfoto/Getty Images)*

Christmas Day in the seamen's mess on the *Tirpitz*, 1942. The slogans on the wall say, "The Führer's Faith is Our Faith" and "The Führer's Struggle is Our Struggle." *(The Trustees of the Imperial War Museum)*

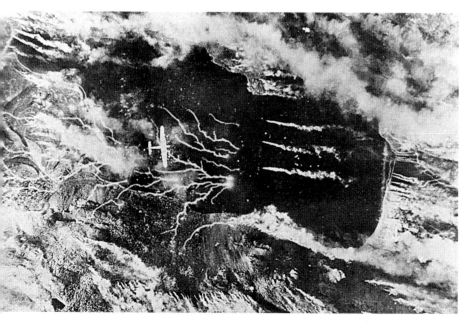

Lancaster silhouetted over Kaafjord during the attack on September 15, 1944. *(ww2images.com)*

Hellcats on HMS *Furious.* (*The Trustees of the Imperial War Museum*)

"Essentially, a shy person": the young "Willie" Tait. (*Courtesy Peter Tait*)

The opening of the final attack, seen from the Lancaster of Bobby Knights. *(ww2images.com)*

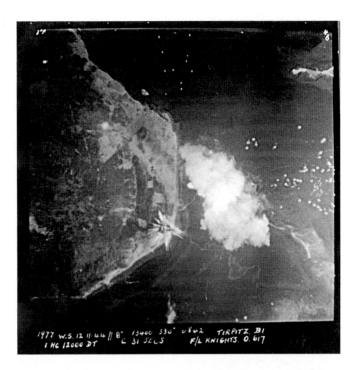

1977 W.S. 12 11·44 || 8" 13400 330° 0842 TIRPITZ B1
1 HC 12000 DT C 31 SECS F/L KNIGHTS. O. 617

Unique photograph of the moment of *Tirpitz's* death, taken by a woodcutter looking south from Tromsø. *(Private collection)*

Klaus Rohwedder at Ehrenfriedhof. *(Author's collection)*

feet towards the lake floor. They were then to wrench open the bypass valve of their oxygen tubes and gasp in the extra gas needed to breathe at extreme depth, allowing some to escape so that it formed a cushion between their faces and the glass visor of the helmet, now crushed by four atmospheres of pressure against their lips and noses. At the same time they were to swallow and breathe hard through their nostrils, squeezed shut by a clip, to combat the agonizing pressure on their ear-drums. Once these steps were taken they were to carry on until they were out of the freshwater patch and back in the seawater which would waft them upwards.

At depths of more than forty feet, there was a tendency to black out. At least three-quarters of those under training did so at one time or another. The convention was to treat it as an occupational hazard, even a joke. For all the discomforts and dangers, for all the trepidation that was inevitably felt as they tried to imagine what it was that they would be expected to do when they finally went on operations, the number of dropouts was tiny.

Once they had mastered the chariot, volunteers moved on to dealing with the obstacles they would have to overcome to reach their targets. Once again they had to find their own solutions. All surface warships were now draped around with defensive nets if they were lying at anchor for any time. There were two types. One was a criss-cross curtain of steel wire, heavy enough to deter a marauding submarine and deep enough almost to touch the bottom. The second was made out of steel rings and was designed to stop torpedoes. Nets were strung on jackstays and hung on buoys in the lake for the teams to practice on.

It was the number two's job to wield the heavy metal cutters stowed in the bo'sun's locker behind him while his number one kept the chariot steady. The anti-submarine nets were relatively easy to cut through. The anti-torpedo defenses were like outsized chain mail and defeated the cutters. The only way past was to dive under them.

Another difficulty was how to attach the chariot's warhead to the target's hull. Again, the crews and their tutors were operating in unknown territory. Dummy attacks were tried on HMS *Titania*, the flotilla depot ship, anchored at Lake Erisort. Eventually, a method evolved. The chariot approached the ship well below the waterline and, when it met the hull, slid underneath. The next step was to detach the clamps holding the warhead to the nose of the chariot. It was packed with 600 pounds of explosive and fitted with a time-delay fuse. The number two charioteer then heaved it into position, fixed it to the hull with magnets, and set the timer. When the job was done the next thing to do was get away as fast and far as possible before the charge went up. The chariots did not have the legs to get back to the mother ships that had delivered them to the target area. The only option left was to head for land and make for neutral territory. In order to prepare his men for life on the run, Sladen devised an exhausting series of exercises in the scree, peat, and heather around Lake Erisort.

Despite the secrecy surrounding the project it seemed obvious to the volunteers that they were being trained to attack the big German ships now lying in the Norwegian fjords and above all *Tirpitz*. Sladen wanted to see his men in action as soon as possible. He was concerned that after three months of intensive training they were beginning to lose their "snap." Almost as soon as the crews arrived in Scotland, moves were underway to put them to use. The failure of the April air attacks followed by the catastrophe of PQ.17 had increased determination to deal with *Tirpitz*. At the Admiralty, the belief grew that the chariots should be given a chance to show what they could do. If they did not succeed, then the midget submarines still in development could be tried at a later date.

A plan was already in the making. In the middle of June, the operational commander of the submarine service, Rear Admiral Sir Claud Barry, had instructed one of his officers, Captain Lord Ashbourne, to work with the Special Operations Executive (SOE) on plans to attack the *Tirpitz* in Faettenfjord. SOE was set up by Churchill in the grim days of July 1940 to establish espionage networks and promote sabotage behind enemy lines. The organization was closely involved with the activities of the Shetland Bus operation and had a Norwegian Section headed by Lieutenant Colonel John Wilson, who had been a luminary of the Boy Scout movement before arriving in the cloak-and-dagger world of SOE. Ashbourne and Wilson began to work on a proposal. It was clear from the beginning that for the plan to succeed it would require the help of the Norwegian resistance—at home and abroad.

The first problem to overcome was how to get the chariots—whose range was severely limited—close enough to carry out the attack. One proposal was to drop the men and craft at night by parachute from a Halifax bomber. Another was to land them by Sunderland flying boat, and five were converted for the purpose. The first idea was abandoned when someone pointed out that it was unlikely that the crews would be able to find their craft in water in darkness. The second was jettisoned when it was realized there was little chance of making a landing undetected.[4] Attention turned to getting the chariots in place by boat. With intelligence provided by the Norwegian underground, a plan emerged to sail teams and machines to the coastal island of Frøya, west of Trondheimsfjord. There they would transfer to a boat supplied by a local resistance sympathizer, which would then bluff its way past the German controls at the mouth of Trondheimsfjord and sail in, with the chariots in tow underwater. The chariots and crews would take to the water to be dropped at the island of Tautra, just to the north of Faettenfjord, where they were just close enough to the anchorage to carry out the attack on their own.

Once Sir Dudley Pound approved Ashbourne and Wilson's plan, it was transmitted in code to E. S. Nielsen, a Norwegian consular official in Stockholm. He had escaped from Norway earlier in the war and was now charged with looking after refugees. He also acted as a link between local resistance groups and the outside world. Nielsen arranged for an agent, Arne Christiansen, to travel to Trondheim to seek the help of the Rørholt network. The network included Birger Grønn, manager of the dockyard, and Herbert Helgesen, the boss of a sausage factory, who posed as a friend of the Germans. They would be in a position to find out the precise details of restrictions and regulations and the documentation required to get around them. Christiansen would then try and find a fisherman in Frøya who was willing to take the huge risks involved in smuggling the chariot team under the noses of the Germans to Faettenfjord.

The attack was initially set for the start of October and given the code name "Title." The sortie against Convoy PQ.17 and *Tirpitz*'s subsequent return to Narvik, however, made that date uncertain. The high tempo of training was unaffected. The crews were given a fortnight's leave in mid-August. They returned to a different headquarters, at Lake Cairnbawn, south of Cape Wrath in the far north of Scotland. It was deep enough to accommodate one of the Royal Navy's biggest and most modern ships, HMS *Howe*, a "KGV"-class battleship. *Howe* was on loan for a few days so that the chariots could mount a practice attack on her. She had a hull of 10.5 meters (34 feet), deeper than the 9.9 meters drawn by *Tirpitz*. This was significant. If the chariots were to approach in the agreed fashion, they would have to descend to below thirty feet, the danger level for oxygen toxicity.

For the exercise the *Howe* was moored tight to the shore, protected on the seaward side by two layers of nets. Hydrophones were extended into the water to detect any disturbance below the surface and a patrol boat plied the water around the ship. Seven chariots would take part in the dummy attack. Their orders were simply to "get your charge under the *Howe* and get away undetected." The crews left the depot ship *Titania* at fifteen-minute intervals under cover of darkness and dived half a mile from the target. Sub-Lieutenant George Goss and Leading Seaman

Trevethian manned the first chariot. They noticed that one net did not stretch all the way to the shore so they came in behind it, dived under the second barrier, and placed their charge under the stern of the *Howe*.

The second team negotiated the nets without trouble and clamped their warhead in place with magnets amidships. The third pair also got in and out successfully. The fourth team hit immediate difficulties when a wire on the nets punctured breathing equipment. They managed to withdraw without being seen. The fifth team had problems with its securing magnets and could not attach the warhead but managed to escape unseen. The next pair got into an unexpected patch of freshwater and plunged seventy feet to the bottom, damaging their eardrums. They decided not to risk compromising the presence of the other craft and returned to the *Titania*. Lieutenant Jock Kerr, who had volunteered for hazardous duties from the Highland Light Infantry five months before, piloted the last. He took his craft so far down that it bumped the bottom. A blast of compressed air sent it floating upward to stop against the vast hull of the *Howe*. The charges were placed and Kerr made his escape, only to be spotted by the patrol launch on the surface. To everyone watching and taking part, the exercise had proved the feasibility of an attack by human torpedoes on large enemy vessels. Another exercise was held the following night with four teams. All four got through but two were spotted as they got away. The exercise only reinforced the positive mood.

A death on the third and final night dampened spirits. Sub-Lieutenant Jack Grogan, a South African reservist, and Able Seaman "Geordie" Worthy dived steeply to get beneath the *Howe*'s hull. There, Grogan blacked out. Worthy moved forward and, while he held Grogan upright, managed to maneuver the chariot out from under the battleship and up to the surface. It was too late to save Grogan. The loss did not alter the judgment that the chariots were now ready for action.

Since returning from its foray against PQ.17, *Tirpitz* had spent the rest of July and the whole of August and September in Bogen Bay, the deep, sheltered anchorage on the north shore of the approach to Narvik. There had been a surge of excitement when it was thought that she might put to sea against convoy PQ.18, which sailed from Iceland early in September. It soon subsided. The experiences of July suggested strongly that aircraft and U-boats could wreak sufficient havoc without it being necessary to risk the Kriegsmarine's greatest asset. So it proved to be, and bombers and submarines accounted for ten of the convoy's forty-five ships.

Tirpitz had been operational for more than a year. Despite having taken part in only two operations she was already due for a refit. Raeder wanted to bring her back to a modern dockyard in a German port with full facilities but Hitler objected, fearing an attack on the homeward voyage. The work would have to be done in Norwegian waters. Bogen Bay was unsuitable. The decision was made to move back to Faettenfjord. First, though, her old berth would have to be improved for the refit to be carried out.

Preparations for Operation Title had continued during *Tirpitz*'s absence. The fact that shore-based anti-aircraft batteries were still in place around Faettenfjord persuaded the Admiralty and SOE planners that the battleship would at some point return there. Some alterations, however, were needed to the plan. Arne Christiansen, the agent sent from Stockholm to alert the local underground, had failed to find anyone on the island of Frøya willing to allow his boat to be used to carry the chariots and their crews to the target area. A man who he had been told might cooperate had refused, on the understandable grounds that he feared for his family's safety if things went wrong.[5]

Colonel Wilson now favored using one of the Shetland Bus fleet for the whole operation. Earlier that year, Sub-Lieutenant David Howarth, a young naval officer working with the Norwegians, had come up with a scheme for using one of the cutters based at Lunna Voe for a torpedo attack on *Tirpitz*. He tried the idea on Leif Larsen, who had landed Bjorn

Rørholt near Trondheim earlier in the year. Larsen agreed it was feasible and volunteered his services. Howarth passed the idea on to the Admiralty where, as he later wrote, it "disappeared into the administrative maze and was never heard of again."[6]

Larsen was already something of a legend. His extraordinary skill and courage made him stand out, even in the company of the Norwegian exiles, themselves a brave and determined bunch. He was the ideal man for the job. Major L. H. Mitchell, who ran the Shetland Bus operation, sounded him out, and he signed up immediately for what would be his most alarming mission to date.

It was left to him to choose a crew. The three men who came to mind were his friend Palmer Bjørnøy, to serve as the ship's engineer, Johannes Kalve, whose worth he knew from several shared Shetland Bus operations as deckhand, and Roald Strand, a trained radio telegraphist. When he approached them, he could not divulge the details of the operation, but he warned them that the chances of returning alive were limited. They all accepted the mission. After some deliberation he decided to use his own boat, the *Arthur*. Work began on adapting her for the job. Two chariots would be used in the attack. They would make the first part of the journey on deck and new hoisting gear was engineered to lift them on and off. For the last part of the journey, a hundred-mile voyage through the islands and inner leads, into Trondheimsfjord, they would be towed underneath the boat with steel hawsers. Two massive eye bolts were machined with threaded ends that meant they could be screwed together through a hole bored through the solid oak of the *Arthur*'s keel. Steel cables were then shackled to each of the eye bolts. These would be connected to eye bolts in the nose of the warheads. It was essential that the work was sound and Larsen himself fixed the keel housing.

Below deck, a secret compartment was built to hide the four chariot crewmen and two dressers who would help them into their diving gear, in the quite likely event of the *Arthur* being stopped and searched by the guard vessels that plied the approaches. Larsen's cover story would be that he was on his way to Trondheim to deliver a cargo of peat, a commodity regularly traded between the coastal islands and the mainland. The hold would be stacked with sacks of the stuff, and with the chariots' warheads buried underneath.

Documents were needed to fool the German bureaucracy. The *Arthur* would have to pass the guards keeping watch from a boat lying off Agdenes at the entrance to Trondheimsfjord, who checked the papers of all who came and went. The Trondheim underground leaders Grønn and Helgesen had been asked to discover what was required. The list was long: registration papers for the boat; identification cards for Larsen and the crew; bills of lading signed by the German harbormasters of all the ports they had visited in the last three months; and authority to enter the fjord, which was a closed military area. As well as this essential information, the agents were also able to supply some of the blank documents. An agent, Odd Sørli, who had accompanied Rørholt on his first trip and was now in Stockholm, traveled to Trondheim at the end of September to collect them.

Safely back in Sweden, he flew to London, disguised as a Lutheran pastor, carrying the papers and details of the underground group's arrangements for helping the attack party to escape after the operation. After dropping the chariots and their crews, the Norwegians and the two remaining Britons were to scuttle the *Arthur* and row in the boat's dinghy to the southern shore of Trondheimsfjord and hide in a hay lorry. After the charioteers had landed, both groups would be collected by the resistance and driven to the Swedish frontier.

The preparations and trials continued until the last minute with scrupulous attention to detail. The *Arthur* was given the identity of a boat similar in size and appearance picked from the Norwegian fishing boat register. Messages were passed to the Trondheim agents to check that it was still in service. The registration documents were rubbed to authentic griminess, then stamped with forged stamps and signed with forged harbormasters' signatures. "When they were finished," said Howarth, "they were masterpieces."[7]

In the first week of October, the *Arthur* sailed with the crew selected by Larsen to Lake Cairnbawn for a final dummy run. Here the Norwegians met the men they would be carrying. The final selection had now been made. One chariot would be crewed by Sub-Lieutenant William Brewster and Able Seaman A. Brown, both of whom answered to the name of "Jock." Sergeant Don Craig, an early volunteer from the Royal Engineers, and Able Seaman Bob Evans made up the other team. Able Seamen Billy Tebb, a cockney wit, and Malcolm Causer, who had been brought up in Brazil but returned home to volunteer at the outbreak of war, would be traveling with them as spare crew and dressers. The target for the exercise was the battleship *Nelson*, and Sir Max Horton was on board to see how it went. At midnight the day after Larsen's arrival, the exercise began. To replicate conditions as closely as possible, the *Arthur* stopped several miles away from the *Nelson*, and the chariot crews prepared to descend into the lake and under the boat. "A little splash was heard as the four men of the deep let themselves glide down into the coal black sea to disappear from sight," Larsen wrote later. "It was quiet on board while the fellows worked under the bottom of the vessel and unshackled the Chariot ... the only thing that could be seen was the phosphorescence and ripples which rose up. Then one machine bobbed up a little way from the side of the vessel. Evans and Craig were holding on to the sides of it and had to [struggle] to mount. Then the other machine appeared."[8]

That night both teams managed to cut through two curtains of nets draped around the ship, dived underneath a third, laid their mock charges, and withdrew without being spotted. A few days later, *Arthur* and the charioteers returned to Lunna Voe to await the order to sail.

Tirpitz arrived back in Faettenfjord from Narvik late on October 23. The following day it was spotted by a PRU reconnaissance flight.

On October 25 a signal arrived in Lunna Voe from Admiral Horton: "Carry out Operation TITLE—target *Tirpitz* in Faettenfjord. D-Day October 31st." That gave them six days to get there.

The *Arthur* left Lunna Voe at mid-morning on Monday, October 26. Crown Prince Olaf of Norway waved them off in the autumn sunshine. The fine weather soon faded. Rain fell and a strong wind blew in from the northeast. The boat plunged and shuddered as it drove head-on through the seas. Even the Norwegians were feeling seasick. They still managed to toast Brewster's twenty-fifth birthday with a shot of gin. It was not until midday on Wednesday, October 28, that Kalve spotted white-capped mountains through gaps in the curtain of fog ahead. As they got closer Larsen identified them as the range that overlooked the town of Bud, south of Kristiansund. Soon afterward the engine faltered and stopped. "We lay for three hours in sight of land, completely help-less," wrote Brewster later. "This was of course rather worrying in broad daylight but no-one came near us."[9] They hoisted a sail to make way while Bjørnøy worked on the engine. After a few hours it was working again, and they were steering northeast toward the island of Edøy where, according to their cover story, they had taken on their cargo of peat. At 8:00 a.m. the next day, as dawn was painting the snow on the hills pink, they anchored in a small bay on an islet west of Edøy, at the entrance to the complex of shoals, skerries, and minefields that led into Trondheims-fjord.

This was the end of the first leg of the journey. It was now time to lower the chariots over the side and lash them to the hull for the next stage of the voyage. The crew and teams got to work, untying the ropes, removing the tarpaulins, and burrowing into the peat in the hold to retrieve the warheads.

As they did so, a German aircraft appeared in the distance and flew straight toward them. They only just had time to haul the covers back over the chariots when it noticed them and swooped down to take a better look. The British scrambled below deck. The Norwegians put on a display of nonchalance for the benefit of the pilot circling sixty feet above, fussing with the net they had dropped over the back. Kalve added authenticity by urinating casually into the sea from the bow. The spotter plane left.

As they resumed work, another aircraft appeared, took another look at them and droned off. There were several more visits that morning. Finally, there was a long enough lull for them to risk another attempt. The warheads were brought up from below and fixed to the noses. When the first chariot was hoisted up on the derrick it was clear to Brewster that the heavy swell in the bay would make it extremely difficult to get it into the water. "It should have been about an hour's job," wrote Brewster later, "but it took a devil of a lot longer."[10] In the choppy sea the *Arthur* started to drag her anchor. There was nothing for it but to set off again, trailing the chariots behind, to seek a better haven.

Night was falling when they found one and "after much cursing and mucking about" made the boat fast to the beach. The charioteers went below to get some sleep. At five o'clock in the pre-dawn darkness of Friday, October 30, they tried again. Tebb and Causer helped Brewster and Evans into their diving gear, and they slipped into the water. They checked the electric motor and instruments then pushed and pulled the craft seven feet below the surface and fixed them under the keel. They lashed ropes underneath, which were fixed to cleats on deck to hold the chariots horizontal. They had just got back on board when the *Arthur* became the subject of more unwanted attention. A rowing boat was approaching, with an old man at the oars. He drew up alongside, held onto the starboard rail, and began a desultory conversation with Larsen.

It was clear that he was in no hurry to leave. He kept up a steady flow of awkward questions, which Larsen, with increasing annoyance and alarm, managed to parry. As they talked, the old man noticed the chariots gleaming in the clear, shallow water. He bent down to get a better look. When the visitor asked what they were, Larsen replied that they were mine-exploding devices. Comprehension dawned on the old man's face. "You fellows go about with the Germans, perhaps?" he asked. Larsen admitted this was the case.[11]

The old man now felt on good enough terms to ask if they could spare any butter. Larsen obliged. As the man prepared to row away, Larsen asked him where he lived and whether he had a family. He supplied the information happily, adding that his daughter lived nearby. In a flash Larsen's friendly manner evaporated. If he breathed a word of what he had seen that morning, he snarled, he and his daughter would pay for his indiscretion with their lives. The old man seized the oars and rowed away, pausing now and again to shout back assurances that he would keep his mouth shut.

Before setting off again, they went over the ship searching for anything incriminating—such as Larsen's British-made pipe—and threw it over the side in a weighted sack. The transmitter, which was one of the most up-to-date yet produced, was also ditched. The machine gun they had been given in case of emergencies, rucksacks, and emergency provisions for their getaway they stowed in the secret compartment.

There were now less than forty-eight hours to go to the attack. Before they approached Trondheimsfjord, there was an important call to make. Larsen headed for the fishing village of Hestvik, on the island of Hitra, fifteen miles west of the mainland. Sørli had made contact with a local storekeeper called Nils Strøm who had promised to help out with details of German activities.

On the way the engine began to knock ominously again. Bjørnøy, the engineer, examined it and diagnosed a damaged piston. Unless it was repaired the *Arthur* would never make it to Trondheimsfjord. They reached Hestvik at eleven that night. Larsen told Bjørnøy to strip the cylinder while he and Strand went to find Nils Strøm. There had been a festival that day, and people were still on the streets. When Larsen stopped someone to ask for directions to the store, he found he was talking to Strøm's son who took him to the shop. A pre-arranged question and answer had been supplied to both Larsen and Strøm that would establish each party's bona fides. But when Larsen uttered the crucial words "Do you need any peat?," Strøm failed to respond to his cue. After some farcical back-and-forth, Strøm finally understood and filled in Larsen and Strand on the latest details of the German checks.

They returned to the boat to bad news. Bjørnøy had discovered that the piston was cracked and would not last much longer. They needed a replacement, or at least the chance to make a repair. Strøm had a solution. The village blacksmith was a reliable man. He would be willing to give Bjørnøy the use of his forge to try and mend it. They woke him up and he let them into his workshop where, for two hours, the engineer hammered away. They returned to the boat and reassembled the engine. When they fired it up the following morning, Bjørnøy's verdict was that it would get them to their destination.

At 9:00 a.m. on Saturday, October 31, they left Hestvik on the last and most dangerous stage of the voyage. From now on they must expect to be stopped and questioned by the Germans at any moment. The British group hid in the secret compartment, machine gun at the ready. The Norwegians had pistols hidden under their jerseys. Just before 10:00 a.m., as they chugged through smooth waters off Trondheimsfjord, a German patrol vessel spotted the *Arthur* and swung toward her. It passed with barely a glance. The cutter was indistinguishable from hundreds of others that worked between the islands and the mainland, fishing and trading.

The inevitable encounter came as they approached the mouth of Trondheimsfjord. Germans from the fortress at Agdenes on the southern side watched the entrance, as did several observation posts and gun batteries. As the cutter moved slowly toward it, a converted trawler with a gun mounted in the bows sailed toward them. Larsen called a warning to the six Britons below, handed the wheel to Bjørnøy, and composed himself.

His main concern was the dead calm of the water. With no breeze to ruffle the surface, the chariots might well be visible hanging down from the keel. His anxiety mounted as he noticed a sailor in the bow of the guard ship staring down at the waterline as the *Arthur* approached. It seemed he was about to say something when the *Arthur*'s hawser landed on his shoulders, thrown aboard by Kalve, who was standing in the bows. The sailor lost interest. The *Arthur* came alongside and the chariots were once again hidden from the Germans' sight.

The lieutenant in charge was brisk and thorough. He jumped aboard and began to examine Larsen's documents, carefully comparing the signatures on the papers with his own records. Crammed in their hiding place between the bulwarks, the chariot teams and the dressers could hear the exchanges between the two in a mixture of German and Norwegian. At last the officer seemed satisfied. He thawed and began to chat. He inquired conversationally whether Larsen knew his old school friend Leutnant Ormann, the harbormaster at Kristiansund, which, according to the documents, had been their last port of call? Larsen mumbled that he did. Was it a trick question? He braced himself for the shout of triumph as the German unmasked him. It never came. The officer was rattling on about the strange coincidences that occurred in wartime and his sorrow that the threat of a British invasion had forced Germany to take over Larsen's country. At last he handed back the documents and after a quick examination of the peat in the hold, he climbed back onto the guard ship and waved them on. The *Arthur*'s propellers turned, the water boiled, hiding the submerged chariots and the boat moved slowly into Trondheimsfjord.

Five hours later, with dusk falling, Larsen thought it safe to allow the men below a spell on deck. The Britons emerged from the hold. They were passing Trondheim where the spires of the cathedral stood out dark against the fading sky. "The weather was quite fine," wrote Brewster. "There were many friendly-looking lights flickering ashore. There certainly didn't seem to be very much concern about blackout. And so we continued peacefully."[12] There were now less than twenty miles to the island of Tautra where they would un-harness the chariots. It was time to get ready. Craig and Evans went back down with Tebb and Causer and began the laborious business of dressing.

Next, it was Brewster and Brown's turn. Brewster found it hard to stay on his feet. A northeasterly wind had arisen and the *Arthur* was thumped and shaken by the waves driving into her bow. Then, Brewster heard "a succession of sharp bumps. The chariots were being swung up against the keel." They were in the grip of a full-blown storm. Larsen slowed the *Arthur* to reduce drag. There was no question of seeking shelter until the weather calmed. They would certainly be discovered. Brewster decided that "the only advice we could give ourselves was to 'press on regardless.'" Larsen explained that these sudden storms often blew themselves out as quickly as they had brewed up. They were only an hour or two away from *Tirpitz*. If they maintained the speed they would still get there in time to launch their attack before daybreak. Brewster and Brown carried on dressing.

They were almost finished when it happened. "We heard a loud, grinding tearing noise," remembered Brewster. "The vessel jerked and shuddered. Something pretty substantial had fouled the propeller. We all guessed what it had been—one of the chariots." It was a blow—but not a fatal one. The remaining chariot could still carry out a successful attack. They steered toward the shore, in search of shelter to check underneath. Bob Evans was fully dressed and ready to dive. When they reached calmer water, Larsen hove to and Evans slipped over the side. When he reappeared he reported the heart-sinking news that there was "nothing there at all."

"We were dismayed," wrote Brewster. "The chariots were gone and the attempt was off. I don't think anyone has ever been so disappointed as we were that night. We were ten miles from the pride of the German Navy; all our obstacles were behind us; and we might as well have been at the North Pole. Looking back I don't remember one single curse. We were all too unhappy for that."[13]

Larsen worried that the disaster was somehow his fault. Evans reassured him that it was the bolts on the warheads of the chariots that had sheared off, not the fastenings on the *Arthur*'s hull, which were still intact and trailing the steel hawsers. It was irrelevant now. All the training, all the preparations, the painstaking intelligence gathering, and the bold subterfuge had been for nothing. *Tirpitz* had been spared by a lucky change in the weather and faulty workmanship.

There was no time to brood. They were immediately absorbed with the problem of how to get away. The original escape plan was now unworkable. It was nearly twelve hours until their rendezvous with the local underground and they could not scuttle the *Arthur* so near the shore without a high risk of alerting the Germans. Nor could they go back the way they had come, as there was no pass from the German authorities in Trondheim to allow them past the controls at Agdenes and no receipt for the peat they were supposed to be delivering. Bjørnøy reported that the engine was, anyway, on its last legs. There seemed to be no alternative to Larsen's proposal to continue eastward to where the fjord swung north, which would bring them closer to the Swedish border. Then they would find a quiet place to sink the faithful *Arthur*, put ashore in the dinghy and start trekking to the frontier.

They abandoned ship in the channel between Tautra and the Frosta peninsula, just north of Faettenfjord, a few miles from where the crew of the *Tirpitz* were standing watch, relaxing off duty or sleeping. They collected their iron rations, maps, and a revolver apiece and rowed ashore in two parties, as the *Arthur* slipped beneath the now calm waters of the fjord.

It was 1:00 a.m. on November 1, 1942. They had no choice but to start moving and keep going as long as they could. They were exhausted, weighed down by fatigue and a feeling of failure. Larsen assumed leadership of the band of ten. It was his country and the four Norwegians had the most to lose. They were wearing their sea clothes: jackets, jerseys, and sea boots. If captured in the company of the British, they would be shot as irregulars. The British, clad in submariners' jackets and naval battledress, comforted themselves with the thought that they at least had the protection of their uniforms.

The tip of the peninsula sloped down gently to the sea. To the east, though, the land rose steeply to a 700-foot ridge, covered with pine trees and bushes interspersed with patches of snow and ice-covered rock. They walked for a while through the darkness, passing an airdrome. Ten men together made a conspicuous sight. They were reasonably safe in the dark, but when day broke they would have to split up. As the sky lightened Larsen called a halt. They slept huddled together against the piercing cold, taking turns to stand watch. At midday they set off again. This time they were in two groups. Larsen led one, with Don Craig as his second in command, together with Bob Evans, Bill Tebb, and Roald Strand. Jock Brewster took charge of the other, with Jock Brown, Malcolm Causer, Johannes Kalve, and Palmer Bjørnøy. Each man had biscuits, chocolate, a tube of condensed milk, two tins of corned beef, and three of sardines. The leaders had a map and compass.

It was fifty miles as the crow flies to the Swedish frontier, sixty-five with detours to avoid villages. The going would be hard all the way but the toughest part would come at the end, when they had to cross the 3,300-foot-high plateau between the Verdal and Stjørdal valleys, covered in snow and scoured by wind. They decided to take separate routes. Larsen's group turned inland. Brewster and his men followed the coast. For a while they kept in sight of each other. Then Larsen's team rounded a hillside and disappeared. The path that Brewster was following began to rise. It was cold but sunny. They were making good progress. They reached the top of the Frosta heights and looked down at the granite-blue waters below. There, tucked securely into the sheltering bowl of Lofjord, were the outlines of a warship. The pocket battleship *Admiral Scheer* laid at anchor, covered with skillfully painted gray and white nets and tarpaulins to blend in with the surrounding land and sea. Apart from some German sailors, enjoying a walk along a path on the slope below them, they saw no one. That night they broke into a hut and collapsed into sleep without bothering to post sentries. "We were all pretty weary and I suppose we took very few precautions," wrote Brewster. "The nature of the whole business was such that it would have been impossible not to leave something to chance. We preferred to put speed before everything else, even at the cost of running some rather unwise risks during the daylight hours."[14]

The luck they had trusted held. The following night they risked knocking on the door of a farmhouse and the farmer took them in; fed them soup, eggs, and potatoes; and gave them beds in his hayloft, in the full knowledge that this hospitality, if discovered, was likely to cost him dearly. The next night they came across a hunting cabin, where they found butter and flour. They mixed them up with the condensed milk from their ration packs and wolfed down a meal of flapjacks.

They reached Sweden on the morning of Thursday, November 5, after struggling overnight over the final range of mountains, wading through wind-whipped snow. Later that day they reached a small village and reported their arrival at the local police station. "We were glad to give ourselves up," wrote Brewster. "We were disheveled, hungry and wearing ten days' growth of beard." Apart from Causer they were all in reasonable condition. He was "in a bad way. He had been in pretty bad pain for the last couple of days but had said nothing about it. It was frostbite of course." The police were friendly. They sent for a doctor and Causer was taken away for hospital treatment. The policemen told them that another British party had crossed the border that morning.

The Larsen group also owed their escape to the kindness of Norwegian strangers. Their journey had been harsh, but they had not hit trouble until the final stretch. Just before they reached the frontier, floundering along in soft snow as they rounded a bend in the road, they came face to face with a German military policeman accompanied by a member of Hirden, Quisling's paramilitary organization. There was no chance to escape. They were questioned briefly and arrested. As they were marched away, Billy Tebb pulled out his concealed gun and opened fire. In the ensuing fight the German was killed and the collaborator ran off. Bob Evans, though, had been hit. Accounts of the seriousness of his injuries are confused. There were many German troops in the area and hanging around meant certain capture. The decision was taken to leave Evans behind. They reasoned that, as a uniformed combatant, he would receive proper treatment and the status of a prisoner of war.

Instead, after being nursed back to health, Evans was handed over to the Trondheim Gestapo chief, Gerhard Flesch. He was then loaned to senior Kriegsmarine officers, questioned about the details of the operation, and handed back to Flesch. His naval interrogators can have been in no doubt about what would happen next. The submariner's jacket had proved no protection. On January 19, 1943, Bob Evans was shot in Oslo as a saboteur. He was twenty years old. The execution was approved by the chief of the German High Command, Field Marshal Keitel.[15, 16]

His companions crossed the border within a mile of the Brewster party. The two groups were reunited at the police station, then locked up in a village house for two days before being moved to an internment camp outside Stockholm. Ten days later they were freed into the custody of the British Mission. Everyone was repatriated over the following days. After a pleasant time in a nice hotel, eating, drinking, and sightseeing, Brewster was flown back to Scotland, arriving in Leuchars on November 17. Larsen went back to Shetland. The operation was marked as a gallant failure. Rear Admiral Sir Claud Barry, who had taken over as Flag Officer Submarines, declared that "the achievement of penetrating to within ten miles of the berth occupied by the *Tirpitz* represents, on the part of the personnel and particularly that of the Norwegians, a fine example of cold-blooded courage."[17] Brewster was awarded the DSC. Larsen received the Conspicuous Gallantry Medal.

All the praise, and all the laurels, could not mask the fact that the operation had been an appalling waste of effort. Great ingenuity and technical skill had gone into the plan. Many men in Norway and Britain had risked their lives to realize it. By the end it stood a real chance of success. Despite the meticulousness of the preparations and the determination to leave nothing to chance, one vital detail had been neglected. The fate of the mission hung on two shackles. When they snapped, a great opportunity was squandered.

The episode passed unnoticed by the men on board *Tirpitz*, who went about their duties in ignorance of the dramas taking place around them. It was only a few days after the date of the intended attack that the discovery of the partially sunk hulk of the *Arthur* off Tautra Island revealed the danger they had been in. The news caused a welcome stir. It was a rare moment of excitement in the routine of shipboard life.

CHAPTER 11

THE IRON CASTLE

A miasma of boredom hung over the decks and messrooms of the *Tirpitz*. The crew's frustration at their inactivity was tempered by awareness that they were living a pampered existence. The knowledge produced mixed emotions. "We are living like lords," wrote the ship's administration officer, Kurt Voigt, guiltily to his wife early in 1942. His conscience had been pricked by an article in a weekly magazine describing how "millions on the Eastern Front have to hunker down in snowstorms next to the horses."[1]

Moored in Faettenfjord, and later further north at Bogen and Kaafjord, the Russian Front was not far. As they ate their three meals a day with only the faint prospect of an air raid to concern them, the crew had every reason to count themselves lucky. The ship had become their universe. On first setting eyes on the *Tirpitz*, most had been struck by its immensity. Once on board they continued to be awed by the scale of everything about her. Klaus Rohwedder, a young conscript, was "stunned. Everywhere there was noise; rumbling, humming. I was quite disoriented by the size and the noise."[2]

The ship swallowed them up. They lived a life that was strangely disconnected from their surroundings. Above deck they looked out on a timeless landscape of rock, wood, and water, where nature ruled and the red-roofed timber houses of the local people seemed no more substantial than lichen on a tree trunk. Below, everything was mechanized and modern. They passed their leisure hours at hobbies, sport, and games, watching films and newsreels in the ship's cinema, reading a book from the library or leafing through the ship's newspaper, *Der Scheinwerfer* (*The Searchlight*). It was tepid stuff, four pages of improving articles on subjects like the history of chess, caricatures of onboard personalities, little poems sent in by the crew, and feeble jokes. Among the cartoons and word puzzles, though, there were uncomfortable reminders of the outside world. While they were stagnating in a Norwegian fjord, their fellow sailors were carrying the war to the enemy. "In the last few days and weeks, a fanfare of special reports has called the German people to the radio," ran the main article of the April 17, 1942, issue. "The familiar words: 'German U-boats have sunk … off the American coast …' have revealed the amount of tonnage dispatched into the deep by the German U-boat weapon, far from their home bases."

Apart from the tedium, there was nothing to complain about. The accommodation was spacious by maritime standards. Kapitän Topp's quarters were palatial, a large day cabin and a sleeping cabin with bathroom attached. There was a similar suite reserved for visiting admirals. The two were separated by a large saloon which doubled as a dining and conference room. His senior officers all had their own cabins complete with sink and table. Junior officers shared and the men slept below decks in hammocks. Each night everyone drifted off to sleep to the husky voice of Lale Andersen crooning "Lili Marleen" over the loudspeakers.

The hardships of war barely touched them. Voigt had responsibility for the company's victuals and comforts and seems to have had considerable success finding supplies. His letters home are full of descriptions of food and drink. "I ate a pound of crabs for dinner tonight, quite fresh from the fish market in the town," he wrote on February 20. "On the other hand I did not get any lunch." Skipping a meal does not seem to have been a regular occurrence. Early on he complains that he is "getting fatter, though it has not yet become ridiculous." His duties took him ashore regularly. When *Tirpitz* was in Faettenfjord, he held meetings with army colleagues at their headquarters in Trondheim. They had set themselves up at the city's best hotel, the elegant stucco-fronted Britannia, and took their meals in the glass-domed palm court. On February 6, 1942, he drove slowly with Topp and a party of the ship's senior officers along the icebound road that ran along the south side of Trondheimsfjord to have dinner with the army brass. "We were received in the hall by many army people in a very friendly way," he wrote. "Charming waitresses in white and black outfits handed us a welcome drink. The prettiest were engaged to German soldiers. Then we started the food which was extremely tasty: first Irish stew, then bread and sausage or rollmop herrings." Afterward they "spread out on the charming furnishings" to drink coffee, beer, and champagne. "There is a rather classy standard of living here," he noted. "Three women were with us, officers' daughters who were working with the army." They were "very disappointed" when the party had to break up at 11:00 p.m. in order for the visitors to return to their ship. The trip back took two hours "through the white moonscape, over hill and dale, as well as a short further journey to get on board."

If Voigt lived well he did his best to see that the men did, too. Just before setting off for Norway, in the depths of a north German winter, he had managed to lay his hands on supplies of apples, oranges, and walnuts. Once in Trondheim such exotic treats were unobtainable. He did what he could with local markets, buying in cod, halibut, and herrings, and, when the weather improved, fresh vegetables. He bought some pigs that were reared ashore and planted a kitchen garden to provide salad. Potatoes were a staple of the company's diet and they had brought an enormous quantity with them from Germany in two holds on the deck next to the funnel. Voigt records that in one hold alone there were "450 zentner," that is, more than twenty-two tons. Keeping them from going rotten was a constant preoccupation. Electric heaters from the cabins were requisitioned to prevent the cargo from freezing.

Voigt's purchasing trips brought him into contact with the local people and he found them courteous and often hospitable. On April 21 he went for a stroll ashore, climbing up the hillside above the anchorage by way of a fifty-meter path that a work party had cut into the rock. They came across a farmstead where they had heard "there was milk to be had. On the barren meadow in front of the house a couple of sprightly lads were jumping about with a pointer dog. To the great joy of one of them we played football with him. We then went into the very basic house and asked for some milk. A friendly woman was just cleaning the tidy living room but stopped immediately and brought us a couple of stools. Then a friendly girl aged about sixteen with very thin legs brought over a small table with a cloth on it and put a large jug with two glasses on a tray on top of it. Everything was simple, the furniture simply painted, meagre like the land, but the people are friendly ... I left quite soon but the milk tasted fantastic."

Living close to the ship, the farmers had little choice but to be amiable and the German sailors were, anyway, on their best behavior, paying for everything or offering cigarettes, schnapps, or other luxuries in exchange for some milk, eggs, or butter. Other Norwegians, though, were genuinely welcoming. While *Tirpitz* was anchored at Bogen in the mid- to-late summer of 1942, Voigt made the acquaintance of "an intelligent, once beautiful" woman, the wife of a prosperous farmer. On his first visit she "prepared coffee in the main room" which, unlike the spare surroundings of the Faettenfjord homestead, was full of "highly polished furniture beneath wood-paneled walls." He noticed a bookcase filled with "well-read volumes, the history of the area, a large dictionary and a copy of *Mein Kampf* in Norwegian." The lady sent him away with two cauliflowers, some cream, and two eggs. Later, at her invitation, he went back "to dine on chicken and mushrooms." A few days later he visited the farm again and met the farmer ("a Quisling") with whom he made a deal to supply cauliflower to the ship. The farmer's wife gave him "some lovely milk and green plums from the south of the country" as a parting gift. Later she sent a present of flowers to the ship and another invitation to dine.

Voigt's impressions of Norway and the Norwegians were positive. He found Trondheim dreary in its wartime austerity and complained about the "lazy buggers" who were too idle to shovel the snow from the precincts of the cathedral. On the whole he subscribed to the official view that the local inhabitants were pretty much like himself and his kin—good Aryans with the potential to become honorary citizens. One day in mid-September he went ashore at Bogen with two of the ship's doctors to forage for wild mushrooms, strawberries, and raspberries. They went past a farmyard where four children were playing. Among them was a girl of seven or eight who "ran up and astonished us with her beauty and queenly bearing and expression as only a northern German can demonstrate." They gave her a sweet and "it was a delight for us to see the way in which this girl took [it] and ate it." The contrast with an encounter at a nearby dockside three days later could not have been greater. There, as he supervised the loading of supplies, he watched "Russian prisoners stamping up and down the quayside, most of them with Mongol features, taking in the strange world around them with wounded, animal eyes."

Voigt's job meant he had more contact with Norwegians than most. While *Tirpitz* was at Trondheim, ordinary crewmembers were allowed into town once a fortnight. There was little opportunity, though, to engage in the traditional pastimes of sailors on a run ashore. Military policemen kept a close eye on them and instead of whiling away their time in bars and brothels the only entertainment on offer was at the "German House" which had formerly been a Masonic lodge. It had a reading room, two cafeterias, and a concert hall, where faded variety performers turned up from time to time. The strongest drinks were cocoa and coffee. The hundred or so German women, imported to carry out secretarial duties at the military headquarters, "lived like nuns" according to Voigt and had to seek official permission to go out on dates. He himself formed a friendship with a Fraülein Francke, a thirty-year-old spinster who, despite a limp, was "not ugly and quite nice." Together they enjoyed meals, strolls in the country, and skiing trips.

Without distraction it was easy to succumb to what the crew called "Polarkoller"—polar fever. The sense of confinement was reflected in the ways they referred to their ship. The young midshipman Adalbert Brünner called it the "iron box," Voigt the "iron castle." Kapitän Topp saw their frustration and worried. Boredom was not merely irksome. It could be dangerous. A stale ship's company could easily turn uncooperative, even hostile. The memory of the Kiel mutiny in 1918, when the lower ranks of the Kriegsmarine who had been sitting idle in harbor for two years refused orders to put to sea on a last foray against the Royal Navy, was still fresh. Admiral Raeder ordered a leaflet to be printed and distributed to all officers with instructions on how to identify and suppress trouble. The ship's executive officer, Fregattenkapitän Paul Düwel, had responsibility for onboard discipline and he instructed officers and NCOs to report any whispers of subversion to him.

At the same time Topp did everything he could to keep his 2,400 men occupied. He encouraged them to go ashore to climb the hills around Faettenfjord, or hunt for gulls' eggs in nests that were identified using the ship's powerful Zeiss optics. Rat hunting was another diversion. Despite all precautions, the ship was plagued with them. "They had already come on board via the steel cables in Germany," remembered Herbert Ludwig, a young anti-aircraft gunner. "Many more came on board in Norway since there was always something to eat. They gnawed our bread sacks open at night and helped themselves. The creatures traveled through the ship via the air ducts. My hammock, a meter under the deck, was right under an air duct opening. One morning I found a rat in my hammock. Whether I crushed it or whether my shipmates had put it there I do not know. But I eagerly claimed the five marks we were given when we handed in a dead rat."[3]

Topp did not stand on his dignity and, when the occasion warranted it, could take a joke. He hated beards, once ordering a subordinate who dared to grow one "to take that sauerkraut off your face." Shortly after arriving in Trondheim, the men maneuvered him into growing one himself by promising to pay a sizable sum into an army charity if he did so. If he refused, he would have to make an even bigger donation. "Those of us who knew our Charley Topp knew what an ordeal this was for him," remembered Brünner. "I can't remember him giving us blacker looks." He gamely wore the whiskers for four weeks before shaving them off on Army Day, the climax of the money-raising activities. The Tag der Wehrmacht was celebrated on March 22. Before the war it had been a recruiting event but on board *Tirpitz* it had, according to Brünner, developed into an occasion for institutionalized high jinks. "On that day we had a fool's license towards our superiors," he wrote. "We celebrated with a great deal of tomfoolery and mischief making."

Topp set the tone by playing a harmonica over the ship's loudspeaker. The ship's chaplain broadcast extracts from a saucy book. Rank was turned on its head. Senior officers served as waiters in the canteens and NCOs scrubbed tables and the medical officers were ordered by their charges to report sick.[4]

Topp had early on spotted the recreational potential of the small island of Saltøya, a mile or so astern of the ship at the entrance of the fjord. He requisitioned it, and work parties were moved in to spruce it up. A cluster of dilapidated buildings which had once housed a sanatorium were refurbished to provide sleeping huts and a mess. The teams built log cabins, painted them bright colors, and named them after their officers. They decorated two of them, the Hindenburglager and the Krillstube, in the style of rustic inns to remind them of home.[5]

The center was officially opened on May 30, 1942, with beer and snacks, including stuffed gulls' eggs, cocktail sausages, potato salad, and beer, while the ship's orchestra played on the island's bandstand.[6] The crew nicknamed the place "Tipito," a Germano-Norwegian approximation of "Tirpitz Island." It was, said Brünner, "a small holiday encampment." The sailors went there to "take it easy—pursue a hobby or go swimming. In short, to forget everyday life."

There were, however, rules. Notices posted around the place detailed a long list of *verboten* activities including smoking in the huts, picking flowers, collecting gulls' eggs without authorization, pulling branches off trees, trading with Norwegians, and receiving guests who were not Germans. This last restriction would bring about the end of the idyll. Soon crew members were arranging to ferry in girls from Trondheim and the surrounding area. The forbidden revels came to light when a fisherman who had carried some of the guests to and from the island was arrested for stealing supplies from the stores. At the hearing he revealed the goings-on. The headquarters at Trondheim ordered Tipito to be closed down.[7]

During the sojourn at Bogen in the summer of 1942, there were concert parties and rowing races and football tournaments with teams drawn from each of the ship's company's twelve "divisions." One of the officers constructed a puppet theater. On August 21, after a dinner of "herrings and new potatoes soaked in butter," Voigt watched a "charming puppet show ... the figures were half the size of a human and fantastically realistic." It was "a brilliant performance that released waves of laughter." Heinz Assman, who took over from Düwel as executive officer after the return to Trondheim, was a piano virtuoso and had a concert grand brought on board on which he gave regular recitals.

All this relentless displacement activity was no substitute for the excitement of operations. Topp tried to keep his crew honed with the sort of drills that precede a major sortie. Brünner described how they would haul in the anchors to the frantic waltz tempo of the "Lampenputzer Galopp" blaring from the loudspeakers. "But then nothing happened," he wrote wistfully. "Every 'anchors aweigh' was just an exercise."

Everyone wanted action. The desire was natural. By the end of 1942, the captain and many of the crew had been on board for nearly two years. They had taken part in innumerable exercises and dry runs. Yet in all that time they had put to sea only twice with the intention of engaging the enemy. It was an inglorious situation. At times it felt ignominious. Every day, news trickled in of the epic struggle taking place a few hundred miles to the east. Many of the crewmembers had families back in Germany's big cities who were in greater danger than they were. By now Bomber Command was getting into its stride. The first thousand-bomber raid had struck Cologne on the night of May 30–31, killing at least 469. On the night of September 14–15, Wilhelmshaven, where *Tirpitz* had started life, suffered its worst raid to date. Seventy-seven people were killed. Voigt's mother lived there but had been out of town at the time. He saw the headlines on the report of the attack in an old newspaper. He told his wife how he read it "with great trepidation, but no-one we know was listed ... the old city hall was destroyed along with a load of damage in the Villen quarter [in the center of town]. How sorry I feel for the people."

The growing frequency and power of the raids only sharpened the desire to fight. Beyond the placid fjords of Norway the war had intensified into a struggle for Germany's existence in which it seemed that everyone but the *Tirpitz* and her crew were involved. Any doubts about Hitler appear to have been overtaken by the need to win the struggle—or at least to survive. There seems, anyway, to have been little antipathy towards the Führer. The detached, maritime nature of the Kriegsmarine and the fact that its traditions predated the arrival of the Nazis had given it a degree of independence that its commander, Raeder, fought to protect. That did not mean that its sailors were not good and obedient patriots. Hitler's portrait hung in Topp's day cabin, next to that of Admiral von Tirpitz wearing full dress uniform and the Grand Cross of the Imperial Eagle, looking stern and patriarchal with his bald skull and long, forked beard. The Führer's picture also hung in the messes, one of which was decorated with exhortations—"Our leader's struggle is our struggle" and "Our leader's faith is our faith." On Hitler's birthday, Topp gave a speech to the entire crew and the officers toasted their leader's health with sparkling wine.

But despite routine displays of patriotism, it was impossible for some to suppress doubts as to where the Führer was leading Germany. Karl Voigt was a thoughtful man who appreciated good books, films, and music and took a keen interest in his surroundings. He was also a loyal German. But in his letters to his wife, buried among the endearments and minutiae of his existence, it is possible to detect a murmur of doubt as to whether the war was worth it.

One day in August, the reality of the war in the east was brought home to him again when one of the ship's doctors showed him photographs in a medical journal of soldiers whose eyes had been damaged in action. "My God, how appalling" he wrote to his wife. "How much men suffer today at the effects of this horrible war where the heroic sudden death seems more merciful than the alternative." He predicted that "every day in the East will one day be engraved in golden letters in a history of Germany." But he goes on to wonder, "what are they compared to what these battles have done to the mothers, the women, and the brides of the dead and badly wounded heroes?"[8] He was ready to fight if the circumstances arose. It was not to be. At the end of October he left the ship to be reunited with his beloved "Klösel" and his family in Berlin.

The mood of frustration led directly to one episode which provided a stark reminder to all on board that they were in the business of life and death. One morning in August 1942, while *Tirpitz* lay at Bogen Bay, the early muster revealed that one of the crew was missing. His name was Bernhard Turowsky. He was eighteen years old and served as a gunner on a flak battery. Inquiries revealed that he had last been seen the previous afternoon. The ship was searched but there was no sign of him.

The authorities on shore were alerted and after four days Turowsky, wearing civilian clothes and guarded by two military policemen, was dragged back on board showing signs of having been beaten. He had been captured thirty miles away, close to the Swedish border. He was carrying a compass and pistol, stolen, it turned out, from one of the ship's Arado pilots.

A few days after his capture, Turowsky appeared before a court martial convened in the main lecture hall. He was condemned to death with the sentence to be carried out the following day. That night, Turowsky was allowed to eat a last supper with his comrades. Among them was Herbert Ludwig, who knew and liked the condemned man. "They had cut all the buttons off his uniform and removed the swastika," he recalled. "He had ordered himself a good meal as his final wish and, to our astonishment, had eaten quietly with no complaining or recriminations. We said our good-byes full of emotion. We, not he, had tears in our eyes."[9]

The motives that led Turowsky to swim ashore and head for the border, fully aware of the penalty for desertion, remain unclear. He was reported to have told the court martial that he was driven by simple boredom. A story went round the ship that he was intending to head for the United States—either to join up with the Allies or deliver a plea for peace, according to who was telling it. Ludwig maintained that "he was badly bullied by his battery officer." However, Hein Hellendoorn, a flak artillery officer, friendly with the officer who defended Turowsky, "never heard that he had a difficult time on board."[10]

On September 4 the sentence was carried out in front of the entire ship's company. The ship's log recorded a cloudy day and a choppy sea. The execution was timed at 3:50 p.m. Shortly before, Turowsky was brought up from below, blindfolded, and led to a point behind the after gun turret. The firing squad was made up of eight men from Turowksy's battery. One of the rifles was loaded with blank ammunition. Turowsky was tied to a rail. Pastor Müller, the ship's chaplain, spoke a few words of comfort and asked him if he had anything to say. Turowsky simply thanked the pastor for his kindness. "At the command 'Fire' his body straightened and fell to one side," remembered Ludwig. His corpse was taken to a military cemetery ashore but the authorities there refused to bury it. It was returned to the ship and later sewn into a weighted sack and dropped into the fjord.[11]

Tirpitz's time at Bogen was coming to a close by then. Despite her inactivity and a careful regime of maintenance, she was due for a major overhaul. A report drawn up by the ship's technical officers on September 15, 1942, listed a large number of necessary repairs and improvements, ranging from the engines and guns to the freshwater drinking tanks and fire extinguishers. The hull's magnetic field also had to be neutralized to prevent it triggering mines—"degaussed" in technical parlance. Proper port facilities were required to do the job properly, and they were not available in the Narvik area. After Hitler again judged the risk of sailing her to Germany was too great, she set off back to Trondheim, weighing anchor on October 23, and arriving in Faettenfjord the following day.

Two days later the *Arthur* put to sea from Lunna Voe with the chariots and their crew on their mission to destroy the battleship. In the flap that followed the failed attack, *Tirpitz* started to shift her mooring frequently, moving around a succession of berths, all at the eastern end of Trondheimsfjord, and divers made regular inspections of the hull. At the end of November a PRU reconnaissance flight reported seeing her at Lofjord, the neighboring narrow inlet to the north. Her hull was painted in dazzle camouflage with broad black diagonal strips on the port side at the bow and the stern, designed to make her look considerably shorter than her true length. Another ship, identified as the *Stavangerfjord*, a depot ship for the workers brought in from the Kiel dockyard to carry out the refit, was alongside. A few days later a local agent reported the presence of a 100-ton floating crane and that major repairs were under way.[12] The work threw the orderly world of the ship into chaos. "The noise really was appalling, fraying our nerves," Adalbert Brünner remembered. "It was astonishing how poorly sound-proofed [the] iron box was. Everywhere you turned there was something in the way: cabling, air and gas pipes, transformers, tools of every kind and, lastly, the workers themselves." By December 17, the refit was completed and the workers had all gone home.

Tirpitz was at full readiness once more, and the mood on board was optimistic as Christmas approached. The crew threw their energies into celebrating it in style. A tall fir tree was erected on the afterdeck and decorations festooned every cabin, mess, and gangway. "Snow lay deep all around and stillness settled on the landscape," wrote Brünner. "It was like going back to childhood days." On Christmas Day, Topp stood on the afterdeck in the thin gray northern daylight, beneath the tree flickering with candles, and gave a speech that "emphasized the Christian nature of the holiday." Then the company, apart from those on watch, settled down to enjoy themselves. They ate and drank and listened to a concert given by a mixed choir.

There were more celebrations on New Year's Eve. There was a special dinner and every man got a bottle of wine, extra tobacco, a packet of sweets, and a book. In the wardroom they held a mock trial and one of the officers did an impression of the Führer. At midnight Topp addressed the company over the loudspeaker. He repeated the message in his New Year's greetings card, distributed to all the crew, in which he spoke frankly about the frustrations of the last twelve months and his hopes for the time to come. He recalled the adventures "we all dreamed about during the dash from Wilhelmshaven to Trondheim … sorties to the northern seas, the Arctic seas, the North Atlantic and the coast of France" where they would find "success and the laurels of victory." Instead, they had been denied "a free ranging war against merchant vessels on the vast extending oceans." There was, however, nothing to be done. "We grit our teeth and bow to the decision of our superiors, even if it is often difficult. We are soldiers and we obey." His message finished on a rousing note: "Let us enter the New Year as Adolf Hitler's truest and best soldiers, with unyielding faith in our victory and Germany's future, and with the sure expectation that the great hour when we can prove ourselves will arrive."

As the festivities continued, five hundred miles to the north other German ships were locked in battle. In the Barents Sea, a force led by the heavy cruiser *Admiral Hipper* had clashed with British escorts protecting the second part of convoy JW.51B, on its way to Murmansk. The German force was led by Vizeadmiral Oskar Kummetz, the Kriegsmarine's commander of cruisers. A U-boat sighted the convoy on December 30. Kummetz was on board *Hipper* at Altafjord and immediately put to sea. He had with him the pocket battleship *Lützow* and six destroyers. Ranged against them were two British cruisers, the *Sheffield* and the *Jamaica*, and six destroyers. The German ships were bigger and better armed than their British opponents, and when battle was first joined they seemed sure to overwhelm the convoy and its escorts. In the middle of the morning of December 31, in the brief and thin midwinter twilight, the destroyer escort was attacked by *Hipper* from the north. HMS *Onslow* was hit and the escort commander, Captain Sherbrooke, badly wounded. A little later, *Lützow* appeared on the convoy's southern flank but instead of attacking immediately her captain decided to hold back until the weather improved. *Hipper*'s guns, meanwhile, sank the minesweeper *Bramble* and crippled the destroyer *Achates*, which had been emitting smoke to conceal the convoy.

Just as a massacre seemed imminent, the British cruisers arrived and opened fire on the *Hipper*. They were mounting 6-inch guns against the enemy's 8-inch main armament. They nonetheless managed to do enough damage to force Kummetz to retire.[13] The cruisers then sighted two of the German destroyers and attacked, sinking the *Friedrich Eckholt*. Shortly afterward, Kummetz ordered his squadron back to port. The *Sheffield* and the *Jamaica* gave chase but, by 2:00 p.m., *Hipper* had been swallowed up by the Arctic darkness. The British could feel considerable satisfaction at the outcome. They had held off a significantly more powerful force with the loss of only one sunken minesweeper and one damaged destroyer. All fourteen ships of the convoy had escaped serious damage and continued to Murmansk unmolested to join the fifteen others that had arrived safely on Christmas Day.

For the German navy, the Battle of the Barents Sea, as it became known, was a humiliation. Hitler's anger at the outcome created a crisis that was to affect profoundly the future of the Kriegsmarine. In the weeks that followed, *Tirpitz* was in greater danger than it had ever faced in its short life. The threat, however, came not from the enemy but from its own Commander in Chief.

CHAPTER 12

ENTER THE LION

t took a while for the storm to break in Berlin. The initial reports of the battle had been sketchy but promising. A U-boat reported back from the Barents Sea that the enemy convoy was under attack and Hitler settled back "in delighted impatience," according to Raeder, to hear the details of its complete destruction. The news, though, was slow in coming. Kummetz maintained radio silence on the way back to Altafjord. Once he got there, his report was delayed by a breakdown on the teleprinter line from north Norway.

Instead, Hitler learned the truth via the BBC, which announced that the raiders had broken off their attack and the convoy had got through without loss. Hitler assumed that he had been kept in the dark about the failure and "flew into a towering rage." Raeder's liaison officer at headquarters said, "in the first outburst of anger, Hitler had expressed his views on the uselessness of our heavy ships and caused them to be recorded in the war log as his considered opinions."[1] The judgment had been gestating for some time. Six weeks before, on November 14, 1942, he had met Raeder at Berchtesgaden and questioned him as to why the Kriegsmarine's big ships had done nothing since July. Raeder had a reasonable excuse. The navy was being starved of fuel. Operations involving the large surface units used up vast quantities of precious oil. The sortie by the *Tirpitz* squadron in March against the convoy PQ.12 had swallowed 8,000 tons, equivalent to one month's production from the Romanian oil fields. The Battle of the Barents Sea seemed to suggest that even when capital ships were allowed off the leash, the results hardly justified the material costs.

Raeder was told to report at once at the Führer's headquarters. He managed to delay for a few days, excusing himself on the grounds that he needed to acquaint himself with all the facts of the episode. On January 6 he met Hitler at the *Wolfschanze* (Wolf's Lair), the Führer's heavily protected headquarters buried among woods and lakes near Rastenburg in East Prussia where he oversaw the campaign on the Russian Front.[2] It was soon clear that Hitler's views had not softened. He subjected Raeder to a lecture that lasted more than an hour, much of which consisted of a "spiteful and quite unobjective attack on the Navy," Hitler coming close to accusing his commanders of cowardice. The navy's performance in the Barents Sea, he said, was "typical of German ships, just the opposite of the British who, true to their tradition, fought to the bitter end."[3]

"Apart from the submarine arm, he could not find a good word to say about the German Navy throughout its whole history," wrote Raeder. "Our heavy ships—which had always particularly interested Hitler and of which he had once been particularly proud—were now condemned as useless." Not only did they not do anything, they required constant protection by the Luftwaffe and by smaller vessels. In the event of an

Allied attack on Norway, a scenario that continued to loom large in Hitler's imagination, the air force would be much better employed attacking an invading fleet than shielding the battleships. He had therefore come to the conclusion that the Kriegsmarine's heavy ships had no further role to play in the war. They were to be taken out of commission and broken up. Their guns would be salvaged and mounted in shore batteries where they might actually do some good. His resolve was "firm and unalterable."[4]

This was an extraordinary proposal, even for Adolf Hitler. The big ships were the Kriegsmarine's scepter, orb, and crown. *Tirpitz*, in the words of Topp's New Year's message, was "still the strongest and sharpest sword in the German armory." Now it seemed it was to be melted down. German workmen would voluntarily carry out a task that the Royal Navy and Air Force had spent hundreds of lives and untold effort failing to achieve.

As Raeder listened silently to the diatribe, he thought he detected the malign influence of Hermann Göring, who frequently denounced the failings of the navy and army to Hitler in order to enhance the achievements of his Luftwaffe. He disagreed profoundly with everything that was said. The modern Kriegsmarine was largely Raeder's creation, and Hitler was intent on dismantling his life's work. The rant had convinced him that he could not continue as head of the German navy. Listening to it had been a disturbing experience. Hitler had "been very excited, and from time to time had allowed himself to go further than he had ever gone before in his dealings with me." Raeder, the chilly Prussian, judged that "the fact that he had allowed himself to lose his self-control in my presence showed me clearly that he regarded the differences between us as more than purely objective."

He asked for a private audience, so Field Marshal Keitel, who was also present, and the two stenographers recording the proceedings left the room. Raeder then told Hitler he wanted to step down as Supreme

Commander of the Navy as he clearly no longer enjoyed Hitler's confidence. "As always when he found himself resolutely opposed," Raeder recalled, "Hitler now climbed down and tried to qualify his previous observations." It was too late. Raeder's stiff mind was made up. A few days later he wrote a memorandum setting out his views on the role of capital ships in which he argued strongly for their retention. He also made two recommendations as to who should succeed him. His first choice was Admiral Rolf Carls, who commanded Naval Group North. The other was the head of the U-boat service, Karl Dönitz. Hitler chose Dönitz.

It was decided that Raeder would soldier on until the end of the month, allowing him to complete ten years at the top under the Hitler regime. This could be presented as a suitable milestone for retirement and minimize the impression that the relationship had ended in bad blood.

His replacement was another Prussian who in later life was candid about the effects his background and upbringing had in determining his outlook and actions. Dönitz came from a long line of modest landowners, yeomen rather than Junkers, whose estate lay close to the River Elbe on the frontier with Poland. Later generations had produced clergymen, men of letters, and military officers. Dönitz's father, Emil, had been an engineer. He later wrote, "as a family we were devoid of any sense of personal individuality." Instead they were "deeply conscious of the corporate spirit of the Prussian community to which we belonged." When he entered the navy, in 1910, "both the exercise and the acceptance of discipline came quite naturally to me. As a child I had been imbued with the conviction that fulfilment of my duty came before everything else."[5]

This attitude made it possible for him to accept the elemental changes to Germany brought about by the arrival of Hitler without deviating from the career course he had set himself. Nor did his subsequent disagreements with the direction in which the Führer was taking

Germany deflect him from pursuing his tasks with extraordinary drive and efficiency.

He joined the Imperial submarine service in October 1916. Two years later, with the end of the war only a month away, he was commanding *UB-68* in the Mediterranean when British ships sunk it after forcing it to surface in the middle of a convoy. He and the other survivors were picked up by a destroyer and taken to a prisoner-of-war camp on Malta. When he returned to Germany in July 1919, he found the country in chaos. He was twenty-seven years old. All the notions of duty, national unity, and patriotism that had underpinned his short life seemed to have been swept away and replaced with shrill factionalism. Like Raeder he was able to hang onto his commission, which kept him afloat during the years of unemployment and inflation. He moved up the service ladder, holding a series of staff jobs including one dealing with political developments that affected the navy, as well as discipline and the application of military law.

He struggled to remain aloof from party politics. Members of the armed forces were not allowed to vote, a circumstance that later proved useful to those wishing to distance themselves from the Nazi regime. Dönitz admitted frankly, though, that he had welcomed the arrival of Hitler. In the street-fighting years of the late twenties and thirties when left- and right-wing thugs battled in German cities, he found himself taking part in conferences on how the armed forces would react to a complete disintegration of internal order, a prospect that often looked quite likely. As the German nation moved to the extremes of the political spectrum and the moderate center shriveled, a civil war could not be ruled out. The military was simply not strong enough to hold the ring. They would have to choose their side. "That they could not come down on the side of the Communists was obvious," wrote Dönitz after the war. "It was as a result of this process of reasoning that they welcomed the appointment of Hitler as German Chancellor."

Dönitz himself "believed that Germany had chosen the right path." Nonetheless there would be occasional points of friction between the navy and the Nazi Party, and in particular the SA. When Hitler moved against them in the 1934 Night of the Long Knives, Dönitz regarded the bloody purge as an unfortunate necessity. The *Kristallnacht* outrage caused him a mild crisis of conscience. Like Günther Lütjens, he wrote a letter of protest to Raeder who endorsed the sentiments and passed them upward to the Führer.

He had not welcomed the coming of war, fearing that Hitler had failed to understand the dangers of taking on Britain and its navy. It was "with a feeling of extreme skepticism" that he learned of the "allegedly unavoidable attack on Poland," and the declaration of war by Britain and France that followed, although anticipated, was "a bitter blow." Even so, he believed that it was "the moral obligation of every fighting man unreservedly to support the government of his country when it goes to war." He maintained this attitude to the end.

Despite his reluctance to engage in a war with Britain, Dönitz had strong ideas on how it should be fought. He advocated a concentrated campaign against her transatlantic shipping using U-boats. In October 1939 he was appointed Rear Admiral Commanding Submarines and in a position to prove his point. He brought a hunter's instinct to the business of tracking down and destroying merchant ships as they plodded gamely across the great gray plains of the Atlantic, organizing his submarines into "wolf packs" which, once they had found their victims, would hang around for days, appearing and disappearing, and picking them off with cold, lupine efficiency. His men called him after another predator. His nickname was *der Löwe*, the lion. His tactics were highly successful. During the course of 1942, U-boats sank nearly eight million tons of Allied shipping, at one point reducing Britain's stocks of commercial oil to two months' supply.

With this background, Dönitz might be expected to share Hitler's pungent views on the utility of submarines and the uselessness of the big ships. At their first meeting at the Wolfschanze on January 30, 1943, Hitler repeated again his determination to scrap the surface fleet. When he asked for Dönitz's views, the new Chief of the Navy did not immediately concur with the plan but said that he did not feel qualified to give a response and needed time to study the details.

Dönitz was nonetheless inclined to go along with Hitler's wishes. On February 8, he returned to Rastenburg to present detailed proposals.[6] Most of the big ships were to be paid off. He asked for complete priority to be given to U-boat construction, maintenance, and repair and for his ships to be provided with adequate air cover by the Luftwaffe—a request that Raeder had forlornly repeated on numerous occasions with limited results.[7] He also asserted his sole right to order such surface units of the Kriegsmarine that remained after the reorganization to sally out on operations and laid down the principle that, when in action, commanders should be left alone to fight without interference from above.

Back in Berlin, as he worked his way through the details of the plan, unwelcome doubts stirred in Dönitz's mind. He had before him Raeder's memorandum on the subject, drawn up as his last act as Commander in Chief. Raeder maintained that despite their record of inactivity the heavy ships in Norway were making an important contribution to the war effort. As long as the main body of the surface fleet was in the northern fjords, the Allies were obliged to maintain at least an equal number of capital ships in northern Scotland and Iceland. While holding themselves ready for a breakout, they could not be put to more effective use in either the Mediterranean, where their presence would help greatly to secure the Allies' communications, or the Pacific, where they would add to the difficulties of Hitler's Japanese partners.

This was not an argument for continued passivity. In the same document Raeder advocated more vigorous action by the big ships. It was Hitler himself who had handicapped offensive operations by insisting that the battle fleet could only venture out when there were no aircraft carriers among the enemy forces.

Further restrictions were imposed by the dearth of aircraft in the area to provide reconnaissance and to cover the ships when they were at sea. The aircraft that had been switched to Norway to support the shift of the surface fleet northward had since been moved away to answer the pressing needs of the army in North Africa and on the Eastern Front. In December 1942, there were only fourteen serviceable Me 109 fighters available in the Trondheim area.[8] Progress on the building of the navy's sole aircraft carrier, *Graf Zeppelin*, had always been jerky as priority was given to more pressing work like building U-boats. In February 1943 it stopped altogether. For all these handicaps, Raeder managed to finish his memorandum on a positive note. "The possibility of scoring a success most certainly exists," he wrote, "provided that the fleet remains constantly on the alert for every possible contingency and waits for the favorable opportunity. Even without adequate air cover and reconnaissance, opportunities will always occur when, by making full use of favorable conditions, we can achieve surprise and strike a worthwhile blow."[9]

Dönitz was persuaded. "As a result of this further scrutiny," he wrote, "I came to the conclusion that withdrawing these ships from service would not result in any appreciable increase in either manpower or material, and that the implementation of the project could not but react politically and militarily to our disadvantage." Actually dismantling them as Hitler had proposed "was an even less attractive solution for it made considerable claims on labor and technical rescources."[10]

The change of heart was unfortunate. Hitler's reaction to such a swift about-face was not hard to imagine. Before committing himself, Dönitz took soundings from his senior commanders, to see if they agreed with

Raeder's analysis, particularly on the question of the fleet being put to more active use. Both the admiral commanding the fleet, Otto Schniewind, and Admiral Kummetz agreed that "the ships, given a favorable opportunity, could undoubtedly still be committed to battle."[11]

Dönitz revised his plans accordingly. On February 26 he traveled to another Eastern Front headquarters, Vinnitsa, on the western borders of Ukraine, to announce the result of his deliberations and to put his case to the Führer. He started on an uncontroversial note by saying that the heavy cruiser *Hipper* and the light cruisers *Leipzig* and *Köln* had outlived their usefulness and would be decommissioned. The same went for the antiquated battleships *Schlesien* and *Schleswig-Holstein*.

But while he was willing to pay off some of the surface fleet, he was not going to agree to scrapping all of it. The Russian convoys, he declared, made excellent targets and he considered it his duty to relieve the pressure on Germany's soldiers on the Eastern Front by attacking them. He therefore proposed sending the *Scharnhorst*, currently lying in the Baltic, to join *Tirpitz* and *Lützow* in Norway. Together with six destroyers they would make a formidable force to menace the Arctic routes.

Dönitz was effectively asking his leader to revoke his "firm and unalterable" decision and cancel his orders to scrap the surface fleet. The response was predictable. The Führer was "highly astonished and indignant." He was "disagreeably surprised since he had not expected that I, as the former Flag Officer, Submarines, and the man who had always pressed for the expansion of the U-boat war would adopt this attitude." Dönitz was now subjected to a Force 9 tantrum in which Hitler denounced the crews of his capital ships whom he presented as enjoying an extended winter holiday while their comrades froze and died in the east.[12] Eventually, though, his anger subsided. He could not risk another resignation by the head of the navy so soon after Raeder's departure. Hitler, wrote Dönitz, "very grudgingly agreed, and I was ungraciously dismissed."

It had taken some courage to contradict the wishes of a leader as capricious as Hitler, and Dönitz wondered for a while whether his "days as Commander-in-Chief were not already numbered." The crisis, though, had passed. Soon afterward, Dönitz issued a directive in which he defined the role of the Norway-based fleet and the conditions under which it could go into action.

Its purpose was to defend Norway against invasion and attack Arctic convoys when the chance arose. Dönitz admitted that the restricted and clearly finite resources the German navy could muster meant opportunities would be limited, given the strong escorts the enemy was sending. If a lightly defended or undefended convoy did appear, however, the chance "must be seized with determination." The directive also kept alive the possibility that it might become necessary to attack heavily escorted convoys with all available forces "if the convoy in question is deemed to be of such value that its destruction is of primary importance to the situation as a whole."[13]

These instructions created an atmosphere of imminent action. Spring was creeping across the north and change was in the air. The *Tirpitz* was undergoing a transformation. Her atmosphere and moods, the outlook and way of life of her crew had, to a significant degree, been determined by the character of her master. On February 21, Captain Topp left the ship for the last time. In keeping with tradition, he was rowed ashore by midshipmen while the crew waved blue gingham sheets from the top decks until he was out of sight. He had been promoted to rear admiral and was heading off to a staff job in Berlin. His replacement was Captain Hans Meyer, who lacked Topp's flamboyance. One sleeve of his uniform was pinned to his tunic. He had lost an arm fighting with the right-wing Freikorps against the Spartacist revolutionaries during the uprising of 1919.[14] After Topp, Adalbert Brünner, who served as Meyer's adjutant, found him "a more quiet person. He was a man of genuine modesty and integrity."[15]

The feeling that events were gathering pace intensified when, in March 1943, *Tirpitz* was ordered northward to a base closer to the convoy routes. She stopped first in the familiar waters of Bogen Bay. Spring was early and Brünner remembered it as a "sublimely beautiful day." Basking in the welcome sunlight he felt he was on a "Strength through Joy cruise in the high northern spring" rather than on a battleship. The stay was short. *Tirpitz* was soon on her way again and this time to a new and remote location. On March 24, 1943, she dropped anchor in Kaafjord, a narrow spur of Altafjord, a large inlet that pierced the coast of Finnmark, close to Norway's most Arctic extremity, the North Cape. It seemed to Brünner that it was hard to find a place much further away from what the sailors regarded as civilization. The nearest town was Alta, a much smaller and less sophisticated place than Trondheim. It was too far "even for seasoned seamen to reach by foot," and even if they had, "they would certainly not have found any kind of *Reeperbahn* there."

On the other hand, there were signs that other excitements might be in the offing. By the end of March the surrounding waters were thick with warships. Alongside *Tirpitz* were the *Lützow* and the *Scharnhorst*, which, after two attempts to break through from the Baltic to the North Sea, had finally made it to northern Norway. The fleet was supplemented by destroyers and torpedo craft as well as eighty U-boats which had been made available for operations in the area. The force in Altafjord became known as the Northern Task Force and was put under the command of Admiral Oskar Kummetz.

In Britain, the drama of Raeder's departure and Dönitz's promotion had been followed closely. The concentration of forces in northern Norway led the Admiralty to an obvious conclusion. It seemed to Admiral Tovey that Dönitz was more inclined than his predecessor to take risks and there was now a greater prospect that *Tirpitz* and the other big ships might dare a convoy attack. There was even a chance that the enemy might "venture all on a desperate breakout" into the Atlantic, a development that would not be unwelcome. Tovey felt that with the new circumstances came "a chance for us to accept fleet action under conditions of exceptional favor." In other words, there was now perhaps an opportunity for a full-blooded high seas battle.[16]

For *Tirpitz* to be tempted out, though, there had to be a target. After the successful arrival in Murmansk of the second half of convoy JW.51 following the Battle of the Barents Sea, the pressure from the Soviet Union to keep the supplies coming was unrelenting. Stalin's demanding voice was amplified by his ambassador in London, Ivan Maisky, whose tone and persistence grated on Churchill's nerves. On January 9, 1943, he told the Foreign Secretary Anthony Eden that "Maisky should be told that I am getting to the end of my tether with these repeated Russian naggings and that it is not the slightest use trying to knock me about any more."[17]

Even so, another small convoy, the fourteen-ship JW.52, sailed that month. The Arctic darkness kept air attacks to a minimum and the seas were unseasonably kind. The passage was swift and the escort kept the U-boats at bay, aided by the new direction-finding wireless reception equipment which intercepted submarine signals and pinpointed their whereabouts. All but one ship, which turned back early, reached the Kola Inlet safely on January 27. After a two-day rest the three cruisers, which had shepherded them all the way through, escorted the returning convoy RA.52 home, losing one of the eleven ships to a U-boat on the way.

The next eastbound convoy, JW.53, was made up of twenty-eight ships and sailed from Iceland in mid-February. By now the darkness was receding and a stronger "summer-scale" escort was thought necessary. The convoy was covered by three cruisers with a large force of bigger ships waiting at a distance to intervene if needed. This time heavy gales scattered the merchantmen. Twenty-two were rounded up and continued on their way. Despite a following pack of U-boats and occasional bombing raids, all reached port safely. The returning convoy was not so lucky. It was shaken apart in a heavy gale. U-boats closed in on the iso-lated merchantmen, sinking three, and another foundered in the wild seas.

The risks to the convoys mounted as the days grew longer. As well as the submarines and aircraft, the escorts now had to contend with the threat from *Tirpitz* and her companions lurking in Altafjord. From now on, dispatching a convoy carried the risk of a clash between the escorts and the *Tirpitz* squadron. It was a prospect that Tovey was happy to consider if the battle took place at a meridian of the Allies' choosing, preferably west of Bear Island where the full power of the covering force could be applied without too much danger from aerial attack. That seemed unlikely, however. The expectation had to be that Dönitz would wait until the convoy was deep in the Barents Sea, and inside the Luft-waffe's striking range, before launching an attack.

Tovey's misgivings were reinforced by the behavior of his Soviet allies. The Russians seemed to regard civility, let alone camaraderie, as a sign of weakness. In the first few months of 1943, they ground down the sympathy of their Allied partners with a campaign of obstruction. Two British wireless stations in northern Russia were closed down with-out explanation, and RAF ground crews needed to service the aircraft that flew from bases in the area were refused entry.

The question of how far into the year to keep the convoys running was eventually decided by Dönitz. In March 1943, the Battle of the Atlantic approached its climax. Dönitz threw all his submarines into an effort to cut the transatlantic lifeline. The immensity of the odds dwarfed all other considerations. Every ship available was needed to stem the losses that the wolf packs were inflicting. The next planned outgoing and returning convoys were canceled. Churchill explained the decision in a letter to Roosevelt, who had maintained firm pressure on Britain to keep the convoys sailing whenever possible. In the middle of March one of the biggest convoy battles of the war was fought in the North Atlantic.

Dönitz concentrated a force of forty U-boats against convoys HX.229 and SC.122 sailing from New York. In two days, they sank seventeen ships. The disaster, wrote Churchill, was "a final proof that our escorts are everywhere too thin. The strain on the British Navy is becoming intolerable." Roosevelt was sympathetic. At the end of March, convoys to the Arctic were postponed and the ships that would have protected them were transferred from the Home Fleet to Western Approaches Command, which had responsibility for the Atlantic routes. It would be the autumn before another Arctic convoy set sail.[18]

On board *Tirpitz* and the other warships in Altafjord, the days of perpetual daylight dragged by. The commanders struggled to find new ways to lift the blanket of boredom. There were berry- and mushroom-gathering expeditions ashore. An athletics tournament, the Polar Championships, was mounted on a gravel playing field on the shore of Kaafjord. The truly desperate could enroll in a raffia-weaving course. None of these diversions was likely to prove satisfying for long. News of the destruction raining down on their homes was reaching the sailors, many of whom came from the industrial towns of the Ruhr. The commander of the *Scharnhorst*, Kapitän Friedrich Huffmeier, noted the "uncomfortable feeling we have that up here in the north we are much safer than are our loved ones, exposed as they are to constant bombing attacks." Frustration stoked the urge to strike back. "The desire to avenge these attacks on families and friends with the aid of the ships or in some other way is very widespread."[19]

Back in Berlin, Dönitz was equally anxious to give the crews something to do. At last a target came to mind. Spitsbergen is a large, mountainous island of 15,000 square miles, part of the Svalbard archipelago, lying 450 miles north of the North Cape. The Norwegian and Russian communities that made a living working in the islands' coal mines had been evacuated at the start of the war. Since then it had been reoccupied by the Allies who set up a meteorological station at Barentsburg, monitoring weather, sea temperature, ice formations, and the like and radioing reports back to Britain. It was a dismal place, a sprawl of huts and machinery, dotted with coal heaps, one of which had been set on fire in late 1941 and was still sullenly burning. In September 1943 it was manned by a force of 134 Norwegian soldiers, mostly former seamen who had received basic training in Scotland, together with nine officers and men from the Norwegian navy. Five British ratings and an RNVR liaison officer were also stationed there.

Spitsbergen was of minimal strategic importance. Its destruction hardly justified the large amounts of precious fuel that would be used to get the fleet there and back. Dönitz, however, considered an attack worthwhile as it "gave the [*Tirpitz*] group and the destroyers attached to it a chance to work together."[20]

The action was more like an exercise than a real operation of war. The risks were minimal. The fleet could be back in port by the time the British ships put to sea to catch them. The men on *Tirpitz* were nonetheless delighted when, on September 6, with Admiral Kummetz aboard, they put to sea together with *Scharnhorst* and an escort of ten destroyers. They had not been told their destination. The news that they were on their way to Spitsbergen did not dampen their spirits. "Our excitement ran high," remembered Adalbert Brünner. As they approached Barentsburg on September 8, Kummetz ordered all the ships to run up the white ensign as a *ruse de guerre*. The deception was hardly necessary. The tiny force was in no position to resist the might of the two biggest ships in the German navy.

The garrison had been told that they would receive ample warning of any German attempt to take the base as it would be impossible for a major seaborne operation to go undetected. In the event of a landing, they were to destroy sensitive equipment and retreat to the interior.

A raid by U-boats was thought more probable. The inhabitants had three 4-inch naval guns and eight Bofors and Oerlikon anti-aircraft cannon with which to defend themselves.

On the night of September 7, Esmond Dabner, a Navy code specialist, ate a supper of boiled beef and dumplings with the rest of the British team before retiring to bed in his hut at 11:30 p.m. Dabner was a quiet, scholarly man who had been quite content with his prewar existence as a clerk with the Midland Bank. Like hundreds of thousands like him, the coming of war swept him from his comfortable obscurity into a world of peril and adventure. After his capture he wrote down his experiences in one of the wartime logs for British prisoners that the YMCA sent to POW camps via the Red Cross in Geneva. On the first page he inscribed Lord Macaulay's famous words about the global effects of the ambitions of Frederick the Great: "The evils produced by his wickedness were felt in lands where the name of Prussia was unknown, and in order that he might rob a neighbor whom he had promised to defend, black men fought on the coast of Coromandel, and red men scalped each other by the Great Lakes of North America."

Reflecting on the fortunes of war and the strange circumstances in which he found himself, Dabner wondered if the British team, composed of "a librarian, an insurance official, two commercial men and two bank clerks, who drew graphs by the light of the Midnight Sun" were the counterpart of those "black men" and Spitsbergen was their Coromandel.

At 2:30 on the morning of Wednesday, September 8, he was woken by Duggie Arthur, another member of the British team, with the news that ships had been seen in the approaches to Barentsburg. The assumption was that they were British but the order had been given to sound the alarm. Dabner dressed and made his way to the meeting point at the wireless station. On his way he saw the ships in the distance and was "somewhat shaken to hear gunfire."[21] The party had their steel helmets but not their rifles and mountain packs which were stored in the research station. It looked as if they had left it too late to retrieve them. Dabner could see the ships looming in the bay now. It seemed to him that the wisest course of action would be to beat a rapid retreat. Instead, the light guns on the shore were pumping shells at two German destroyers, the *Z29* and the *Z33*, which were rapidly approaching the dock.

"The inevitable reply to this was a hail of missiles which left us with no alternative but to lie down in a small gulley," he wrote. On board *Tirpitz* the crew watched delightedly as the turrets of Anton, Bruno, Caesar, and Dora swiveled; the muzzles of the 15-inch guns belched smoke and flame; and the air wobbled as shells reduced the shore installations "to matchwood," according to Adalbert Brünner, who was among the spectators.

Very soon the shore batteries were silenced, but not before they had managed to score some hits on the two destroyers, forcing *Z33*, the second in line, to falter and then turn away. Peering up from his gulley, Dabner saw "the greater part of Barentsburg in flames." *Z29* had now docked and advance parties were swarming ashore, moving through the coal and slag heaps while the covering volleys from the destroyers whistled overhead. They "proceeded to spread fire to such few places that had so far escaped it and to ferret out the occupants." Two Arado seaplanes from *Tirpitz* flew back and forth spraying machine-gun bullets. Soon the defenders' fire slackened and then stopped altogether. Engineer teams started to lay charges to demolish the settlement's installations.

Dabner and his companions saw that flames were creeping closer to an ammunition store near their hiding place and decided it was time to move. They split up, heading for the higher ground. Dabner, together with his commander, Lieutenant Watson, Duggie Arthur, and two Norwegians took cover in a disused mine entrance. Watson told Dabner to stay put and ran down the hill with Arthur to the research station, which was still intact. Dabner emerged from the mine and watched them enter the building. He heard later that they had managed to destroy some records and put the transmitter out of commission. They sloshed petrol around the rooms, set fire to it then ran out of the building straight into the arms of the Germans. Dabner considered following them at a distance but "there seemed little sense in all keeping close together, encouraging as that would have been."

Looking down at the base he was "very much aware of the hopelessness of our situation. Everything was burning. *Tirpitz* fired an occasional salvo from her big guns, not now towards Barentsburg, fortunately." Instead they were concentrating their fire on the coal tips and oil depots. Some of the landing party had reached the slopes behind the settlement. Dabner decided that "there was no alternative but to go to ground." He returned to the mine and lay face down inside the entrance. The two Norwegians stood behind him. "Two hand grenades settled our business," he wrote. "All three of us were hit. Looking up I saw four German soldiers some 6–8 yards away. It appeared to be time to go. We went."

They were taken down the hill to the jetty at gunpoint, hobbling from their wounds. The journey "seemed like a dream." They had not gone far when Dabner had "the unhappy experience of seeing the body of my good friend David Rae," one of the British party, lying on the ground. At the jetty they were put on a destroyer. Another Briton, Stan Johnson, was already aboard. He had been with Rae when he was shot but was "not allowed to do anything for him." Lieutenant Watson and Duggie Arthur arrived shortly after. Dabner's wounds were hurting him. He had more than a dozen grenade splinters in his legs. "A very pleasant German" treated him and told him that they would be moving to the more spacious surroundings of the *Tirpitz*. Sure enough, a little later he was lashed to a stretcher and lowered into a launch flying a Red Cross flag where other casualties, including a badly wounded German, were waiting.

They drew alongside the huge flank of the battleship and were hauled aboard. Dabner took a final look back at the "island of pointed mountains" where he had spent the last three months. Then he was hurried along the deck, to the sound of clicking cameras as the crew snapped away, and down into a comfortable bed in the *Tirpitz*'s well-appointed hospital.

The ships did not linger. They were eager to reach the safety of Altafjord before a British force could mount a retaliatory operation. The Home Fleet did put to sea when news reached the Admiralty of the raid but it soon turned back when it was accepted that there was no chance of an interception. The weather turned bad on the return but Brünner and his shipmates noted proudly that the ship barely seemed to notice. "Our Toni Paula [as the crew affectionately nicknamed the ship] made its way sedately, even though she was under full steam, towards the Norwegian coast." Some booty had found its way aboard, mostly Russian cigarettes. A mysterious chest seemed at first as if it might hold something more interesting. "It looked amazing, with illegible Russian writing all over its tin cladding," remembered Brünner. Once it was opened up, it was found to contain nothing but salt. It might have been a metaphor for the Spitsbergen operation. Despite the unimportance of the action, however, Brünner and the rest of the crew were in high spirits. "Now there was something new to talk about on board," he wrote. "Nothing earth-shattering had occurred but *something* had happened." As they neared their haven they were left wondering whether their adventure was not the prelude to "a great endgame."[22]

CHAPTER 13

MADMEN

The Spitsbergen raid was essentially a morale-raising exercise. It was also a provocation. It had the effect of drawing attention once again to the threat still posed by *Tirpitz*. Churchill needed no reminding. Throughout 1943 the ship had broken into his thoughts, often when it might be imagined there were greater matters at stake. On February 16, he sent a sharp note to Pound at the Admiralty, Harris at Bomber Command, and Mountbatten at Combined Operations, asking if they had "given up all plans for doing anything to *Tirpitz* while she is at Trondheim? ... it is a terrible thing that this prize should be waiting and no-one able to think of a way of winning it."[1] It fell to Pound to reply on April 15 with a six-page situation report. There were in fact several plans, he reported. The navy was pressing forward with its midget submarines and human torpedoes and the RAF was experimenting with a new bomb—"Highball"—designed by Barnes Wallis, which it was hoped could be put to use against the battleship. It was based on the same concept as his "bouncing bomb" which would be used a month later in the raid on the Ruhr dams. None of these weapons, though, was ready for use and the problems of getting at *Tirpitz* were as great as ever. Slotted into her Faettenfjord anchorage, protected by flak, fighters and smokescreen, "the ship could hardly be in a less vulnerable situation."[2]

Churchill was not placated. On May 1 he told his scientific advisor Lord Cherwell that he was thinking of asking Pound for a monthly report on the anti-*Tirpitz* activities. "This will keep things lively," he promised.[3] A few days later another nagging missive was on its way. "I trust all concerned are alive to the importance of sinking this ship," he wrote to the First Sea Lord, "and that it is realized that reasonable losses must be risked in order to do so."[4]

At this point it was the navy that felt the pressure for results most. Bomber Command was entering into the most terrible phase of its campaign to smash Germany from the air, and Harris could reasonably argue that he had other priorities. The navy was also locked in its own mortal battle in the Atlantic. However, there was pride at stake. The failures to bring *Tirpitz* to action on the high seas or to blow her up in her anchorage rankled at the Admiralty, deepening the determination to finish the job.

By late summer it seemed that unorthodox tactics with unconventional weapons still carried the best hope of success. The gallant failure of Larsen and the charioteers in October 1942 had not dampened enthusiasm for human torpedoes, and they would go on to be used in further operations in the Mediterranean and the Far East.

In the case of *Tirpitz*, though, it was time for midget submarines to have their chance. There were now two types in existence. The Welman was a one-man submarine developed by the SOE's Technical Section following a request from the Admiralty for new ideas on dealing with

Tirpitz. It never seemed a very convincing weapon. An early version envisaged human propulsion with the operator pedaling the craft like a bicycle. Later models lacked a periscope and vision was restricted to glass panels in the small conning tower, which made navigation almost impossible.

X-Craft seemed a much better proposition. A prototype had been launched in conditions of great secrecy at Portsmouth in March 1942 and intensive trials and modifications had been going on ever since. They could travel almost a hundred miles submerged and carry two concrete detachable charges, clamped port and starboard to the hull and each containing two tons of Amatol explosive—surely enough to penetrate even the *Tirpitz*'s far from soft underbelly. They were fifty-one feet long—small enough to reduce the chances of detection and sufficiently maneuverable to find a way through or around the mines and nets festooned about the battleship.

During the spring and summer of 1943, work continued on an attack plan. It would be carried out by teams drawn from the body of men who, like the charioteers, had answered the Admiralty's call for "volunteers for hazardous operations." The response had been good and a steady flow of officers and ratings had gone through special training at Portsmouth. They were a diverse bunch, ranging from seasoned merchant seamen to adventure-seeking playboys, and included South Africans, Irishmen, Frenchmen, and Australians, among them a young reserve officer called Maxwell Shean.

Shean was twenty-four and had been brought up in Perth, where his father taught him how to sail and build small boats. He was mechanically minded and was halfway through an engineering course at the University of Western Australia when war broke out. Shean had never been to Britain; nor had his immediate family, yet he "felt a great affinity for England." His uncle had fought in the Great War and been grotesquely disfigured by a wound to the face. Shean did not feel inclined to follow him into the colors. Then came the disaster of Dunkirk. "You couldn't ignore that," he said later. "Until that time I had confidence [we could] keep the Germans at bay."

He went with a friend to the Australian navy depot in Fremantle and tried to join up. They were told it would be better for them and the navy if they first finished their degrees. But their initiative had made them restless. When an advertisement appeared calling for volunteers with sailing experience to be trained for anti-submarine operations, they both applied. This time they were accepted and after initial training in Sydney were on their way to Britain aboard a refrigerator ship loaded with frozen lamb. Shean's first posting was as a sub-lieutenant to HMS *Bluebell*, an anti-submarine corvette, based in a Blitz-scarred Liverpool. At school and at home, the old country had been "presented as a fairyland. Everything in England was beautiful. But Liverpool didn't look pretty at all. It looked desperate and I hated it."[5]

Bluebell was on convoy duty, covering the sailings to and from Gibraltar. For fifteen months Shean endured the harrowing routine. "I was homesick and I was seasick and those two don't go well together," he remembered. "I used to go up on the bridge with oilskins, sou'wester and a bucket. It was very hard to hold up your dignity as an officer when you go up there with a bucket in your hand." The first trip was a "dream run," and the U-boats left them alone. The return journey was different. Shean was on the middle watch, from midnight to four in the morning. "The graveyard watch they called it. You turned in as soon as you had your supper and tried to get a bit of sleep." It was during the pre-watch rest period that the U-boats would attack. "You'd hear the explosion, hear the odd crump, and then ten seconds later the alarm bells would ring—action stations. You always slept in your clothes. You'd turn out of your bunk, put on your oilskins because it was always wet up top, dash up there and see a ship burning in the distance."

Sometimes, as the nearest ship to the stricken vessel, they would race to pick up survivors. "All merchant seamen had little red lights on their shoulders. You would see a forest of red lights. We would pull them out with boat hooks ... grab them and haul them up." They would "finish up with a dozen chaps lying on deck vomiting." Some would die and later be buried at sea. "You couldn't hang around to get everyone. The captain had to decide to move on, otherwise you would be the target. It was very depressing." Shean spent fifteen months with *Bluebell*. When he left he "felt as though I was leaving home. I felt sort of homesick again."

While ashore in Liverpool in mid-1942, he had seen an Admiralty Fleet Order calling for volunteers from officers and ratings for "special and hazardous service." It specified that they should be less than twenty-four years old, unmarried, good swimmers and "of strong and enduring physique." The order gave no more details of what the duty would entail and Shean had thought little of it. Back on board *Bluebell* the captain, Lieutenant Geoffrey Walker, told him that he intended to volunteer. "Obviously he wanted a response to this," he recalled. "I thought as quickly as possible." He was coming to the end of his time on *Bluebell*. He would soon be moved to another post. At least by volunteering he was able "to choose my shift rather than where anybody else thought best so I said right, put my name down too please."

Shean and Walker were called to HMS *Dolphin*, the home of the navy's submarine service in Portsmouth, for interviews. Walker was rejected on the grounds that he could not be spared from convoy duty. Shean was accepted. By now he had been told that the mysterious new mission was connected with midget submersibles. He was going from hunting submarines to sailing in them.

Shean started his initial training in August 1942 at HMS *Dolphin*. It involved repeated practices with the Davis Submarine Escape

Apparatus—the invention of Sir Robert Davis of Siebe Gorman. This comprised an oxygen bottle strapped to the wearer's front and connected by tubes to a lung-like rubber breathing bag and a tight-fitting face mask. The flow was controlled by a tap. Trainees were placed into a diving tank about forty feet wide and thirty feet deep which was filled with tepid water, and made to carry out tasks while instructors watched through windows set in the side. The drill doubled as a psychological as well as a physical test. It was easy to panic as the tank flooded. Some volunteers soon realized they would never be able to control their fears and dropped out.

As the course progressed, they were allowed to know the basics of the mission they were training for. They were going to be sent to attack enemy ships in harbor. They also learned more about the craft they would be operating in. "We were told that these small submarines, which were called X-Craft, were fitted with equipment to enhance their chances of entering and leaving an enemy harbor undetected and that provided we weren't detected we had a pretty good chance of successful attack and retreat. It wasn't a suicide mission. The risks were pretty high but the reward was great."

John Lorimer was another of the assorted company of volunteers. He was tall and lean and blessed with a sense of the absurd, a valuable asset in the world he was joining. He was born in Kelso, Scotland, the son of a Scottish doctor who had served in the navy in the previous war and later set up practice in Norfolk. Lorimer had tried for Dartmouth at the age of twelve but narrowly missed selection. In 1940, aged eighteen, he joined up as an ordinary seaman and spent six months on a destroyer shepherding convoys through the Channel, "going very slowly as the Germans lobbed shells over," before being commissioned as a sub-lieutenant. Early in 1942 the Admiralty's appeal caught his eye. Almost seventy years later he could still not identify what it was that made him or his comrades respond. "Perhaps we were all mad," he said.[6]

The majority of those in training were officers but there were a substantial number of non-commissioned volunteers. Vernon "Ginger" Coles had left a boring job as a toolmaker apprentice in a tin box factory in Reading to join the Royal Navy at the age of seventeen in July 1938. He had been in the thick of the Norway campaign on the destroyer *Faulknor*, and had seen more action in the Mediterranean. After a spell in Portsmouth qualifying as an engine room artificer (ERA)—the technicians who kept the navy moving—he felt that "after all the excitement we had had in the *Faulknor* it was a bit boring to be stuck in a naval barracks not knowing what ship you were going to get on." Egged on by a Glaswegian messmate and fortified by a session in the pub, the pair signed up for the submarine service. After five trips to sea he was still in search of more excitement. In September 1942 he saw an appeal for ERA volunteers for special service. "I looked at this and thought 'Shall I or shan't I? Shall I or shan't I?' And in the end I thought, yeah, I'll have a go." Like Lorimer—like everyone it seemed—he was unable to understand exactly why, when danger was already freely available, he chose to seek out more. It was out of "excitement or stupidity, call it what you will," he said many years later. "When you're twenty-two years old, you look at life differently."[7]

In the autumn of 1942 work was continuing on two prototypes, *X-3* and *X-4*, developed at Varley Marine in their Hamble factory, around the corner from Portsmouth. Command of *X-3* had been given to Donald Cameron, a lieutenant in the Royal Navy Reserve. He was twenty-six, and past the official upper age limit, a detail the selectors chose to overlook. He was born in Carluke, in the Lanarkshire coalfields, and went to school at Shawlands Academy in Glasgow, leaving at seventeen to go to sea with a local shipping company, the Baron Line, where he earned a reputation as a brilliant navigator. He was commissioned in the Royal Naval Reserve in 1939 but brought a merchant marine officer's sometimes skeptical outlook to the service and its ways. He was serving on the submarine HMS *Sturgeon* when he volunteered for hazardous duties. Cameron never spoke about his reasons for doing so. To his son, Iain, he was "a natural loner. That doesn't mean he wasn't perfectly gregarious on occasion but he preferred to be on his own and to be his own boss."[8] He also had a romantic streak, reflected in his love of the Scottish Highlands and in the thoughtful and whimsical letters he wrote to his wife.

Cameron had spent much of 1942 in Portsmouth carrying out the secret initial trials on the prototype. He had been obliged to move out of the mess to escape the curiosity of his companions and had found digs in a large house on the Hamble belonging to a widow called Mrs. Kilpatrick. Soon Cameron was ensconced and courting her eighteen-year-old daughter, Eve, a driver with the WRNS. They found they both liked the same things. "We got on," she remembered many years after their first meeting. "He painted watercolors beautifully."[9] Romance worked fast in wartime and they soon got engaged. The selection criteria had specified that candidates be single but the Admiralty was sensible enough not to interfere. They were married in June 1942.

By the end of 1942, the other prototype, *X-4*, was in the hands of Godfrey Place. Place was a regular RN officer among a host of RNVR reservists. He was the son of a barrister who had served in the trenches and emerged with an MC and a DSO. At fourteen he was sent to Dartmouth and come out near the top of his class. He had a reputation for mild eccentricity, "the scruffiest naval officer I have ever seen," according to Lorimer, with a habit of making off with other people's clothing. He was on the cruiser *Newcastle* when the war broke out but joined the submarine service in 1941 and served in the Mediterranean aboard *Urge* and *Una*. After a spell as liaison officer in the Polish submarine *Sokol*, he joined *Unbeaten* as first lieutenant and won a Distinguished Service Cross after sinking the Italian U-boat *Guglielmotti*.

As the summer of 1942 faded, the X-Craft operation moved north. Real training was about to begin in the waters of Loch Striven, a narrow seawater inlet plunging between the hills of the Cowal peninsula in Argyllshire, that replicated the conditions of a Norwegian fjord. On his way to the station for the train to Glasgow, Max Shean walked past HMS *Victory* sitting in her place of honor in a dry dock. He was wondering what he had let himself in for. "I thought, I'm not in the right group here. This is not me. I'm not that sort of person." As he approached the ship he saw that it had been damaged by one of the many bombs the Germans dropped on Portsmouth. He climbed down under the concrete plinth on which the hull rested. Looking up, he noticed a "fragment of the oak hanging off the keel." He "reached up and broke it off and stuck it in my pocket ... that was my treasure. [It] made me feel a little bit better."

The 12th Submarine Flotilla, as the force was now called, was billeted in the Kyles Hydropathic Hotel on the island of Bute. It was a gray-stone Edwardian structure, overlooking the small fishing village of Port Bannatyne, where in peacetime rheumatics had gone for the curative effects of the waters. There were fifty in the group, and, despite Shean's fears, no easily definable "sort of person." What did bind them together was a certain restlessness, a taste for adventure, and a willingness to take mighty risks.

The early exercises had followed the usual process of trial and error with the usual quota of hair-raising accidents. On November 4, 1942, John Lorimer took *X-3* for a training dive with two other volunteers, Sub-Lieutenants "Taffy" Laites and Len Gay. Training took place in a deserted stretch of Loch Striven, which was hidden from Port Bannatyne across the water by a convenient headland. They boarded the craft, wriggled through the hatch and stood by to submerge. Lorimer opened the valves to flood the buoyancy tanks and, in a disconcerting symphony of gurgling and gulping noises, the hull began to sink. As they slid below the surface, water started to cascade through the hull. The valve shutting off the induction pipe that vented diesel fumes when running the engine at periscope depth had stuck open.

Things happened quickly after that. Lorimer recalled that as they struggled to staunch the flow, *X-3* tipped up and "went down arse first into 120 feet of water." He ordered the ballast tanks to be blown, which would have taken them safely back to the surface. But as the others scrambled for the spanner to turn the wheel, it dropped between the deck boards and into the bilges. The vertiginous descent continued, with water coursing through the control room and into the engine room in the stern. "*X-3* was terribly badly designed, as it had the batteries aft," Lorimer recalled. As the seawater mixed with the battery acid, clouds of poisonous chlorine gas began to form, and soon the control room was filling up.

At the same time a shudder ran through the craft and the lights went out. They had hit the bottom of Loch Striven. Lorimer heard himself telling the others, in a remarkably calm voice, to don their Davis Submarine Escape Apparatus (DSEA). They had one set each, plus a spare. These would save them from the poisonous effects of the chlorine gas and give them enough breathing time while the hull filled up and the water pressure inside and out equalized sufficiently for them to get out.

The important thing was not to panic. Panic made you breathe faster and rapid breathing burned precious oxygen. The others sat as still as they could and tried to control their bodies and their imaginations. Lorimer unscrewed the hatch cover, opened the seacocks and sat back as the seawater bubbled in and crept up around them. "I was quite convinced I was going to die," he remembered later. "I was sitting in this bloody thing for an hour as the water was coming up, waiting until we could open the hatch. I was thinking, well, my parents will get a telegram tomorrow, telling them it's the end of their little son." He realized with some surprise that he "wasn't frightened."[10]

It took forty minutes for the compartment to fill up. They sat there in the dark listening to the beat of blood in their ears struggling to keep their breathing shallow, regular, and economical. They were 120 feet under the sea, and they felt the water clasp them tight as it crept up their bodies. Before he was completely submerged, Lorimer removed his mouthpiece and gave the pair their final instructions. Gay was to go first, then Laites.

Eventually, when the compartment was three-quarters full, the pressure inside and outside the hull equalized and the water stopped rising. Gay stood up and pushed at the hatch cover overhead. It was hard work and he was down to his last few lungfuls of oxygen before he forced it open. Water rushed in. He pulled himself through the hole and shot upwards in a cloud of bubbles. Now it was Laites's turn. Lorimer could see nothing. He waited for him to push past but there was no movement. He began a groping search of the control room and his hands closed on an inert figure. Laites's oxygen had given out. Lorimer's mind raced furiously in what he later called a "miserable debate" with himself. His own oxygen was almost exhausted. If he tried to help Laites he would use up what was left in his cylinder manhandling him through the hatch. If he abandoned him, though, he would save himself.

Lorimer made his decision. He remembered the spare apparatus. He tore Laites's useless oxygen set from his face and hurriedly attached the new one. He switched on the supply but it seemed to make no difference. Laites didn't move. He hooked his hands under his thighs and pushed him toward the hatch. As he shoved him through, the oxygen set was torn off. At least he was free now and on his way to the surface. Lorimer followed him, then kicked toward the pale ceiling of sunlight tilting and shimmering overhead. "I was unconscious I think when I went up," he recalled, "but I held up, and the gunner's mate who pulled me out said 'You're bloody lucky, sir, because there was only one "guff" of oxygen left in your cylinder.'" It was forty-eight hours later, when the adrenaline had worn off, that the full scale of the drama struck him. He had been strangely calm throughout the ordeal but now "by God ... I was shit-scared."[11] Gay and Laites put in for a transfer. Lorimer, though, decided to stay on. After a week's leave he was back in training.

The following month, *X-4* suffered a fatal mishap. Godfrey Place and his crew were on exercise in the Sound of Bute when a storm blew up and Sub-Lieutenant Morgan Thomas was washed out of the W&D compartment and drowned. The waves swamped the compartment, tipping the craft almost perpendicular and trapping Place and ERA Willie Whitley for two hours.

It was a relief when, in January 1943, the new, modified X-Craft began arriving from the Vickers-Armstrongs yard in Barrow-in-Furness. The prototypes had not inspired much confidence when the volunteers got their first look at them. Ginger Coles had been taken with some fellow volunteers to see *X-4*, lying in an unassembled state in a heavily guarded workshop in Portsmouth Dockyard. "Our stomachs turned upside down when we saw the size of her," he recalled. Lorimer had reacted the same way, "thinking how incredibly small everything looked and wondering how such a frail craft was expected to cross the North Sea."[12] The improved versions seemed quite impressive, however, and Lorimer, who had been to Barrow-in-Furness to take delivery of *X-6*, judged that "Vickers had done a good job."

They were indeed midgets, far smaller than the navy's conventional submarines. S- and T-class subs, of the type they would work alongside, were twenty-seven and forty times heavier respectively. The only area in which X-Craft matched their big sisters was in their ability to reach safely the same sort of depths. Otherwise they were slower, managing only a maximum speed of 6.5 knots on the surface and 5.5 knots submerged against a T-class submarine's fifteen knots above the water and nine knots below.

From the outside, an X-Craft looked like a cigar tube, tapered at both ends. Unlike a conventional submarine, it lacked a conning tower.

A narrow deck ran along the top of the hull, pierced by a forward and aft hatch and cluttered with lockers and shackles. It submerged and surfaced by means of three ballast tanks, fore, aft, and amidships. They were filled by opening seacocks and pumped out with compressed air cylinders. It could go down as far as 300 feet. Below that depth the seams would burst and the hull crumple, squeezed flat by the pressure of the water. Submerged, it was propelled by an electric fan motor driven by two large batteries. On the surface a diesel engine pushed it along, the same type that powered London double-decker buses and which also recharged the electric batteries. Aquaplanes were used to maneuver the craft up and down when cruising below the surface and small trimming tanks could be emptied and filled to keep it straight and level. The periscope was slender to reduce the chances of detection. It allowed the captain a limited view of what was going on around him. There was a second, short periscope, used to observe and direct the diver as he went about cutting the nets. Unlike conventional submarines, X-Craft had no guns or torpedo tubes. Their sole weapons were the two charges or mines, each weighing four tons in total including explosive, which fitted snugly over the curved sides of the hull. They were released by turning a small wheel inside the control room. As they came away, a copper strip peeled off, unsealing a buoyancy chamber which filled up with water, sinking the charge to the bottom. There it would lie until exploded by a clock timing device, set before release.

You could fit five X-Craft alongside the hull of a T-class submarine with plenty of room to spare. All submarines were cramped but these felt like coffins and great self-control was needed to suppress the claustrophobia that most felt at their first submersion. Even with the improvements, it took great deftness to maneuver around the tiny control room amidships where the four-man crew had to live and work. The only place where it was just possible to stand upright was under the dome of the periscope. Elsewhere, the widest point was only four and a half feet high or wide and the crew scrambled and crawled to get around.

The captain sat at a tiny chart table next to the periscope, from where he navigated the craft through the shoals and skerries, nets and mine-fields, they would meet on the way to the target. The first officer's post was an arm's length away at the after end of the control room, monitor-ing the gauges, wheels, and levers that controlled the direction, speed, and trim of the craft. The ERA shifted around, maintaining the instru-ments and engines. With the diesel and electric motors, the wiring and the mechanics, there were an extraordinary number of things to go wrong. To reach the diesel engine in the stern he had to crawl through a two-foot-wide hatch, lying flat on the fuel tank to work in spaces where clearance was only a few inches. The diver, meanwhile, helped out with all the jobs when not performing his specialized task.

The suffocating proximity, the intense interdependence on which success and survival depended, engendered an egalitarian atmosphere. According to John Lorimer, it ran "through the whole submarine ser-vice ... from the captain down to the ship's cook you're all equally responsible. You make one mistake and you kill the rest. You're a great team of chums and you call each other by Christian names."[13]

Sleeping, eating, and ablutions arrangements were all improvised and spartan. There was room for one man, two at a pinch, to stretch out on the boards that covered the big batteries, now shifted to the bow. In the control room amidships, there was a gap on the port side. As Max Shean discovered, by putting your head under the chart table and arranging your legs around the pipes and pumps it was possible to get some rest. "For all the inconvenience of this bunk," he wrote, "the few odd hours, or even minutes, which I was able to spend in this position were golden."[14] They ate prepared meals, heated up on a carpenter's double-boiler glue pot. The head was an Elsan, located in the wet and dry (W&D) compartment in the forward section from which the diver left and re-entered. The air they breathed was cleaned by a Protosorb filter which was reasonably efficient. Submariners tried to be as fastidious as conditions allowed. But life below the waves was not for hygiene fetishists.

Crews would be spending a lot of time aboard. To carry out the attack, the X-Craft first had to get to their targets. Various means of transporting them to Norway were examined, including dropping them from aircraft. It was decided in the end to tow them to the target area behind full-sized submarines. The voyage would take at least five days using passage crews for the first stage, leaving the operational crews fresh for the attack.

In the wardroom at the Kyles Hydro on Bute, renamed HMS *Varbel* after Commanders Cromwell Varley and T. I. S. "Tizzy" Bell, who had designed and supervised the building of *X-3* and *X-4*, the young men smoked, drank weak wartime beer, and wrestled with the problems that the training exercises continually threw up. They had also been given the use of Ardtaraig House, a shooting lodge at the northern end of Loch Striven. Eventually it was leased to the navy and became "Varbel II," and the flotilla's diving training center. "Life there was much more informal and rural," remembered Peter Philip, one of the team, "with cows, sheep and poultry on our doorstep, home grown dairy produce and vegetables, and mugs of beer and long yarns around the roaring log fire at night."[15] Bell was a fitness enthusiast and encouraged long, early-morning runs. Shean joined the runners but recorded that there was "another school of thought that argued that the best way to train for life in a poorly-ventilated submarine was to take all the rest available and to spend off-duty time becoming accustomed to a self-generated tobacco fug before the log fire in the officers' mess, sipping gin."[16]

Eve Cameron, by now "rather pregnant and fat," was given leave from the WRNS to spend a few weeks with her husband. They were given a room in a gamekeeper's cottage on the "Varbel II" estate. The project was still top secret and those engaged in it were forbidden from discussing it even with their spouses. Eve had picked up enough during her travels around Portsmouth to have a shrewd idea of what was involved. One Sunday morning they were sitting in their little room. Don was reading the paper, which contained an article on the Japanese navy's midget submarines. She could not resist telling her husband "I know what you're up to."[17]

For the attack to succeed, they had to find a way through the nets that protected *Tirpitz*. It was standard practice on both sides to drape steel mesh around larger surface vessels if they were at anchor for anything but the shortest periods. The X-Craft had to penetrate an outer perimeter of anti-submarine netting, then a curtain of nine-inch steel hoops suspended from buoys like chain mail to stop torpedoes. There was no question of cutting through the anti-torpedo netting; the hydraulic shears available were not strong enough. The available intelligence suggested that the German nets were the same as the Royal Navy's, which only stretched about ten feet below the hull of a ship. It was thought to be relatively easy simply to steer underneath them.

The submarine nets could hang much lower, however, too deep for an X-Craft to dive beneath. They were made of thick steel wire woven together in a diamond pattern. These would have to be cut. It was the diver's job to exit the craft, retrieve the cutter stowed in a locker on the front deck, and shear through the wire. He then shepherded the X-Craft through the gap before rejoining the boat. He entered and left the craft via the Wet and Dry compartment. This was a watertight tank situated below the forward hatch, just big enough for a man to crouch inside.

The diver first had to struggle into his two-piece rubber and canvas diving suit. Then he strapped his breathing apparatus onto his chest and inserted the mouthpiece, which, to Max Shean, always "felt that it was lubricated with the previous wearer's saliva." He then climbed into the tank and began to pump in water from the number two main ballast tank directly below into the W&D compartment.

Shean had done his initial diving training in Loch Striven in an old-fashioned, one-piece suit complete with metal and glass helmet and brass breast and back plates. He had quite enjoyed the experience, taking the opportunity to collect scallops from the lake floor to augment the "Varbel" rations. Initial anxieties calmed when he saw the shimmering light of the sky through the water above, which was "always friendly and always there. If things go wrong you can come to the surface." The first time he experienced the inside of a mock-up W&D suspended from a pontoon, he hated it. "You're filled up with water and you're in this steel compartment. It's pitch dark and you're under water. It's the most unnatural set of conditions you can imagine ... at that time you wish you'd never been born."[18]

As the "water rose to visor level there was a natural tendency to panic." He resisted it successfully only to feel another "shock to my feeling of well-being" as the water covered his head. It was a relief when the tank was full and the water pressure equalized. When he pushed the overhead hatch to make his escape, though, "nothing happened." After forcing himself to relax he tried again and "suddenly all was light. It was like Wagner's Sunrise that preceded Siegfried's Rhine Journey." He "floated up, shut the hatch ... and swam to the surface." Soon afterward he had to reverse the process. Getting back in was no easier than getting out. The outside hatch opened smoothly enough but closing it again "was the most difficult act of all." The diver was weightless and had to wedge himself inside the walls of the W&D and struggle to force down the lid. Eventually he was able to close the hatch and open the valves to pump the compartment dry.[19]

The attack had initially been scheduled for March when the Arctic night would still be long enough to provide protection. The ninth of

March was considered the last practical date when the mission could go ahead. As well as the cover of darkness there would be a glimmer of moonlight to help the X-Craft on their final approach.[20] But as the date drew nearer, it was clear that more preparations were needed. Several practical problems remained. Among them were the difficulties the crews were having with the anti-submarine nets. As the summer arrived, the craft were taking too long to wriggle through the holes cut by the divers. Several divers had blacked out during exercises. One had died. On May 31, Sub-Lieutenant David Locke surfaced after a test dive in X-7, gave a thumbs-up sign, then disappeared—the victim, apparently, of "Oxygen Pete." "It upset me no end," said John Lorimer. "He and I had joined the Navy together."

Further exercises were canceled until a safer method of net-cutting had been found. Shean was summoned by Commander D. C. Ingram, one of the triumvirate who ran the 12th Submarine Flotilla, and told to take command of X-5 and work out a solution to a problem that now looked as if it might ruin the entire operation. He was to "concentrate on net cutting until you've solved it."[21] He relished the job. It was "interesting, challenging, exciting and sufficiently uncertain to inspire the boldest with a sense of care and awareness." He would be working with Sub-Lieutenant Henry Henty-Creer, as his number two. Henty-Creer was another Australian, the son of a naval officer. He was twenty-two years old, sandy-haired and dashing. He had worked in the film business before signing up for the navy in the autumn of 1940. His last assignment had been in Canada shooting *49th Parallel*, a Michael Powell and Emeric Pressburger production starring Laurence Olivier and Leslie Howard, designed to persuade an as-yet-undecided America to join the war. After selection for officer training, he passed out near the top of his intake and volunteered for hazardous duty.

Apart from their Australian birth and a shared taste for adventure, the two men had little in common. Where Shean was scientific and methodical, Henty-Creer was romantic and rash. While Shean kept to himself in the mess, "Henty" was the life and soul of the party, amusing senior officers with jokes and tales of his colorful and glamorous life. Opposites often worked well together in wartime. Men who in peacetime would have been unlikely to meet, or if they had, given each other a wide berth, frequently formed effective teams when flung together by the crisis, supplementing and canceling out each other's strengths and weaknesses. This was not to be the case with Shean and Henty-Creer.

They started their task by interviewing all the divers. Shean discovered that cutting the nets was relatively easy. The difficulty was doing it in such a way that the X-Craft could then slip through without fouling on the wires. He devised a means of making the minimum number of cuts to produce the maximum-sized hole, and a drill by which the diver made hand signals to the captain, watching through the auxiliary periscope, to ensure the craft was trimmed straight and level and less liable to snag when it passed through.

Soon afterward, with Henty-Creer, an ERA and a stoker, he boarded X-5 to put it to the test. Henty-Creer volunteered to make the first attempt. "That was typical," said Shean many years later. His partner, he said, "was a very proud fellow" who always needed to be "center, stage-front." Shean let him have his way. They dived to thirty feet and Henty-Creer struggled into his diving suit and climbed into the W&D compartment. Above, on the gray surface of the lake, a naval rescue boat with a diver on board looked out for any signs of trouble.

At first all went well. The operation of the W&D valves could be monitored from outside and Henty seemed to be doing the right things in the right order, beginning with pumping the compartment full of water. Then Shean noticed that he was "starting to do some strange things with the valves." He took over and reversed the valves so that the water could be pumped out again. When he opened the door "there was Henty obviously having a fit so I pulled him into the control room,

pulled out his mouthpiece and opened his visor and got him breathing…."
There was something wrong with the breathing apparatus. Shean took
the craft to the surface, put Henty-Creer on board the rescue boat and
helped him out of his suit. He made a rapid recovery and insisted he was
fit to carry on the exercise. This time he would keep the craft steady while
Shean did the cutting.

Shean managed to exit the W&D compartment without difficulty.
First he signalled to Henty-Creer to trim the craft level. Then he retrieved
the hydraulic cutter from its locker and began work. "With a steady hiss
the blade moved slowly out from its guide toward the wire held in the
hook. When they met, the blade continued as if there were no wire.
Crunch, snap and the wire fell apart."[22] He made three more cuts. The
hole widened and Shean watched X-5 slip through, "nice and easily, nice
and slow. All around the green water was very clear and it was a magnificent sight to see."[23] When he emerged from the W&D compartment,
Henty-Creer told him that the whole operation had taken twelve minutes.

When the other crews followed the procedure they had equal success.
The way was now clear for the final preparations for the attack. In July
1943 the flotilla shifted its base, this time to Loch Cairnbawn, on the
west coast of the Scottish Highlands. From there, six of the X-Craft
would set off on their extraordinary mission. The plan for the operation,
code-named "Source," was now approaching completion. *Tirpitz*, which
had settled into its anchorage at Kaafjord and looked likely to remain
there for some time, was the main target. But *Scharnhorst* was also in the
area. With any luck the X-Craft might dispose of Hitler's last operational
battle cruiser as well as his last battleship.

They would be towed into place by six S- and T-class submarines,
which, after slipping their charges, would stand by to pick up the crews
when they returned from their mission. The submarines also had a

secondary mission. If the attacks caused *Tirpitz* to run for the safety of the high seas, they would be there to cut her off.

A passage crew would man each X-Craft during the initial voyage. They would then hand over control to the operational crew traveling aboard the mother submarine, which would then carry out the attack. Tests were conducted to monitor the endurance of men cooped up in a tiny craft for long periods. "We did a six-day trial to see if we could stand it," remembered John Lorimer. "Just tooling around the Isle of Bute, six days non-stop." They were fortified with Benzedrine pills, which "kept you awake if you wanted to be awake but if you wanted to go to sleep you could sleep."[24]

Towing trials with HMS *Tuna* revealed that the passage crew's task would not be easy. Shean found that "in the first minutes we had bother keeping the X-Craft under control." It had a tendency to "porpoise, that is to go deep until they get to the stage where the tow pulls them up again, then ... break surface and go deep again." As it reared and plunged, the crew and any loose objects were "apt to slide along the deck." They eventually found that by constantly trimming the tanks and keeping to a depth of forty or fifty feet it was possible to maintain fairly smooth progress. Preventing "porpoising," however, was going to need constant vigilance.

Another source of trouble was the tow cable itself. Despite the ingenuity that went into the design of midget submarines, little thought was given to this most basic aspect of the operation. The debacle of the chariot operation the previous year had revealed painfully the fact that the fate of the mission could hinge literally on the fastening linking the weapon to the towing vessel. Yet at this stage the only material made available for the vital task of towing was Manila hemp. The success of the mission was to a large extent dependent on a 600-foot length of rope. It was clear from the outset that the Manila tows were less than trustworthy. According to Vernon Coles, during the final exercises they were "breaking wholesale ... they didn't last more than four or five days. We persevered with these things. They put bigger ones on and they still broke."[25] The crews were told "not to worry because the towing submarine had a spare cable." It did not take much imagination to envisage the difficulties of reuniting with the towing submarine if the cable snapped, or the problems of connecting a new line in anything but perfect conditions.

Everyone knew that more robust and reliable cables existed. The RAF had developed nylon ropes with the strength and elasticity to tow gliders. Only three reached the flotilla. When they arrived, Don Cameron made sure he got one for *X-6*. The others went to *X-5* and *X-10* while the rest had to make do with something that would have been recognizable to the crew of the *Victory* or the *Golden Hind*.

In July, the final crew selection was made for passage and operation crews. Don Cameron and John Lorimer would be sailing with Sub-Lieutenant Richard Kendall as diver and ERA Edmund Goddard as engineer in *X-6*. Dickie Kendall was slim and athletic, just twenty-one, a former public schoolboy who had joined the navy as a rating at the outbreak of war and served on a destroyer before being commissioned and moving to submarines. He had impressed Cameron who had managed to wrest him away from *X-10*, where he was originally supposed to go. Eddie Goddard, who had been educated at St. Edward's School, Oxford, was notable for his jet-black hair, good nature, and extraordinary ability to keep things working. For six weeks they lived side by side with the other crews in a large house near the loch, repeating drills and exercises until they had the unthinking familiarity of instinct. Godfrey Place was now a married man, having just wed his sweetheart, Althea Tickler, a Wren who worked in the coding office at "Varbel." He would lead *X-7* on the attack. Two Australians, Brian "Digger" McFarlane, a short, cheerful regular navy officer from Victoria, and Ken Hudspeth, were in operational charge of *X-8* and *X-10*.

Initially it seemed that Max Shean's training had been in vain. To his annoyance, Henty-Creer would be captain of *X-5* on the attack. Shean believed that "Henty" had used his "winning personality" to "obtain command." He had "a flair for top billing and would not be happy playing second fiddle to anyone for long."[26] Then a last-minute decision by two French crew members to pull out meant Shean would go after all. Together with Vernon Coles he got what the navy called a "pierhead jump," landing aboard *X-9* under Terry Martin.

By the end of August a date had been set and all further leave was canceled. Operation Source would begin on September 20. At that time of the year, nights were long enough to provide some cover but the Arctic autumn with its storms and gales had not yet set in.[27]

Contingency plans were made in case *Tirpitz* moved to Narvik or Trondheim but three PRU flights on August 14, 15, and 21 reported that she was in her "usual berth" in Kaafjord, where she had been for the last five months. Not only *Scharnhorst* but also the pocket battleship *Lützow* was there. Work intensified on amassing the latest data on the defenses the X-Craft would have to contend with. The evidence of agents on the ground reinforced the photographic reconnaissance. Early in August, at the instigation of MI6 and the Norwegian intelligence service in London, a twenty-three-year-old student called Torbjørn Johansen was sent to the area from his home in Tromsø. He took the coastal steamer to Alteidet, then cycled more than sixty miles to Alta. The road took him past Kaafjord and the *Tirpitz*, *Scharnhorst*, and *Lützow*. He hid among the rocks and undergrowth of the hillside and hurriedly sketched locations, net arrangements, and the positions of surrounding gun emplacements. His sharp eyes caught a detail that would prove vital. The double anti-submarine net that was supposed to close the entrance to the fjord was left partly open on the southeastern side to allow ships to come and go.

Johansen was also tasked with trying to obtain water samples from Kaafjord to establish its salinity and buoyancy. With extraordinary coolness he set off in a boat, equipped with a rod and a set of containers. "He went all round the fjord fishing and secretly scooping up samples," remembered another young member of the Tromsø resistance, Terje Jacobsen. "Every time he caught a fish the Germans watching him from the ships' rails applauded."[28] Johansen returned to Tromsø where his brother Einar operated the clandestine radio post. The basic information was radioed back to Britain. The maps and samples went by courier to Stockholm, then on to London.

Unknown to him, another agent was also operating in the area. Torstein Raaby had established his resistance credentials while working in the meteorological station on Jan Mayen Island in the winter of 1941–42 and had used the cover to send reports of German reconnaissance flights and submarine movements to Britain. He had moved to Tromsø where he operated a clandestine radio station but fled to Sweden after a tip-off that the Gestapo was onto him. In March 1943 he reached Britain and spent four months training before being sent back by the Admiralty to conduct close surveillance of the German ships in the Alta area. He was landed by Norwegian submarine south of Trondheim, equipped with eight special transmitter-receiver sets and a large bundle of cash, and made his way north.

In Alta he teamed up with an old friend, Karl Rasmussen, who worked in the municipal roads department, and Harry Pettersen, who ran a taxi service in the town. Much of Pettersen's trade was ferrying junior officers back and forth to *Tirpitz*, and their chatter helped to build the picture of the routines, dispositions, and atmosphere on board. The town had five thousand inhabitants, small enough for the two men to know whom they could trust. There was no shortage of informants.

Local women boarded *Tirpitz* every day to clean and work in the galleys. They noted new developments and monitored the notices on the bulletin board. The information was collated and fed to Raaby, whom Rasmussen had fixed up with a job in the roads department. At night he sent his reports via a transmitter hidden in his office, which he hooked up to an aerial conveniently erected by a German officer billeted next door.[29]

All was set for the final preparations. On Sunday, September 5, the X-Craft were winched on board the flotilla's depot ship HMS *Bonaventure* to be provisioned and fueled and fitted with their side charges. As the charges were being fitted to *X-6*, sparks from a welder's torch started a fire on deck. The workforce fled in all directions and it was left to John Lorimer to find a hose and douse the blaze—unnecessarily, as it turned out, for a detonator was needed for the explosive to go up. That evening the crews received their first detailed briefing on their targets.

It was the first time they had been officially informed of the ultimate purpose of all their exhausting and dangerous preparations. Most of them had already guessed the targets, but it was nonetheless a solemn moment. They were about to attempt one of the boldest strokes of the naval war. Success would bring them fame and glory. It would also make a large and measurable contribution to the war effort. Lorimer wrote later about the sense of "tremendous responsibility" that descended on the crews. "If they succeeded in destroying or crippling the *Tirpitz*, the British Home Fleet could give its protection to the U-boat-haunted Atlantic convoys and the lives of thousands of merchant seamen might be saved."[30] The air of arousal and apprehension that precedes a great adventure hung over the base. "The adrenaline started flowing," remembered Ginger Coles. "The boats were ready, the crews were ready ... everyone was keen to go."[31]

On September 7, a PRU Spitfire took off from Vaenga airfield near Murmansk, where the Russians had granted the RAF facilities, and headed to Kaafjord to confirm that *Tirpitz* was where it should be. Instead of the familiar outlines, the pilot saw a much smaller shape in the water, which he identified as the *Lützow*. The news caused alarm when it reached London the following morning. As the Admiralty's intelligence staff sifted the possible scenarios, *Tirpitz* was bombarding the shore installations of Spitsbergen. It took a few hours before they learned of the operation. The question now was whether the force would return to Altafjord or head for Narvik or Trondheim. Another flight on September 9 gave no clue. *Lützow* still sat inside *Tirpitz*'s old berth. It was only on Friday, September 10, that a PRU Spitfire sighted the battleship and the rest of the squadron back safely in their old anchorages. Operation Source was set in motion.

The Commander of Submarines, Admiral Claude Barry, flew to Loch Cairnbawn, anxious to be there to "witness the start of this great enterprise." He invited the captains of the operational and passage crews to dine with him that night on the *Titania*, the depot ship for the big submarines towing the X-Craft. The navy's social codes may have dissolved during the eighteen months of training, but they were back in evidence on the eve of battle. "The officers had a wonderful party in the wardroom," remembered Ginger Coles, "but not we people on the lower deck." Instead, the six ERAs were given the use of "a little cowshed on the beach where a barrel of beer was put and a Naafi manager and we had mud up to our ankles. That was our farewell party to go on the attack."[32]

When the hilarity generated by alcohol and excitement had subsided, fears and doubts edged in. Ralph Mortiboys, the fourth member of Henty-Creer's crew on *X-5*, missed the cowshed party. A premonition had warned him he would not return from Kaafjord, and he stayed aboard *Bonaventure* to write to his widowed mother.[33] Don Cameron had been keeping a log of the preparations for Operation Source. It was intended for Eve, now back in Portsmouth with their seven-month-old son, "for your enjoyment I hope, and for Iain's when he is old enough to take an interest in such matters." The talk at Admiral Barry's dinner had been "very optimistic, perhaps a trifle too much so." He emerged from it into a "lively, clear night, moon almost full," promising "good weather ahead, thank God." After a few more drinks with his comrades he turned in "for my last night in a comfortable bed."

The following day, the good weather that Cameron hoped for failed to materialize. There was a strong southwesterly breeze and the sea was choppy. He brought in X-6 to complete victualing and congratulated himself on having secured one of the "extra strong" nylon towing ropes. He made out his will and visited the paymaster "in case something goes wrong." He felt, he confessed, "rather sheepish but best to be on the safe side." There was a last flurry of chart and photograph consultations before a quiet lunch. Then came the final inspection of his boat before Lieutenant "Willie" Wilson and the passage crew went aboard. At 4:00 p.m. they led the flotilla out of the lake. Cameron looked back at his native land from the conning tower of the towing submarine, HMS *Truculent*. As they rounded the point and headed for the open sea he felt "slightly depressed" that he had mislaid a lucky red cap. He comforted himself with the reassuring presence of a little wooden dog, "Bungay," Eve's first present to him, which he always carried in his pocket. "Why should I, a product of modern civilization, be affected by such things?" he wondered. "No logic in it, but there it is. I look at the familiar hills and islands and wonder when I shall see them again. Said a little prayer for all of us darling...."[34]

CHAPTER 14

THE GREAT ADVENTURE

One by one, over the next eighteen hours, the submarine pairs made their way out to sea. They would be traveling on the same course, parallel and ten miles apart. The route would take them north, leaving Cape Wrath and the Scottish mainland to starboard, passing between the Faroes and the Shetland Islands then turning northeast toward Norway's Arctic coast.

Admiral Barry went out in *Bonaventure*'s launch to wave them off and wish them a "grand trip." He regarded the expedition as "undoubtedly one of the most hazardous enterprises undertaken in [the] war." He recalled later that "any doubts I might have entertained about its outcome could not possibly have survived the infectious confidence of these young men who were just leaving us. They were like boys on the last day of school, their spirits ran so high."[1] The crews did nothing to dispel this fantasy. Lieutenant Martin Jupp, the captain of HMS *Syrtis*, towing *X-9*, had brought along an old-fashioned car horn which he honked from the conning tower as they left. When Barry came alongside and called out "good luck and a safe return," he gave a few more blasts and shouted back "Thank you sir. If we have any trouble we'll take a taxi."[2]

There were a few initial dramas as the passage crews adjusted to the business of steering while being dragged fifty or sixty feet below the waves by a 200-yard-long line attached to the parent ship on the surface. Their work was uncomfortable and exhausting. Towing vessel and charge never seemed to move smoothly together. In rough weather the X-Craft slid up and down as the submarine negotiated the peaks and troughs of the oncoming or following seas, sending everything that was not tied down tumbling around the control room and pitching the crew against the many sharp and hard surfaces.

As there was no need for a diver, it had been decided that a crew of only three would suffice. This, it soon became clear, was a mistake. The weight of work meant there was little time for rest or to maintain the interior, which needed constant wiping down to prevent electrical failures. Of the two men on duty, one spent his time watching the dials on the ballast tanks, the depth gauges and the bubble of the inclinometer which showed the angle of the hull, for any deviation from the norm. Failure to react quickly could easily result in catastrophe. The other was kept busy steering and checking and maintaining the circuits and motors.

In between tasks, they ate, quite well in the circumstances. They heated up tomato soup, tinned lambs' tongues, peas, and baked beans in the carpenter's glue pot that served as a stove, and finished off with canned blackberries, loganberries, and condensed milk. Cooking added to the sheen of condensation which dripped down every surface, reappearing almost as soon as it was dried. The damp was all-pervading, the air hot and fetid. The only escape was the blissful fifteen minutes they spent above water when, every six hours or so, the craft surfaced to "guff through" the living space with fresh air and to run the diesel engine to recharge the batteries. Real sleep was almost impossible. Rather, they dozed, stretched out on the pallet in the forward battery compartment. When exhaustion approached, there was Benzedrine to help.

They met their privations with good humor and stoicism. On the morning of the fourth day of the voyage, the captain of *X-7*, Peter Philip, who in his previous existence had been "Uncle Peter," the presenter of South African radio's *Children's Hour*, recorded his tribulations as the weather worsened. "We are rolling as well as pitching and every few minutes our bows are hauled over to port with a corkscrew motion. We heel over and rise, then go down in a power dive. Perfectly bloody. I expect the tow to part at any moment. Also I have a vague suspicion that one if not both of our side charges have gone or are at least flooded." He ended with a cheery "heigh ho."

Philip was wrong about the side charges but his fears about the manila tow rope would prove correct. At 4:50 p.m. the same day he felt something ominous in the way the craft was moving and a few moments later the stern dipped down and began a steady descent. He gave the order to blow the ballast tanks and after a few heart-pounding moments the bows rose again. They emerged into gray, jagged waves that crashed over the hull, coursing down the hatch when Philip pushed open the cover. He fought his way out and forward along the casing to see the reassuring bulk of *Stubborn* ahead. A lookout had spotted the line break and the submarine had already hove to. A rubber dinghy was launched with *X-7*'s operational diver, Bob Aitken, on board. Clutching a line attached to the replacement tow, he let the wind and waves carry him the seventy feet to *X-7* where Philip was clinging to the upper casing. He hurled the line and Philip miraculously caught it and made it fast. Now Aitken had somehow to row back, against the run of the seas, to *Stubborn*. There were no willing hands to pull him back to the mother ship as the line connecting him to the submarine had snapped. He could see only one solution. He reached down and grabbed the waterlogged manila tow rope he had just delivered and, hand over hand, hauled himself back to the ship.

Earlier in the day, at 4:00 a.m., *X-8* had also come adrift. In this case, though, it took *Sea Nymph*, the towing submarine, two hours to notice. The captain, Lieutenant John Oakley, ordered the ship around in the hope that his charge had surfaced and proceeded on the same heading. By noon there was still no sign of *X-8*, and in the high wind and rough seas the chances of sighting her were small. The signs were ominous. Then, by an extraordinary stroke of luck, *X-8* was spotted. It was *Stubborn* who encountered her, not once but twice. On the first occasion the submarine mistook her for a U-boat and dived. The second sighting occurred as she came into view just as *Stubborn* was passing the replacement tow to *X-7*. This time there was no mistake and *Stubborn*'s captain, Lieutenant Arthur Duff, yelled through a megaphone to Jack Smart, the passage crew commander, to proceed northward with him on a course of 046 degrees until daybreak, by which time he would have alerted *Sea Nymph* and arranged a rendezvous. The wind whipped his words away. Smart misheard and understood he was to steer 146 degrees. The compass is divided into 360 degrees with 0 degrees as north, 90 degrees east, 180 degrees south and 270 degrees west. The mistaken course Smart now steered took him further and further away from his savior.

When dawn broke at 3:00 a.m. on Thursday, September 16, Duff scanned the surrounding water in vain. Soon after, *Sea Nymph* appeared. Duff had little information to offer, and all Oakley could do was head southward in the hope of another miraculous encounter. Fourteen hours later it came. At 5:00 p.m., *X-8* was sighted. The crewmembers were crushed by fatigue. There was no question of them carrying on. On board *Sea Nymph*, Digger McFarlane decided that the operational crew would have to take over.

X-9 was also being towed by a hemp line. At 1:20 a.m. on Thursday, September 16, she came up for the obligatory fifteen minutes to ventilate and recharge, and then submerged. There was no communication between her and *Syrtis* when either dived as the telephone line had snapped the day before—manila stretched while the wire did not. A signal for resurfacing had been arranged: three grenades dropped in the water. Shortly after 9:00 a.m. the explosions went off for *X-9* to come up again. When, after fifteen minutes, she still had not appeared, the crew began hauling in the tow. Their alarm mounted as they felt no resistance. Another line had parted. The urgent need now was for *Syrtis* to retrace her course in the hope of seeing her charge on the surface but as the rope was hauled in it snagged around the submarine's port propeller. It fell to Max Shean, as *X-9*'s diver, to try and free it. Shean put on his diving suit, which was not insulated and gave no protection from the bone-numbing cold of the sea. Nor was it fitted with sinking weights. They improvised with lumps of steel from the engine room and he was lowered overboard. Lieutenant Jupp urged him "to be quick [as] if we were surprised by enemy aircraft we would have to dive immediately." He "climbed, with a lifeline attached, onto the after hydroplanes, switched to oxygen and launched myself under the North Atlantic Ocean. It was cold. When my face went under it took my breath away. I was floating. The weights were not only too light but loose as well."

He tried to force himself under. "The water was absolutely clear. In the few moments that I could remain submerged I noted the shafts of sunlight descending into the depths. It made me feel giddy. I tried to see the propellers but as *Syrtis* pitched in the heavy swell, the hydroplanes smacked the surface with an almighty splash which forced me to the surface again."

Shean was proud of his skill and sangfroid, which he had demonstrated over and over again in training, but this was not Loch Striven and he was wearing the wrong kit. His suit was acting like a life jacket, buoying him up, pushing him to the surface with every swell. As he tried again and again to fight his way under, he knew that, unless he succeeded, the submarine would be half crippled, relying on the starboard propeller alone to make progress. He swam clear of the hydroplanes and forced himself under again. The light filtering down lit up the stern and this time he was able to see the propeller clearly. The rope was looped loosely round the screw. He broke the surface and directed the crew as they pulled and pushed at the line until it floated free.

The submarine was at last able to go in search of its lost ward. It swung round and set off with all speed the way it had come. Six hours passed, then a lookout spotted a long oil slick staining the surface. There was no point in searching further. Sub-Lieutenant Edward Kearon, Able Seaman Harry Harte, and Stoker First Class George Hollett were gone.

Shean and the *X-9* operational crew felt a double jolt of sorrow. They had shared the rigors of training together and the pleasures of relaxation. Shean had a common bond with the commander, "Paddy" Kearon, "a cheerful Irishman, short, slightly on the heavy side of average, fair with a broad countenance and a smile to go with it." Kearon's girlfriend was a Wren and based at Dundee where Shean's girlfriend, Mary, was also posted. On his last leave he had done Shean a favour and delivered a letter to her for him. He remembered "Darkie" Harte as a "quiet industrious Londoner," and "Ginger" Hollett as a "ball of fire, always cheerful, always doing something in the boat of his own initiative; a very good submariner." But there was another element to their dismay. The loss of *X-9* meant the end of their hopes of glory. Their part in the enterprise was over.[3] *Syrtis* proceeded north to a point inside the Arctic Circle where it was safe to radio the news of the loss to the Admiralty.

There were more setbacks to come. When Digger McFarlane and the operational crew boarded *X-8* later that Thursday afternoon to relieve the exhausted passage team, they soon discovered major problems.

Water was leaking into the empty ballast tank on the charge on the starboard side, spoiling the balance and creating an alarming list. No amount of trimming helped. McFarlane decided to jettison it, reckoning that they could still carry out their attack with the remaining one. He set the timing device to "safe," which should have meant that the charge sank harmlessly to the ocean floor. They felt the craft rock over to port as the weight dropped away, and adjusted the ballast chambers to compensate. Fifteen minutes later they were knocked off their feet by a massive shock. Somehow, the charge had exploded. McFarlane hurriedly checked the controls. No harm seemed to have been done. They started off again. As the hours passed, the craft began to develop a list again, this time to port. They carried on, trimming as best they could, but it was no good. It seemed that the blast had damaged the copper strips sealing the buoyancy chamber on the other charge, which also began to fill up with water. McFarlane decided that it, too, would have to go. This time he was taking no chances. He set the timer to two hours and sent it to the bottom. Up above, *Sea Nymph* had been told by telephone what was going on. She moved away at nine knots in order to get them both to a safe distance before the Amatex went up.

At the set hour the charge went off with spectacular force. Even at such a distance, the shock wave reverberated through *X-8*'s casing, buckling the seams. Inside, the wiring sparked and crackled as circuits shorted, pipes burst, and the W&D compartment started to fill up with water. The shock was felt on board *Sea Nymph* but when her commander, Lieutenant Oakley, tried calling his charge on the telephone, he heard only the hiss of static. Some hours later the line miraculously came to life again. McFarlane reported that the midget submarine was slowly filling up with water. They struggled on but it was clear the end was approaching. He took her to the surface and opened the hatch. *X-8* was in no condition to continue. Oakley brought his submarine alongside her. He shouted to McFarlane that he was launching a dinghy to take them off. There was one last thing left for the crew to do. "Scuttle her," he ordered. "The show's over."[4]

It was now Saturday, September 18. They had been at sea for a week. Of the six X-Craft that had set out four were left, and they had not yet reached their slipping positions off the Norwegian coast, when the submarines would say goodbye to their charges and they would continue alone. There was still every hope that the remaining craft could carry out a successful attack. The losses, though, meant that the plan would have to be revised. PRU Spitfires had revealed in two overflights on Tuesday, September 14, that *Tirpitz* remained in her usual place, inside her net cages in an anchorage thirty fathoms deep, on the western shore of Kaafjord. It was a snug berth. The fjord was only a thousand yards wide and the shore curved protectively around the battleship. *Scharnhorst* lay at the entrance, in deeper water, behind the Auskarneset headland. The third target, *Lützow*, was in Langefjord, another inlet of Altafjord, nine miles to the north.

On the basis of this information the Admiralty had chosen Target Plan Four from the range of options before them. Under this, *X-5*, *X-6*, and *X-7* would go for *Tirpitz*. *X-9* and *X-10* would attack *Scharnhorst* and *X-8* the *Lützow*. With the losses, the plan now changed. *Tirpitz* remained the great prize and Henty-Creer, Cameron, and Place would concentrate on her. Hudspeth would have to tackle *Scharnhorst* alone and *Lützow* was struck off the list. It meant little to the overall success of the operation. The pocket battleship was the least of the targets and on its own represented little threat.

In Kaafjord the mood of celebration that had pervaded *Tirpitz* since the Spitsbergen raid lingered. The crew was still disposing of some of the loot captured from the Barentsburg stores. The haul included chocolate, butter, and Russian cigarettes. The goods went back and forth, won and lost in the poker schools that assembled all over the ship.

Beer and schnapps flowed at celebrations to mark the many gongs awarded. Four hundred Iron Crosses, Second Class, were distributed to crew members. Only 162 had gone to seamen on the *Scharnhorst*, a disparity that caused some ill feeling among the crew. Neither ship had played much of a part in the attack. What fighting there had been had largely been done by the destroyers *Z29* and *Z31*. Nonetheless, the crew of *Scharnhorst* felt that the *Tirpitz*'s share of decorations was unmerited. In the course of the war, the battle cruiser had seen far more action than the battleship. She had sunk the aircraft carrier HMS *Glorious*, spent two months of 1941 roaming the Atlantic, and pulled off the Channel Dash. *Tirpitz* had sunk nothing and never strayed more than a few days' sail from her safe Nordic havens. Relations between the two units were already cool. *Scharnhorst* sailors did not regard *Tirpitz* as a happy ship. Their views were colored by reports from stokers loaned to the battleship who returned from time to time to drink with their old messmates and complain about Captain Meyer's disciplinarian attitude.

The awards were indeed extravagant. The operation had been virtually risk-free, compared with the dangers facing troops on the Eastern Front. The boost to morale, however, was thought to justify the largesse. The outing had provided a welcome outlet for the sailors' energies. Admiral Kummetz, the northern task force commander, who was flying his flag in *Tirpitz*, was convinced that more such sorties were needed not just to raise spirits but to improve efficiency. "I cannot emphasize how important it is to mount frequent operations of this kind that last for several days," he wrote to naval headquarters. "They are essential to the maintenance of the Battle Group's effectiveness and striking power." He had been disturbed to read in his commander's reports of the Spitsbergen action that during the voyage north "a lot of men became seasick when the height of the waves was no more than two to three meters." He concluded that "a Battle Group that never leaves its base loses its edge. It will never be capable of meeting major challenges."[5]

The desire for more operations clashed with practical realities. All big warships required perpetual attention if they were to remain effective. This was not just a matter of continuous, minor running repairs but regular, exhaustive overhauls. At the same time as he was urging more action, Kummetz recommended that, with winter closing in, it was a good time to send *Tirpitz* for another refit. Long nights and the likely bad weather, he believed, would provide enough protection for her to make the passage safely to a German yard.

As the crew of *Tirpitz* basked in the fading afterglow of their modest adventure, the men sent to destroy them were getting ready to say good-bye to the submarines. On Sunday, September 19, the captain of *Truculent*, Lieutenant Robbie Alexander, held a service in the control room. The submarine was now submerged to avoid detection from German aircraft operating from the Norwegian coast. The crew of *X-6*, Don Cameron, John Lorimer, Eddie Goddard, and Dickie Kendall, by now bristling with ten days' growth of beard, stood with hands clasped and heads lowered and listened to the captain reading from the Book of Common Prayer. He had chosen the Naval Prayer, with its appeal to God to "preserve us from the dangers of the sea and the violence of our enemies," and its heartfelt wish "that we return in safety to enjoy the blessings of the land."

Cameron recorded in his private log how he looked round at his crew and marveled at how confident they seemed. "Is it a pose or do they really feel that way?" he wondered. "If so, I envy them. I have that just-before-the-battle-mother feeling. Wonder how they will bear up under fire. ..." The difference between the exercises in Port Bannatyne and Loch Cairnbawn, where, "if things went wrong, up you popped and came alongside *Bonaventure* for a gin," and the real thing was all too apparent. His thoughts went back to his wife and infant son, waiting for him in Portsmouth. "I can't help thinking what the feelings of my next of kin will be if I make a hash of things," he wrote.[6]

Later, in the dying light of the evening, *X-6*'s passage crew surfaced for the last time. A rubber dinghy carrying Cameron and Goddard set off from *Truculent* through steep waves and icy spray. The captain, Lieutenant "Willie" Wilson, emerged from the hatch and clung to the air induction trunk as the little craft rocked and wallowed. It seemed to Cameron that "in the half light of an Arctic night, Willie [looked] pretty shagged."[7] Wilson made his report to the new captain. The ballast tank of the starboard charge was beginning to let in water and the gland that sheathed the main periscope was leaking slightly. Otherwise, *X-6* was in good shape. There were stilted farewells and Wilson, together with another crewmember, Bill Oxley, scrambled onto the dinghy and were hauled back to the relative luxury of *Truculent*. The voyage had lasted nine days. They were stiff, dirty, and all but wiped out.

Lorimer and Kendall were waiting on the casing. Standing there in the desolation of an Arctic autumn twilight, Lorimer was swept suddenly by doubt. "I lost my nerve," he recalled. "Then the [rubber] dinghy came alongside the stern of *Truculent*, and after Wilson and Oxley climbed out, I thought I heard air escaping from it. In fact I insisted it was leaking, but the seaman lending a hand quite rightly assured me that the noise was the water rising and falling over the stern of *Truculent* and running out of the holes in the casing." Once aboard the dinghy he "felt much better, the seamen wishing me 'good luck' and 'see you in two days time sir.' Then there wasn't time for any more doubts."[8]

With John McGregor, the last member of the passage crew, safely away in the dinghy, they were on their own. Cameron set about trying to deal with the problems caused by the leak in the starboard charge. The craft had a list of 15 degrees. That would make maneuvering it very difficult, especially in the fresher water of Kaafjord, which was sixty miles from the open sea. He decided to throw overboard all surplus supplies, including the prized tins of Florida orange juice, and shift the rest to the port side in an attempt to correct the list. Then he had a proper look around his boat. He was pleasantly surprised at its condition. "Wilson and his crew must have had a field day before handing over," he wrote. "Everything was spic and span. There was a little dampness on the hull, and except for the leak in the top periscope gland, she appeared first rate. The list decreased to 10 degrees when submerged, and one got used to it in time."[9]

By the dawn of Monday, September 20, all four operational crews were on board and ready to move to their respective slipping positions where they would part company with their parent submarines and continue the journey alone. The submarines, meanwhile, would wait offshore to pick up the crews when—and if—they returned. At 11:00 a.m., *Stubborn*, which was towing her charge, *X-7*, spotted a contact mine which had broken loose from its mooring bobbing ominously in the water ahead. They watched as it slipped by, the detonator horns almost brushing the hull. Once past them, though, the mooring wire caught in the rope towing *X-7*. Soon the mine was hooked over the bows of the midget submarine. By now the commander, Godfrey Place, had emerged to see what was going on. He saw, rising and falling in front of him, the spherical steel casing and sinister spikes that, if they struck hard enough, would put an end not only to him and his craft but to *Stubborn* as well. Peter Philip, who had commanded *X-7* on passage, watched from *Stubborn*'s conning tower as Place inched to the bow and put one sea boot tentatively against the mine "a little as if he were shooing off a small animal." He gave it a shove but it was no good. The mooring cable was wrapped firmly round the tow. He bent down and started laboriously to disentangle it, while the men of *Stubborn* looked on in horrified fascination. It took him seven minutes. Then he grasped the prongs and gave a hefty push. It floated harmlessly away, to relieved cheers from the conning tower. "That's the first time I've ever shoved a mine clear by its horns," he called back.

Just before 7:00 p.m., with dusk yet to descend, *Stubborn* hauled in the towrope and *X-7* slipped free. Philip and the others waved goodbye as "she disappeared inshore, creaming along on her engine, bound for the Great Adventure." Elsewhere, as darkness gathered, the other remaining craft said farewell to their big sisters. They were now less than a hundred miles from Kaafjord, where *Tirpitz* lay at anchor, ignorant of the attempt being made on her life.

CHAPTER 15

A "BLOODY
GREAT BANG"

The little submarines were on their own now, but Don Cameron, aboard *X-6*, felt a curious sense of relief at the parting of the ways. "Free at last and left to my own resources," he wrote in his private log. "Monarch of all I survey, a little tin god in a little tin fish." They had agreed on "patrol routine" while surfaced, with two men on watch for two hours at a time while the other two tried to sleep. Cameron stayed on top for the first watch, crouched in the open hatch above the wet and dry compartment, chilled by the evening air and soaked by the freezing spray, occasionally touching "Bungay," his doggy talisman, for reassurance and watching the water ahead. He felt "very much alone" but also "quite excited ... at the prospect before us, and only hope that everything will be OK."

The first obstacle was the minefields laid off Sørøy Island, which guarded the entrance to Stjern Sound, leading to the inner fjords in which the German fleet lay. The dangers were relatively slight. Mines were designed to blow up big ships and were anchored well below the surface. It was estimated that the X-Craft's shallow hull would mean they would skate over the top without disturbing them.

So it turned out. Shortly after 9:00 p.m. they were clear of the mines. Cameron watched a "wonderful display of Northern Lights" which pulsed mysteriously in the heavens at this time of the year. The night passed quietly. X-6 was listing to 10 degrees now as the starboard charge slowly filled with water but she handled reasonably well. They traveled submerged most of the time, and at 1:00 p.m. passed into Altafjord. They were now only about fifteen miles from Kaafjord and *Tirpitz*. It had been agreed that the four craft would rendezvous in the waters between the small islands of Tømmelholm and Brattholm, five miles north of Auskarneset, the headland that stuck out into the entrance to Kaafjord. At 6:30 p.m., Cameron brought X-6 to the surface. He felt an air of "great tension in the craft" as he opened the hatch and crawled out onto the casing to have a look. It was a "beautiful evening, atmosphere clear and everything still." He could see the lights of Alta and the German logistics base at Bossekop glimmering on the edge of the water to the south. He decided to find a quiet bay on Brattholm where they could ventilate and recharge in peace. They hove to twenty yards from the shore when light blazed from among the trees and voices drifted over from an unseen house. Cameron decided they were unlikely to have been spotted and stayed put. Then, a small vessel with the sleek lines of a torpedo boat appeared, heading in their direction. Dickie Kendall was looking forward to the eggs, cocoa, cheese, and sardines that John Lorimer was busy preparing when the hatch crashed down and Cameron reappeared shouting for them to cut engines and dive. Kendall remembered later how they could hear the sound of the engines getting nearer, "straight towards us. Twenty feet. Nearly on us—had they seen us? Thud, thud, thud of the twin propellers—40 feet. We waited for the crushing effect of depth-charges. None came, and gradually the noise died away." Cameron took her up again. Dinner lay spread over the control room floor.

They stayed on the surface for the rest of the night undisturbed. Cameron sat on the casing and brooded about what lay ahead. To the south, searchlights illuminated the boom that lay across the entrance to Kaafjord. Thanks to the efforts of the Norwegian resistance and the RAF's photographic reconnaissance from Russia they knew that it was not as formidable as it seemed. The constant traffic of boats ferrying supplies from the logistical base at Bossekop to the ships in the anchorage meant it was too much trouble to keep opening and closing it so a gap was always left at the southern end. Cameron noticed the headlights of a car bouncing off the hillside as it made its way along the shore road and amused himself with the thought that it might be carrying Admiral Kummetz himself. The moon was rising above the mountains and "everything was brushed with silver." He wondered if his wife Eve would be looking up at it from her home overlooking the Solent and if his infant son Iain was behaving himself. He felt "very homesick indeed." The "elation of sitting in the middle of [the] enemy fleet's anchorage vied with [the] feeling of a small boy very much alone and wanting someone to talk to." He cheered himself up with "visions of my leave and the thought of having waited two years for this…."[1]

At midnight Lorimer took over and Cameron went below. He busied himself setting the timings on the side charges. He had decided on a six-hour delay. This would give him plenty of time to escape through the boom where he could hide in the broad waters of Altafjord when the inevitable hunt began, before heading to the open sea and the waiting submarines. He started with the starboard charge. Despite being flooded, the clock worked perfectly, and he switched it to a six-hour setting. When he tried to do the same on the port charge, though, the fuses blew. The timer was now jammed at a mere two hours, leaving scant time to escape the tight confines of Kaafjord before the explosive went up. In addition, a hole had appeared in the number one ballast tank in the bows which meant that, unless fully submerged, they left a trail of bubbles on the surface which might be noticed by an alert seaman on board one of the many boats lying in Kaafjord.

There was yet another cause for concern. There was no sign of the other X-Craft in the surrounding waters. The surviving crews had not been told that *X-9* had sunk without trace and that *X-8* had been scuttled. Admiral Barry had decided to withhold the information about these mishaps on the grounds that it "might have had a slightly dampening effect."[2] Cameron had no means of communicating with the other craft to find out where they had gone. A rendezvous was not essential for the attack to go ahead but it was certainly desirable. It would mean they could coordinate their movements to all arrive in the target area at the same time. If they could get in together undetected, they would retain the great advantage of surprise and the combined effect of their charges would maximize the damage to the target.

There were many imponderables that Cameron had to weigh as the night wore on. He did his thinking on the casing as the night sky lightened. He reckoned that if he did attack on his own "and was successful, only one of my charges might explode but the gaff would be blown and the enemy on the lookout for [the others]. If I waited for a day, the others could make their attacks and I could limp around and perhaps do a little damage." On the other hand, there was no indication that they had made it as far as he had and they might be in a worse state than he was. To add to his troubles, the periscope was leaking and misting up constantly. Soon it might be completely unserviceable, and an attack would be out of the question. He decided that there was really only one course of action. *X-6* would have to press on alone.

In fact, Cameron did have company that night. Godfrey Place and *X-7* were lying on the bottom of Altafjord, just on the other side of Brattholm. After slipping from *Stubborn* they had negotiated the minefield without incident. Off the island of Sørøy, Place had caught a glimpse of Henty-Creer, crouched in the hatch of *X-5*. They had yelled across the waves, wishing each other "good luck and good hunting." Then each was lost to the other in the darkness. It was the last time anyone would see Henty. The voyage into the fjords went smoothly. The main excitement was the sight of a large ship lying off Arøya Island at the north of Altafjord. It looked like *Scharnhorst*. If that was the case, she would not be where she was supposed to be, lying in her usual anchorage in the lee of Auskarneset, when *X-10* launched her attack.

At that moment, though, *X-10* was in no position to menace anyone. Ken Hudspeth and his crew had got into difficulties almost immediately after casting off from *Sceptre*. The passage crew reported problems with the periscope when they handed over on the evening of Sunday, September 20. By early on Monday the electric motor that hoisted the heavy mechanism up and down had failed and it was stuck fast. The electrically powered gyrocompass, which kept true north no matter how the craft was configured and by which the crew steered when submerged, was wandering. At this point it would have been reasonable to decide that *X-10* was in no condition to continue. There was nothing in Hudspeth's background or prewar career to suggest an unusually developed determination to get to grips with the mother country's enemies. He was the son of a technical school principal and when the war broke out was headmaster of a small school in the idyllic far south of Tasmania.

Instead of turning back, he decided to find a quiet anchorage off the island of Stjernøy where they could carry out running repairs. They headed for the inlet of Smalfjord on the north coast. *X-10* arrived at 7:00 a.m. and sank to the sandy bottom at the head of the fjord. They spent all day dismantling the periscope motor, then drying, greasing, and reassembling it. They did the same with the gyrocompass. When they tried them out they were still in less than proper working order. Hudspeth nonetheless gave the order to carry on and just before midnight they entered the northern end of Altafjord.

Ninety minutes later they were forced to dive when they found themselves on a course with an oncoming enemy ship. They leveled out at fifty feet and tried to continue steering by the gyrocompass. Once more, it started to wander wildly. There was no way of knowing which direction they were traveling in and nothing to do but to go up again. As they neared the surface, Hudspeth tried to raise the periscope. There was a burst of sparks and the smell of burned rubber filled the control area. The hoisting motor had gone again.

Hudspeth was forced to bring the craft up to vent the smoke. He climbed out onto the casing and looked around. Dawn was now breaking. Kaafjord was only about five miles away. Close by he could see the island of Tømmelholm. He steered the craft toward it then dived to the bottom, nearly two hundred feet down, just to the southeast of the island. They began the repair work all over again. The attack was due to start in a couple of hours. Judging by the time the job had taken before, it seemed impossible they would be there at the start. Cut off from any knowledge of the whereabouts or state of the others, unaware that *Scharnhorst* was no longer there for them to attack, Hudspeth still believed his duty lay in carrying on.

Cameron and Place were by now both entering the final stage of their missions. Admiral Barry's orders had forbidden an attack before 1:00 a.m. to allow all craft time to get into position.[3] Shortly after the deadline passed, Place gave the order to blow the tanks and she rose from her resting place on the bottom off Brattholm and steered southwest towards Kaafjord's narrow mouth. As they approached the boom, he brought her up to periscope depth and took a look around. The Auskarneset headland laid dead ahead, and stretching across the water below it was the boom. As predicted, and as hoped for, it lay partially open at the southern end. Half submerged, with a complete absence of drama, *X-7* slipped through the gap and into the narrow sleeve of water that held their target.

The relief of the entry was soon dissipated by the sight of a mine-sweeper coming towards them, heading for the gate in the boom. Place gave the order to dive and they sank rapidly to a depth of seventy-five feet. They moved slowly ahead. After a few minutes they stopped. Something was blocking their way. It was too soft to be a rock. Place decided they had hit an anti-torpedo net. His guess was correct. It was not one of the *Tirpitz*'s defenses but was surrounding the empty berth where *Lützow* had until recently been moored. There they remained stuck for what Place later called "a rather exasperating hour," nosing forward and reversing, maneuvering in every direction the steering allowed. Then, when they were starting to despair, they were suddenly free. The pulling and pushing had shaken the gyrocompass off the gimbals that held it level. To continue the attack they needed to see their way. Place took the craft cautiously to the surface. Then, with only the periscope showing, they steered towards the corner of the fjord where *Tirpitz* lay, protected by a layer of anti-torpedo nets.[4]

Cameron and the crew of *X-6* set off from their resting position a little after *X-7*, at 1:30 a.m. The list caused by the flooded starboard charge had got worse and when Cameron tested the periscope he found it was virtually useless. There was a "green film over the eyepiece except for a tiny pinhole in the top left hand corner."

By 4:45 a.m. they were approaching the boom. A trawler was just ahead of them, traveling in the same direction. Cameron took his chances and brought *X-6* to the surface, fired up the diesel and tucked in behind it, trusting that their low silhouette would be lost in the white water churned up by the ship's propellers. There were men on deck, making a lot of noise. They seemed to be sailors, returning from a night out. If so, they were in no state to notice the dark shape in their wake.

As the trawler chugged away, Cameron looked around at the flat waters of Kaafjord, dotted with nearly twenty vessels including the 23,000-ton supply ship *Nordmark*, and studded with buoys holding up torpedo nets. Nowhere was there any sign of alarm. In the near distance, only a couple of miles away, the bulk of the *Tirpitz* stood out in the clear morning light. They sank to periscope depth and resumed groping their way forward.

Aboard *Tirpitz*, another working day had begun with its usual routines. At 5:00 a.m. hands were called to their posts. On shore the anti-aircraft batteries came to full readiness. A launch made its way to the anti-torpedo net, at a point nearest the port bow of the battleship which jutted toward the entrance to Kaafjord. The men on board unhooked the net from its buoys and peeled it back, effectively opening a door that would allow small craft to pass in and out. At the same time, the hydrophones that had been listening for suspicious sounds in the surrounding waters were switched off. Both these measures, as Admiral Kummetz was keen to point out in his subsequent report, were perfectly defensible. Leaving an entrance in the net barrier by day was "in keeping with the existing situation of constant boat traffic," he wrote. The hydrophone operators would have "lost their alertness" if kept at their posts twenty-four hours a day and there were anyway not enough trained men for non-stop surveillance. Kummetz conceded that the British had demonstrated their ability to launch unorthodox seaborne attacks in 1942 with the unsuccessful attack by "torpedo riders" at Faettenfjord. But the idea that they could launch another one at such long range and succeed in penetrating the successive lines of defenses was assumed, he said, to be "out of the question."[5] His main concern continued to be attack from the air, and he had faith in the effectiveness of the anti-aircraft defenses.

That morning Kummetz rose, dressed in breeches and riding boots, and ate breakfast. He was intending to start his day as he did most mornings with a ride along the shore, and there was nothing to suggest he should alter his routine. He would be going home soon. His request for leave had been granted, and he would spend the winter with his family in Berlin, exchanging the gloom of an Arctic winter for the dangers of the increasingly battered capital. Although the news had not yet been made public, most of his Battle Group would also be departing. The order had already been given for *Lützow* to sail to the Baltic for an overhaul. It was expected that *Tirpitz* would follow in November, leaving *Scharnhorst* as the sole big ship on active service in the far north.

As he set off for his morning hack, *X-6* and *X-7* were slowly closing on his ship. On *X-6* the periscope was playing up again. Cameron dived the craft and started to clean the delinquent part. The others watched with a "look of dejection." He shared their dread that the great enterprise was about to collapse. "We had waited and trained for two years for this show and at the last moment, faulty workmanship or bad joss was doing its best to deprive us of it all." He felt a "bloody-minded" determination not to be thwarted. He replaced the eyepiece, brought *X-6* toward the surface and tried to raise the periscope again. There was a shower of sparks, a puff of smoke, and a stink of burning rubber. Just as in *X-10*, the hoisting motor had burned out. The constant breakdowns were, as John Lorimer said later, hardly surprising. After all the practice trials and the long voyage from Scotland, *X-6* was just "knackered." Edmund Goddard had another go at mending it. After more stripping and reassembling he and Cameron succeeded in restoring the viewfinder to a condition when it was just possible to make out vague shapes in the surrounding water. They edged toward the northern bank of the fjord.

There was only one obstacle now separating them from their target—the anti-torpedo barrier. The nets were curtains of circular steel grommets, a hand's width in diameter. They were impossible to cut through but the intelligence briefings had said there would be no need. Torpedoes ran at shallow depths. The anchorage in which *Tirpitz* lay was thirty fathoms—180 feet. It was calculated that the nets would hang down no more than fifty feet, leaving ample room for the midget submarines to pass beneath them.

Shortly before 7:00 a.m., *X-6* was creeping along at two knots, just below periscope depth. Through the small glass scuttles set in the hull Cameron could make out the bank rising on his starboard side "and a few fish." There was a black shape overhead, "shaped like a pontoon with wires hanging from it." They nosed forward gingerly and gently rose to the surface. The periscope was hopelessly fogged but Cameron could just discern some "dark blobs" which he took to be the floats holding up the anti-torpedo net. There seemed to be a gap. He "pushed towards a space in this chain" and suddenly they were in open water. *X-6* had found the gate in the net through which a small picket boat had just passed. To his port side, less than two hundred yards away, lay the bow of the *Tirpitz.*

Cameron kept on his course, moving parallel to the battleship's flank. His intention was to veer sharply to the left, to bring himself under the stern, then slide along the keel to drop his first charge, as instructed, under the after big gun turrets—Caesar and Dora—and then move on to Anton and Bruno. Placed there, the explosions would break the battleship's back, an injury from which it could never recover. As *X-6* started to turn, there was a sickening collision that sent all four of them reeling. They had struck an uncharted rock. The impact pushed them upwards and the bow broke the glassy surface of the fjord in a swirl of foam and bubbles. Cameron threw *X-6* into reverse and she slid below again into deeper water. It was 7:07 a.m.

There were twenty-four men posted as lookouts on the deck of *Tirpitz* and several saw the commotion in the water. The shape they glimpsed, twenty yards from the shore, was black and sleek. Among the witnesses was a flak gunner who shouted a warning to his battery commander, Leutnant zur See Hein Hellendoorn. Hellendoorn swept his binoculars to the spot his gunner pointed out. There was nothing there now. Hellendoorn was skeptical. It seemed impossible that a submarine could have penetrated this deep into their defenses. Elsewhere others who had seen the apparition were being mocked for mistaking a large fish for a U-boat.

But then, five minutes later, the shape appeared again. This time it was only sixty or so yards from the ship and, as the ship's diary noted, it was clearly recognizable as a "briefly surfaced mini submarine." The ship now erupted in a flurry of excited energy. The siren sounded five times, the signal for all the watertight bulkheads to be closed. The ship's first officer, Kapitän Wolf Junge, hurried down from the bridge to the commander's cabin where Kapitän Meyer had just finished breakfast, and told him that a small U-boat had been sighted inside the anti-torpedo net. Meyer was skeptical but hurried out on deck.

By now everyone on board was blazing into the water with rifles and some were throwing grenades at the black shape in the water. The ship's guns were useless. The submarine was too close to the hull for them to be brought to bear. Meyer ordered an Arado plane off to search for other submarines and the door in the nets was closed. At the same time he called for steam so that they could escape the anchorage. No tugs were available and *Tirpitz* would have to make her own way out.[6]

Oberleutnant zur See Herbert Leine, who had been on his way to relieve the officer of the watch when the drama erupted, rounded up some men and set off in a launch from the stern of the ship, armed with rifles, and steered for *X-6*, which was now only fifty yards from the side and heading for the bow. The boarding party peppered the hull with rifle fire and lobbed grenades, but to little effect. The craft slid below the surface again to reappear thirty yards from the stern. As the launch sped toward it, they saw a hatch on the casing clang open. One by one, four men emerged, raising their arms in surrender.

Leine ordered his men to hold their fire and warily they bore down on X-6. One of the sailors jumped across and made fast a towline. The casing was awash with water. Without saying a word to their captors, Cameron, Lorimer, Kendall, and Goddard stepped into the launch. Leine then attempted to tow the craft away from the battleship. The ship's diary recorded that they had only gone twenty meters when it became apparent that "since the valves had been opened the submarine could not be captured." It then "sank having been towed some fifty meters."[7]

Cameron and the crew sat huddled in the launch, recovering from the most frantic ten minutes of their lives. After hitting the rock and shooting to the surface, they had dived again to seventy feet. The gyrocompass was swinging wildly and Cameron had to guess which course would take him under the target. They could see nothing out of the scuttles. He tried a different tack, only to get fouled in some wires hanging down from the ship's port side.[8] They pushed forward and pulled back, blowing water from the ballast tanks, but to no avail. Then, suddenly, they were free and X-6 rose uncontrollably to where the crew of Tirpitz was now waiting with guns trained. They broke the water into a blizzard of small-arms fire and hurled grenades. "They seemed to think they were under attack from a fleet of midget submarines," said John Lorimer. "They were shooting at anything that moved, even seagulls."[9] Cameron remembered the bullets bouncing off harmlessly but making "a helluva noise, like a lone dockyard riveter." As they were shielded by the ship's overhanging bulk, most of the grenades "plopped … into the water and exploded well out of effective range."[10]

They dived once more. This was their last chance to drop their charges. X-6 was now pointing away from the ship so Cameron called for reverse and a minute later the craft was scraping and bumping under the hull. They had arrived at the front of the ship, abreast of Bruno, the second of the two forward big gun turrets. It was as good as they could have hoped for. Cameron gave the order to let go both the charges. Kendall took the port side release wheel and Lorimer the starboard and they started to turn. A moment later the charges dropped away and slithered down the hull to settle nearly 100 feet below, close to the port bow. Freed of their weight, the craft rose sharply. There was no chance of escape now. X-6 was blind and leaking. The boom would be closed and every ship in Kaafjord would be looking for them. Depth charges would soon be plunging around them and the end would come in an explosion of buckling seams and a rush of freezing water. It was time to surrender. They set about smashing instruments and burning their maps and charts. Then they pumped in air and X-6 surfaced for the last time. Just before they opened the hatch Cameron gave the order to open all the valves.

At about the time that X-6 had first been spotted, X-7 reached the anti-torpedo net, a few hundred yards in front of the ship's bow. Place timed the charges to go up in one hour—a very short setting if they were to get away—and descended to seventy-five feet, expecting to clear the bottom of the barrier. The net, though, was still there. He dived deeper, to ninety feet, but the result was the same. He reversed and moved forward, then, after what he later described as "a little wriggling," they were free again and in the clear—whether he had found the boat gate or slipped through an unforeseen gap he was never able to decide. "We came right up to the surface, not more than thirty yards from *Tirpitz* with no more nets ahead of us," he said. "We went straight for her. We collided with her just below the surface and slid gently underneath." They let go the first starboard charge on the port side of the fore end of the ship near where Cameron's mines dropped earlier. Then they slid another 150 to 200 feet along the bottom and dropped the second charge amidships. As they did, they heard the sound of muffled explosions booming through the water—the sound of the grenades being hurled from the deck at X-6. The crew's satisfaction at having dropped their explosives was tempered by the realization of what would happen when they went off. The seconds were hurrying past. If they were still there when the charges blew, the blasts were likely to kill them all. But as they tried to escape they "ran into one net, got out of it and were at once in another."

Their exertions were draining their oxygen supply. Eventually, in desperation, Place came up as near to the surface as he dared and tried a new technique. Putting the motor full ahead, he took a run at the line of floats from which the net was suspended and slid up and over. They had emerged on the battleship's starboard bow. By now the decks of *Tirpitz* were crowded with watching sailors and X-7 was hit by a squall of gunfire that forced her under again. She dived to 120 feet. Without the compass, they had no clue as to which way to head to get away. Despite the certainty of being shot at, they would have to ascend to periscope depth. Place recalled later that, when they reached sixty feet, "it was extremely discouraging … to run into yet another net." They were still wrestling with it when, at 8:12 a.m., the explosion came. Instead of crushing them, the blast shook them free from the net. They surfaced briefly, and Place was dismayed to see that *Tirpitz* was still afloat. They dived again to 120 feet and wondered what to do next. They had suffered some damage from the blast but the hull was intact, and the engine seemed to be unharmed. Place announced they would try to make a run for it on the surface. It was, as everyone knew, a forlorn hope.

They broke the surface to *Tirpitz*'s starboard, a hundred meters from the net and were immediately engaged by machine guns and flak. Unlike the rifle bullets that had ricocheted harmlessly off X-6, the heavier rounds drove through X-7's hull. She dived but as they went down, water gushed in through the holes and she was forced to the surface, to meet another wave of fire. Again they dived but Place had accepted the inevitable. Whoever went through the hatch first to signal their surrender was placing himself in mortal danger. It was the captain's job. Place pushed open the cover and scrambled out. In one hand he waved a white submariner's sweater. The gunners ignored it. Rounds clanged and whined off the casing. The boat was still moving forward. It was heading for a large raft, used as a platform for target practice. The bow slid underneath and Place leapt onto it. Behind him, water sluiced into the hatch of *X-7* and she began to sink. The firing died away. Place was safe but, beneath the platform, his boat was going down for the last time.

Cameron and his crew were taken aboard *Tirpitz* and marched to an upper deck where the ship's English-speaking intelligence officer, Rolf Woytschekowski-Emden, began to interrogate them. Cameron found the atmosphere "rather frigid." Presumably because of the great distances involved, his questioner "would not believe we were British and maintained we were either Russian or Norwegian saboteurs." The ship's diary noted that "from the demeanor of the prisoners on board it is to be assumed that the submarine has completed its mission." That was, they guessed, to lay explosive charges under or at least near the ship.

The crew was now working frantically to shift the ship away from where the first X-Craft had been seen—and where the charges had presumably been dropped. In the absence of power or tugs, they used the anchor cables to shift her, slackening the port line and hauling in the starboard hawser to winch her sixty yards further away from the shore.

It was too late. At 8:12 a.m. the diary recorded "two heavy detonations." The entire 50,000-ton weight of the *Tirpitz*, ship, men and stores, "bounced vertically and sharply." The blasts were almost simultaneous. The charges had been designed so that an explosion by one would detonate any others in the vicinity. The shock waves surfed through bulkheads and down passageways, ripping up decking and slamming men into hard metal. On deck, a twenty-two-year-old seaman, Fritz Adler, was flipped into the air, landing on his head on a mound of anchor chain to be killed instantly. Others suffered broken limbs and cracked skulls. The real damage, though, was to the ship. The forward charges split the port side plating but it was *X-7*'s charge amidships that did the greatest harm, tearing a gash more than twenty feet long, swamping the port outer compartments and partially flooding engine rooms. Everywhere electrical synapses crackled and shorted and all the lights went out.

Kendall had been held on the quarterdeck with Goddard when the others were taken below. He later recalled how his "knees buckled as the explosion hurled the ship out of the water." All around there was "complete chaos. Seamen ran in all directions … injured men were being brought up on deck. Machine gunners imagined they saw submarines everywhere … it was impossible to take it all in. All around was confusion … I suddenly felt tired to death, yet with a wonderful feeling of relief."[11] John Lorimer was in the captain's cabin being interrogated in pidgin English by Kapitän Meyer when he felt a "bloody great bang. He went flying one side of the desk and I went flying the other."[12]

Until now his captors had been proper and correct. With the blast, however, the mood darkened. The interview came to an abrupt halt. Lorimer's guards dragged him back up to the others on the quarterdeck where "all hell was reigning. Sailors were rushing about. There was a lot of fist shaking and all the guns seemed to be firing."[13] Cameron also rejoined them, and they were lined up against a bulkhead, facing a squad of men carrying machine guns. Lorimer was sure this was the end. "They were very angry," he said. He was convinced that "we were lined up to be shot." The officer in charge, pistol menacingly in hand, kept demanding to know how many other submarines were out in the fjord. Then, the angry voices quieted. Admiral Kummetz had arrived. He heard the explosions from the shore while on his early morning ride and hurried back to his flagship. Still wearing his jodhpurs and boots, he swept past the four men, but paused to talk to the officer in charge. It seemed to Lorimer that he was saying "you can't shoot these men, they're prisoners."

Tempers calmed and, as the admiral hurried off to confer with Meyer, Lorimer felt they were safe.[14]

The dramas of the morning were not over. At 8:43 a.m. a third submarine was spotted, beyond the torpedo net, 600 meters away on the far side of the fjord. Fifty-six hours after she was last sighted, in the minefield at the start of the voyage, X-5 had reappeared. The guns opened up again. The ship's log noted laconically that the intruder was "hit in several places. Probably sinking."[15] John Lorimer was standing under guard on the quarterdeck when its periscope showed above the "millpond" calm of the fjord. He saw it take a "direct hit with a 4-inch shell." He was in no doubt that he had witnessed "the end of Henty-Creer."[16] It was the end, too, of Sub-Lieutenants Tom Nelson and Alastair Malcolm and Ralph Mortiboys, the ERA who had missed the eve-of-operation party at Loch Cairnbawn to write a last letter to his mother. His premonition had proved correct.[17]

As the first rush of alarm on board subsided, and the crew busied themselves with emergency repairs, the Germans broke off the interrogation. Woytschekowski-Emden had the four taken to a mess deck where they were given coffee and schnapps. They were provided with hammocks and told they were free to sleep. Before they settled down to their first proper rest in seventy-two hours, Place arrived, clad in the long johns and sea boots he had been wearing when he clambered onto the target platform.

A little later they were joined by another of their comrades. Lieutenant Bob Aitken, X-7's number three, had been picked up in the fjord at 11:25 a.m. He was alone. He was too exhausted to speak at first but later, when they had woken from their deep sleep, he told the story of what happened after the craft disappeared under the waters of the fjord.

The ballast tanks had been holed by gunfire and she immediately sank 120 feet to the bottom. Lieutenant Bill Whittam, the second in command, took charge. There was no question of making another

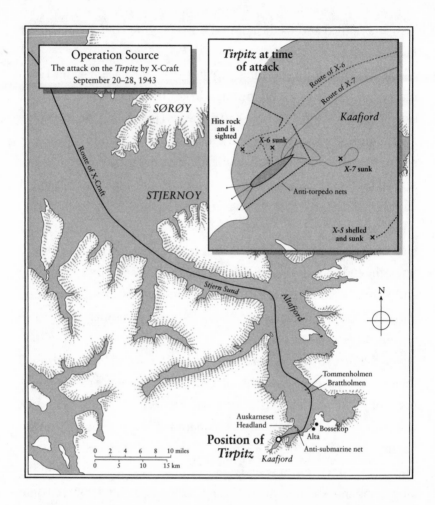

attempt to surface. The craft was finished. Whittam and the ERA, Willie Whitley, started to put on their Davis escape kit. Aitken, the only trained diver, climbed into his rubber tunic and waist-high boots. He strapped on his breathing apparatus. It contained a large and a small oxygen cylinder connected by a rubber pipe to the facemask. It also carried two "oxylets" to inflate a buoyancy bag incorporated in the DSEA and turn it into a life jacket in an emergency. They could provide a few extra lungfuls of oxygen. He made sure that the others had their escape kits on correctly. Then they tried to work out how they were going to get out.

The obvious exit was by the W&D compartment, but it was too late for that now. It took at least half an hour for the chamber to fill up with water. It seemed to Aitken that it was better to flood the entire craft and leave via both the W&D and control room hatches. Whittam agreed and they opened the seacocks. While they waited they rehearsed the drill. It was immediately clear that it wouldn't work. In the tiny space it was impossible for the three men, two kitted out in their DSEA gear and one swaddled in a diving suit, to get past each other. Whittam ruled that as Aitken was nearest the W&D chamber he should exit first, waiting outside to help the next man through.

The water gushing in was agonizingly cold, colder than anything they had experienced in Scotland. As it crept up their legs, Whittam and Whitley climbed onto seats, bending double under the low upper casing. The process was desperately slow. After thirty minutes the water reached an electrical circuit. The fuse wires spluttered in a spurt of flame and gas began to leak from the batteries. It was time to switch on their breathing apparatus. They stood now in total darkness, listening to the groaning of stressed metal and the sound of their own breathing. They fought to suppress the ghastly scenarios bubbling in their imaginations, willing themselves to stay calm.

Minute by minute the water crept up their bodies until it reached chest level. "Its icy grip was like a vice," remembered Aitken. *X-7* had filled with enough water for him to think it worth trying to raise the W&D hatch, but "the pressure wasn't balanced yet. I had to go on waiting." His main oxygen bottle was nearly empty. He groped his way back into the control room to where he had last seen Whitley, propped against the periscope, to ask for a hand with the lid. He reached out to touch him but there was nobody there. Then his foot touched something solid. Whitley was on the floor. He "leant over and put my hand on his face, his chest, his oxygen bottle. The breathing bag was empty, flat, completely flat. The two emergency oxylets were empty too. Poor old

Whitley couldn't be still alive, and even if he was, I couldn't hope to lift him.… He moved forward, groping vainly in the freezing water for Bill Whittam. He was down to his last few lungfuls of oxygen. He remembered "scrambling back into the escape compartment for one more go at the hatch. Then things went black and I must have fainted." When he came to he was speeding upward towards the sunlit canopy of the surface where a launch from *Tirpitz* hauled him aboard.[18]

The next day they were transferred to Tromsø hospital before being sent on to Germany for further interrogation. It was four months before Eve Cameron heard the news that her husband was alive and a prisoner of war. She was pushing Iain in his pram along the seafront near her home overlooking the Hamble when she saw "the telegram man, on a bicycle go past. I thought, I bet that's for me." She did not draw the obvious conclusion. "I knew that if anyone would come through it, it would be him," she said.[19] Donald's lucky charm "Bungay" had worked. The Germans found it when they searched him. It was listed along with his fountain pen, pencil and lighter as a "pipe tamper, wooden, mastiff."[20]

The Admiralty had to wait several days before learning of the outcome of the raid. A planned overflight on the day of the operation failed, and the PRU reconnaissance on September 23 showed *Tirpitz* in her usual place but with no obvious sign of damage. The following day, a radio news bulletin from Berlin announced that an attack by British submarines "of the smallest type" had taken place but failed. This was the first indication that the attack had in fact taken place.

No photographic reconnaissance was possible between September 24 and 26. On the evening of September 28, though, pictures were taken that showed a two-mile-wide oil slick issuing from the ship. Then, on September 30, there was came cheering news. *X-10* had spent the day of the attack lying on the bottom near Tømmelholm, four and a half miles from the entrance to Kaafjord, while repairs to the periscope persisted. By the time darkness fell, they were still without a working periscope or compass. That only left them the option of a suicidal approach on the surface. Ken Hudspeth reluctantly abandoned the attack. After many hazards and hardships they made their rendezvous with their mother submarine, *Stubborn*, on September 30. They were able to pass on to the Admiralty the very welcome information that at the time the attack was scheduled, the thump of big explosions had reached their anchorage.

When Admiral Barry's first dispatch on the operation appeared on November 8, he was still only able to say of the results achieved by the X-Craft that "it may well be that the damage done was considerable." Barry's guess was correct. Beneath the serene exterior she presented to the overflying PRU cameras, *Tirpitz* was a mess. The first reports calculated that 800 cubic meters of water had swamped the lower decks, contaminating fuel and freshwater tanks. All but one of the eight motors of the generators providing the ship's electricity was knocked out. Without electricity the boilers could not be fired and the ship was, for the time being, crippled. One of the after gun turrets, housing two of the ship's main 15-inch guns, had been lifted out of its bearings by the blast and was now inoperable. With no electricity, the fire control systems and electrical range finders were useless. By the end of November the navy headquarters in Kiel was predicting that the battleship would be "out of use for several months" to come.

What Barry was in no doubt about was the extraordinary bravery and determination shown by his men. "It is clear," his dispatch concluded, "that courage and enterprise of the very highest order in the close presence of the enemy were shown by these very gallant gentlemen, whose daring attack will go down as one of the most courageous acts of all time."

The Germans, too, could not hide their admiration. In the words of the official report on the attack, their British enemy had once again shown himself "a master of cunning and devious weaponry which he is not afraid to deploy in situations where the stakes are of the highest order if he thinks the goal is worth it."[21] Hitler was sufficiently impressed to approve the construction of fifty midget submarines as well as "one-man torpedoes" to counter an invasion of Northern Europe.[22]

Churchill had followed eagerly the progress of Operation Source and emissaries from the Admiralty provided verbal updates. As the picture of the operation filled out, he was anxious to broadcast the tidings of a venture that exemplified the virtues of daring, courage, and ingenuity that he held dear. On the morning of Tuesday, October 12, readers of *The Times* learned of a "very gallant enterprise" involving "hazards of the first order."

Men like Ginger Coles, who had endured all the hardship and dangers of the long preparations, received the news with mixed feelings. For him, the raid had been only a partial success. "I honestly thought that *Tirpitz* would have been blown sky high and if everything had gone according to plan she would have been," he reflected. That the operation had not played out perfectly was hardly unexpected. It was a military cliché that no plan survived contact with reality. The X-Craft crews, though, were cheated of a more complete victory by avoidable mistakes. Equipped with nylon towropes, perhaps all six would have made it into Kaafjord. The chances of success would surely have been further improved if they had taken the shorter passage from a base in the Shetland Islands rather then setting out from the mainland of Scotland.

In Churchill's eyes, though, a partial success was better than none. Operation Source had hurt *Tirpitz* more grievously than had any previous attempt against her. This was, he wrote, "an agreeable new fact" in his calculations as to how best to pursue the war in northern waters.

CHAPTER 16

NORTH CAPE

For Churchill, the crippling of *Tirpitz* had come at a fortunate moment. It offered the chance of—at least temporary—relief from the stream of complaint issuing from Moscow concerning the Arctic convoys. There had been no sailings during the spring and summer of 1943. The middle of the year saw the climax of the Battle of the Atlantic. There was no question of the Royal Navy's warships being diverted to escort duties in northern waters while the outcome hung in the balance. The result was that by the beginning of the autumn only a third of the volume of the previous year's supplies had been delivered to northern Russian ports.[1] This was bad news for Stalin. The tide had turned on the Eastern Front and he needed American and British tanks and aircraft if his armies were to exploit their gains.[2] He was deaf to the Allies' excuses, and Churchill and Roosevelt were subjected to continual badgering from Moscow as to when the convoys would resume. By the end of the summer, Allied air and sea countermeasures had begun to alter the balance in the Atlantic and pressure on the Home Fleet eased. Assets would now be available for convoy duty. The fact that *Tirpitz* was *hors de combat* reduced further the risks of the enterprise. Churchill was eager to resume sailings and had already been pressing the navy to reopen the Murmansk pipeline.

An era was ending at the Admiralty. Dudley Pound was dying, in the same dutiful and uncomplaining way that he had lived. The brain tumor he tried to conceal could no longer be hidden. On August 25, while attending the QUADRANT meeting in Quebec where Churchill, Roosevelt, and their staffs discussed the forthcoming invasion of Europe, he turned down a fishing trip with his fellow chiefs of staff, saying "he did not feel well enough to accompany them."[3] He had in fact suffered a stroke, but carried on to Washington when the conference moved there. On September 7 he visited Churchill in his bed-sitting room in the White House "and said abruptly, 'Prime Minister, I have come to resign. I have had a stroke and my right side is largely paralyzed. I thought it would pass off, but it gets worse every day and I am no longer fit for duty.'"[4] He died the following month, on October 21, Trafalgar Day, to be replaced eventually by Sir Andrew Cunningham, a far more skeptical and combative personality.

In the meantime, the Vice Chief of the Naval Staff, Sir Neville Syfret, filled in for him. On September 25, he received a message from the Prime Minister asserting the duty "if humanly possible" of restarting the Arctic convoys and running one full-sized sailing a month, from November until March. Churchill found the response "not satisfactory." The Admiralty remained doubtful. They were unconvinced that the benefits merited the risk involved, and it was by no means clear that the Battle of the Atlantic was yet won. With the "agreeable new fact" that *Tirpitz* was no longer a menace, the admirals' resistance could not be sustained

for long and on October 1, Churchill sent a long telegram to Stalin telling him "with very great pleasure" that the convoys would resume in
November. He made it clear that while this did not constitute a binding
contract it was "a declaration of our solemn and earnest resolve."

He took the opportunity to try and extract something in return for
the Allies' largesse. Relations between British units in north Russia and
their hosts were fractious. The Soviets seemed to regard their allies as
potential fifth columnists rather than friends. They made endless difficulties about issuing visas. Those who obtained them, and made the
journey to the bleak waters and dreary tundra of the White Sea and Kola
Peninsula, had to endure numerous petty restrictions on their actions
and movements and constant interference from officials.

One incident in particular had raised British hackles. In July and
August 1943, the cargo ship *Dover Hill*, which had been stuck in Russia
since February when the convoys were suspended, was lying in Ekonomiya on the North Dvina River. There was nothing much to do and
the hours hung heavy on the crew. One day, the ship's bo'sun was returning from a run ashore when he met a local who harangued him over
Britain's supposed failure to support its Soviet allies. In the ensuing
scuffle, the bo'sun laid out his critic. Two militiamen then accosted him
and tried to arrest him. The *Dover Hill*'s cook, passing by, came to his
rescue and a brawl ensued. Both Britons were finally subdued. Elsewhere
it would have amounted to no more than a quayside mêlée. Here, it
quickly developed into a diplomatic incident. Unfortunately for the
bo'sun, the man he assaulted was a local Communist Party official. He
and the cook were sentenced respectively to seven and four years in
prison.

Churchill touched on the case in the long list of requests for better
cooperation that he attached to the telegram. It included an easing of
visa restrictions and an end to bureaucratic bullying, measures he judged
"modest ... considering the efforts we were now to make."[5] Stalin did

not agree. He fired back a telegram, smoking with real or manufactured indignation, describing Churchill's unwillingness to make a contractual obligation to sail the convoys as "a kind of threat addressed to the USSR." Familiar though he was with the marshal's violent language, Churchill was surprised and even hurt. For once his professional equanimity was jolted. He told the new Soviet ambassador to London, Fyodor Gousev, that he would not formally accept the telegram and handed it back to him, saying the Foreign Secretary Anthony Eden would deal with the contents on his forthcoming trip to Moscow. His patience with Stalin was reaching exhaustion point. He wrote to Roosevelt, telling him of the exchange with "Uncle Joe," the ironic nickname they had given their sinister ally. "The Soviet machine is quite convinced it can get everything by bullying," he said. "I am sure it is a matter of some importance to show that this is not necessarily always true."[6]

In his determination to face Stalin down, he was now prepared to support canceling the Arctic convoys. "It would be a great relief," he confided to Eden, "to be freed from the burden of these convoys and to bring our men home from North Russia." He concluded: "If this is what [the Soviets] really mean and want, we ought to oblige them."[7]

Tempers cooled. Churchill decided against sending an inflammatory reply he had drafted in response to Stalin's insulting message. It was just as well. When Eden reached Moscow he found the Soviet mood had softened. On October 22 he met Stalin and told him of Churchill's anger at the telegram with its implication of bad faith. Eden reported back to London that "the Marshal said that this had not been intended." He acknowledged the bad blood between British and Soviet personnel in north Russia but lamented that "if only our people ... had treated his people as equals none of these difficulties would have arisen." If the British were prepared to do that, then "we could have as much personnel as we liked."[8]

The meeting generated a more cooperative spirit and some of the British grievances were redressed. As a token of good faith, the brawling bo'sun and cook of the *Dover Castle* were freed. By a combination of courtesy and resolve, Churchill had forced Stalin into a retreat and to offer the nearest thing to an apology he was capable of making. There was nothing now to stop the convoys from sailing.

On November 15, the first half of convoy JW.54A left Loch Ewe for Iceland. Then, covered by a strong escort and protected by cloud and mist from the eyes of the Luftwaffe, it set off for the Arctic. Eleven days later all nineteen ships had docked in Murmansk and Archangel without loss. The second half of the convoy, JW.54B, set out a week later and arrived unharmed. Two homecoming convoys, RA.54A and RA.54B, also made the trip safely.

The news that the convoys were sailing again was received with alarm in Germany. By the autumn of 1943 Hitler was retreating on all fronts. The "one bright spot"—as he had described it—provided by the successes of the U-boats in the Atlantic had faded as the Allied navies gained the upper hand in the battle of attrition. The German army had been driven out of North Africa, and Allied forces were ashore in Italy. In the east, the Red Army was clawing back the conquered territories, smashing the Wehrmacht at Kursk and Kharkov, while in the air great masses of Yak fighters were clearing the Luftwaffe from the skies. The reconnection of a supply line that would further strengthen the hand of the Soviet forces could not be overlooked. Forceful, even desperate action was needed to shut it off. In the circumstances, the chronic caution that had characterized the attitude of Hitler and his admirals toward their fleet in the north would have to be abandoned.

As it was, there were few assets to bring into play. Not only *Tirpitz* was out of the reckoning. So, too, was *Lützow*, which had quit Narvik on September 26 to return to the Baltic for a refit, dodging a force of Fleet Air Arm torpedo bombers on the way. The only large ship remaining was *Scharnhorst*, still lying at Kaafjord after escaping the attentions of the X-Craft.

It was Dönitz's unenviable duty to report to Hitler on the X-Craft attack in Berlin, three days after the event. He spread out the maps and took him through the operation, emphasizing carefully the extensive precautions that had been in place to protect the ship. The Führer took the news surprisingly well. No explosion of rage was recorded, and Hitler listened as it was explained that extensive repairs were needed if *Tirpitz* was ever to put to sea again.

In Dönitz's opinion there was no question of towing her back to Germany. It had been proposed, before the attack, that she would sail back to home waters for a refit. Admiral Kummetz had considered this feasible, as winter and darkness would shield her from Allied attacks. That might be so if she sailed under her own power. Under tow she would be easy meat for British aircraft and submarines. Hitler agreed that the work would somehow have to be done in Kaafjord and experts from the Wilhelmshaven dockyard were soon on their way to decide if this was possible.[9]

The question remained of how to close off the Murmansk pipeline, which was flowing abundantly once again. On December 12, nineteen British and American merchantmen left Loch Ewe in a convoy designated JW.55A. The second half of the convoy, JW.55B, was due to sail eight days later. At Iceland they picked up an escort of eight destroyers while three cruisers, *Belfast*, *Norfolk*, and *Sheffield*, under the command of Vice Admiral Robert Burnett, provided distant cover. When it appeared that the convoy had been sighted by a German reconnaissance flight, Admiral Sir Bruce Fraser, who had taken over command of the Home Fleet from Tovey in May, put to sea in his flagship *Duke of York*, accompanied by the cruiser *Jamaica* and the destroyers *Savage*, *Scorpion*, *Saumarez*, and the Royal Norwegian Navy's *Stord*.

Fraser was hoping that the temptation presented by the convoy would be irresistible and a German force, possibly led by *Scharnhorst*, would put to sea. The sighting seems to have come too late for the Kriegsmarine to react and the convoy passed unchallenged. Fraser stayed with it throughout, taking his squadron all the way to the Kola Inlet on which Murmansk lay, arriving on December 16. It was the first time the Russians had seen a capital ship of the Home Fleet. Fraser had spent six weeks in a Bolshevik prisoner-of-war camp in Baku after being captured in the Black Sea during Britain's intervention in the Russian civil war, a fact that made him an object of particular suspicion to the pathologically mistrustful Soviet Commander in Chief, Admiral Arseni Golovko. Like many Communist officers and officials in northern Russia he resented bitterly the need to seek capitalist largesse. By the end of the trip, though, Golovko's Arctic hostility had thawed a little. On paying a call to Fraser aboard *Duke of York*, he was surprised when a member of Fraser's staff immediately brought up the business of his chief's incarceration by the Reds. He went on to say that Fraser was grateful for the experience. "This time I really was astonished," recalled Golovko. The "triumphant" officer went on to explain, "Admiral Fraser was badly fed in the prison where he was confined and this enabled him to recover from an ulcer that was plaguing him." Fraser "who was present throughout the conversation confirmed this with a smile."

With this sally, the admiral and his team seem to have located the Russians' well-concealed sense of humor and for the duration of the visit ideological differences diminished and they were sea dogs together. "Like a good host Fraser showed me over the whole ship, which indeed made a powerful impression [wrote Golovko] and even invited me into the ship's bakery where we were regaled with some good newly baked buns. After eating one I praised both it and the bakers, little suspecting that this would lead to a surprise. When we had disembarked from the battleship a bulky sack was lowered onto the deck of the launch containing a vast quantity of buns. What you might call the acme of hospitality!"

The following day Fraser and his staff returned the visit. Golovko gave a dinner in their honor, and afterward there was a concert by the fleet choir. "The visitors were delighted," he remembered "especially by the dances and the few songs sung in English. They even entreated me to let them take the choir to Scapa Flow and Rosyth for a fortnight. All in all we received our British visitors as real allies."[10]

Fraser now returned to Akureyri in Iceland to refuel and await developments. He did not have to wait long. On December 19 and 20, Dönitz and other members of the high command met at Hitler's Wolfschanze HQ in East Prussia to discuss the coming year. All theaters of war were reviewed and the preoccupations of everyone present were overwhelmingly defensive. Dönitz's report was pessimistic. He bemoaned the "wholly inadequate" long-range air reconnaissance that was vital if his U-boats were to return to the offensive in the Atlantic, and the shortcomings of naval radar which by now was significantly inferior to that used in the Allies' ships. Despite these problems, he ended on a belligerent note. He told Hitler that "if a successful operation seems assured," he would send the fleet to sea against the next Allied convoy that sailed for Russia.

Even so, there were doubts among Dönitz's own staff as to whether these circumstances would ever arise. The concealing darkness and storms of winter made air reconnaissance very difficult. If a convoy was spotted and tracked, the attackers would almost certainly have to contend with a strong escort as well as carrier-borne aircraft. The Kriegsmarine had only one big ship in play—*Scharnhorst*. Caution argued for leaving her in Kaafjord and mounting a small-scale foray with destroyers alone against the next convoy.[11]

Dönitz, though, was inclined to be bold. The pressure to act was of his own making. It was he who had persuaded Hitler not to scrap the surface fleet after the debacle of the Battle of the Barents Sea the previous Christmas and had promised him that it would be put to aggressive use. Sending *Scharnhorst* to sea might be a gamble, but the stakes were high. A successful attack would not only assist the German armies struggling through another horrific winter; with luck, it might also lead to a further suspension of the Arctic convoys, and perhaps a crisis in the relationship between "Uncle Joe" and his partners.

Another opportunity to strike was beckoning. On December 20, the nineteen ships of JW.55B, the second half of the convoy, left Loch Ewe and sailed east. On December 22 a Luftwaffe aircraft on a meteorological flight spotted them. The next day a force of Ju88s attacked the convoy, without result. At the same time, U-boats had fallen in behind it, launching an attack that was beaten off by the escorts' depth charges.

The following day, an Ultra decrypt revealed that *Scharnhorst* had been put on three hours' notice to sail. Fraser and the Home Fleet were in Iceland. The moment he had been waiting for had arrived. Bruce Fraser entered Dartmouth in 1904. He was fifteen years old, the son of General Alexander Fraser of the Royal Engineers, a distinguished empire builder who constructed railways, lighthouses, and docks the length and breadth of the Indian subcontinent. Almost from the beginning, young Bruce was marked out for a distinguished career. His superiors' confidential reports as he ascended the hierarchy praised his zeal, intelligence, and tact. The only fault his senior officer could find with him after he completed two years commanding the light cruiser HMS *Effingham* in 1932 was that "with his kindly disposition he is apt to allow his heart to rule his head in dealing with his subordinates."[12]

Those aboard *Duke of York* found him friendly and informal, puffing on a pipe as he did his rounds, dressed for comfort rather than smartness. "He was the ideal commander," remembered Julian Richards, an eighteen-year-old midshipman. "He would spend the first part of the day... just talking to ship's companies and captains, and giving them the lowdown about his intentions. In the afternoon he would spend two or three hours thinking things over in his own mind, preparing for all eventualities. He was the sort of laid-back commander who let people get on with their work and not harry them all the time as others did."[13]

On the afternoon of December 23, he ordered a refill of the bunkers and went ashore for a walk to clear his head with the *Duke of York*'s commanding officer, Captain Guy Russell. Back on board he ordered the Royal Marine band up on deck to play Christmas carols. The familiar tunes, with their powerful reminders of hearth and home, "brought tears to your eyes," he recalled later.[14] At 11:00 p.m. that night of December 23, preceded by four destroyers and with the cruiser *Jamaica* following behind, *Duke of York* put to sea. As well as his own squadron, which he designated Force Two, he also had at his disposal Burnett's cruisers—Force One—which had turned round after delivering the previous convoy and were now headed west to cover JW.55B.

The convoy steamed eastward throughout Christmas Eve at no more than eight knots, protected by the Royal Navy destroyers *Onslow*, *Onslaught*, *Orwell*, *Impulsive*, and *Scourge*, and the Canadian navy's "Tribals," *Haida*, *Huron*, and *Iroquois*. The weather was terrible. A gale was blowing from the south, driving huge seas against the flanks of the merchantmen and their escorts. None of them displaced more than 10,000 tons, and they were thrown from wave top to trough in sickening succession with no hope in the forecasts of an improvement. As she hurried to catch up from the west, even the *Duke of York* was suffering. The pounding of the sea as it swept over the low bow tore away Oerlikon anti-aircraft guns mounted forward, and icy water poured into the bolt holes left in the decks, drenching those below. Julian Richards was in charge of two of the guns. "Anything that was loose on the upper deck went overboard," he remembered. Even a big ship like the *Duke of York* was "plunging and rocking." For insulation from the force 8 and 9 winds, those on deck had a duffel coat, layers of pullovers, long stockings, and rubber boots. A woolly hat, though it "was not part of the official uniform ... a balaclava, knitted by mummy, was essential."[15]

The Germans had been shadowing the convoy by air and U-boat since Christmas Eve but, by lunchtime on Christmas Day, a decision to attack had still not been made. The situation seemed to match Dönitz's criteria for a successful operation. At this point it was not known that Fraser had put out to sea. On the available facts, the convoy's escort was no match for the *Scharnhorst*. The target's speed and course were established and the wall of polar ice encroaching from the north limited its room for evasive action. Air reconnaissance had not discovered any heavy enemy unit in the vicinity. That did not mean that there was not a battleship lurking out there somewhere. Dönitz calculated that, even if there were, "it must have been a long way from the convoy, and the *Scharnhorst* seemed to have every chance of delivering a rapid and successful attack." Dönitz and the naval staff agreed that "here was a splendid chance for the *Scharnhorst*." He sent the order for the battle cruiser and the 4th Destroyer Flotilla to put to sea.[16]

Scharnhorst was at anchor in Langefjord when the news came through. Vizeadmiral Erich Bey, who was in temporary command of the northern task force while Kummetz carried on his home leave, was not, however, on board. He was a dozen miles to the south, in a *Tirpitz* stateroom, sitting down to Christmas lunch with Kapitän Meyer. The crew of *Scharnhorst* seems also to have been in festive mood, despite the heightened state of alert. Survivors later told their interrogators that they had "been looking forward to a cheerful and relaxed Christmas." Some of them had spent the morning skiing and extra rations of sweets and cigarettes were handed out, overseen by their commander, Kapitän zur See Fritz Hintze, a popular figure who his men admired for his attention to their welfare.[17]

At 3:00 p.m. the order came to prepare to weigh anchor. Shortly afterward, Bey arrived from *Tirpitz* aboard a tug, and at 7:00 p.m.

Scharnhorst steamed northwest up Altafjord with five destroyers leading the way. Once clear of the coast, they headed due north, straining to make twenty-five knots in the dark, wind-humped seas. The launch of the operation produced a quickening of signals flying through the freezing ether between the ship and headquarters in Kiel. In Hut 8 at Bletchley Park, the naval team worked intently, deciphering the traffic and passing it on to London. At 4:00 a.m. on December 26, as the morning watch relieved the middle watch aboard *Duke of York*, Fraser was handed a slip of paper which read: "Admiralty appreciate that *Scharnhorst* is now at sea."

The news sent a ripple of excitement through the ship. The convoy and its escorts were now fifty miles south of Bear Island, butting along at eight knots and heading east-northeast. Ahead, 150 miles to the northeast, the cruisers of Force One—*Belfast*, *Norfolk*, and *Sheffield*—were hurrying in their direction. Behind, just over two hundred miles away, approaching from the southwest, further support was on its way from *Duke of York*, the light cruiser *Jamaica*, and their four destroyers.

As *Scharnhorst* steamed northward her destroyers were finding it hard to keep up. Their upper works were encrusted with frozen brine and a heavy following sea jostled them. Bey had reported his problems back to base, only for Dönitz to reply that if the flotilla could not maintain speed, *Scharnhorst* should attack the convoy alone.

At 7:30 a.m., when there was still no sign of the convoy, he detached his destroyers and sent them off on a search to the west. *Scharnhorst*, meanwhile, followed on a zigzag course behind. The first leg of the maneuver put the ship on a northward tack. *Scharnhorst* was now on a collision course with the advancing cruisers of Burnett's Force One.

At 8:45 a.m. a blip on a cathode screen aboard Burnett's flagship *Belfast* revealed a single ship steaming slightly north of west. The vessel was only fourteen miles away. At 9:21 a.m., lookouts on *Sheffield* glimpsed the outlines of a large ship, ghostly in the murk, on the port beam, about seven miles away. There was no doubt what it was. The signal lamps flashed the message to Burnett: "Enemy in sight."

At this point, *Scharnhorst* was outnumbered but she was not out-gunned. She mounted nine 11-inch and twelve 5.9-inch guns. The heaviest guns the cruisers could muster were the eight 8-inchers on *Norfolk*. *Belfast* and *Sheffield* each had twelve 6-inch guns. The superior reach and power of *Scharnhorst*'s main armament should have been enough for her to do serious damage to one or more of the cruisers without getting within range of their weapons. Her slight edge in speed gave her the advantage in a chase. But Bey and Hintze were hindered by a serious handicap. The limited range of their radar compared with the British equipment meant they were unlikely to sight the enemy before the enemy sighted them. At 9:24 a.m. the gloom was pierced by the first star shell, fired from *Belfast* to light up the target. A few minutes later, real shells were plunging into the surrounding waters.

Scharnhorst was just turning south when she was spotted, and the shells from *Belfast* and *Sheffield* all missed. *Norfolk* was luckier. Her radar-controlled 8-inch guns fired six broadsides and scored three hits. One smashed *Scharnhorst*'s main radar aerial, and another wrecked the port high-angle gunnery director. In a few minutes her armament advantage had been severely reduced, and she was now operating in semi-blindness.

Bey ran for it. He turned *Scharnhorst* southeast, and hurried off at thirty knots, making smoke as he went. Despite the encounter, he was still determined to attack the convoy. He ordered his destroyers to steer northeast on a heading which he believed would take them onto the southern flank of the convoy. He, meanwhile, would race round to the far side, to attack it from the north.

Burnett decided not to give chase. His ships were too slow to over-haul their quarry. He guessed, correctly, that *Scharnhorst* was still full of fight and would make another attempt on the convoy. His place was therefore alongside the merchantmen, and he ordered his squadron north and west, from where JW.55B was approaching.

Fraser, aboard the *Duke of York*, received with dismay the news that Force One had lost touch with the enemy and was returning to the convoy. It seemed to him that *Scharnhorst* was more likely to return to Norway rather than continue the operation. A German flying boat had spotted Fraser's flagship. News of the presence of a battleship in the area would surely cause Bey to beat a rapid retreat. If so, Fraser was still too far away to cut her off. The prospect of glory was fading. Fraser could not hide his chagrin. At 10:57 a.m., nearly an hour after the engagement had ended, he signaled to Burnett: "Unless touch can be regained by some unit, there is no chance of my finding enemy."

Bey had indeed received a report of the flying boat sighting but it was shorn of a crucial detail that, had it been included, Dönitz was later to claim could have altered the whole course of the drama. At 11:00 a.m. he had been told that five warships had been seen far to the northwest of the North Cape. The original report had included the information that one of the vessels was "apparently a big ship." The senior air officer removed this detail before relaying it to naval headquarters on the grounds that he did not wish to pass on what he regarded as conjecture.

The result was confusion. Admiral Schniewind at Naval Group North in Kiel made the incorrect guess that the ships were probably the destroyers Bey had sent off when they could not keep up with him, and therefore no threat. Dönitz maintained that, had he been given the full message, he would "probably have immediately ordered the operation to be abandoned." What Bey made of the information is unknown. Whatever his appreciation of the situation, he decided to carry on.[18] By noon *Scharnhorst* was to the north and east of the convoy. So, too, were Burnett's cruisers. Once again it was the *Belfast* radar operators who picked up a lone ship on their screens, and the *Sheffield*'s lookouts who first laid eyes on the target. At 12:21 p.m. the signal lamp once more flashed the message: "Enemy in sight."

Burnett gave the order to engage. At the same time, he sent his destroyers darting forward, seeking a line on which they could fire their torpedoes. The sight of the advancing destroyers resulted in *Scharnhorst* making several violent course changes, before heading away on an east-southeast heading. As the first shells crashed around her, she returned fire, concentrating on *Norfolk* whose shells were not propelled with flash-suppressing charges. The great tongues of flame leaping from her guns lit her up and gave the German gunners, working without radar, a point for their optics to range on. Their aim was good enough to land one 11-inch shell, which struck a gun turret and knocked out the cruiser's main radar sets, killing seven and seriously wounding five more.

Scharnhorst did not linger. She broke away, heading southeast, piling on as many knots as her turbines could muster. Once again her superior speed told and she was soon lost in the gloom and smoke. Although being slowly outdistanced, the cruisers were still able to shadow her for the next few hours by radar, and even as *Scharnhorst* was escaping from one set of pursuers she was running straight into the path of another.

By now Fraser was in a position to cut off her escape. His frustration had given way to cautiously rising hopes as he traced Burnett's reports onto the chart before him. Then, at 4:17 p.m., a bright point of light glowed on the *Duke of York*'s long-distance radar screen. *Scharnhorst* was just over twenty-five miles away. When the distance had closed to eleven miles, he ordered his destroyers to prepare their torpedoes but to await his signal to attack.

It was only when the two ships were seven miles apart that he swung *Duke of York* onto a starboard course to give all his guns and those of *Jamaica* behind him their chance. The bombardment opened with a salvo of star shells that hung in the dark sky, bathing the sea in a flat, harsh light. There, outlined like a great silver ghost, was the *Scharnhorst*. She had been taken by surprise. Her guns were still pointing forward and aft, away from her nemesis. At 4:51 p.m., *Duke of York* shook with the recoil of a full broadside. Shells flew from her ten 14-inch guns on an almost flat trajectory toward their target. One struck *Scharnhorst's* forward turret, wrecking it. The ship swung away from its attackers, heading northward—back toward the guns of the shadowing cruisers of Force One. Soon she was under fire from *Belfast* and *Norfolk* and turned to the east, still firing at her pursuers from her rear turret as she fled. *Scharnhorst* still retained one advantage: she was a full four knots faster than *Duke of York*. As she pulled away, *Duke of York* fired broadside after broadside. The shocks swept through the ship, smashing the valves in the gunnery radar system, temporarily disabling it.

One of the 14-inch shells struck *Scharnhorst's* starboard boiler room, slowing her down to ten knots until the steam pipes were jury-rigged to bring her back up to twenty-two knots. It was enough to draw her out of range. At 6:20 p.m., after firing fifty-two broadsides, the *Duke of York's* guns ceased firing and her exhausted crews slumped back in a despondent daze. It seemed to be all over. Fraser signaled Burnett that he "saw little hope of catching *Scharnhorst* and am proceeding to support convoy." His destroyers, though, had not given up hope. Despite the heavy seas they had managed to gain on the battle cruiser. Just as Fraser had decided pursuit was hopeless they arrived astern of *Scharnhorst* and began maneuvering to launch attacks on either beam, with *Savage* and *Saumarez* on the port side and *Scorpion* and *Stord* to starboard.

The *Scharnhorst's* gunners soon picked up the portside attackers but, blinded by star shell, failed to notice the ones approaching from starboard until the destroyers were only two miles away. Hintze swung his ship toward them in an effort to comb the tracks of the torpedoes that would soon be racing her way. He almost succeeded. Sixteen torpedoes leaped from the tubes of *Scorpion* and *Stord*, and only one struck.

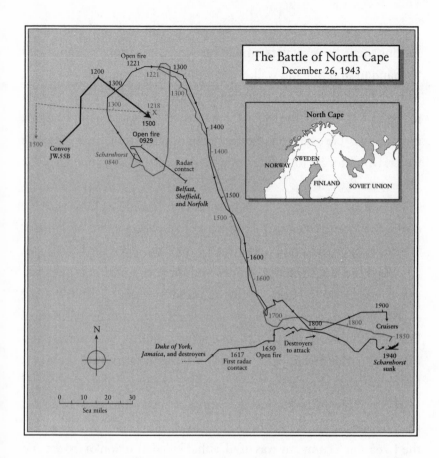

The change of course, though, brought him into the arcs of the torpedo tubes of *Savage* and *Saumarez*. At almost point-blank range they loosed off twelve torpedoes. Two exploded, knocking out another boiler room and bending a propeller shaft. *Scharnhorst* shuddered and slowed. Soon she was rolling and pitching, barely able to scrape ten knots. *Duke of York* and *Jamaica* swept toward her, opening fire again at six miles. Burnett's cruisers, moving to join up with the Commander in Chief's squadron, joined in. Under the pounding she staggered and slowed. The cruisers moved forward and lanced her burning sides with torpedoes. Then it was the turn of the Force One destroyers.

The decks of *Scharnhorst* were strewn with the dead and dying. Among them, the survivors, smoke-blackened and deafened, mustered to abandon ship. She was wallowing, almost on her beam-ends. Hintze, who had led them with perhaps more kindness than skill, was fatherly to the end. "Don't go overboard to starboard," he told them through a megaphone. "Go over from the port side and slide from the rail into the water. Don't forget to inflate your life-jackets and now one after the other, over the rail."[19]

On the deck of *Duke of York*, Julian Richards could no longer see the outlines of the stricken ship, "just a lot of smoke and a lot of flame."[20] Witnesses spoke of a dull underwater explosion. Then the black night absorbed the last, flickering flames and there was nothing. Bey's last signal, addressed to Hitler, had announced, "we shall fight to the last shell." There was no doubt about his bravery or the courage of his men. But in truth he had mishandled an engagement that had offered a significant chance of success. Certainly among the survivors there was bitterness that she had not put up a better show. After an hour of searching, only thirty-six men, all ratings or petty officers, were picked up. They had been lucky enough to clamber into a life raft. The rest of the 1,765 ship's company was dead, either killed in action or frozen and drowned within a minute of entering the sea.

Scharnhorst had taken a lot of sinking. She had probably received thirteen full hits from *Duke of York*'s 14-inch guns and about as many from the smaller armament of the cruisers, as well as eleven torpedo strikes, and yet she had not blown up. "Once again," remarked Stephen Roskill, "the ability of the Germans to build tremendously stout ships had been demonstrated."[21]

The loss shook the German fleet. Dönitz struggled to understand why Bey broke off the first fight of the day when, in his judgment, he had it in his power to overwhelm Burnett and his cruisers. "The correct thing to have done … would have been to continue the fight and finish off the weaker British forces, particularly as it was plain that they had already been hard hit," he wrote. "Had this been done an excellent opportunity would ... have been created for a successful attack on the convoy." Why, when he fled after the second clash, did he not use his advantage of speed and weight to steer a westerly course into the wind and heavy sea that would have made it very difficult for the lightly built British cruisers and destroyers to keep in contact?[22] The answer would never be known. Bey and Hintze had been swallowed by the Barents Sea.

CHAPTER 17

TUNGSTEN

A hundred miles to the south, the crew of *Tirpitz* heard the news and shuddered. The death of *Scharnhorst* "cast a long shadow over the ship's company," remembered Adalbert Brünner. Among the dead were some of their own comrades who had been lent to the battle cruiser to fill in for men absent on leave.[1] Now *Tirpitz* stood alone, the last of Hitler's capital ships left in commission. A sobriquet began to attach to her—the "lonely queen of the North." It was obvious to all on board that their enemies must once again be eyeing her up for annihilation. The tiny shape of reconnaissance Spitfires overhead provided regular reminders that the RAF was following every step of their ship's return to seaworthiness. So, too, were the Norwegians.

The information gleaned from photo reconnaissance and signal interceptions was being supplemented by the eyewitness reports of

Norwegian agents. In February 1944 Terje Jacobsen set off from his home in Tromsø on a mission to check on the progress of repairs. He had just turned nineteen and had joined the local resistance network as soon as the occupation began. He was blond, blue-eyed, and athletic, the Nordic type that some Germans liked to think of as kin.

Jacobsen had no natural antipathy toward them. He had visited Germany before the war and spoke the language fluently. It was the behavior of the occupation forces in Tromsø that drove him into the resistance. "You could practically hear the screams from the Gestapo headquarters in the street," he remembered.[2] Even in one of the furthest outposts of their territories, the Nazis hunted their victims with appalling zeal. On June 18, 1941, the Gestapo began to arrest Tromsø's Jews. There were only eighteen of them and eventually all were picked up and sent to Auschwitz. The youngest was two and half years old. None survived the war. Among them was Conrad Caplan, a schoolfriend of Jacobsen's, whose father owned a department store. "He was one of the happiest boys in the class," he remembered. He perished on January 10, 1945, seventeen days before Soviet troops liberated the camp.

Jacobsen's mission was explained to him by his controller in Tromsø, a policeman called Olaf Aasegg. British and Norwegian intelligence in London wanted detailed information on the condition of *Tirpitz* after the X-Craft attack, and the progress of repairs. He was to go first to Alta, then Kaafjord. If questioned, he was to say he was visiting a friend from Tromsø who, conveniently, lived in the area. To get to Alta he would take one of the steamers that plied the coast to the little port of Alteidet, then continue by road to Isnestoften, at the head of Altafjord, to take another boat to Alta where a local contact would take care of him.

The first boat was full of German soldiers. Jacobsen got into conversation with a young SS officer who was impressed by his command of German. Their matey conversation was observed by the boat's captain, a relation of Jacobsen's on his mother's side who "looked at me as if he would gladly throw me overboard." On arrival there was no public transport. The German officer offered his Norwegian friend a lift and Jacobsen spent the night as his guest in a barracks. At Isnestoften he took another steamer and met another German, a naïve, well-mannered young man of his own age who was surprised to see him reading a book of German poetry. The poet was Heinrich Heine, a Jew whose books had been burned by the Nazis. "He had never heard of him," said Jacobsen.

At Alta he went to the house of Freddie Tscholari, a friend from Tromsø. Tscholari was head of the telegraph office. He found him a bed in official accommodations and lent him his bicycle to make the journey to Kaafjord, five or six miles away. The following day he set off on the icy road. As he was laboring up to the head of the pass that led down to Kaafjord, he turned a bend and there before him were a group of German soldiers, some of them high-ranking, judging by the red tabs on their lapels. Jacobsen had learned that "the Germans weren't stupid but they had one weak point and that was their superiority complex." He decided to play on it. "I looked a bit dumb and I had this fur hat down on my ears. I looked at this German guard rather stupidly and said 'Do you have any cigarettes?'" He was rewarded with "a kick in the behind" and an order to clear off.

At the top of the pass he had "a beautiful view of the whole scene. It was very impressive." The battleship lay in its usual haven in the lee of the hills on the northwest side of the fjord. Nearby loomed a floating crane, the repair ship *Neumark*, and next to it the *Monte Rosa*, a former liner that was now the home of eight hundred workers from the Blohm and Voss Hamburg shipyard. It was the same ship that earlier in the war had carried his friend Conrad Caplan and many other Jews on the first leg of their journey to the death camps. Even at this distance he could sense the bustle and energy below. He lingered as long as he dared, memorizing as much detail as he could. Back in Alta he made notes and sketches that were smuggled by rail to the Norwegian Embassy in neutral Sweden, then on to London. On a second trip he learned from one of the local contractors technical details about the repair program. It was going very well. On his third visit, in March 1944, Jacobsen witnessed the battleship heading out into Altafjord for initial speed and gunnery trials. His reports reinforced the intelligence gleaned from the Enigma transmissions passing back and forth between Kaafjord and Germany. On March 17 the battleship reported that its "hull, guns and power installation were from a material point of view fully operationally effective."[3] It was clear that the "period of easement" welcomed by Churchill was over.

Three convoys had sailed to north Russia in the first three months of 1944 and three sailed back. Exceptionally bad weather shielded them from the Luftwaffe but not from U-boat wolf packs which harried them all the way. The submarines had only limited success, sinking a total of four merchantmen and two destroyers. The relatively light losses were a tribute to the determination of the escorting destroyers, corvettes, and carriers, whose Fleet Air Arm crews were sometimes so frozen at the end of their sorties that they had to be lifted from their cockpits.[4]

With *Tirpitz* out of action, the Admiralty had not judged it necessary to cover the movements with battleships and cruisers. Now that she was back in commission, she reassumed the function of a "fleet in being," and once again the navy felt compelled to maintain a counterforce to deal with her if she ventured out. The Allies now dominated the seas of the northern hemisphere. They had contained the U-boat threat in the North Atlantic and neutralized the Italian fleet to give them command of the Mediterranean. Apart from *Tirpitz*, the German surface fleet had been reduced to two pocket battleships—the *Lützow* and the *Scheer*—and the heavy cruiser *Prinz Eugen*, all now skulking in the Baltic, and a few training ships. Yet despite this overwhelming superiority, Churchill and the Admiralty remained greatly impressed by the battleship's menace.

The importance they bestowed on it reflected a new perception. As well as threatening the convoys, *Tirpitz* appeared to pose another potential danger. The invasion of Normandy was approaching. As long as she remained afloat, she would absorb naval assets that were essential for the success of the landings. If left unguarded, she could sail south to perhaps sink a troopship crossing the Atlantic, or when the landings began, menace the invasion fleet. As the repair work reached completion, *Tirpitz* loomed again in the Admiralty's imaginations.

It seemed clear that it was the navy that would have to deal with her. There was little enthusiasm in the RAF for an air attack, and none at all from Arthur Harris at Bomber Command. He had decided that the long distances involved and the strength of the battleship's anti-aircraft defenses meant there was no more chance of his crews succeeding in 1944 where they had failed in 1942. He, anyway, had no wish to divert them from what he considered their primary task of smashing German cities. He had sidestepped nimbly Churchill's demands for action, suggesting that the US Army Air Force's Flying Fortresses with their superior bombsights were better placed to do the job. If, however, *Tirpitz* was to return to Germany, he graciously offered to mount "the heaviest possible attacks against the German port where she lies."[5]

The RAF had already been drawn into one abortive effort to finish off *Tirpitz*. In the spring of 1943 a new weapon appeared which promised to succeed where conventional bombs—and the hopeless spherical "roly-poly" mine—had signally failed. Its creator was Barnes Wallis whose bouncing bomb was dropped by 617 Squadron—the Dambusters—on their spectacular raid of May 16–17. The new invention, code-named "Highball," was based on the same principle. It was cylinder-shaped, weighed half a ton, and contained a 500-lb. charge.

Wallis saw it as a naval weapon and hopes soon rose that it might be used to the same devastating effect on *Tirpitz* as its sister had on the Möhne and Eder dams.

A new Coastal Command squadron, 618, formed in April 1943 at Skitten, near Wick, in northeastern Scotland and began secret preparations for an attack, code-named "Operation Servant." Specially converted Mosquito Mark IVs dropped Highballs in dry runs on the old French battleship *Courbet* in Loch Striven but the results were disappointing. Plans were nonetheless made for twenty Mosquitoes to attack *Tirpitz* in Kaafjord that summer, operating—if the Russians agreed—from the Vaenga airbase. It was shelved when Coastal Command's chief, Air Marshal Sir John Slessor, ruled that it was "not a reasonably practical operation of war" given the difficulties of delivering a Highball on target in the narrow confines of the fjord and the likelihood of high casualties at the hands of the ship's anti-aircraft defenses.[6]

There was another alternative. The north Russian airfields were only three hundred miles from the target. The British Senior Naval Officer in the area, Rear Admiral Ernest Archer, spent the first few months of the year issuing "almost daily" requests to Admiral Golovko for action. The only result was a half-hearted effort launched on the full moon night of February 10–11 by fifteen aircraft each carrying a 2,000-lb. bomb. Snow blotted Kaafjord and only four of the raiders dropped their bombs, none of which did any damage.

At the turn of the year, the Fleet Air Arm seemed to offer the navy the best hope of success. British naval aviation had at last struggled into the modern era. It had a new monoplane torpedo bomber, the all-metal Fairey Barracuda II, which replaced the wood and canvas Albacore biplanes. The specification for an up-to-date torpedo bomber had been issued in 1937, but the priority given to production of RAF aircraft meant that it did not start reaching the FAA's squadrons until January 1943. It performed best as a dive-bomber, helped by large flaps that held it steady as it swooped on its target. The Barracudas were supported by a new generation of very effective carrier-borne fighters, American-manufactured Corsairs, Wildcats, and Hellcats.

The FAA had been the target of some sniping from Churchill, who in July 1943 flicked an ill-considered memo at the stolid First Lord of the Admiralty, Albert Alexander, noting the "rather pregnant fact" that out of the service's 45,000 officers and ratings, "only thirty should have been killed, missing or prisoners during the three months ending April 30." It seemed "clear proof of how very rarely [the FAA] is brought into contact with the enemy." This was despite the "immense demands ... made on us by the Fleet Air Arm in respect of men and machines."[7]

It fell to the Fifth Sea Lord, Vice Admiral D. W. Boyd, to draw up a response. Boyd was "naturally astonished at the spirit of the Prime Minister's minute." The draft reply, coldly indignant in tone, claimed that it was "a matter beyond dispute that, in proportion to its size, the Fleet Air Arm has given bigger results than any branch of any other service." In the end Alexander decided against rising to the provocation.[8] Action, not words, were needed. The fact was that at the time of Churchill's memo it had been more than a year since the Fleet Air Arm had sunk a ship—a Vichy French armed merchant cruiser, the *Bougainville*, off Madagascar. The resurrection of the *Tirpitz* threat would give the navy the chance to show what its aviators could do.

The initial plan was to hit *Tirpitz* in her Kaafjord anchorage early in March 1944, just before repair work was expected to end. The attack would be spearheaded by two striking forces, embarked on the big fleet carriers *Furious* and *Victorious*. Each one would be made up of twenty-one Barracudas. An escort of forty fighters would protect them, some on the fleet carriers and the rest on three smaller escort carriers, *Emperor*, *Pursuer*, and *Searcher*. More fighters on board *Furious* and another carrier, *Fencer*, would protect the fleet itself from air and submarine attack. The operation carried the code name "Tungsten."

Despite the large scale of the enterprise, the Home Fleet commander Bruce Fraser seems to have had little faith in its chances, and, according to the First Sea Lord Andrew Cunningham, had to be "practically bludgeoned" into agreeing to it.[9] As it was, he handed over responsibility for Tungsten to his number two, Vice Admiral Sir Henry Moore.

Intense preparations for Tungsten began in February. Crews flew from Hatston in the Orkneys for exercises around Loch Eriboll, in northwest Scotland. The steep surrounding hills could pass for Kaafjord, and the Barracuda crews got busy accustoming themselves to the maneuvers needed to reach the anchorage, line up on the target, complete the dive, and slip back over the hill tops and out of reach of the anti-aircraft batteries bristling on ship and shore.

Barracudas carried a crew of three: a pilot, a navigator, and a telegraphist air gunner (TAG), who sat, one behind the other, in the long cockpit. For Alan Thomson, a twenty-two-year-old Glaswegian, flying as a TAG with 830 Squadron, the exercises were the overture to his first big operation. In the loch "was an island. There was an area laid out, about 900 feet by ninety and we practiced bombing that first with practice bombs, then with a 500-pounder." As yet the target was a secret but the crews did not need to be told. "There were not many things that were 900 feet by 90 feet so we knew where we were going."[10]

As was often the case, training activities were almost as perilous as the real thing. One misty morning they were flying over the loch when they glimpsed a tug in the waters below. They had not been told to expect any shipping in the area. A few seconds later, shells were whistling around them as a nearby warship which had just come into view opened up with a broadside aimed at the target that the tug was trailing.

The Barracudas were flown by 827 and 830 Squadrons of the FAA's 8 Torpedo Bomber Wing, and 829 and 831 Squadrons from 52 Wing. Normally, 8 Wing was based on *Furious* and 52 Wing on *Victorious*.

Moore wanted the wings to operate as complete units, but embarking them together on their mother ships meant the time needed to take off and form up from a single flight deck would delay and complicate proceedings. He decided that 827 would sail on *Victorious* alongside 829 and 830 Squadron on *Furious* with 831 Squadron. At the given time, the squadrons of each wing would take off from their respective carrier, join up in the air, and set off. The attack would be made in two waves, starting with 8 Wing. The strike forces would be protected from fighter attack by a top cover of Corsairs from *Victorious* and a close escort of sixty Hellcats and Wildcats from the other carriers, which would shoot up anti-aircraft batteries on ship and shore and strafe *Tirpitz* from stem to stern.

This was a huge and novel operation, "of a character which hitherto had not been attempted by Allied aircraft in the European theatre," in the words of Captain Michael Denny, commander of *Victorious*. It was the first time in the war that such a large force of dive-bombers had been launched at a single ship. The weight of numbers was supplemented by a correspondingly powerful load of ordnance. The shortcomings of British bomb design had finally been addressed and the Barracudas would be carrying bomb loads which, it was promised, had the capacity to cut through *Tirpitz*'s thick carapace. To reach the battleship's vital parts a bomb had to plunge through two layers of deck then penetrate the armored deck that ran along the waterline, protecting the engine and boiler rooms and the magazines. According to the intelligence estimate, the steel plating was three and a quarter inches thick over machinery and four and a quarter inches over her magazines.

A new bomb—the 1,600-lb. AP (armor-piercing)—was now available which, it was claimed, could penetrate at least the lighter layer of armor plating, thereby putting the ship out of action if not actually sinking her. To be effective though, it had to be released at a height of above 3,500 feet.

Of the forty-two Barracudas in the strike force, nine would be armed with these weapons. Twenty-two would carry three 500 lb. semi-armor-piercing (SAP) bombs, which, if released above 2,000 feet, would smash through the upper deck and devastate the living spaces below. The other ten would be loaded with 500 lb. and 600 lb. high explosive and anti-submarine bombs intended to kill anyone not under cover if they hit the ship, and to cause underwater damage if they missed.

Tungsten was originally timed for between March 7 and 16. As the date approached, *Victorious* was still in the Liverpool dockyard being fitted with new radar and the operation was postponed for two weeks. This turned out to be convenient. Convoy JW.58 was due to put to sea at the end of the month with a huge cargo of war materiel for an impatient Stalin. The escort required to cover the movement would provide excellent camouflage in which to conceal the carriers and the Tungsten strike force.

A huge armada assembled for the two operations. It was divided into two groups. Force One, led by Fraser flying his flag in *Duke of York*, would initially provide distant cover for the convoy. He would be accompanied by Henry Moore on the battleship *Anson*, together with *Victorious*, to provide air support if needed. Force Two was made up of *Furious*; three escort carriers, *Emperor*, *Pursuer*, and *Searcher*; four cruisers; and four destroyers. They were to sail directly to the rendezvous point where, once the convoy was out of danger, the operation would commence. Another carrier, *Fencer*, would also be at sea with twenty-eight aircraft to attack any lurking U-boats.

Convoy JW.58 left Loch Ewe on March 27, followed three days later by Fraser and Force One from Scapa. On the mainland, spring was in the air but the northern seas were as vicious as ever. Spray and sleet froze solid as they hit the deck and upper works and on board *Victorious*, Captain Denny ordered the engines of the Corsairs parked on deck to be run up every two hours to prevent them seizing in the cold.

Denny had taken over the previous December and believed that "the aroma of the ship's previously unrewarding efforts" against German battleships "still remained in the nostrils of the Naval Air Arm." A Swordfish from *Victorious* struck *Bismarck* with a torpedo in the chase of May 1941 but failed to inflict serious damage. The carrier had taken part in the bitterly disappointing air attacks on *Tirpitz* in March the following year and a few months later shared in the collective guilt of the PQ.17 catastrophe. An opportunity for revenge had now arisen, but Denny worried that preparations had not been thorough enough to make the most of it. His ship's own squadrons were only recently formed and "few of them had ever engaged in an offensive operation before." At his reckoning, "85 percent of them had never proceeded to sea in a ship other than in the smooth waters of the Clyde."[11]

At this point it still seemed possible that, even though trials were not complete, *Tirpitz* might venture out against the convoy. The tanks and aircraft on board would add greatly to the burden of misery being borne by Hitler's armies, now falling back all along the Eastern Front. A short sharp foray—particularly if, as with the previous three sailings, the merchantmen had only a light escort—might be worth the gamble.

By the morning of April 1, however, Fraser was coming to the conclusion that this would not happen. German air reconnaissance picked up the convoy and tried, unsuccessfully, to home U-boat packs onto it. But there had been no wider search to establish if JW.58 was being covered by a powerful force. "This apparent lack of interest," wrote Fraser later, "suggested to me that *Tirpitz* was unlikely to threaten the convoy." He decided to send off *Victorious* to join Force Two and advance Tungsten by twenty-four hours, while he withdrew westward to await events.[12]

On the afternoon of April 2, the two forces met up 250 miles northwest of Altafjord. None of the crews got any sleep that evening. They were called to a last briefing at 1:30 a.m., "that hour," wrote Denny, "when man's stamina is at its lowest." On board *Victorious* was a former naval officer, Anthony Kimmins, who had switched careers to become an actor and prolific film director. He was now back in the service and described the "feverish activity" in the hangars as the fitters and riggers "swarmed over their aircraft making final adjustments … great yellow bombs were being wheeled down the narrow gangways, loaded up and fused," each with a chalked message for the *Tirpitz*. The Barracudas, with their wings folded back along their bodies seemed "like enormous beetles."

After the crews had eaten a hot breakfast he followed them up to the flight deck where, to their relief and surprise, they found "perfect conditions—calm seas, clear skies with patches of cloud" and were assured by the met officer that the weather was even better inland. It seemed to everyone that "providence was very much on our side. Even in the summer one would have been lucky to find such conditions, but at this time of year it was almost unbelievable."

At 4:00 a.m. they boarded their machines. "At exactly the pre-arranged minute, Commander, Flying, shouted the welcome order 'Start up!' The words were hardly out of his mouth before there was a roar of engines. Gloves laid on the wings during the final adjustments went whisking over the side. Ice which had formed on the flight deck was sent scurrying in all directions." As the ship swung into the wind for take-off "lumps of ice shot up in the air and went slithering down the flying deck, got whirled up in the propeller slipstreams and went cracking against the flight deck crews, clinging to the wingtips and lying on the deck tending the chocks."[13] Then the flight deck officer waved a green flag, and the first Corsair went racing away over the bow. The fighters were followed by twelve Barracudas of 827 Squadron. A few minutes later nine Barracudas from 830 Squadron left *Furious*. They circled above the fleet forming up with their comrades from 8 Wing. It seemed to Denny, looking up at them, that "they left the carriers' decks in the greatest of heart and brimful of determination … taking departure to the target exactly as if [in] a parade ground movement."[14] Lieutenant Commander Roy Baker-Falkner led the wing; he was a twenty-seven-year-old professional naval officer who had taken part in the attack on the Italian navy at Taranto and whose action-filled war to date was a reproof to Churchill's suggestion that the FAA was slacking.

They set course to make landfall at the island of Loppa, cruising at fifty feet over the flat calm sea to slip in under the radar. Above them darted the blunt-nosed Wildcats and Hellcats, which would swoop to blast the onshore anti-aircraft batteries and strafe the decks of the *Tirpitz* while the Barracudas delivered their bombs. Visibility was perfect. Ahead, the crystal Nordic light bounced off the jagged snow-blanketed hills and silver inlets ahead. Twenty miles from land the strike force started to climb. At 5:08 a.m. they flashed over the coast at 7,000 feet, easing onto a course that would take them south of Altafjord and over the western end of Langfjord, before looping around to launch their attack from the south over the hills rising from Kaafjord.

Sub-Lieutenant John Herrold, a young New Zealand Barracuda pilot with 827 Squadron, looked down on "a picture of incredible beauty." The mountains "were bathed on one side with the pink light of the sun." The snow sweeping down the mountain sides to the fjords "wasn't the white snow of a Christmas card. It was so brilliant it was more of a light blue color."

Alan Thomson, hunched over his guns several aircraft behind him, saw two small ships lying in Langfjord, which opened fire. They were way out of range and the "smoke puffs hanging there" did not disconcert him. About ten miles from the target, Baker-Falkner ordered the 830 Squadron aircraft to fall in behind the twelve Barracudas of 827 Squadron. By now Herrold could see the ridge beyond which lay Kaafjord. "As I looked at this hill it seemed to come towards me so slowly, then suddenly, with a surge we were over the top and there beneath us lay the *Tirpitz*, and in exactly the place we'd been told to look for it."[15]

She was lying in her berth, bows pointing northeast toward the entrance to the fjord. The first wisps of smoke were starting to curl from the artificial fog generators on ship and shore but far too late to spoil the bombers' aim. Surprise had been almost total. *Tirpitz* was due to set sail for high-speed trials in Stjern sound, at the entrance to the open sea, at 5:30 that morning. Her five destroyers had already set off down the fjord, the net defenses were open and the crew were casting off cables and weighing anchor when the radar warning came of approaching enemy aircraft. Kapitän Meyer ordered everyone to action stations but when the first airplanes appeared, flak crews were still scrambling to their posts and below decks watertight doors hung open.

As soon as the ship came in sight, Baker-Falkner broke radio silence and Herrold heard him order "all fighters anti-flak!" The gun crews were still trying to bring their weapons to bear when they were set upon. The Wildcats of 882 Squadron "whistled down over forested hills ... [and] shot across the fjord in a straggling line abreast," their CO, Lieutenant Commander A. J. Cooper, reported later, "shooting into the battleship ... various missiles appeared to be whizzing in all directions ... very exciting."[16] Moments later, at 5:29 a.m., they were followed by the Barracudas, led by Baker-Falkner. Herrold watched him "doing a half-roll and plunging towards the target. We peeled off and dived down behind him." He could see the fighters "strafing the anti-aircraft gun positions and the ship, spraying their machine gun fire ... at incredibly close range." The result of these attentions was "a very slight and very ragged flak opposition during the whole operation."

Herrold was fourth in line, swooping at an angle of fifty degrees. He "had the nose of my aircraft pointing just below the funnel of the *Tirpitz* ... and kept her nose glued to that point." He could see the swastika painted on the forecastle and the "white faces of the ack-ack crews looking up." And then "a great sight." Two of Baker-Falkner's three 500-lb. high explosive bombs hit near the ship's two big forward turrets.

Seconds later, with his altimeter showing 2,500 feet, Herrold let his three 500-lb. SAPs go, "then pulled over and started weaving to dodge the flak."

Bombs were bursting all over *Tirpitz*. Baker-Falkner was followed by Sub-Lieutenant H. R. Emerson, carrying a single 1,600-lb. AP, and it seemed to Sub-Lieutenant I. G. Robertson, hard behind him, that he had landed it "aft of amidships." This was dreamlike accuracy and as each subsequent pilot tilted onto the target, they reported repeated huge red flashes and orange flames. It only took a few seconds for smoke from the explosions to roll over the ship. When the first 830 Squadron aircraft went into its dive the observer, Lieutenant J. Armitage, noted that "amidships and forward parts of the ship were wreathed in smoke." The result was that he was unable to follow his own 1,600-lb. bomb all the way down. Thereafter the aircraft were aiming into the smoke and flame. Alan Thomson's Barracuda was the last of the Barracudas to dive. As his pilot, Sub-Lieutenant Dickie Williams, put the nose down to sixty-five degrees he "experienced negative G for the first time, I had a signal pad strapped to my knee and it floated as high as my eyes." As they hurtled down he saw "our bombs disappear into the smoke and fire … I don't know if we had hits or not. But the flashes suggested we did."

As they turned to escape he noticed "five columns of smoke on the shore." He thought for a moment they might be the result of bombs that overshot. In fact they were produced by land-based fog generators starting up, "but they'd left it too late and they had been caught with their trousers down." Williams took the aircraft around, waiting for a chance to dart through a gap in the bowl of hills to the west that was their best route out. A "gun battery ashore was concentrating fire on that point and it was a case of watching for the fire and trying to nip through before the next salvo came up." When they passed safely through, the skies over Kaafjord were empty. The whole attack from first to last had taken, Baker-Falkner proudly reported later, "sixty-seconds exactly."

In the roiling smoke and flame below, the crew of *Tirpitz* was experiencing for the first time the real shock of war. The exposed upper decks had been crowded with men engaged in casting off when the attackers arrived. In seconds, the orderly drills were replaced by chaos, and the spotless decks were slippery with blood. Karl Rohwedder reached his action station commanding one of the light flak batteries and started to return fire at the blue-green bombers skidding down the sky toward him at 230 mph. "We kept on firing but could not get any more ammunition via the lift that usually brought it up and had to rely on our existing supplies," he remembered. Flash from a blast scorched his face, but he kept at his post until eventually persuaded to go below for treatment. "The hospital area had taken a hit and we sat in the dark and waited. There were people who were a lot more seriously wounded than I was. It was terrible sitting there in the dark with all the shouting and screaming and in the end I couldn't stand it." A nurse gave him a bandage, and he tied it on himself before climbing back on deck to await a further attack.[17]

At 6:19 a.m. the first aircraft began landing on *Victorious*. By 6:38 a.m. the Barracudas were safely back on board their carriers. "All aircraft returned in flight formation with a unanimous broad grin," reported Captain Denny. Only one was missing. Aircraft "M" from 830 Squadron, with Sub-Lieutenant Thomas Bell, Leading Airman George "Paddy" Burns, and Sub-Lieutenant Robert Drennan on board, had been seen by another aircraft "going down in a controlled glide" over a lake on the return journey. Alan Thomson was friendly with Burns, who earlier in the year declined to fly with a pilot because he doubted his competence and was assigned to Bell instead. There was no time to reflect on the vagaries of fate. Thomson went below with the others for breakfast and a shot of rum. It felt like the start of a victory celebration.

By now the second wave of Barracudas was already over the target. The two squadrons of 52 Wing started taking off at 5:25 a.m. One developed engine trouble and there had been a fatal mishap when another, from 829 Squadron, crashed into the sea with a 1,600-lb. bomb on board, killing Sub-Lieutenant Francis Bowles, Lieutenant John Whittaker, and Leading Airman Colin Colwill. Shortly after the remaining nineteen crossed the coast, they could see, forty miles away, a dark cloud polluting the virgin blue of the sky, the product of the fog generators and the smoke from the onboard fires. As they approached Kaafjord the wing commander, Lieutenant Commander V. Rance, ordered them into two double columns, hoping this dispersal would make them a less concentrated target for the flak. Once again, the escorting Hellcats went in first to shoot up the onshore batteries while the Wildcats sprayed the ship.

Following the first attack, the ship had maneuvered into a position where she was lying broadside across the fjord, with her bow facing west, apparently the better to bring her guns to bear in the direction of the next anticipated attack. It made little difference.

The close-range flak guns opened up as soon as they saw the approaching aircraft which, as Rance insouciantly reported, was "much too early" to do any damage.[18] As they prepared to dive, a canopy of flak began bursting at about 3,000 feet. Undeterred, Rance led his men into the dive. It was 6:36 a.m. At intervals of a few seconds, the Barracudas slid toward the ship, showering two 1,600-lb. AP bombs and thirty-nine 500-lb. and 600-lb. bombs onto the still-visible shape below. A bare minute later the attack was over. Rance reported that "*Tirpitz* had ceased firing by the time the last aircraft dived." Not, though, before its gunners claimed one of the attackers. An 829 Squadron Barracuda, with Sub-Lieutenants Hubert Richardson and Andrew Cannon and Leading Airman Ernest Carroll, was hit over the target but carried on the attack, only to be seen crashing into a hillside in flames.

The rest made their getaway over the mountains to the north and west. Forty minutes later they were landing on *Victorious* and *Furious* with reports of hits, explosions, and fires. There was no doubt in Captain

Denny's mind that the operation had been a success. At 6:28 a.m., while the first-wave aircraft were still landing on *Victorious*, he signalled Admiral Moore on *Anson*: "It is certain that Tirpitz is badly hit by first strike." He spent the rest of the day studying the crew debriefing notes and the photographs from the cameras of the bombers before delivering his preliminary assessment of the results. He judged that the first wave hit *Tirpitz* with three 1,600-lb. APs, four 500-lb. SAPs, and three 500-lb. high explosive bombs. The second wave landed four SAPs and two 500-lb. and one 600-lb. anti-submarine bombs on target. One of the big armor-piercing bombs struck in the "vicinity of the fore superstructure." Other bombs landed on the forecastle, amidships, forward of the bridge, on the starboard side of the mainmast, and close by two of the big gun turrets. At 5:37 p.m. he sent his report to Moore with the bold conclusion: "I believe *Tirpitz* now to be useless as a warship."

The emphatic tone was understandable. The great plumes of smoke visible in the photographs painted a dramatic picture of the destruction wrought. The superstructure of *Tirpitz* was a mass of twisted metal. The deck was rent with jagged holes, and everywhere were spurting flames and billowing smoke. The ship's hospital was overwhelmed by the 316 men wounded in the attack and the passageways were lined with casualties awaiting treatment. Another 122 had been killed. Kapitän Meyer was badly wounded, and command of the ship passed to his second in command Kapitän zur See Wolfe Junge. Once she was back in her berth and no further attack arrived, a proper assessment of damage was possible. It soon emerged that the damage, though spectacular, was essentially superficial. Denny's tally of hits was not far from the findings of the ship's chief engineer, Fregattenkapitän Eichler, who counted twelve strikes and four near misses. None of them, though, did critical damage. Holes had been blasted in the port side of the deck, wrecking galleys and the officers' mess and reducing the grand piano, on which Kapitän Assman once entertained the company, to matchwood and wires.

One of the 1,600-pounders landed in the water, holing the hull below the armored belt and causing extensive flooding and a list to starboard. But none of the other big armor-piercing bombs had done its job. One exploded on the port side of the upper deck. Two reached the armor deck but failed to penetrate it. One failed to explode at all. The vital parts of *Tirpitz* remained intact, and the damage to its big guns was slight and easily repairable. Nonetheless, despite their escape, the mood on the ship was somber. Among the casualties, the flak gunners had been particularly hard hit. Many of the guns had no armored shields, and the crews had no protection from the Wildcats' bullets. "We missed the men who had sat down to eat with us, who had operated the turret gun with us," wrote Adalbert Brünner. "It was bitter to take down the photos of wife, parents, and children from their lockers and to send them home."[19]

Subsequent analysis of the operation advanced the idea that the very zeal of the aircrews may have undermined the effectiveness of the 1,600-lb. bombs. They were supposed to be most efficient at heights over 3,500 feet, yet almost all the pilots carrying them dropped below 3,000 feet. The interpretation was that in their enthusiasm to hit the target they had gone in too low. Some doubted whether they would have pierced the armor deck at whatever height they were delivered. Among them was the civilian Director of Naval Construction, the astringent Sir Stanley Goodall. In the course of the post-operation evaluation, the Director of Naval Intelligence, Rear Admiral Edmund Rushbrook, queried the precise thickness of the armor over the *Tirpitz* magazines. Was it three and three-quarter inches as stated in one document or three and a quarter as in another? The reply came from the DNC's office that it made no difference. "Whichever of the figures ... is correct, the armor could not have been defeated by the bombs."

The crews knew nothing of this as they toasted each other in Pusser's rum and endlessly replayed the morning's events. The day wore on, and they began to wonder whether they would be called on to repeat the performance the following day. As they lay in their hammocks, catching up on lost sleep, Thomson heard some "831 personnel, [who] possibly had a stickier [time] than we had, [start] to grumble about the thought we were going back next morning. I just piped up and said, if you don't shut up and get some sleep you'll not be fit to go anywhere in the morning." They did not have to worry long. During the afternoon, Admiral Moore had indeed planned to repeat the performance at first light. On receiving the first reports that *Tirpitz* had been seriously damaged and Denny's verdict that she was now "useless," he reconsidered. He also took into account the "fatigue of the crews and their natural reaction on completing a dangerous operation successfully." Enough was enough. He "decided against a repetition and ordered the forces to withdraw."

At 4:40 p.m. on April 6, the fleet arrived back in Scapa Flow. "It was beautiful," remembered Alan Thompson, aboard *Furious*. "The carrier opened up to thirty knots and we were cheered around the fleet." They took the applause standing on parade without greatcoats in a freezing Orkneys wind. There were letters of congratulation from King George VI and Churchill who praised a "brilliant feat of arms." But the Prime Minister and the First Sea Lord Admiral Cunningham were unable to relax. *Tirpitz* was still afloat. Cunningham had doubted whether the Barracudas' bombs were heavy enough to put *Tirpitz* out of action and confined himself to hoping that "her AA armament, controls and upper works are badly smashed up."[20] He regretted Moore's decision not to launch a second assault the following the day. As serious analysis of the damage got under way, backed with agent reports and photographic reconnaissance, it became clear that the most that could be hoped for was that *Tirpitz* would be out of action for six months. The Germans had already demonstrated their ability to overcome huge logistical difficulties and work at a rate that confounded their enemies' optimistic estimates.

On April 13, ten days after the attack, Cunningham called Moore in and asked him to repeat the operation. He appeared "quite ready to do it." When Cunningham rang Fraser to tell him of developments he found the Home Fleet's commander "in a most obstinate and truculent mood." Fraser had been skeptical about Tungsten's worth from the outset. He told Cunningham now that "he had held a meeting with his admirals and captains and made the decision that 'Tungsten' was not to be repeated." Cunningham "reasoned with him," arguing that the decision was not irrevocable and that the Admiralty must have a say in which operations were to be carried out. Fraser was adamant and said "if we were not satisfied we must get another C-in-C and in fact indicated that he would haul down his flag (resign) if ordered to repeat 'Tungsten.'"

Cunningham told him to sleep on it and to call him in the morning. When they spoke next day, Fraser seemed in a more acquiescent mood. Later on, however, the vice-chief of the naval staff, Neville Syfret, told Cunningham that Fraser was once again talking of resigning. Later in the day he seemed to have softened enough for Cunningham to risk sending a signal ordering the operation.

Fraser's subsequent version of events was less dramatic, and he denied having threatened resignation. He remained convinced, however, that the favorable conditions of the first attack were unlikely to be replicated. The nights were shrinking and there was little hope of achieving the same surprise. As no convoys were scheduled for the next few months, there would be no sailing to divert the enemy's attention. There were also fears that *Tirpitz* now had fighter protection, and the free run the bombers had enjoyed to and from the ships would not be repeated.

Nonetheless he agreed—weather conditions permitting—to try again. As his destroyers were needed at the end of the month to take part in exercises for the Normandy invasion, he proposed that a new operation be mounted before then. Once again, he left his number two in charge. Moore sailed on April 21 with a similar force, planning to strike three days later. Fraser's pessimism was borne out. There was no recurrence of the freakishly fine conditions of Tungsten and the operation was called off, defeated by the weather. Intelligence from Alta suggested that the repair program was progressing fast. On May 9 Torsten Raaby's clandestine wireless station at Alta sent a report that *Tirpitz* had her engines going and two hundred workmen had arrived from Germany to speed along the work.

On May 14, another operation, Brawn, was launched, but the strike force was recalled before it reached the coast as the target was completely covered by cloud. A fortnight later, Operation Tiger Claw was also thwarted by bad weather. With the Normandy landings, attention was diverted away from *Tirpitz*, but not for long. On June 14, the man who might have called a halt to the succession of expensive and fruitless missions departed. Bruce Fraser relinquished command of the Home Fleet to take over the Eastern Fleet and was replaced by Henry Moore. Moore was determined to carry on with carrier-borne attacks, and plans were laid for Operation Mascot, scheduled for mid-July. The strike force took off on July 17 in the near-daylight of an Arctic midnight. Improved radar cover picked up their approach. When they arrived in Kaafjord, *Tirpitz* was blanketed in smoke and none of the bombs dropped hit the target.

With each failed operation *Tirpitz* was returning to something like full health. Watching her progress from Stockholm, the energetic naval spy Captain Henry Denham reported she was making daily trips up and down Altafjord, reaching a speed of twenty knots, and her guns were in full working order. At the end of July she put to sea for an exercise with destroyers. The defenses around Kaafjord were steadily growing stronger. More smoke generators had appeared along the shore. In the minds of the Admiralty, all this activity suggested that an aggressive sortie was imminent and that Kaafjord was being turned into a secure base for operations.

The summer of frustration only intensified the determination for another effort. This time, the biggest force the Fleet Air Arm had ever mustered was to be thrown at the ship. The operation was timed to coincide with the sailing of Convoy JW.59. On August 20 a huge fleet assembled off the Norwegian coast for the launch of Operation Goodwood. At its core were three fleet carriers, *Indefatigable, Formidable*, and *Furious*, together with the smaller *Nabob* and *Trumpeter*, their hangars crammed with forty-eight Barracudas, twenty Avenger torpedo bombers, and a hundred Corsair, Wildcat, and Seafire fighters. Moore oversaw events from his flagship, *Duke of York*, and the armada was attended by swarms of destroyers and corvettes.

Sub-Lieutenant Cyril Price, an observer in an 828 Squadron Barracuda embarked on *Formidable*, looked down while conducting an anti-submarine patrol at the sight of the ships and marveled at the array of craft "spread over a vast, vast distance ... unbelievable." Even at this stage of the war, with Allied armies pushing out from the Normandy beachheads, the objective was still identified as of vital significance. Before leaving Scapa the crews were given a special briefing by civilian officials who "told us how important it was that we did our very best ... [*Tirpitz*] was tying down the Home Fleet and was a terrific threat to the convoys."[21]

Goodwood was due to start on August 21 but bad weather caused a day's postponement. August 22 dawned cloudy and there were further delays until finally the first aircraft launched at 11:00 a.m., only for the Barracudas to be recalled when it became clear that thick cloud would make bombing pointless. Fog the next day ruled out another effort, but on August 24 the weather cleared sufficiently by the afternoon for another attempt. The strike force was made up of thirty-three Barracudas, each carrying a 1,600-lb. AP, as well as five Corsairs and ten Hellcats armed with armor-piercing bombs. By now it took only ten minutes for the smoke generators to blanket Kaafjord and by the time they arrived

Tirpitz was invisible. From 12,000 feet, all Cyril Price could see "was smoke down below." He and his pilot decided to aim at the flashes from the ship's guns and "put the nose down and dived down through the smoke, hoping we were aiming in the right direction." He found "the scary part was pulling out of the dive at the bottom because you were in the smoke, surrounded by mountains, with all these aircraft dashing around."

Out of the shower of bombs, two found the target. One 500-pounder hit the Bruno turret, doing minor damage. The other was a 1,600-lb. AP which for once achieved what it was designed to do, plunging through the ship at an angle to penetrate the armored deck and ending up jammed lengthwise with its nose pointing at the bow in an electrical switch room below the water line. A detonation would, as the report later acknowledged, have done "immeasurable" damage,[22] but the bomb failed to explode. The team given the delicate job of defusing it could find no obvious reason for the failure, noting only that the "detonation device" was "damaged." The fuse was too awkwardly placed to remove immediately so they neutralized the bomb by sluicing out the explosive. The ship's log summed up: "The hitherto greatest attack has not resulted in any lasting damage."[23]

The fleet hung around for five more days, buffeted by gales and shrouded in fog, before launching a final attack on August 29. Sixty aircraft took part, only to be frustrated again by the smoke generators. That evening the great armada began to disperse, with seventeen aircraft and forty airmen fewer than they had arrived with. The Fleet Air Arm's greatest operation of the war had ended in failure. It was now time for the RAF to take up the challenge.

CHAPTER 18

THE THIRD MAN

One morning at the end of August 1944, a group of airmen was playing football on their airfield at Woodhall Spa, Lincolnshire, when there was an interruption. "Somebody arrived on the touchline and asked for our CO, Willie Tait," said Tony Iveson, a twenty-four-year-old flight lieutenant. Tait disappeared and came back later "to say that we had a special job." The game broke up and later that day the players were in the air on the first of a series of cross-country flights.

All the jobs the airmen did were special. They were members of 617 Squadron—the Dambusters—and they had spent the summer carrying out attacks requiring exceptional accuracy on vital targets in France. Tait did not tell his men the nature of their next mission and speculation bubbled. That afternoon the engines on Iveson's Lancaster were fitted with flow meters and he and his crew took off for seven and a half hours of tests at different heights and speeds to find the most economic rate of fuel consumption. Wherever they were going, "we all knew it was going to be a long trip. It struck one or two people that *Tirpitz* was a possible target."[1]

Even before the Fleet Air Arm's great effort had definitively failed, new plans were being hatched to dispose of *Tirpitz*. The repeated operations of the summer had revealed a simple truth: the Barracudas were simply not fast enough to get to Kaafjord in time to beat the smokescreen. At a meeting of the Chiefs of Staff Committee on August 19—the day after the Goodwood force put to sea—Admiral Cunningham raised the possibility of using the RAF's faster Mosquito bombers, carrying 2,000-lb. armor-piercing bombs, to launch an attack from one of his carriers. The idea was passed up to the headquarters of General Eisenhower—who, in order to obtain the tightest coordination in preparations for the Normandy landing, had been given control of the strategic bombing force—and also to Bomber Command. The answer came back that the Supreme Allied Commander did "not consider diversion of Mosquito bomber effort justifiable at this moment." This rejection produced a sharp reaction from the Admiralty. It retorted that Eisenhower "was not in a position to appreciate the significance which an attack on 'Tirpitz' would have on the overall strategic plan" and dared to suggest that the direction of the bomber force should revert to the RAF.[2]

The admirals' indignation was stoked by their conviction that even in her diminished state *Tirpitz* still posed a serious threat to Allied shipping and a major obstacle to their plans. Cunningham had told his fellow chiefs that eliminating her would "have an important effect ... on world wide dispositions of battleships and fleet carriers and on the early strengthening of the Eastern Fleet."[3] The importance of finishing her off was emphasized in an August 23 report of the inter-service Joint Planning Staff which claimed that *Tirpitz* was still "capable of carrying out limited operations, or of returning to Germany [where] a period of a few months in a German dockyard would ... fully restore her fighting efficiency." If left unmolested she might "risk everything in a final effort" against a Russian or Atlantic convoy, or even attack a troopship bound for France. Her destruction would not only neutralize this menace; it would also remove the need to hold the minimum of "one fast battleship and one fleet carrier" at the ready in case of a breakout.[4]

At this distance in time, these fears seem exaggerated. *Tirpitz* remained afloat but she was battered and enfeebled. Despite the heroic efforts of the repair force she could only muster twenty knots, against the twenty-eight knots of her British equivalents. In this condition she was unfit for serious operations. If she did try to regain a German port, she would be vulnerable to attack by Allied surface ships, submarines, and aircraft on passage. If she survived the voyage, she would then be assured of the attentions of Bomber Command.

Admiral Dönitz had no intention of sending *Tirpitz* off on a last, death-or-glory sortie. The strength of the enemy, in the air and above and below the waves, meant the chance of success was minimal while catastrophe was virtually assured. He also recognized that it would have been "impossible for her to undertake the long journey home through the North Sea without being detected by the enemy and subjected to attack by superior sea and air forces." The ship had no role to play elsewhere. Her uses were therefore limited to "protection against any enemy landing in the area" and "[tying] down the enemy heavy ships to the north European zone and [preventing] them being sent to some other theatre of war."[5]

Of all the rationalizations for continuing the assaults, then, it was the argument that putting an end to *Tirpitz* would release heavy warships for duty in the Far East that had the most validity. The war in the central Pacific—a struggle in which aircraft carriers were of paramount importance—was moving toward a climax. The Americans were poised to close on the Philippines, and the Royal Navy's Eastern Fleet needed reinforcements to play its part in the Allied plan and to assert its right to a continued presence in the area when peace came.

The solution to the Admiralty's problems now lay in the hands of a man who until recently had demonstrated little interest in *Tirpitz* or its destruction. Arthur Harris regarded battleships as pointless relics of a vanished age, whose survival owed more to the *amour propre* of admirals than to strategic necessity. Following the COS committee meeting of August 19, Harris had also been asked for his opinion of Cunningham's proposal for an attack by Mosquito bombers. Nine days later, Sir Douglas Evill, the Vice Chief of the Air Staff, visited him at Bomber Command's High Wycombe HQ to hear the response. Harris trashed the plan. He doubted "very much" whether Mosquitoes were fast enough to get to the battleship before the smokescreen rolled in, and he doubted the capacity of the bombs to do serious damage. Nor did he want to divert his Mosquito force from its regular raids on Berlin.

Lurking in this disparaging assessment, though, was a possible solution to the navy's problems. According to Evill's report to his chief, Sir Charles Portal, Harris told him that Bomber Command "had for some time been considering the problem of bombing the 'Tirpitz' and the only reason they had not pressed on with it was because they did not realise the importance the Admiralty placed on this attack."

The last part seems to have been an example of Harris's knockabout wit. No one could have been ignorant of the titanic efforts of the Fleet Air Arm throughout the summer. He appears to have realized that he may have overstepped the mark for when a copy of Evill's report reached him, he protested that he had been misrepresented and the account was "quite incorrect." The true reason for holding back was that "the only bomb suitable for an attack on 'Tirpitz' is the 'Tallboy,' the supply of which has been barely sufficient to cover the Command's immediate commitments." This version was duly inserted into the official record.[6]

In his 1947 memoirs Harris nonetheless presented a colorful account of how Bomber Command came to be engaged once more in the great campaign against *Tirpitz*:

> During all this period the Admiralty continued to worry about the German navy and in particular, in the autumn of 1944, about the *Tirpitz*. Our own battleships with their usual large complement of ancillary craft, were kept hanging about at home in case the Germans should decide to send the poor old lone *Tirpitz* to sea, and it was felt that some use might be found for these large units of the Royal Navy in the Pacific. I was accordingly asked to intervene in this fantastic 'war' between these dinosaurs ... I was quite willing to do so, but only if this did not seriously interfere with more important operations; I gave an undertaking that we should sink the *Tirpitz* in our spare time.[7]

This interpretation, amusing though it was to Harris with its implication of a despairing Admiralty imploring Bomber Command for deliverance, is not quite in accordance with the record. At the meeting with Evill, Harris already had a fully-formed plan up his sleeve. He told him that he could have twenty-four aircraft available for an operation ready by September 7—only ten days away. They would attempt to fly on a round trip from the far north of Scotland to Kaafjord and then back again to a base in the Shetlands. If the return journey looked risky, arrangements could be made for the bombers to carry on to north Russia, to land and refuel at Murmansk. Inquiries had already been made and it appeared suitable facilities were available.

Harris seems to have been in no doubt that the plan would be accepted and preparations were well under way by the time the final approval was received from Eisenhower's headquarters on September 5. The operation was to be carried out by his two Special Duties units, 617 and 9 Squadrons. They lived a few miles apart from each other in the rich, flat fields east of Lincoln. Of the two, 617 was by far the best known. It was 9 Squadron, however, that had the oldest pedigree. While 617 was only seventeen months old, having been formed specifically for the Dams raid, 9 Squadron dated back to 1914. After disbandment in 1919 it re-formed in 1924 as a night bomber squadron, later acquiring a bat as its badge symbol and the motto "Per noctem volamus" (We fly through the night). It started operations on the first day of the war, attacking shipping at Brunsbüttel at the mouth of the Kiel Canal, and losing two Wellingtons to ground fire or fighters. Since then it had been in the vanguard of the strategic bomber campaign, returning night after night to blast German cities and ports and suffering staggering casualties in the process. In 1943 it lost fifty-seven aircraft, nearly three times the squadron strength. In the spring and summer of 1944, it had been occupied with invasion targets, led by Wing Commander James Bazin, a former fighter pilot who flew Hurricanes with 607 in the Battle of Britain. Now it was to be switched away from the grind of "main force" operations and join 617 on special operations, swapping its conventional bombs for the streamlined sophistication of the Tallboy.

The Tallboy was the latest invention of Barnes Wallis, "our Number One Wizard" as Harris called him. Wallis was a creative engineer, and in the words of his friend and biographer J. E. Morpurgo "saw creative engineering as an art and himself as a sort of poet."[8] In the crucible of wartime, his prodigious talent and energy had produced some remarkable and valuable inventions.

The idea for the Tallboy dated back to 1940 but Wallis had only been put to work on developing it in the summer of 1943, when it was discovered that the Germans were close to deploying flying bombs and long-range ballistic missiles—the V1s and V2s. The only defense available was to bomb the sites where they were being developed or stored. A mass raid by nearly six hundred aircraft dropped 1,937 tons of bombs on the V2 missile research center at Peenemünde on the Baltic coast on August 17, 1943. This was a huge attack, but forty aircraft were lost and the program was set back by only two months. The blunt instruments that were all Bomber Command had available could not do the job. Something more precise and deadly was required.

Wallis had foreseen the need for a bomb for use against "targets ... of the most massive nature ... practically invulnerable to attack by existing aerial methods."[9] It was axiomatic that the bigger the bomb, the greater its destructive potential, but in the first years of the war, aircraft lacked the lifting power to carry monster weapons. With the arrival of the Lancaster, capacity increased. Tallboy was not just a very big bomb; it was designed to bury itself in the ground and explode, producing an earthquake effect. Shockwaves ripple more powerfully through earth— and water—than they do through air. Thus, a Tallboy did not have to score a direct hit to destroy its target.

To achieve the penetration needed for the best results, the bomb had to be dropped from high altitudes. It needed to be tough and aerodynamically efficient to withstand the impact. Wallis's bomb was made of molybdenum steel, sufficiently strong and light to carry a high proportion of explosive—5,000 pounds of Torpex in an all-up weight of 12,000 pounds It was twenty-one feet long, tapering to a point that was as sharp as a pencil and fitted comfortably into the Lancaster's thirty-three-foot bomb bay. According to its inventor, "previously bombs had just [been] made [of] thin steel casings which dropped from the sky. But I gave this bomb [a] perfect aerodynamic shape and arranged the fins so they would impart to it an increasingly rapid spin. As the bomb attained a high velocity it actually passed through the speed of sound and penetrated the ground to a depth of about a hundred feet."[10]

The loss of accuracy that grew with increased altitude was offset by the use of the Stabilized Automatic Bomb Sight (SABS). With conventional sights, the bomb aimer had to guide the pilot up to the moment of release. The delay between instruction and adjustment left an inevitable margin of error. The SABS was the most sophisticated aiming device to date. Shortly before arrival at the objective the navigator passed data on airspeed, altitude, and wind direction to the bomb aimer, lying in the nose of the aircraft, to be fed into the instrument's computer. He then peered through the lens of the sight, speaking into the captain's earphones, calling "left, right, steady" as needed until the target lay at the tip of a lit-up sword symbol reflected on a sheet of glass. As the target grew closer he held it in place, sliding down the blade of the sword, with two control wheels. These activated an instrument mounted in front of the pilot—the Bombing Direction Indicator. A needle on the face then told him the slight adjustments needed to keep the aircraft on track. Then, at the optimum moment, the bomb was released automatically. An experienced aimer could drop a bomb from 20,000 feet with an average margin of error of only eighty yards. To do so, of course, he needed to have clear sight of the target. Over cloud—or smokescreen—the SABS was useless.

Throughout the summer of 1944, 617 Squadron had been using both Tallboy and the SABS in specially modified Lancasters against V weapons sites buried deep under concrete in the Pas-de-Calais. In the month of August, prior to the summons to prepare for a "special job" they had repeatedly and successfully bombed the previously invulnerable submarine pens at the Biscay ports of Brest, Lorient, and La Pallice.

A new commander led them into these attacks—Wing Commander Tait, who for reasons never established was always known as "Willie."

His arrival at 617 Squadron in July marked the opening of another remarkable passage in what was already an extraordinary wartime career. If there had never been a Second World War, James Brian Tait's service career might have passed in obscurity. As it was, he emerged from it laden with decorations and bathed in the esteem of his comrades. Tony Iveson placed him in the highest rank of the aces of the war "alongside Guy Gibson, Leonard Cheshire, Donald Bennett, Johnnie Johnson and Douglas Bader." Unlike them, Tait would never become widely known in the world outside the RAF. That was exactly how he liked it. "He had no interest in being the center of attention," said his son, Peter. "Ever."

There was, in his antecedents, some hint of what the demands of war might uncover. According to Iveson, "bravery obviously ran in the Tait family" as James's father, Alexander, had been decorated for his exploits in mining operations under the German lines on the Western Front.[11] Tait was born on December 9, 1916, in Manchester, where his mother had gone to stay with relatives while her husband was in France. At the age of twelve, he was taken by his father to watch the Schneider Trophy races off Portsmouth, and, like many other boys of his generation, was soon smitten by the world of flying. He was sent off to board at Wellingborough School in Northamptonshire, from where, in 1934, at seventeen, he won a prize scholarship to the RAF College at Cranwell.

Despite his love of flying "the intention was that he was going to develop an engineering career in the RAF," said Peter Tait. Throughout his service he maintained his knowledge and practical skills, to the extent of taking courses at the RAF apprentice school at Halton which qualified him to do some maintenance work on engines. This was unusual. Few officers had a detailed understanding of the functioning of the machines they flew in. Leslie White, the mechanic responsible for maintaining Tait's aircraft in 1942 told of him visiting the hangar on the morning of an operation to discover that his bomber was unserviceable due to a coolant leak in one of the engines. Tait asked how long the repair would take. White replied that he could not say, as the rest of the crew had been moved to another job and he was working alone. Reminding his old boss of the incident years later, White recalled: "You said 'I want that plane for tonight because I am leading the squadron on the raid ... start getting the cowlings off and I will go for some assistance.'" He returned half an hour later with several men. He then removed his cap and tunic, climbed into overalls, mounted a maintenance platform and got busy with spanners. The problem was fixed, and after an air test Tait led the squadron on that night's raid.[12]

At the start of the war he was with 10 Squadron, equipped with Heyford biplane bombers. "I don't think he had the temperament for flying fighters," said Peter. "The Taits are not flamboyant." He flew on his first operation in May 1940, and went on to do a hundred more. His emergence alive owed something to skill but also to what Iveson called "that luck which was essential to survive in Bomber Command."

As the boundaries of the bombing campaign advanced, he was always at the frontier. He took part in the first trip to Berlin—dropping leaflets—on the night of October 1–2, and the first raid across the Alps to Turin. In February 1941, now commanding 51 Squadron, he led a small force of Whitleys from Malta to drop a team of parachutists tasked with blowing up an aqueduct near Tragino in southern Italy, the first British airborne operation of the war. The feat won him his first DSO.

He dodged death again and again. After joining 35 Squadron, the first to be equipped with the four-engined Halifax, he led a daylight raid on Kiel. When he landed at Linton-on-Ouse, he was the only one of his crew who did not leave the aircraft on a stretcher. He flew on the first thousand-bomber raid, to Cologne in May 1942. One of his engines failed on the outward journey. He had every excuse to turn back but pressed on to the target.

In July 1942, he took over 78 Squadron and flew regularly alongside his men, disregarding the advice that squadron commanders should go on no more than one operation a month. In the spring of 1944 he was base operations officer at RAF Waddington. Again, he was discouraged from regular operational flying. Nonetheless, in his first six weeks he went on nine missions, joining inexperienced crews with two Australian Lancaster squadrons. The idea was to give them confidence. "He insisted on first of all flying over the target to 'acclimatize' them," said Peter Tait. They then carried out the actual attack. Just as the novice crews thought their baptism of fire was complete, he "insisted on flying low over the target to see what the damage was like." Perhaps his intention was to inoculate them with his own contempt for death. It was, however, Peter reflected, "an experience they never wanted to have again."[13]

In May he returned to full-time operations and was appointed master bomber of No. 5 Group. On the eve of the Normandy landings he controlled a force of two hundred Lancasters tasked with smashing the coastal batteries covering the American landing beaches on the Cherbourg peninsula. The success of the mission earned him a second bar to his DSO. Once again, he took enormous risks, circling low, calmly floating around on what looked like a sea of flak while his cool, precise voice guided the bombers in.

What enabled Tait to remain so serene when all around him combat-hardened men were fighting panic? His comrades discussed it frequently. There were theories as to what drove him on when he had used up his fair share of luck long ago and in statistical terms should have been dead several times over. There was a theory that he was seeking revenge. Peter Tait recalled a rumor "that father had a grudge because a German plane had succeeded in bombing the house that his fiancée had lived in. Totally untrue. I don't honestly think he felt the slightest enmity for the Germans."

If anything, he had sympathy for them. His favorite composers were German and Austrian: Beethoven, and, especially, Schubert, in whom he took an academic interest. "He always used to say that the Germans were our traditional allies against the perfidious French," said Peter, "and that the First and Second World Wars were aberrations really, historically speaking."

Squadron was founded in March 1943 under Guy Gibson. There were two brief appointments between Gibson's departure in August and the arrival of Leonard Cheshire in November. Squadron Leader George Holden was in command for six weeks before he was killed in a fruitless attempt to breech the banks of the Dortmund–Ems canal on the night of September 15–16. Flight Lieutenant Harold "Mick" Martin, a brilliant Australian pilot, took temporary charge but the Bomber Command hierarchy decided against formalizing the appointment. Tait was thus the third man in a triumvirate of extraordinary figures to leave their mark on the Dambusters. The memory of Gibson was beginning to fade by the time he arrived on July 12, 1944. Cheshire, though, was still a palpable presence. In his time with the Dambusters, he had managed to inspire affection—even love—as well as awe in a group of men who were not easily impressed. He did it by a unique mixture of strength, humor, and humility and an unusual concern for those under his command, aircrew and ground crew alike. "It was very difficult to follow a man like Cheshire," said one of his long-serving pilots, Bobby Knights. "He [had] an aura that made everybody else rather small beside him. I hero-worshipped him."[14]

There were obvious differences between the two. Cheshire was a would-be writer, playful and sophisticated, married to an American actress, Constance Binney, whom he whirled off to the Ritz for cocktails when in town. Tait was a RAF professional, with no interest in the high life. But there were similarities, too. Both had quick and questing minds. Above all they shared an uncanny interior calm. An old friend of Cheshire's noted that "he did everything with an air, but that there was at the same time a withdrawn quality about him, a secret self-sufficiency."[15] It was the same inviolable inner stillness that people sensed in Tait. There was another quality that united them—a flinty determination to achieve the objectives they had been set whatever the risk to themselves.

The two knew each other from Linton, when Tait had commanded 78 Squadron and Cheshire 76 Squadron. Tait liked Cheshire enough to make him godfather to his first child, Celia. "As a fellow squadron commander there could be no finer person to work with," he wrote in a private memoir. "His clear, logical brain always picked out the essence of any problem." The two worked harmoniously together "free from the petty jealousy which was all too common between squadron commanders on the same station."[16] Cheshire admired Tait sufficiently to try to convert him to Catholicism. It was never very probable. According to Peter, his father's religiosity extended only to being "Church of England in an agnostic sort of way. He liked the ceremonial."

He was unlikely to reproduce the warm relationship with his men that Cheshire had fostered. As Tait acknowledged, "the charm of his personality was unique. It never broke down under stress, and in fact his endurance was remarkable. I have known nobody who could get more out of men than him, simply because they would do it for him. He was a leader and not a driver."[17] Tait was himself an understanding boss, who, despite his own background as a prewar professional, had little patience with attempts to impose service bull on men whose spirit was that of civilians in uniform. "He certainly had a mind of his own," said Peter Tait. "On one station, there was a rather tedious group captain who wanted to put the airmen on parade. Of course bomber crews weren't much good at parades, so father said we're not going to [do it]. We're going to play football … he was threatened with court martial for that." The episode ended with him being sent to Harris for reprimand. "Butch" lectured him, but then, as Tait was turning the door handle, spoiled the effect by saying, "Well done, I'd have done the same thing myself."

In the mess he "looked like a hawk that had touched down for a drink beside a pool."[18] He was a listener not a talker, standing quietly with pipe in hand and a modest half-pint tankard tucked under his arm. When he did speak it was with intensity more appropriate to a university seminar than a barroom chat. Lawrence "Benny" Goodman, who arrived on the squadron in August, felt this reticence indicated diffidence rather than aloofness. "He didn't keep himself to himself for any other reason than that he was, essentially, a shy person."[19] Tait's social appearances were brief, and Tony Iveson found he had to coax him to descend from his bedroom and join the squadron in the bar. While others roistered, he was "more likely to be listening to Beethoven quartets on his gramophone," said Peter.

Tait took over a squadron in flux. When Cheshire left, his three flight commanders, Dave Shannon, Les Munro, and Joe McCarthy, moved on, too. They had been with 617 from the beginning, and with their departure went the last of the original Dambusters. Those who remained were an individualistic and international bunch, all of them competent, experienced, and self-confident. In the summer of 1944, Sir Ralph Cochrane, the commander of 5 Group to which both 617 and 9 Squadrons belonged, felt the unit was strong enough to be able to absorb new crews with less combat experience. In the case of Goodman and his comrades, they had none at all. They had been astonished to hear that as a "baby" crew they were being posted to the most famous squadron in the air force and arrived "feeling very much like the underdogs, frightened to say boo to a goose." The old hands, though, treated the new boys as equals "and it soon became clear to us that we'd been accepted."[20]

Despite his awesome record, Tait seems to have felt the need to demonstrate from the beginning that he would be leading from the front. His first operation with the squadron was on July 17 against the V2 rocket site at Wizernes, in the Pas-de-Calais. Tait flew as pathfinder in a Mustang fighter, as Cheshire had done, dropping red spot flares on the target for the Lancasters to aim their Tallboys at. "When they got [to] the target [it] was covered in cloud," said Peter Tait. "So he dropped to a lower altitude and circled and said 'Look for me.'" Another version of the story had him waggling his wings to catch the sunlight providing those above with an aiming point. The result was that he "got thoroughly shot up, and came back with a Mustang full of holes ... after that, no one was going to question his leadership."

By the end of August, Tait and his men were adept at dropping Tall-boys on land-based targets. The *Tirpitz* operation, though, would be the first time one had been used on a ship. It had soon become clear that with the distances involved, a round trip would not be feasible. The plan was changed so that after the attack the two squadrons would fly on to an airfield in north Russia. The initial choice of the Murmansk area was dropped as it was feared that the force would be vulnerable to attack by German fighters while on the ground. They settled on a base further east. A Soviet naval air station at Yagodnik, on an island in the Dvina River twenty miles southeast of Archangel, seemed suitable even though it had only a grass runway. After consultations with the Russians—who, now that victory was approaching, had adopted a more comradely attitude—Yagodnik was chosen.

The attack was code-named Operation Paravane, and all was due to be ready by September 8. Good weather was crucial to success. Clear skies were essential if the 617 bomb aimers were to see the target. With preparations completed, the crews waited for a favorable forecast. Hanging about at Woodhall Spa was no hardship. The officers' mess was housed in Petwood, a mock-Tudor mansion built for an heiress of the Maples furniture family, and the oak staircases, large rooms, and sweeping lawns represented wild luxury in the monochrome austerity of wartime. By now, the crews knew the nature of their mission. On September 8, 9 Squadron were driven the few miles over the flat Lincolnshire fields from their base at Bardney to join 617 at Woodhall for a secret briefing. The briefing room floor was covered with a large-scale model of Kaafjord complete with a miniature *Tirpitz*.

The mission was more complex and potentially dangerous than the short trips to the continent of the summer. Every aspect of the operation was problematic. The intention was to fly to Lossiemouth on the eastern tip of Scotland and refuel there before setting off for Russia. The Lancasters had been fitted with extra fuel tanks that took up much of the fuselage. Even with these, the 2,100-mile journey stretched the bombers' endurance to the limit. There were no radio beacons to guide them in until the last stage of the journey. For most of the way navigators would have to rely on dead reckoning and map reading to get to Yagodnik. On the actual attack they could expect to face fiercer flak than they encountered over France. There also remained the threat of fighters which, despite intelligence that they were present in the area, had mysteriously failed to come up to defend *Tirpitz* from the Fleet Air Arm.

Next day the forecast was bad again, and there was a PT session to fill the time. There was one more day of standing by and then, on September 11, the weather prospects brightened. Harris, who had taken a close interest in the operation, grasped the chance. At this last moment, he decided on a change of plan. Instead of bombing on the way to Russia, the aircraft would fly to Yagodnik first and launch their attack from there. The shorter distance involved meant a greater opportunity to catch the clear skies that were essential if the Tallboys were to be dropped with any accuracy. There was also the chance that the Germans would not be expecting an attack from Russia. An approach from the east might evade the radar and catch the ship's defenses off guard.

Harris called the Air Staff with the details of the new arrangements and the news that he intended to dispatch the bombers that evening. The deputy chief, Sir Norman Bottomley, received the announcement with some irritation. He complained that the plan should have been cleared with the Russians first. "I pointed out that this was very short notice, especially in view of the possibilities of failures in recognition, if warning was not received in time, with consequent untoward incidents," he huffed in a back-covering memo. Harris was unconcerned, telling him that there was "no material change" to the situation and that he had, anyway, already given orders for the aircraft to proceed. As it was, the Russians accepted the new plan without fuss. The hurried departure, however, did cause problems, which, but for luck, might well have proved catastrophic.

With no detour to Kaafjord on the outward journey, it was thought that the Lancasters had the range to reach Yagodnik from their home bases. At 5:00 p.m. on Monday, September 11, 1944, eighteen bombers from 9 Squadron left Bardney and twenty from 617 took off from Woodhall, each making their own way to their destination. Two Liberators loaded with spares, stores, and ground staff, who headed first to Lossiemouth to refuel, preceded the 9 Squadron force. A Lancaster carrying three RAF cameramen, a BBC radio reporter, and an Associated Press war correspondent went with the Bardney force to record the hoped-for triumph. It was piloted by Flight Lieutenant Bruce "Buck" Buckham, a twenty-six-year-old Australian who had survived a tour with 426 Squadron, winning a DFC for struggling home on two engines after a raid on Essen and was on transfer with his aircraft "Whoa Bessie" to the RAF film unit. A PRU Mosquito would join later to carry out weather reconnaissance. Twenty-six of the attacking force carried a single Tallboy. The others were loaded with JW "Johnny Walker" antiship mines. No one had any confidence in their efficiency. They were "supposed to fall into the fjord, reach the bottom and jump about in the hope that in one of their jumps they would strike the underside of the *Tirpitz*," said Tony Iveson. "I cannot think of anything more stupid than the JWs we carried that day."[21] The weather forecast for the journey was good. The force was expected to land at Yagodnik at dawn and, if fine conditions persisted, to carry out the attack later the same day.

The crews took off as the early autumn afternoon was fading to dusk, climbing over the fens and flatlands, glancing back for a last look at the towers of Lincoln Cathedral lit by the setting sun, and turned over the limitless plain of gray water stretching north and east. The navigator was kept busy with his charts and calculations but for the others the time passed mostly in monotony, and in their minds, apprehension changed places with boredom, then back again. When they reached the Gulf of Bothnia, things livened up. Tony Iveson looked down from the cockpit at lights glowing in the darkness below from neutral Sweden. To see a town illuminated after years of blackout was somehow shocking. Then there were other lights. As Flying Officer Bill Carey of 617 crossed into Finland, streams of flak rose towards him. He swung his aircraft off its straight and level course but there was a thud of impacts. The Lancaster was still flying and nobody was hurt but now a different danger was looming for everyone.

The good weather they had enjoyed for most of the journey was worsening. As dawn came up and they crossed the Finnish border into Russia, they were advancing into a wall of cloud, up to 6,000 feet thick and hovering only a few hundred feet above the ground. It was not what they had been told to expect. Traveling in one of the Liberators was Group Captain Colin McMullen, a thirty-six-year-old 5 Group staff officer, who left his home in Australia as a young man to join the RAF and was charged with controlling the operation from the ground. The appalling weather was "hardly in keeping with the forecast anticipated," he wrote in his subsequent report. The speed of departure meant that no forecast had been sought from the Russians, who were much better placed to give an accurate prediction. At the last Met briefing, the crews had been told to expect a cloud base at 1,500 feet and visibility of six miles at Archangel.[22]

The aircraft were forced lower and lower. The bomb aimers looked down from their perches in the nose, hoping to identify some feature that would point them in the right direction. The landscape was a "waste of marsh or endless pine forests and innumerable small lakes."[23] The maps they had been given did not show towns and railways. Their best hope of help was from the Russians. During the final briefings the crews were given a radio call sign, which, when tapped out in Morse, would raise Yagodnik. The letters were in English. The Russians worked in Russian. The signals meant nothing and the dots and dashes streamed out unanswered into the ether.

They rumbled on, through the murk and rain squalls, scouring the treetops below for some feature that might point the way. Tony Iveson finally saw an expanse of water that he hoped was the White Sea. There was a town and an airfield on the shore and he made it the start point for his search for Yagdonik, figuring he could always put down there if he didn't find it. They quartered the land to the east but eventually, with fuel running low, gave up and landed to be met by Russian soldiers, "unshaven, wearing German greatcoats, carrying rifles and looking as if for two roubles they would do us." Another Lancaster had also landed, piloted by Nick Knilans, a Wisconsin farm-boy who, after being turned down by the US Army Air Force, joined the Royal Canadian Air Force and finally the RAF. They were all driven to the seaside town—Onega as it turned out—and taken to the office of the mayor who asked through a female interpreter where they had come from. "They had a map on the wall," remembered Iveson. "I pointed to Lincolnshire and they couldn't believe it."[24]

All over the area other crews were making their own unscheduled landings. Of the forty-two aircraft that left from Britain, only twenty-one made it to Yagodnik. The rest roamed the skies as their tanks ran dry, eventually putting down in any airfield they could find or ditching with their wheels up in the least daunting looking stretch of tundra. Four Lancasters from 9 Squadron and two from 617 were written off in crash landings. McMullen felt they had got off lightly. "It is amazing that no one was injured in any of these crashes and it is even more extraordinary that so few crashes occurred," he recorded. "A loss of at least half the force might have happened in the circumstances."

It was obvious that there would be no operation that day as the original orders had optimistically and unrealistically proposed. Throughout the rest of the day, Lancasters arrived at Yagodnik, and their crews went off in search of a bed leaving them to the attentions of the ground staff. Not all the aircraft that landed undamaged were serviceable and one Lancaster needed an engine change. It seemed that twenty-eight Lancasters, including the film unit aircraft, might be ready for operations the following day. Then came another unpleasant surprise. They had been told that three 5,000-gallon and five 2,000-gallon tankers would be available at the base. In fact there were six with a capacity of a paltry few hundred gallons each, and refueling all the aircraft for the attack would take eighteen hours.

All through Wednesday, September 13, the ground crews worked ceaselessly on the wet and windy airfield, servicing and pumping fuel and taking it in turns to grab a few hours' rest. The others hung around waiting on the weather reports. The base was bleak, a place of "weather-beaten hutments, dun-colored flat earth and gray winding river," in Tait's description.[25] The Soviets, though, were assiduous hosts. The surly resentment of the earlier stages of the war had given way to a keen desire to impress. They were playing host to 325 RAF personnel—seventy-five more than they had been told to expect—and they were determined to be hospitable. "WELCOME THE GLORIOUS FLIERS OF THE ROYAL AIR FORCE" declared a banner stretched over a paddle steamer, *Ivan Kalyev*, moored on the Dvina, where some of the officers were billeted. The extra numbers meant the rest of the party were crammed into underground huts, where along with the overcrowding they had to contend with bed bugs. On the first night everyone, with the exception of Tait, was bitten, proving, it was said, that "even communist bugs have respect for rank."

Early on Thursday, the PRU Mosquito took off with Flight Lieutenant George Watson at the controls and Warrant Officer John MacArthur navigating to scout the weather in the Kaafjord area. They came back with bad news. Operations were officially scrubbed and the crews settled in for another day of inaction. In the afternoon, 617 took on an immaculately outfitted Soviet team from the base at football and were beaten 4–0—"a diplomatic defeat which was fruitful," in McMullen's view.

The meals were good, served up on nice china with proper cutlery and linens. The largesse, McMullen was to discover later, was a touching deception. He and a few colleagues had to linger on for another ten days after the main party had departed for Britain and found that the quality of the food deteriorated to the point where they were forced to live off the tinned emergency rations they had brought with them from Britain. In addition, "various amenities such as cutlery, table napkins, crockery etc were removed until there was insufficient for the small party that remained." He speculated that his hosts had expected the RAF to stay only a week, after which time all the "show items" had to be returned to some central store in Moscow. They were "somewhat disconcerted that they did not possess the facilities to keep up the pretense for longer … we were correspondingly sympathetic, even if somewhat uncomfortable."[26]

While they waited, Tony Iveson killed some time playing bridge with the BBC reporter Guy Byam, a "very impressive, tall good-looking man." Byam-Corstiaens, to give him his full name, was twenty-seven years old, an intellectual forced by war into the life of a man of action. He was born in Buckinghamshire and went to school in Brighton and France, going on to study at the Sorbonne and Jesus College, Cambridge. He joined the RNVR and was a sub-lieutenant aboard the armed merchant cruiser

Jervis Bay when it was sunk in a gallant action in November 1940. The ship was the sole escort of thirty-seven ships returning to Halifax, Nova Scotia, when the *Admiral Scheer* appeared. The commander of *Jervis Bay*, Captain Edward Fegen, told his charges to scatter while he took on the pocket battleship. There could be only one outcome and *Jervis Bay* was sunk, with the loss of 190 men including Fegen, who was later awarded the VC. Byam was one of the sixty-five survivors, but he had been blinded in his right eye during the battle and invalided out of the navy.

He had hopes of being a writer before the war and had written for the fashionable literary magazine *Lilliput*. He had given a talk on Canadian radio after the sinking, written a screenplay about the incident, and submitted a script to the BBC. BBC seemed an obvious place for a man with literary ambitions and no hope of returning to active service. He was fluent in French and in October 1942 found a job as a sub-editor writing scripts for broadcasting to occupied France. A report a year later by his supervisor praised his "bright and ingenious mind ... nice style and occasional flashes of brilliance."[27] His reporting took him across the Atlantic and around Britain, and as the invasion approached he was transferred to the BBC's War Reporting Unit. He underwent parachute training and won a place at the center of the action in Normandy, dropping with airborne forces on D-Day and sending back vivid dispatches from the front line. He was about to produce another.

At 4:37 a.m. on Friday, September 15, Watson and MacArthur set off for a weather reconnaissance. The crews were gathered in the open for a briefing when they returned at 8:50 a.m. They did not bother to land to report the good news, swooping low over the airfield and firing off a green Very cartridge, the signal that the skies over Kaafjord were clear. "In no time the airscrew blades of the huge bombers commenced to whirr in aggressive chorus as they warmed up for take off," recorded a RAF internal narrative of the action. "The battle was on!"[28]

At 9:30 a.m. the first bomber took off, piloted by Flying Officer Frank Levy of 617, followed by twenty-six more Lancasters at one-minute intervals. Twenty-one of them were carrying Tallboys and the rest Johnny Walker mines. Tait's aircraft was fitted with two VHF radios to direct the other captains during the attack and its wings were painted with heavy white markings to identify his position in the order. They flew in a loose "gaggle" formation, keeping low to avoid the radar, and Byam had a clear view of the lonely landscape below. "It was a lovely day [he broadcast later] and soon we were flying over ice floes below us in the Gulf of Archangel. And then over Finland, over the Petsamo road, the famous motor road that goes into the Arctic Circle. We could see it below stretching northwards into the pine forests. And then on, over Finland and millions of lakes. And the Lancasters in the skies were all around us, and their camouflage hardly discernible against the greens and browns and the blues of the countryside. And on to the Norwegian frontier. And the country more hilly and undulating now."[29]

At the Finnish border they climbed and set course for the rendezvous point, a small lake about a hundred miles south of the target. *Tirpitz* lay moored in front of a spit of land projecting from the southern shore of the fjord, with her bows pointing toward the entrance. The approach would be from the south and west, bombing her from stem to stern. Before they again set off they got into battle order. They were grouped in ranks of five, roughly 500 yards apart and with the same distance between waves, stacked at varied heights. The loose formation made it difficult for the flak gunners to concentrate their fire. Each wave would follow immediately on the tails of the other. This, said Tait later, meant that "the aircraft in the fourth wave could release their bombs before the bombs from the preceding attackers actually hit and by exploding perhaps obscured the target in smoke."[30] Before they lined up, two aircraft from 9 Squadron took wind measurements to feed into their automatic Mark XIV bombsights—regarded as less accurate than 617's SABS.

As they turned northward, they had nothing to fear from the weather. The skies were clear. The one thing that could thwart the attack was the smokescreen. The film unit Lancaster was flying several thousand feet higher than the rest. From this vantage point, Guy Byam described what happened next.

> And now up to 16,000 feet, oxygen height. And far ahead of us, the white-capped hills and the sea. And then through the sparse cloud, the black granite, split by something. Yes! Water. A fjord. Altenfjord! [*sic*] And now it was touch and go because the Germans were known to have the biggest smokescreen in the world stretched around that fjord. We had to beat the smoke to enable our bombers to get a good sighting of the *Tirpitz* itself. We were coming in close now and the Lancs were flying steadily on, and scores of English and dominion airmen were around us, high in the sky over the cream of the German navy, high in the Norwegian sky, eighteen hundred miles from home … and Buck our pilot checks his instruments momentarily with his eyes, and Doc the Scotch engineer checks the engine temperatures, and out there in the sun in the Arctic haze scores of crews are doing the same thing, doing it in that calm, imperturbable way, as they've done it over Berlin and Stuttgart. And then below us a fork of water and a ship.
>
> The *Tirpitz*! And like thin white streamers, the smoke is coming up from the hills around, covering the whole of the approaches to the fjord. But Wing Commander Tait, who is in the leading Lancaster, looks as if he will beat that smoke. He and another plane about two thousand feet below us are in on their bomb run. And they hold steady, steady as the flak comes up, and the flak comes up again all around the fjord

and little spurts of light and there's flak all over the sky. And then the bombs go down. They go down from the two leading aircraft—two great five ton bombs. And leaping away from each Lancaster and going down and down. And then gathering speed and going down and down towards the ship to be lost out of sight. And the smoke is almost over the ship by now and we weave and turn away sharply. And there's lots of talk going on between the planes. English talk mixed with RAF slang going from plane to plane high over the Norwegian hills.

And one voice says calmly: "Can I have another run in over the target please?" And the answer is "yes." And two others go in with him. And far below ... another party of bombers are swinging in. They almost seem to be flying on top of the smoke clouds and then for a moment in the middle of the vast billowing clouds of white smoke, a dull red glow hangs for a second and then dies down ... and we swing away now, towards the coast. The country below us is lovely. There are blues and browns in the white of the snow. And then a last look at the target where the black and brown smoke billows up from the clouds of the white smoke screen. We won't know for some time the exact results but they look very promising....[31]

With that Buckham set course for Waddington, to carry back what seemed like very good news.

When Tait arrived, the tip of one mast was still poking out from the smoke and it was on this that his Canadian bomb aimer, Flying Officer Danny Daniel, sighted his SABS. Alongside Tait was Flight Lieutenant James Melrose of 9 Squadron who bombed simultaneously. At their bombing heights of above 14,000 feet the ship already made a small target. As its narrow outlines disappeared, there was nothing to aim at but the smoke. Jim Bazin, 9 Squadron's leader, was seventh in line to bomb, but an inconvenient scrap of cloud obscured his bomb aimer Pilot Officer Joe Gran's view of the scene below, and they went round again. "Huge mushrooms of smoke and water rose up through the smokescreen," he reported later, "and my bomb aimer was again unable to get the ship in his sight. But at that moment the *Tirpitz* started to fire her … light ack-ack guns and the flashes below the smokescreen provided a perfect marker so we bombed the center of the flashes."[32]

The combination of flak, fog, and bomb smoke was impressive, but it was impossible to know how much damage had been done. As they turned for home, Tait was "cheered considerably" by "a single plume of thick black smoke emerging from the white." The flight back was uneventful with no sign of the enemy fighters which they believed to be based somewhere along the return route. They landed at Yagodnik at teatime after a 1,300-mile round trip, to be met by a brass band and a welcoming committee that included "six local belles."[33] That night they drank vodka, steamed in the "Russian baths" laid on by their hosts, and talked about the day's events. The PRU Mosquito had carried out an afternoon reconnaissance. Cloud now covered Kaafjord, but Watson and MacArthur saw enough to confirm that *Tirpitz* was still afloat. It seemed unlikely, though, that she had not been harmed. A few of the aircraft, unable to get an aiming point, had returned with their Tallboys and JWs. There were not enough bombs to merit hanging around to wait for another opportunity. The next day Tait and Bazin and their men climbed back on board their Lancasters and set off for England where they would await full analysis of the results and learn whether they would have to return to *Tirpitz*.

CHAPTER 19

"MY GOD MAC, THEY'VE HAD IT TODAY"

A s the departing bombers vanished over the mountains, the crew of the *Tirpitz* surveyed the destruction they had left behind. Georg Schlegel, the chief engine room officer, groped his way forward through smoke and twisted metal to see "a huge gaping hole, like a barn door. The whole of the side had been ripped open and the bow started to sink ... all the cabins and holds in the bow had disappeared ... it was pretty much mayhem."[1]

Despite the devastation, the ship's company had got off lightly. Five men were dead and fifteen wounded. It was clear at once to Kapitän Junge, who took command after Meyer was injured in the Tungsten attack of April, that severe structural damage had been done. The engines and guns were still working. The bow, though, was a wreck. One Tallboy had struck the foredeck and sliced through the ship, exiting via the hull and exploding on the starboard side, tearing a forty-foot hole. The front compartments were swamped with two thousand tons of seawater, dragging down the bow. Other bombs missed narrowly, but the shock waves rippling through the water had buckled plates and blown out bulkheads. *Tirpitz* was still afloat, but with the great hole in her bow she would sink if she tried to move. It was obvious, though, that she could not remain in Kaafjord. One of the Tallboys had landed on Straumsneset point just behind the anchorage. The hole it blasted in the rocky soil was unlike any bomb crater anyone had seen. When Adalbert Brünner, now manning a lookout post onshore, went to inspect it with his comrades "it took our breath away."[2] It was clear that the British had a new weapon, far more powerful than anything they had experienced before and, if they stayed where they were, it was certain they would be subjected to it again. The attack confirmed that the smokescreen and flak batteries, the ship's main defenses in the continued absence of fighter cover, provided insufficient protection. *Tirpitz* would have to move.

Admiral Dönitz sat down with his staff in Berlin on September 23 to discuss *Tirpitz*'s immediate future. The meeting heard that it would take nine months to make her seaworthy again, and the work would have to be done on the spot. This was no time for a program of lengthy repairs. Four days before the meeting Finland had switched from the losing to the winning side, abandoning an alliance of necessity with Germany to sign an armistice with Moscow. The northern front was crumbling. A big Soviet offensive was brewing. It seemed probable that German forces would soon be falling back, and Kaafjord would have to be abandoned. Even if the repairs could be carried out, there seemed no realistic scenario in which *Tirpitz* might play the role for which she had been created. Dönitz now came to a crucial decision about the fate of Hitler's last battleship. It was no longer to be considered as a seagoing vessel. Instead, "in future, *Tirpitz* would be used merely as a floating battery, in defense of northern Norway."[3]

But where now should she go? Even though Allied armies were advancing on Germany's western borders, Hitler's belief that Norway was threatened by invasion remained firm. Tromsø, a major port, 120 miles to the west and south, seemed a likely enemy objective. If *Tirpitz* could be shifted there, her big guns might at last be put to some good use, opposing an Allied landing. As October progressed, it looked more likely that they would be employed to landward, part of the new defensive line drawn only forty miles to the east as German forces retreated in the face of the Russian push. There was another potential benefit. If the true extent of the damage to *Tirpitz* remained unclear, she might still serve as a fleet-in-being and, in Dönitz's words, "continue to tie down enemy forces and by her presence ... confound the enemies' intentions."[4]

Konteradmiral Rudolf Peters, who moved from command of the U-boat force in Norway to take over what remained of the northern task force in June, was told to find a suitable new anchorage in the Tromsø area. Dönitz specified that it must be shallow, so that if the ship was hit again she would stay above the surface and continue to serve as a gun platform. In the meantime *Tirpitz* was patched up for the move. A repair ship was brought in and new plates welded over the hole. By the middle of October, Junge thought she was fit to make the 170-mile voyage up Altafjord and south to Tromsø. Relieved of his onshore watch duties, Adalbert Brünner came aboard to "notice a change on *Tirpitz*. The repairs looked rather makeshift and there was a more frantic atmosphere, not the nonchalance we were used to."[5]

Konteradmiral Peters tried to rally spirits with an address to the company before the ship limped away. "We are living in momentous but difficult times," he said. "I feel assured that in these changed circumstances, all the men ... under my command will, with undiminished vigor and determination, do their duty until victory is ours." It was a hollow exhortation. By then he had been told that his—by now notional—task force was being disbanded. He recorded in his diary his chagrin that he had "not been able to lead it in battle against the enemy," despite it being full of "capable, well-trained men, eager to fight."[6]

At midday on Sunday, October 15, *Tirpitz* left Kaafjord for the last time, pushing through the water at a cautious seven to ten knots, escorted by tugs and every available destroyer in the area. At 3:00 p.m. the following day she dropped anchor at Haakøy, a low-lying island two and a half miles west of Tromsø. That afternoon, an agent, Egil Lindberg, mounted the stairs to the room on the top floor of the town's hospital where he hid his transmitter and radioed the news of her arrival to London. The significance of the move was not immediately clear. Reconnaissance flights over Kaafjord had failed to provide conclusive proof that she was *hors de combat* and incapable of mounting a last sortie.

Intercepted messages ordering U-boats to patrol at the entrance to Altafjord had given warning that *Tirpitz* might be departing, and the fleet carrier *Implacable* had put to sea as a precaution. Early on October 18, Firefly fighters flew off to try and get pictures of *Tirpitz* in her new berth. A reconnaissance Mosquito was also dispatched for a marathon eleven-hour round-trip flight from Dyce, near Aberdeen. The images they brought back showed the ship anchored on the southern side of Haakøy with her bow facing east toward the island on which Tromsø sat. She was already surrounded by nets. There was no sign of any smoke generators but flak batteries were in place on shore and demonstrated their efficiency by managing to put some holes in the Mosquito. Having shot up an airdrome at Bardufoss, forty miles south of Tromsø, the Fireflies returned to *Implacable*. Her commander, Captain L. D. Mackintosh, requested permission from the Home Fleet to launch an attack on the battleship. The commander, Sir Henry Moore, wanted no more gallant efforts from the Fleet Air Arm, especially as *Implacable* did not have the aircraft on board to suppress the defenses prior to dive-bombing. "Return to Scapa," he ordered. "Do not, repetition not, try and bomb in the face of heavy flak with your inadequate anti-flak fighter strength," prefacing the signal with a cheery "well done."[7]

The photographs revealed little new about the state of the battleship. The evidence of agents, and the slow pace of the voyage to Tromsø, though, suggested that she was not in a seaworthy condition. On October 1, the Alta resistance cell radioed that their agent in Kaafjord, "a solid and reliable man," reported that she had received "a direct hit on the starboard side which made a hole ... so large that large motor boats could go in."[8] Public confirmation that *Tirpitz* no longer posed a genuine threat seemed to have been given, obliquely, in a BBC radio talk by Wing Commander Bazin of 9 Squadron as early as October 5. He concluded his broadcast with the words: "It is understood from the Admiralty that she is now no longer a menace to our shipping."[9] This was certainly how Arthur Harris later claimed to see it. In his postwar account, he stated that after the September 15 attack "we had very good reason to believe that the ship could never be made fit for operations before the probable end of the war and was therefore quite useless to the enemy." This, however, "did not seem to cut much ice with the Admiralty." It came as no surprise when he was "therefore pressed to attack the *Tirpitz* again."[10]

Looked at from a distance of many years, the effort involved in another attempt, against what were known to be strong flak defenses and the threat, mercifully unrealized as yet, of fighter attack, seems wasteful. The lives of brave men—some of whom had completed a hundred operations—were being risked against what was surely a spent force. It was reasonable now to conclude that the threat from *Tirpitz* had faded to insignificance. For her to venture out against the Arctic convoys, about to sail again after the summer lull, would be suicidal. Within the Kriegsmarine's pitifully depleted armory, the U-boats still operating in northern waters were, anyway, potentially a far more efficient weapon.

Passage to a German port was possible, but the journey would expose her to equal danger from ships, submarines, and aircraft.

These, though, were peacetime considerations. Britain had been at war for five years now and was impatient for the end. Blood was up and the mood was for settling accounts and closing unfinished business. Even if the Admiralty and the Air Staff had wanted to leave *Tirpitz* in peace, it was unlikely that they would be allowed to do so. Churchill's eye was still fixed unwaveringly on the battleship. On October 26, he informed Admiral Cunningham: "I think it will be regarded as a very serious misfortune if the TIRPITZ succeeds in returning to Germany. I consider that every effort should be made to attack this ship, even if losses have to be incurred."[11]

The First Sea Lord was quick to respond. "I fully agree," he replied the following day. By now intercepted messages had revealed Dönitz's intention to keep *Tirpitz* where she was and he concluded that "it is most improbable that the long passage southward to Germany will be attempted at present." He was able to tell the prime minister that "Bomber Command has planned an attack on the ship in her present berth as soon as weather conditions are favorable."[12]

It was fear of further air attacks that had prompted *Tirpitz's* move to Tromsø, but, as everyone on board understood, there could be no hiding place. They were now in fact an easier target than before, for the shift south and westward had edged them a fatal step closer to British air bases. The 5 Group planners calculated that modified aircraft, operating from forward airfields in northern Scotland, would just have the range to carry out a direct attack on the battleship and return home.

Once again it was 617 Squadron and 9 Squadron that would carry it out. Both squadrons had been busy since their return from Russia. Satisfaction at a partial success, achieved without loss, was overshadowed by an accident on the homeward journey. Flying Officer Frank Levy, a

Rhodesian with 617, flew into a mountaintop in Norway, killing himself, his six crewmembers, and two additional aircrew traveling as passengers.

Now both squadrons were to experience more casualties. On the night of September 23–24, 9 Squadron took part in a raid on a night-fighter base outside Münster. Two of their aircraft were shot down and all but one of the fourteen crewmembers killed. Another crew was lost on the night of October 19–20 over Nuremberg. The luck of 617 Squadron, which had pulled through the summer with remarkably few losses, seemed to have changed. On September 24 the crews took part in a mass attack on the Dortmund–Ems Canal, a strategic waterway that linked the Ruhr with the North Sea. Their Tallboys smashed the banks, draining a seven-mile stretch and rendering it un-navigable for six months, but 10 percent of the attacking force was shot down, including the Lancaster piloted by Flight Lieutenant Geoff Stout, on whom night fighters pounced as he left the target. Stout stayed at the controls while the crew bailed out and went down in flames with his aircraft. Two of those who escaped subsequently died of their wounds.

On Saturday, October 7, a small force of thirteen Lancasters set off on a mission that would require particular sangfroid and skill. They were to bomb the Kembs barrage, on the Rhine just north of Basle. It held back a huge quantity of water which it was feared the Germans would unleash on American and French forces as they advanced from the south. The purpose was to preempt the move by triggering the flood before the Allies got into the danger area. Seven aircraft were to drop their bombs from 8,000 feet while the other six went in at 1,000 feet to lay delayed-fuse Tallboys alongside the lock gates of the dam. Tait, as always, led from the front. Despite intense light flak, he and the three aircraft following him dropped their bombs and emerged without serious damage. One of the last two, the Lancaster piloted by Squadron Leader Drew Wyness, was hit on the approach and crashed into the Rhine, apparently with the loss of all on board. In the other, Flight Lieutenant Christopher Howard made one pass without dropping a bomb and despite being told by Tait, "Kit, abandon, abandon," went round again. By this time the gunners had found their range and according to Tony Iveson, who was in the high level force, Howard's aircraft was "shot to pieces."

By now Iveson was used to the loss of comrades but, he said later, "Drew's death affected me more than anybody else because we were very close." He had taught Wyness while instructing in Rhodesia and felt a protective affinity for his amiable, big-hearted comrade. With others, "although I knew them, it wasn't the same. The feeling was, well, hard luck, poor bugger. Like everyone else, I knew it might be me tomorrow." [13, 14]

No one was untouchable. A few days after their return from Russia, the squadron had heard that 617's first leader was dead. On September 19, returning from a raid in Germany, Guy Gibson's Mosquito had crashed in Holland. Only a few weeks before he had come over from Coningsby to have a drink in the mess at Petwood, even though none of the men he had flown with were still in the unit. The evening ended in the customary high jinks and Gibson was divested of his trousers.

The flamboyant personalities of Gibson and Cheshire colored the squadron's own character. If Tait lacked their obvious charisma, what he had instead was an enigmatic quality that in its way was equally potent and inspirational. As preparations began for another attack on *Tirpitz*, this awkward, modest man was about to carve his niche in the 617 pantheon.

The new operation was called Obviate. The crews had long ago given up wondering how the names were chosen. The mission would test their endurance and the skill of the navigators to the maximum. It meant a round trip of 2,250 miles which, depending on conditions, could take nearly fourteen hours. For the Lancasters to make it there and back, they would have to carry every extra gallon of petrol they could cram on board and lose every pound of superfluous weight.

Each aircraft was fitted with two extra tanks in the fuselage to boost the fuel load to 2,400 gallons, a tedious job which required removing the rear gunner's turret. The mid-upper turrets were stripped out and the front guns and ammunition, spare oxygen bottles, and even the armor plating behind the pilot's seat removed. This still left a total weight of airplane, bomb, and fuel of nearly thirty-two tons, which was over the safety limit. To get the extra lift, Tait organized the replacement of the existing engines with more powerful Merlin T-24s and paddle-bladed airscrews, achieving the "the stupendous task of scouring the whole of Bomber Command for the new equipment and installing it ... in five amazing days," according to an official RAF account of the operation.[15] To shrink the distance a little, the squadrons would take off from three bases in northern Scotland: Lossiemouth, Kinloss, and Milltown. By mid-October, everything was in place and the crews stood by to await the Met reports.

In Tromsø, *Tirpitz* was struggling to establish herself in her new home. For better or worse, it seemed that she would not be leaving it soon. On arrival, six hundred men—most of them engine-room hands—were moved ashore, leaving about 1,700 men on board. Dönitz had insisted on a shallow anchorage, but the best that could be found, off Haakøy, lay in open waters with no steep hills nearby to deter attacking aircraft like those that had protected her at Faettenfjord and Kaafjord. The water was still too deep. Nor was the seabed beneath it stable, consisting of fifteen feet of mud topped with a layer of sand. Plans were made to use dredgers to raise the seabed, but to those on board it seemed that they had exchanged a dangerous situation for a fatal one. Smoke generators were brought from Kaafjord to set up on shore though it would be a while before they were installed and working. More were mounted on boats nearby but Hein Hellendoorn, second in command of the ship's flak batteries, worried that the fog they produced would be more likely to hinder his gunners than hide the ship. "It was clear to us at that point that we were on borrowed time," he said later. The crew began talking about their new duty as "a mission to heaven."[16] Kapitän Junge did not inspire the same confidence as Topp and Meyer, for "he had little sea experience and we disliked him." The feeling settled on the ship that the end, not just of *Tirpitz* but also of Germany, could not be far off. "Nobody believed in victory any more," said Hellendoorn. There was continuous propaganda of new miracle weapons but "no one really gave them any credence." It was unwise to speak one's mind too openly. According to Klaus Rohwedder, a sailor who was arrested for drunkenness was found to have written "defeatist" letters home and was court-martialed and sentenced to death. He was killed in the September 15 attack before the sentence could be carried out.[17]

The evidence of impending defeat, however, was all too visible, just across the water on Tromsø. The town was full of refugees, flooding back from the Soviet advance. The homes they left behind were now ashes, consumed in the fires of the scorched earth tactics of the retreating German forces. The citizens saw the anxiety on the faces of their conquerors and inwardly exulted. But the presence of the big gray ship across the bay was ominous. Their town had been dragged onto the front line. Whenever the skies cleared they braced themselves for the appearance of the bombers.

On the morning of Saturday, October 28, Cochrane listened to the favorable reports of the weather over Tromsø and gave the signal for Obviate to begin. At Bardney and Woodhall Spa, the Lancasters of 9 and 617 Squadrons took off, one by one, and set course for northeast Scotland. They touched down at their allotted airfields for refueling and a final briefing. By now it was officially conceded that the battleship was "unfit for sea-going operations." The 5 Group operation order, however, claimed that "it appears likely" that an attempt would be made to get it back to a base in Germany. "So long as TIRPITZ remains afloat," it concluded, "it continues to be a threat to our sea communications with Russia."[18]

The force was made up of eighteen aircraft from each squadron and a Lancaster from the RAF film unit. The Johnny Walker experiment had been abandoned. All the bombers would carry Tallboys. The first leg of the journey took them 237 miles north before turning due east to make landfall halfway between Bodø and Trondheim, where there was a gap in the German radar. They then crossed into neutral Sweden and swung north to rendezvous at a lake south of Tromsø for the final approach. In case of emergencies, aircraft were to press on to Yagodnik or Vaenga.

At 2:30 a.m., in gusting rain, they started to take off. There was a near catastrophe at Milltown when one of the engines on Tony Iveson's aircraft failed to develop sufficient power and he slewed off course on take-off, skimming over Benny Goodman on the perimeter track. "All I could see was two massive main wheels and I thought 'this is it,'" Goodman remembered. "It's a funny thing—there was no panic. I thought he was going to scrape along our canopy but he just got airborne. Thirty seconds later we'd all forgotten it."[19]

They headed out over the sea, each aircraft making its own way, staying low at 1,500 feet to avoid radar. As they approached the Norwegian coast they saw daylight streaking the eastern sky. Once over, in Tait's account for the official RAF record, they began "climbing steadily to get over the mountains ... heading apparently for Russia. Soon they were ... over the low country of northern Sweden and now they turned abruptly over lifeless wasteland for the rendezvous." They met up over Torneträsk Lake, 100 miles south of the target. It seemed extraordinary to Benny Goodman that they had all arrived at the right place at the right time, armed only with maps and dead reckoning. "It was a navigators' trip not a pilots' trip," he said long afterwards. "I just flew the course I was given."[20]

They circled around, getting into bombing formation, and then set off for Tromsø, climbing to their bombing heights of 13,000 to 16,000 feet. Visibility was excellent. It was all going suspiciously well. Then, according to Tait, "the fliers' luck, which had held so well, now began to go against them as the nearer they got to Tromsø, the more obvious became a large sheet of low cloud with its tops at 6,000 feet almost completely shielding the … battleship from the bombers' view." It had come up very quickly. Tait could see the target clearly on the approach but by the time he arrived it was disappearing. They carried on, showering strips of "Window" to confuse the radar. Despite the conditions, Tait bombed anyway. The thought of flogging home with a 12,000-lb. bomb in the belly swamped pious injunctions issued at briefings that precious Tallboys should not be used unless there was a strong prospect of success, and all but four of the thirty-six Lancasters dropped their bombs. Then it was time to get out. The flak batteries below were now well tuned to air attack and smoke and flame blossomed around them as they closed. After several circuits looking for a hole in the gray blanket below, Easy Elsie, flown by Bill Carey, an Australian pilot with 617, had dropped its bomb and was heading south for home when it was hit. The flak knocked out an engine and damaged the hydraulics, leaving the bomb doors jammed open. Elsie would never make it back. Carey turned for Sweden and after an increasingly anxious search for a landing place amid the hills and forests, put her down in a field. He smashed his knee in the impact but all emerged alive to be interned and, shortly afterward, sent back to England.

Everyone else returned safely after a record twelve-and-a-half-hour flight, "tired out" according to Tait's report and "despondent at the frustration of their skilled and strenuous effort." Two 617 pilots claimed to have scored or seen a direct hit. It was obvious, though, that the job had not been done. The most persuasive testimony came from Bruce Buckham, once again flying the film unit Lancaster. He descended to 8,000 feet to try and get pictures and saw two bombs exploding about a hundred yards from the ship and two more hitting the net defenses. As he left her guns were firing and she was still definitely afloat.

On board *Tirpitz*, satisfaction at the performance of the flak gunners soon evaporated. The first inspection showed that although they had suffered only three casualties and escaped any direct hits, a near miss had damaged the port engine shaft and rudder and caused more flooding. The gloomy certainty that the bombers would be back hung over the ship. Once again they had received no help from the Luftwaffe.

On November 4 *Tirpitz* got a new captain. Junge left to be replaced by the ship's executive officer, Kapitän Robert Weber. Dredging had begun to reduce the depth of water under the keel but it would be a long, slow job before the bed of the fjord was raised to the required six and a half feet. Weber was desperate to get the protection of the aircraft now arriving at the airbase at Bardufoss, less than fifty miles to the south. An underground telephone cable was laid between the ship and the Luftwaffe's air warning center in Tromsø. This received and broadcasted reports of enemy air activity, collected from radar stations and observation posts, most of which looked out to sea in expectation of an Allied attack. The center was controlled from the Bardufoss base.

On Friday, November 10, Hein Hellendoorn visited the Tromsø office with the ship's first gunnery officer, Korvettenkapitän Willi Müller, where the commander, Oberleutnant Walter Härer, assured them that enough warning would be received to get fighters airborne in time to defend *Tirpitz* from another attack. Two days before, a squadron of aircraft from the Jagdeschwader 5 fighter wing had arrived in the area after being driven out of Finland by the Soviet advance. They were to be based in Bardufoss while they converted from their Messerschmitt 109s to new and superior Focke-Wulf 190s. They were under the temporary command of Major Heinrich Ehrler, a twenty-seven-year-old former butcher and enthusiastic Nazi who had become one of the stars of the Arctic air war with 199 "kills" to his account. Härer told his visitors that "the fighters would be informed of any expected attacks ... they were there only to support and defend us." When Hellendoorn returned to *Tirpitz* and told his shipmates the good news, they "felt safe for the first time in years. Now nothing bad could happen to us. The fighters were there for us."[21]

Nonetheless, as each new dawn broke the crew scanned the skies, praying for cloud and cursing the clear, windless weather that seemed treacherously prevalent in the first days of November. They longed for the end of the month to come, when the sun sank below the horizon, not to reappear until January.

In England, the 5 Group planners watched the approach of near-perpetual darkness with increasing alarm. From November 26, *Tirpitz* would be safe from attack for several months, and repairs could go on unhindered. The experience of Obviate had underlined the lesson that success depended on the weather. Every day a Mosquito from the Met Flight took off from Sumburgh in the Shetlands and climbed high over the target area to gather temperature and humidity data. On its return, Cochrane and his staff gathered to forecast and weigh the odds. On November 4, the omens seemed good and the crews departed to the Scottish bases, only to return home when a gale warning was announced.[22] Tait noted that "the combination of untoward weather, false starts, ill-luck and the depressing prospect of the descent on Northern Norway of its impenetrable winter blanket at any minute, reduced the spirit of the anxious crews."[23]

As the winter deadline approached, caution dwindled and the temptation to take a chance mounted. On November 11, with the weather prospects still uncertain, the squadrons were ordered north again, arriving at their forward bases that afternoon. Take-off was scheduled for early the following morning and empty hours of waiting lay ahead. At Milltown, the 617 crews were taken off and installed in cozy bedrooms with a coal fire burning in the grate where they lay down and tried to sleep. At midnight they were given the final briefing. The plan of attack had not been altered, and the times and routes were identical to the Obviate operation. There was one ominous new development. The crews learned that there was now hard intelligence that a squadron of fighters was based in the target area tasked with protecting *Tirpitz*. This was very unwelcome news. They were going into battle with only a rear gunner to defend them, in an airplane laden with extra fuel. A single round through the fuselage could bring instant extinction. During the briefing there were more bad tidings. The Met Flight Mosquito had returned with reports of stratus clouds over Tromsø. Cochrane nonetheless decided to gamble. Operation Catechism, as it had been codenamed, was on. The crews trooped off for a last meal of bacon, eggs, and potatoes, then climbed aboard the lorries to take them to their aircraft for a mission that seemed marked for likely failure and possible disaster.

The night was bitterly cold. As the temperature plunged, the ground crews had been busy spraying de-icer over the wings of the Lancasters. Six of the 9 Squadron aircraft were still weighed down with hoar frost when departure hour came. The force took off, leaving Wing Commander Bazin and Flight Lieutenant Melrose, who had been credited with scoring the direct hit during Operation Paravane, grounded.

At 3:25 a.m., twenty-nine bombers and the faithful film unit Lancaster with "Buck" Buckham at the controls were in the air and heading north, out over the Moray Firth, past the Orkneys and the Shetlands before turning east toward Norway, skimming along at a radar-dodging two thousand feet. Once again they were to make their own way to a meeting-up point south of the target to commence the attack. Just off the coast, looking out from the cockpit, Tony Iveson saw a "tiny crack of daylight, like a silver thread on the horizon." He noticed a Lancaster silhouetted against the dawn and pulled alongside it. It was Tait's aircraft. The rear gunner, Micky Vaughan, greeted him by "making rude gestures towards me."[24] They flew along companionably toward the rendezvous point over Torneträsk Lake in the mountains of northern Sweden.

Tait and Iveson reached it first. As they did a circuit, Iveson saw the shapes of the other 617 Squadron Lancasters looming out of the black western sky. Two of 9 Squadron's aircraft failed to make the rendezvous. They could not hang around. Tait ordered a colored flare fired to signal the advance to attack and they swung north. He remembered afterward that "the sun was resting on the horizon so that the snow-covered mountains were turned pink in its light. The sky was cloudless, the air calm and the aircraft rode easily without a bump to disturb the bomb-aimer."[25] The visibility, as they were all to say afterward, was "gin clear." Pleasure at the beauty of the new day and the knowledge that conditions

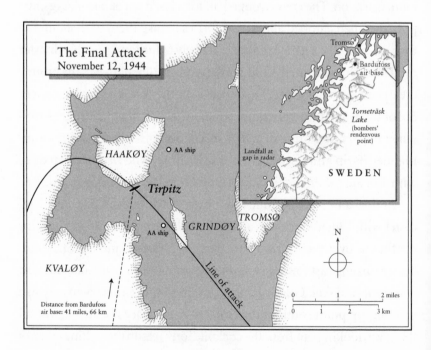

were perfect for bombing were quickly overshadowed by alarm. "We thought, Christ, if it's OK for us it is going to be equally OK for the fighters," said Iveson.[26]

But as they flew steadily along at just over two hundred miles an hour there was no sign of them. When they were still twenty miles away Tait spotted *Tirpitz* "lying squat and black among her torpedo nets like a spider in her web, silhouetted against the glittering blue and green waters of the fjord." He was struck by the peacefulness of the scene. "Everything was quite still," he remembered. "The whole scene, water, mountains, and sky blazed in the cold brilliance of the Arctic dawn." There was no sign of a smokescreen. To Freddie Watts, following close behind, it seemed that they could not fail. Later he recalled "saying to my bomb aimer, my God Mac, they've had it today."[27] Then, when they were five miles away, the peace was shattered.

Tony Iveson was suddenly aware of a "great unfolding golden cloud." It was the explosion from the huge shells pumped out by the big, 15-inch guns in *Tirpitz*'s main turrets, fired at maximum elevation, bursting below. It was a measure of the alarm now gripping the ship. The monster guns had no hope of hitting the approaching Lancasters, which were still only specks in the sky at this range. Then the flak guns opened up. Tait saw the air ahead fill "with smoke puffs as all the guns on the ship and those along the shore combined in a fusillade." He noted that "no aircraft deviated from the formation." The men of 617 and 9 Squadrons were well used to flak by now and this did not seem too bad—certainly lighter than they had faced in the confined space of Kaafjord. So far there was no smokescreen and still no sign of fighters.

The eighteen aircraft of 617 Squadron came in from the southeast with the sun behind them, grouped together in a gaggle, layered at different heights with the lowest at 12,650 feet and the highest at 16,000. Tait was in the lead. He approached on his bombing run at 13,000 feet. The battleship lay straight ahead, starboard side-on, its bow pointing

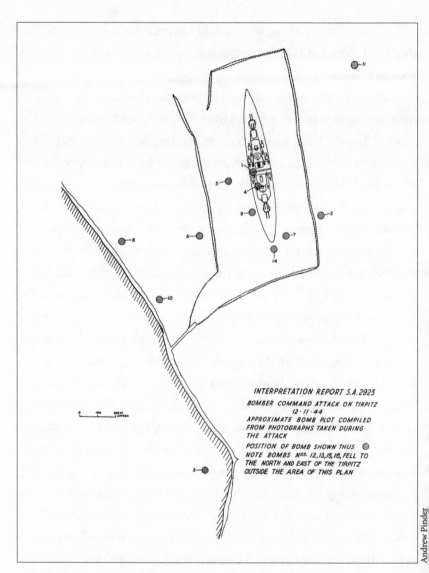

INTERPRETATION REPORT S.A. 2923
BOMBER COMMAND ATTACK ON TIRPITZ
12·11·44
APPROXIMATE BOMB PLOT COMPILED
FROM PHOTOGRAPHS TAKEN DURING
THE ATTACK
POSITION OF BOMB SHOWN THUS
NOTE BOMBS Nᵒˢ. 12,13,15,16, FELL TO
THE NORTH AND EAST OF THE TIRPITZ
OUTSIDE THE AREA OF THIS PLAN

Andrew Pinder

eastward. The old asymmetric camouflage, designed to give the appearance of a much smaller ship, had been obliterated. Her hull now was a dark, uniform gray, with the upper works painted in a paler shade to help blend in with the snow dusting the low-humped hills of Haakøy, whose shore lay four hundred feet away on the port side. He kept on this course for five long minutes as the dirty bursts from the flak guns blossomed ahead and around them. Below, lying prone in the nose, his curly-headed Canadian bomb aimer, Flying Officer Danny Daniel, peered into the sight, speaking over the intercom into Tait's earphones, easing him onto a course that would put the ship on the blade of the sword glowing on the glass in front of him. Tait's eyes were fixed on his instruments, now and again making delicate banking turns to keep the needle of the bombing direction indicator glued to the vertical. Ten seconds before dropping, a red light went on. Then the automatic release mechanism tripped. The Tallboy slid away, and, suddenly freed from its five-ton burden, the Lancaster leaped thankfully upward.

The bomb went into an aerodynamically perfect descent, spinning like a rifle bullet. Thirty seconds later it hit. The nose of Tait's Lancaster was over the target, obscuring the moment when the Tallboy struck, but he "turned and dived hard to port to see what was happening. The ship was almost hidden by smoke. A jet of white steam was gushing out and amidships she blazed fiercely."

The sequence was captured by the film unit Lancaster's three cine cameras. When it first comes into view, *Tirpitz* looks tiny and exposed "like a Dinky Toy," as some of the crews were to say later, lying broadside-on close to the flat shore of Haakøy. Bright lights flicker out of the monochrome as the flak teams frantically work their guns. Then, out of nowhere, a great white mushroom envelops the front of ship. There is a brief stutter of anti-aircraft fire from aft. A bomb splashes down close to the stern on the starboard side. Almost simultaneously an eruption three hundred yards away on the shore of Haakøy flings debris high and wide. It is followed by another white blossoming amidships. Two more bombs crash between ship and shore. After that it becomes impossible to follow the bombardment as the ship disappears under rolling banks of smoke, steam, and fire.[28]

Tait's bomb went down at 8:41 a.m. He was followed by Bobby Knights, James Castagnola, Paddy Gingles, John Saunders, and Bunny

Lee, who came in, ranged in a loose gaggle, and stacked up at between 12,650 and 14,400 feet. By 8:44 a.m., all of 617's eighteen Tallboys were gone. Flight Lieutenant John Sayers of the Royal Australian Air Force dropped the last from his Lancaster, from 14,200 feet. "We followed our bomb down nearly to the ship where it was lost in the smoke," he told the debriefers on his return. "It was either a hit on the bows or a near miss."[29] Then, within seconds, the bombs from 9 Squadron's ten aircraft were falling into the inferno. Flight Lieutenant Harry Watkins was the last to drop. He reported a "glow seen amidships and a pillar of smoke both from bow and stern ... own bomb fell in smoke at stern."[30]

It was difficult for anyone to get an accurate view of what was happening. The speed of the bombs and the almost instant eruption of explosions made the reports the crews gave on their returns sketchy and generalized. Only three aircraft from 617 Squadron and one from 9 Squadron claimed to have scored direct hits. Tait himself reported that "we did not see our bomb burst but the initial bombing was concentrated on the vessel."[31] Most reports speak of seeing their Tallboys fall into the cauldron of smoke. Everyone was sure that the bombing was remarkably concentrated and effective. Bobby Knights gave the fullest account. "Our bomb fell about 10 yds off port quarter," he told the debriefer. "We saw the first 4 bombs go down as follows: On or near starboard quarter, starboard bow, port bow and near funnel." He waited around long enough to see a "large explosion" at 8:51 a.m. and a smaller one two minutes later. As they left "we saw Tirpitz listing heavily to port."

Despite several apparent bull's-eyes, the glow of fires, and the billowing smoke, Buckham, flying the film unit machine, was disappointed to see that the ship was still afloat. "I thought that after all these hits that the myth of the unsinkable *Tirpitz* was true and we were thinking of going home," he said later. Then Flight Lieutenant Eric Giersch, a fellow Australian, looking down from the rear turret "came up on the intercom, saying, 'Hey, Skip, I think she's keeling over. Have a look.'" When he turned again she had already capsized. "All I could see was the red lead hull gleaming in the morning sunshine."[32] By then most of the attackers were on their way home, anxiously scanning the skies for fighters as they hurried away south and west along the fjords that led to the sea and safety.

Tirpitz had awoken to the normal routines of shipboard life. The 1,700 or so men left on board had had breakfast and begun work. The morning was cold, minus eight degrees, and the skies were clear. Just before seven o'clock, the ship's first flak officer, Kapitänleutnant Alfred Fassbender, received a report that observation posts on the coast to the south had seen three Lancasters flying over Mosjøen, apparently heading east into Sweden. A little later there was another sighting of a lone Lancaster near Bodø, going in the same direction. Bodø was 220 miles away, Mosjøen a further 120 miles. Lieutenant Leo Beniers, from the air-warning center at Bardufoss, passed the report to him. The base was unconcerned. The aircraft were probably on their way to Russia. Fassbender was more cautious. The situation, and the weather, reminded him uncomfortably of the Sunday a fortnight before when Lancasters had appeared from the direction of Sweden. He "immediately grabbed the phone" to make sure that the recently arrived fighter squadron was alerted.[33] Such were the complexities of the German system of command and control that he had to contact the Tromsø air-warning center to get the message through to the fighter command post at Bardufoss, even though it was from the base that the alert had emanated. He spoke first to Lieutenant Ewald Hamschmidt, a twenty-three-year-old junior officer whose dozy reaction did not inspire confidence.

At 7:25 a.m. another report arrived saying four more Lancasters had been seen over Mosjøen. Fassbender rang Tromsø again, this time making sure he spoke to the chief, First Lieutenant Härer, with whom he had held a reassuring meeting only two days before, and urged him to "make sure that fighter cover is prepared and because Bardufoss is to provide it, keep them informed."[34] At their subsequent court martial, both Härer and Hamschmidt denied receiving the request.

By now the sighting of the bombers had been logged at Bardufoss. By a stroke of fortune, the first of several for which 617 and 9 Squadrons would be forever grateful, the clerk noting the details took down the wrong coordinates and plotted the incursion over Hammerfest, 125 miles to the north.

Having taken these precautions, *Tirpitz*'s gunnery officers felt reasonably secure. Then, at 7:54 a.m., another warning arrived. A confused, and as it turned out erroneous, report from a coastal battery suggested more aircraft were approaching from the northeast. All over the ship alarm bells jangled, and blue and yellow flags were run up to warn that a raid was in the offing. At 8:02 a.m. the watertight doors slammed shut and the crew hurried to their action stations. Seven minutes later, the first ominous blips began to show up on the ship's Würzburg radar, showing aircraft seventy-five miles to the southeast. They were succeeded by what seemed to be another wave of bombers. Soon the lookouts could see the real thing, tiny specks against the flawless sky. Each new development was passed on to Tromsø and from there to Bardufoss. At 8:14 a.m. the alarm had finally been given at the base, setting in train another chapter of garbled orders, misunderstandings, and coincidences that crippled the fighters' response.

As the crew prepared for battle, Kapitän Weber's voice echoed round the ship. "We are expecting a heavy air attack," he told his men over the loudspeakers, though by now that was hardly news. "The ship's company will fulfil its duty again this time and prepare a hot reception for the bombers." All the guns were trained toward the approaching aircraft. As they grew closer red light gleamed on the Perspex of the bombers' cockpits and some gunners believed the fighters had come to the rescue, but it was only the rising sun glinting off the canopies, and the Lancasters came on unmolested. There were no smoke generators to mask them from their attackers. Only their own guns could save them now. At 8:38 a.m. Weber gave the order to fire. The ship shook with the titanic jolt as the big guns and shells, weighing nearly a ton each, screamed out toward the uneven line of advancing bombers. It was no more than a gesture of defiance and they passed spectacularly but harmlessly underneath.

A minute later the secondary guns and the heavy 37 mm flak artillery joined in. Hellendoorn and his team were stationed on the port side. They began firing their heavy guns, with the shells set to explode at different ranges to provide layered defense. Then they opened up with the 10.5 cm flak. It made no impression on the attackers who came unwaveringly on. On the starboard side of the ship, Klaus Rohwedder was at his action station on the aircraft deck, manning one of the 10.5 cm guns near the funnel. Through his headphones he could hear a stream of information about the distance and speed of the approaching bombers.

He did not need to be told. He had a perfect view of the attackers, streaming straight toward him. He watched a dark shape detach itself from one of the aircraft, but "then we did not see it any more as it was traveling too fast." He felt a "quake" then saw a "huge wall of water" rise from the sea and was suddenly drenched to the skin. Through the headphones the order at last came to fire. Before he engaged he felt "a second quake and the ship almost immediately began to list." The deck was tilting sickeningly to port. He clung to a gun mounting to stay upright, then his "stomach was on the deck and I was hanging onto the railings." He looked around. All his colleagues but one had disappeared. Together they pulled themselves over the railing and clung to the side of the ship.[35]

The transformation was astonishingly quick. In seven minutes the great ship had toppled onto her side. Hellendoorn remembered that during a brief lull between explosions "there was a huge stillness." People seemed bizarrely serene. "Normally every sailor should have his life vest handy but I didn't see anyone with one on." There was "absolutely no panic." He heard someone "asking quite calmly if there was anyone there who couldn't swim and one chap answering, yes." Hellendoorn was a strong swimmer and volunteered to help. "I explained precisely that he mustn't hold on to me, I would hold on to him. But just as I was saying that the tower was hit and the chap I was talking to panicked and jumped into the water and I jumped in after him."

When he surfaced he had to struggle through a thick blanket of oil and emerged blinded and choking. He flailed around in the freezing water, somehow locating his companion who was clinging to a piece of wood. There were others spluttering and gasping, grabbing the torpedo net to stay afloat. Hellendoorn clasped the non-swimmer to him and struck out for the shore, two hundred yards away. Eventually, streaked with oil and all but sightless, he and the man he had saved "crawled ashore, completely exhausted." It was a fortnight before he could see properly again.

That morning Adalbert Brünner was ashore on Haakøy with a work party building a jetty and watched the drama from the moment when the blue and yellow air raid warning flags began to flutter. "Everything seemed to happen so quickly," he recalled. "The hellish roar of the flak set in but the detonations of the English bombs overwhelmed all other noise. Huge geysers of fire, water, and debris covered everything and we had thrown ourselves on the beach to escape the shell splinters." Then, "suddenly, it was quiet—no guns, no detonations." Out of the silence they heard a "chorus of screams that reached all the way to the shore." When the smoke cleared "we could not believe our eyes. *Tirpitz* had gone. The hull stuck out of the water like a giant whale. There was nothing else."[36] It had taken eleven minutes for the ship to capsize. The first bomb exploded amidships, on the port side, and the fourth, a few moments later, just abaft of it. The near misses that followed on the port side rent the hull, further increasing the list. As the ship leaned sideways, the mud and sand of the seabed gave way beneath the keel. The climax came ten minutes after the first bomb struck. A huge explosion, probably the blast from the after magazines igniting, wrenched the Caesar turret from its mounting, flinging it through the air. *Tirpitz* toppled. Her mast and upper works slid below the surface, digging into the unresisting mud and sand of the bottom, and leaving her starboard side and keel naked above the water.

The flank of the ship now provided a haven for those like Klaus Rohwedder who had scrambled over the starboard rail as *Tirpitz* rolled. They slipped and skidded their way toward the rudder. Then, with no rescue boats in view and the plates heaving and lurching beneath his feet, there seemed nothing for it but to swim. Rohwedder flung off his jacket and jumped into the numbing waters, struggling through an oil slick toward a tree trunk and hauling himself onto it. "I saw that there were many people in the water, screaming for help. There were others floating face down—the dead who were being kept afloat by the air trapped in their clothes." He helped a comrade struggling in the water up onto the tree trunk. He could see that the torpedo nets were sagging below the water under the weight of desperate men. Rohwedder turned back for a last look at the ship. Then a trawler with German soldiers aboard was pulling him and his shipmate aboard and he was on his way to a nearby ship.[37]

The catastrophe had been so swift and violent that there was no time for an orderly evacuation. Above decks, many were killed in the storm of fire and blast. Below, the Arctic brine rushed through the great gashes torn by the near misses, paralyzing and overwhelming men as they scrambled for ladder and hatch. Weber went down with his ship, trapped inside the armored control room where he had gathered with his staff to direct the defense of *Tirpitz*.

Others found an at least temporary refuge in the many air pockets that formed in the upturned hull. The first rescue boat to arrive was requisitioned by Lieutenant Walter Sommer who sent to Tromsø for oxyacetylene torches. Teams worked along the length of the hull, cutting through the steel wherever they detected any sign of life. In the first twenty-four hours, eighty-seven men were brought out alive, including Alfred Zuba, with whose story this book begins. The work went on for two more days but no more survivors emerged. Of the 1,700 men or so on board, 971 had perished in the sinking.

From the shores of their hilly island, the people of Tromsø heard the explosions, and watched the procession of dead and wounded arriving from Haakøy, with a mixture of hope and anxiety. Nine-year-old Aud Schreuder had been rushed to the cellar in her family's big white house on the heights of Tromsø, as the anti-aircraft gun the Germans had mounted in the garden began to fire. When she emerged and heard that *Tirpitz* was sunk, she feared there would now be reprisals and the Germans would come for her father, who, along with her six brothers, was a member of the underground. Displays of joy were imprudent. Lars Thøring, Tromsø's town clerk, remembered that "there was great enthusiasm … over the successful attack and the joy manifested itself loudly which resulted in a number of arrests by the Gestapo during the day."[38] Nonetheless, Aud could not help feeling a tremor of sympathy for the victims. "It was a dreadful way to die," she said.[39]

As the Germans surveyed the wreckage of their last battleship, and began burying their dead, the men who had destroyed it were heading home. One 9 Squadron Lancaster had been badly hit by flak. As it departed the target area, it became clear that it would never make it home. For a few anxious minutes it was stalked by one of the Bardufoss fighters that had finally taken to the air, but it then unaccountably lost interest and they were able to make their way east to force-land in Sweden. The rest streamed toward Scotland, trying to keep themselves awake as the adrenaline ebbed and weariness flooded in. After twelve hours in the air they had a tiresome end to their journey, and winds and overcast skies meant many of them were diverted to land away from the forward base they had taken off from.

Just after three o'clock that afternoon they began to touch down. At 5 Group Headquarters, at Bomber Command, everyone was eager for news. As the details were flashed to Harris, he could not wait to pass it on to the man who would appreciate it most. That Sunday, Winston Churchill was in Paris, staying at the British Embassy. At 6:50 p.m., a member of his staff was handed a message telephoned from London asking him to relay a message to the Prime Minister. It read simply: "*Tirpitz* sunk this morning." It was signed "Bert," the nickname by which Harris was known by his peers. Churchill instructed an assistant to telephone the Air Ministry offering "heartiest congratulations to all."

After years of proddings and interventions, urgings and suggestions, Churchill had finally got what he wanted. Before setting out that evening to visit the French and American headquarters, he dashed off a telegram to Stalin. "RAF bombers have sunk the *Tirpitz*," he informed him. "Let us rejoice together." The following day the Marshal replied that he was "greatly delighted" and that "the British airmen may legitimately pride themselves on this deed." Roosevelt had listened frequently to Churchill's concerns about the battleship. On hearing the tidings he dispatched a message: "The death of the *Tirpitz* is great news," he said. Churchill's response carried the sound of genuine thankfulness. "Thank you so much," he replied. "It is a great relief to us to get this brute where we have long wanted her."[40]

Churchill's fascination for *Tirpitz* had seeped into the public consciousness. Since 1940 the ship had become steadily more notorious, a malign player among wartime's dramatis personae, symbolizing both the menace and the hubris of Hitler and the Germans. Official propaganda faithfully reported each attempt on her life. It had never been able to announce her death, and the victory was to be savored and celebrated. On November 14 Willie Tait flew to London for a press conference and later described the attack in a broadcast on the BBC. Squadron Leader Bill Williams, who led 9 Squadron after Jim Bazin was forced to stay behind, went with him and that night was interviewed by Ed Murrow, whose radio dispatches for the CBS network reached millions in the United States and Canada. An interview with Bruce Buckham was relayed on the BBC World Service. By chance his wife Gwen was listening in Sydney when it was aired. It was the first time she had heard his voice in two years.[41] The news was splashed over that morning's papers and applauded in the editorials. "The British people will rejoice at the valor of their airmen and at the final smashing of Hitler's sea ambitions," exulted the *Daily Express*. In cinemas all over the free world, audiences watched the dramatic footage taken from the film unit Lancaster.

As soon as the sinking had been confirmed, telegrams started to pour into the headquarters of 617 and 9 Squadrons, beginning with the royal congratulations of King George VI who conveyed his "hearty congratulations to all those who took part in the daring and successful attack." Crown Prince Olav, the heir to the Norwegian throne, exiled in Britain, joined King George and expressed the "particular delight that we Norwegians hail the achievement of this deed."[42] The Admiralty, who had been denied the prize themselves, praised a "good job well done" and Barnes Wallis the "tremendous courage and skill" with which the crews had deployed his bomb.

There were no lavish celebrations to match the enormity of the event. The first ten 617 crews who landed at Woodhall the day after the raid were greeted by a regimental band and a crowd of ground staff offering congratulations. That night, remembered Freddy Watts, they piled into the small bar at Petwood and all "got very drunk." It was clear now that they would not have to go back again. There was no doubt that *Tirpitz* was finished. A PRU Mosquito flight shortly after the raid showed the ship capsized to port with seven hundred feet of hull poking out of the oil-stained waters of the fjord. The RAF's interpretation unit at Medmenham compiled an approximate bomb plot from the film and photographs taken during the attack. It showed that Tait's Tallboy had been the first to hit the target. The obscuring smoke meant only sixteen bombs could be traced, and it was impossible to say with certainty who had dropped which. Though Tait's name would henceforth be linked to the operation, everyone could claim to have played a part in *Tirpitz*'s doom.

On November 15, Air Minister Sir Archibald Sinclair visited Wood-hall. After lunch in the officers' mess he spoke to the crews assembled in the briefing room. "Gentlemen, we have sunk the toughest ship in the world and I'm sure in the war," he told them. "You are now going on forty-eight hours' leave. Go home and tell your story. Your people have had a hard time in this war, a lot of troubles, losses, suffering. Thank you for all you have achieved in the sinking of *Tirpitz* and good luck to you in the hard fighting which ... lies ahead."[43] The war was not yet won. Survival was distant and uncertain. It was the battles to come rather than recent victories that crowded their thoughts as they departed to their families, wives, and girlfriends.

EPILOGUE

Wilhelmshaven,
November 12, 2010

At 11:00 a.m. a small procession of old men and neat, white-haired women filed into the chapel of the Ehrenfriedhof cemetery on the edge of town for a simple ceremony of readings, prayers, and hymns. Afterward they walked along a rain-soaked path, through an avenue of elm trees to lay a wreath at a granite slab set among the shrubbery. "Schlachtschiff Tirpitz, 1.4.1939–12.11.1944" reads the legend, below an emblem of a Viking ship. Inscribed underneath are the words "Unseren toten zum Gedanken"—in memory of our dead. It is a modest memorial to a ship that in its short life caused the world such trouble.

They stood for a while under the bare trees chatting quietly and taking photographs, before driving back to the hotel, through streets lined with the drab utilitarian shops and apartment blocks that rose in place of the old town after the RAF bombed it flat. Then the solemnity that hung over the morning's events dissolved, and they sat down to a hearty lunch of meat, cabbage, and potatoes, washed down with beer and schnapps. The veterans of the *Tirpitz* comrades association gather every year to meet old friends and tell old stories. For all present, their time on board seems to have been a precious experience, one to be preserved. Among them is Klaus Rohwedder, the young gunner who saw the fatal Tallboy fall. After the war he became a pacifist. "That does not mean, though, that I have turned my back on the community we had on board or the memories that I still cherish today," he said.

The *Tirpitz* survivors can remember their war with pride and without shame. They did their duty and defended their ship to the last. It is the Luftwaffe which gets the blame for its demise. Five weeks after the disaster, seven men went on trial at a military court in Oslo, accused of dereliction of duty. Major Heinrich Ehrler, the commander of Jagdegeschwader 5, was at the head of the list of defendants. He was sentenced to three years' imprisonment but was released after a month. A loyal Nazi to the last, he died on April 4, 1945, over Berlin, reportedly ramming an American bomber after running out of ammunition.

His colleagues at Bardufoss believed Ehrler was a scapegoat in the affair. According to his adjutant, Oberleutnant Kurt Schulze, no specific orders had been issued to JW5 for the defense of *Tirpitz*, whose precise location was not even known to them. Their response had been crippled from the beginning by inaccurate plotting and poor communication.[1] The German defenses were indeed chaotic. Had they been more effective, *Tirpitz* might have stood at the center of a dramatic Allied defeat and November 12, 1944, remembered as the day when the Dambusters squadron and their comrades in 9 Squadron were annihilated.

As it was, she had already achieved much without having to fire her guns. After her move to Norway at the start of 1942, the Home Fleet was forced to manage the threat she posed to the Arctic and the Atlantic sea lanes, dedicating important resources to containing her that could have been put to much better use elsewhere. Her presence was directly responsible for one of the great failures of nerve of the Allied war—the decision to order PQ.17 to scatter. *Tirpitz* was, of course, to be feared. Had she ever cruised among a convoy the results would have been devastating. More appalling still was the prospect of her breaking into the Atlantic, perhaps sinking one of the transports laden with American troops which began arriving in 1942, bringing about both a military catastrophe and an Anglo-American political crisis.

The example of the *Bismarck*, though, showed that the chances of getting through to the North Atlantic undetected were slim, and the prospects of long-term survival small. Surface ships were, anyway, far less deadly to Allied shipping than aircraft and U-boats. From June 1, 1943, to May 31, 1944, warships and armed merchant raiders sank only five Allied ships. The overwhelming majority of the other 319 vessels lost to enemy action were destroyed by U-boats (216) and aircraft (64).[2] While achieving little, the big ships soaked up enormous resources. Vast quantities of scarce fuel were needed for a major operation, a consideration that weighed heavily in the question of whether or not to send them to sea. In this respect, *Tirpitz* perhaps placed almost as much of a burden on the German war effort as she did on British dispositions.

By the end of 1943, she had barely been put to aggressive use, with only an ineffective foray against PQ.12, a brief appearance during the PQ.17 disaster, and the inglorious raid on Spitsbergen to her credit. After the midget submarine attacks of September 22, 1943, she was badly damaged, and put out of action for six months. A cool appreciation by her enemies might have concluded that, following the sinking of *Scharnhorst* in December 1943, *Tirpitz* was unlikely to be risked at sea again. Instead, throughout the summer of 1944, the Fleet Air Arm engaged in a series of full-scale operations against her, handing over the task in the autumn to the RAF. The zeal of the pursuit, whipped on by Churchill, seems excessive now, but wartime created its own dynamic. By the time of the last attack, it was well understood that *Tirpitz* could no longer make any significant difference to the direction of the war. Willie Tait's characteristically cool judgement was that the feat had "not contributed much to the Allied victory."[3] Her death was still a cause for universal celebration. She had come to symbolize the hubris of a terrible regime. Her fate and that of Hitler seemed intertwined. Catharsis, deliverance, required that both should die.

The Lincolnshire Echo, whose circulation area included Woodhall Spa and Bardney, found a parable for "the misguided German people" in 617 and 9 Squadrons' victory. "They have been told that the *Tirpitz* was unsinkable—the RAF have proved that to be a fallacy; they have been told that Hitler was invincible, the reincarnation of the greatest virtues of the German spirit—and the [Allies] have proved that to be a fallacy also."[4]

The conclusion of the war in Europe was still six months away. Some of those involved in the quest to destroy *Tirpitz* would make it to the end. Others would not. They included men for whom peace held bright promise. Guy Byam, the young BBC reporter who flew with the film unit Lancaster on September 15, was captured while reporting at Arnhem. He was ordered by the Germans to help collect casualties, but knocked out his guard and escaped back to the Allied lines. He was killed on a reporting mission when the American 8th Air Force bomber he was flying in was shot down during a daylight raid on Berlin on February 3, 1945, leaving behind a wife and a baby daughter.

The survivors of the X-Craft attack were released from POW camp in May 1944. Godfrey Place returned to the navy, retraining as a pilot and flying with the Fleet Air Arm in the Korean War. He retired as a rear admiral in 1970. Don Cameron also stayed on and was about to take up an appointment at HMS *Dolphin* in Gosport, where his great adventure began, when he died suddenly in April 1961.

After the last *Tirpitz* raid, Willie Tait was taken off operations and spent the rest of the war training Canadian crews. He had flown 101 missions and earned four DSOs and two DFCs. Unlike Gibson and Cheshire he was not awarded the VC. He was recommended for one, nine days after the final attack, by Ralph Cochrane who praised "a great leader who in danger is unperturbed and at all times pits a stubborn will against the enemy's heaviest defences." His operational career, he went on, was "one of prolonged and heroic endeavour continued at his own urgent request far beyond what is normal and reasonable." The proposal was backed by Harris. According to the 617 Squadron veteran, Mick Martin, who, unbidden, delved into the matter, it was turned down by the "political/inter-service committee for high awards." Commenting on Tait's record, laid out in the recommendation, Martin, who was himself one of the best and bravest of Bomber Command's pilots, reckoned it "quite magnificent—the very best of all in my opinion and the opinion of many others."[5] No explanation emerged as to why the award was not granted. It was said in jest that the authorities did not want to give the impression that decoration came automatically with command of 617 Squadron. Tait stayed on after 1945, serving in the Middle and Far East, retiring as a group captain in 1964. He trained as a computer programmer and spent his leisure time studying the lieder of Schubert and tending his allotment. He retained his reserve to the end. Tony Iveson remembers a lunch at the RAF Club in Piccadilly to which Cochrane, Harris, and the great figures of Bomber Command were invited. Tait was naturally included. Before the start Iveson received a telephone call from Tait's wife, Betty, who told him, "he's left home but all I can say is wait outside for him." It was, said Iveson, "quite possible that he would get to the steps of the club and then turn back."[6]

The exiled Norwegians returned home as heroes. Leif Larsen was showered with decorations and became the subject of several books and a film. He remained modest despite the exposure, dying aged eighty-four

in 1990. Bjørn Rørholt went back to his engineering studies, before joining the Norwegian military, inventing in retirement a radar device for
the blind. Torstein Raaby returned to his life as a telegrapher, sailed on
the 1946 *Kon-Tiki* expedition as the raft's wireless operator and later
went back to run the radio station on Jan Mayen Island. He died in 1964
on his way to join an expedition to the North Pole. Terje Jacobsen
escaped to Sweden before the Gestapo closed in on him. After the war
he married an Englishwoman and had a successful career as an architect.
He still lives in Tromsø and now and then takes a visitor to Haakøy
island. Once the war was over, a Norwegian salvage firm moved in to
dismantle *Tirpitz*'s sad carcass. The work was dangerous, with unex-
ploded ordnance everywhere, and often gruesome. Hundreds of corpses
still lay trapped inside the hull. In September 1945, before they began
work, Tait visited the wreck. It made a melancholy sight. "From close-to,"
he wrote, it "was huge, hideous and stank like a charnel house. There
were nearly a thousand bodies still inside the flooded hull and the trea-
cly black fuel oil still seeped out of the rents ... this rusty tomb was
nothing to gloat over. It affronted the Arctic stillness of the unpolluted
hills."[7] When the salvors departed some debris remained, including the
steel rings of the anti-torpedo nets, until they, too, were carted away. But
even now you can still find, amid the rocks and seaweed of the peaceful
shoreline, a hunk of steel, flaking and rusted through, a small memento
of the folly and waste of war.

ACKNOWLEDGMENTS

The *Tirpitz* story took me into new territory historically and geographically, and I am grateful to those who helped me to explore it. As the years pass, the number of participants dwindles. It has been a great pleasure to meet some of those who remain and to hear their extraordinary stories. To them, a heartfelt thank you for the privilege. In Norway I would also like to thank Karen Sofie Aanjesen, Einar Ianssen, Terje Jacobsen, and Aud Schreuder. My friend Nina Watts was the perfect guide and companion. In Germany I am particularly grateful to Kurt-Jürgen Voigt for allowing me access to his father's letters and to Hein Hellendoorn and Klaus Rohwedder and the members of the *Tirpitz* comrades association for making me so welcome at their annual gathering. In Britain I was given every assistance by the Imperial War Museum—especially Edgar Aromin of the sound archive—the

Public Records Office, with special thanks to William Spencer, all the staff at the Churchill Centre in Cambridge, and Jeff Walden at the BBC Written Archives Centre in Caversham. I must also record the debt I owe to earlier historians of the *Tirpitz* saga, notably James Benson, Alan Cooper, James G. Dorrian, Thomas Gallagher, Alf R. Jacobsen, Ludovic Kennedy, Léonce Peillard, John Sweetman, C. E. T. Warren, and Richard Woodman.

The official historian of 617 Squadron Rob Owen was generous with his time and a source of much food for thought. Ian Weatherhead kindly lent me documents relating to the service of his father Wing Commander Trenham Weatherhead at RAF Medmenham, and Ken Lowden provided valuable material on the war in Norway. Thanks too for the hospitality and help of Ian Cameron, Vernon Coles and his daughter Jane, Eve Compton-Hall, Dave Graham, Bridget Lorimer, and Squadron Leader Ian Smith. I was greatly assisted with the research on the German aspect of the story by my former colleague and fellow foreign correspondent Robin Gedye, and Geli von Hase. Arnt Sundstol read the manuscript with a Norwegian eye and saved me from many *bêtises*. Rear Admiral Nick Wilkinson kindly did the same from a nautical perspective and corrected a crop of landlubberly errors. For those that remain, *mea culpa…*

I owe a particular debt to Peter Tait and Irene Bridgmont for their help in my researches into the career of their remarkable father. I would like to pay tribute to the superb professionalism of the HarperCollins team in producing a handsome book, and in particular the editing of Arabella Pike and Kerry Enzor. As always, Helen Ellis was a source of cheer and encouragement. I would also like to thank Alex Novak and the Regnery team for *Target Tirpitz*'s U.S. makeover. To Henrietta and Honor, once again, a thousand thanks for your patience, support, and fortitude.

NOTES

CHAPTER ONE

1. See p. xx, Ranks of the Kriegsmarine, for equivalent British rank.
2. Taken from Alfred Zuba's account delivered to the "Sink the *Tirpitz!*" Symposium organized by the Confederate Air Force Golden Gate Wing, October 21, 2001.

CHAPTER TWO

1. Letter to Ludovic Kennedy.
2. Shirer, William, *The Rise and Fall of the Third Reich*, Secker & Warburg, 1963, p. 467.
3. *The Times*, Monday, April 3, 1939.
4. Von Hassell was a conservative patriot who had been wounded in the First World War and still carried a French bullet in his heart. He was executed for his part in the July 20, 1944, plot to assassinate Hitler.
5. Hassell, Ulrich von, *Die Hassell-Tagebücher 1938–1944: Aufzeichnungen vom Anderen Deutschland*, Siedler Verlag, pp. 87, 88–89.
6. *Daily Express*, Monday, April 3, 1939.
7. Raeder, Grand Admiral Erich, *Struggle for the Sea*, William Kimber, 1959, p. 95.
8. Evidence of Wilhelm Süchtig to Nuremberg War Tribunal, May 16, 1946.

CHAPTER THREE

1. Private Papers of C. T. Collett, IWM 3161.
2. Bercuson, David J., and Herwig, Holger H., *Bismarck*, Hutchinson, 2001, p. 50.
3. Ibid., p. 58.
4. Private Papers of C. T. Collett, IWM 3161.
5. Private Papers of Lieutenant G. P. Allen, IWM 1994.
6. Private Papers of Patrick Mullins, IWM 2432.
7. Harriman, W. Averell, and Abel, Elie, *Special Envoy to Churchill and Stalin*, Random House, pp. 33–34.
8. Bercuson and Herwig, op. cit., p. 241.
9. Ibid., p. 242.
10. Private Papers of Charles Friend, IWM 2751.
11. Private Papers of Lieutenant Commander J. A. Stewart-Moore, unpublished manuscript, IWM 91/291.
12. Interview with author and testimony from Moffat, John, and Rossiter, Mike, *I Sank the Bismarck*, Corgi, 2009.
13. Private Papers of A. E. Franklin, IWM 11581.
14. Bercuson and Herwig, op. cit., p. 298.

CHAPTER FOUR

1. Private Papers of A. F. P. Fane, IWM 7685.
2. Churchill, Winston, *The Second World War*, vol. IV, Cassell, 1951, p. 98.
3. Gilbert, Martin, *The Churchill War Papers*, vol. III, Heinemann, p. 1037.
4. Ibid., p. 1134.
5. Ibid.
6. Ibid., p. 1344.
7. Briefe von der "Königin des Nordens," September 1941–Oktober 1942, ed. Jürgen Voigt, unpublished letters of Kurt Voigt (hereafter Voigt Letters).
8. Interview, *Schlachtschiff Tirpitz: Die Einsame Königin des Nordens*, History Films, 2006.
9. Raeder, op. cit., p. 214.
10. *Fuehrer Conferences on Naval Affairs, 1939–1945*, Greenhill Books, p. 234.
11. Roskill, Stephen, *The War at Sea*, vol. I, HMSO, 1954, p. 116.
12. Sweetman, John, *Hunting the Beast*, Sutton, 2000, p. 15.

13. Brünner, Adalbert, *Schlachtschiff Tirpitz im Einsatz. Ein Seeoffizier berichtet*, Podzun-Pallas, 1993.
14. Sweetman, op. cit., p. 16.
15. Interview with Georg Schlegel, *Schlachtschiff Tirpitz*.
16. Brünner, op. cit.
17. Interview with Georg Schlegel, *Schlachtschiff Tirpitz*.
18. Middlebrook, Martin, and Chris Everitt, *The Bomber Command War Diaries*, Penguin, 1985, p. 165.
19. Peillard, Léonce, *Sink the Tirpitz!*, Jonathan Cape, 1968, p. 40.
20. Roskill, op. cit., vol. I, p. 159.

CHAPTER FIVE

1. See Woodman, Richard, *Arctic Convoys 1941–1945*, Pen and Sword, 2007, for the best account of these operations.
2. Memoir of Able Seaman William Smith DSM, The Second World War Experience Centre.
3. Quoted in Roskill, Stephen, *Churchill and the Admirals*, William Collins, 1977, p. 124.
4. *The Cunningham Papers*, ed. Michael Simpson, Publications of the Navy Records Society, 1999, vol. I, p. 169.
5. Roskill, op. cit., vol. I, p. 188.
6. PRO PREM 3/191/1.
7. PRO CAB 69.
8. Private Papers of R. P. Raikes, IWM 6349.
9. Private Papers of C. Friend, IWM 2751.
10. Wikipedia, Harrison, W. A., Fairey Albacore (Warpaint Series No. 52).
11. Roskill, *The War at Sea*, vol. II, HMSO, pp. 119–23.
12. Sweetman, op. cit., p. 28; Kennedy, Ludovic, *Menace*, Sidgwick & Jackson, 1979, p. 43.
13. IWM 2751, p. 122.
14. IWM 2751, p. 125.
15. Kennedy, op. cit., pp. 43–44.
16. Sweetman, op. cit., p. 31.
17. Kennedy, op. cit., pp. 44–45.
18. IWM 2751, p. 126.
19. Sweetman, op. cit., p. 31.

20.   Roskill, *The War at Sea*, vol. II, p. 123.

21.   Ibid., vol. II, p. 124.

22.   Kennedy, op. cit., p. 45.

23.   PRO PREM 3/191/1.

CHAPTER SIX

1.   Webster, Sir Charles, and Frankland, Noble, *The Strategic Air Offensive Against Germany*, vol. IV, HMSO, 1961, pp. 133–34.

2.   Ryder, Robert, *The Attack on St. Nazaire*, John Murray, 1947, p. 3.

3.   Lt. Bill Watson, quoted in Dorrian, James G., *Storming St Nazaire*, Pen and Sword, 1998, p. 37.

4.   See: www.commandoveterans.org/history.

5.   Ashcroft, Michael, *Special Forces Heroes*, Headline Review, 2008, p. 56.

6.   See: www.history of war.org.

7.   Ryder, op. cit., p. 80.

8.   *The Daily Telegraph Book of Naval Obituaries*, Grub Street, 2005, p. 23.

9.   Private Papers of W. L. Stephens, IWM 1927.

10.   Private Papers of Philip Dark, IWM 3028.

CHAPTER SEVEN

1.   Bennett, Air Vice-Marshal D. C. T., *Pathfinder*, Goodall Publications, 1988, p. 116.

2.   IWM Sound Archive Recording 10310.

3.   Private Papers of A. F. P. Fane, IWM 7685.

4.   PRO ADM 223/87.

5.   Sweetman, op. cit., p. 43.

6.   Ibid.

7.   PRO PREM 3/191/1.

8.   Quoted in Sweetman, op. cit., p. 44.

9.   IWM Sound Archive Recording 9378.

10.   Interview on BBC TV, *Target Tirpitz*, director Edward Mirzoeff, presenter Ludovic Kennedy, 1973.

11.   After the landing the burning bomber melted through the ice and settled on the bottom of the lake. It was recovered in 1973 and is now on display at the RAF Museum at Hendon.

12. IWM Sound Archive Recording 10310.
13. IWM Sound Archive Recording 9378.
14. Interview with author.
15. IWM Sound Archive Recording 9378.

CHAPTER EIGHT

1. Roskill, *The War at Sea*, vol. II, p. 130.
2. Churchill, op. cit., vol. IV, p. 233.
3. Private Papers of R. P. Raikes, IWM 6349.
4. A witty signal is highly prized in the navy and these *bons mots* have been attributed to other captains.
5. Ibid.
6. Roskill, op. cit., vol. II, p. 130.
7. Ibid.
8. Connell, Brian, *Knight Errant: A Biography of Douglas Fairbanks, Jnr*, Hodder & Stoughton, 1955, p. 106.
9. Ibid., p. 112.
10. Kennedy, op. cit., p. 71.
11. Denham, Henry, *Inside the Nazi Ring: A Naval Attaché in Sweden, 1940–1945*, John Murray, 1984, p. 90.
12. Roskill, op. cit., vol. II, p. 136.
13. Kennedy, op. cit., p. 65.
14. PRO KV2/1137.
15. Kennedy, op. cit., p. 64.
16. Kennedy, op. cit., p. 71.
17. Winn, Godfrey, *PQ.17*, Hutchinson, 1946, p. 67.
18. Ibid., p. 74.
19. Roskill, op. cit., vol. II, p. 138.

CHAPTER NINE

1. Norman Denning was one of a trio of remarkable brothers. "Tom" Denning became Master of the Rolls, Britain's senior law officer; Reginald joined the army and ended up a lieutenant-general; and Norman finished his career a vice admiral.
2. Interview, *Target Tirpitz*, BBC, 1973.

3.   Roskill, op. cit., vol. II, p. 140.

4.   Interview, *Target Tirpitz*, BBC, 1973.

5.   Connell, op. cit., p. 173.

6.   Merchant Navy in Second World War website.

7.   Interview with author.

8.   Churchill, op. cit., vol. IV, p. 236.

9.   Roskill, op. cit., vol. II, p. 140.

10. Kennedy, op. cit., p. 84.

11. Winn, op. cit., p. 96.

12. Irving, David, *The Destruction of Convoy PQ.17*, St. Martin's Press, New York, 1987, p. 157.

13. Interview, *Target Tirpitz*, BBC, 1973.

14. Irving, op. cit., p. 153.

15. Quoted in Kemble, Mike, The Merchant Navy in World War 2, www.second worldwar.org

16. Churchill, op. cit., vol. IV, pp. 235–36.

17. PRO ADM 119/913.

18. Roskill, op. cit., vol. II, p. 144.

19. Kemble, op. cit.

CHAPTER TEN

1.   PRO PREM 3/191/1.

2.   Warren, C. E. T., and Benson, James, *Above Us the Waves: The Story of Midget Submarines and Human Torpedoes*, Pen and Sword, 2006, Appendix 1.

3.   Davies, Robert H., *Deep Diving and Submarine Operations*, Siebe, Gorman, 1955, p. 291.

4.   See: www.underwaterheritagetrust.org.uk.

5.   Peillard, op. cit., p. 119.

6.   Howarth, David, *The Shetland Bus*, Shetland Times Ltd, 1998.

7.   Ibid.

8.   Quoted in Warren and Benson, op. cit., p. 51.

9.   Ibid., p. 54.

10. Ibid., p. 56.

11. Ibid., p. 58.

12. Ibid., p. 63.

13. Ibid., p. 64.

14. Ibid., p. 68.

15. The episode was used as evidence in the postwar trials of Flesch and Keitel, which ended with their executions.

16. *Nuremberg Trial Proceedings*, vol. 13, 14 May 1946.

17. Peillard, op. cit., p. 166.

CHAPTER ELEVEN

1. Voigt Letters, 8/01/42.

2. Interview with author.

3. Herbert Ludwig, unpublished memoir.

4. Brünner, op. cit.

5. Peillard, op. cit., p. 95.

6. Voigt Letters, 8/01/42.

7. Kennedy, op. cit., p. 70.

8. Voigt Letters, 8/01/42, p. 102.

9. Ludwig, op. cit.

10. Interview with author.

11. Kennedy, op. cit., pp. 92–93.

12. PRO ADM 223/87.

13. Raeder, op. cit., p. 226.

CHAPTER TWELVE

1. Raeder, op. cit., pp. 226–31.

2. Peillard, op. cit., p. 174.

3. Roskill, op. cit., vol. II, p. 354.

4. Ibid., p. 299.

5. Dönitz, Karl, *Memoirs*, Weidenfeld & Nicolson, 1959, p. 300.

6. Ibid., p. 310.

7. Roskill, op. cit., vol. II, p. 354.

8. Sweetman, op. cit., p. 72.

9. Dönitz, op. cit., p. 371.

10. Ibid., pp. 310–11.

11. Ibid., p. 372.

12. Peillard, op. cit., p.180.

13. Dönitz, op. cit., p. 373.

14. Peillard, op. cit., p. 242.
15. Brünner, op. cit.
16. Roskill, op. cit., vol. II, p. 399.
17. Ibid., vol. II, pp. 397–98.
18. Ibid., vol. II, pp. 400–401.
19. Quoted in Jacobsen, Alf R., *X-Craft versus Tirpitz: The Mystery of the Missing X5*, Sutton Publishing, 2006, p. 113.
20. Dönitz, op. cit., p. 374.
21. Private Papers of E. C. Dabner, IWM 3886.
22. Brünner, op. cit., p. 6.

CHAPTER THIRTEEN

1. PRO PR PREM 3/19/1.
2. PRO PREM 3/191/1, Pound to Churchill, 15.4.43.
3. PRO PREM 3/191/1, Churchill to Cherwell, 1.5.43.
4. PRO PREM 3/191/1, Churchill to Pound, 5.5.43.
5. IWM Sound Archive 28642.
6. Interview with author.
7. IWM Sound Archive 13422.
8. Interview with author.
9. Interview with author.
10. Interview with author.
11. Interview with author.
12. Warren and Benson, op. cit., p. 47.
13. Interview with author.
14. Shean, Max, *Corvette and Submarine*, Claremont, WA, 1994, p. 126.
15. Peillard, op. cit., p. 85.
16. Shean, op. cit., p. 134.
17. Interview with author.
18. IWM Sound Archive 28642.
19. Shean, op. cit., p. 136.
20. Gallagher, Thomas, *Against All Odds*, Macdonald, 1971, p. 50.
21. IWM Sound Archive 28642.
22. Shean, op. cit., p. 154.
23. IWM Sound Archive 28642.
24. Interview with author.

25. IWM Sound Archive 13422.
26. Shean, op. cit., p. 157.
27. Gallagher, op. cit., p. 51.
28. Interview with author.
29. Gallagher, op. cit., pp. 33–35.
30. Quoted in Jacobsen, op. cit., p. 108.
31. See: www.yorkshiredivers.com.
32. IWM Sound Archive 13422.
33. Shean, op. cit., p.169.
34. Quoted in Peillard, op. cit., p. 193. Authenticated by Eve Compton-Hall (Cameron's widow).

CHAPTER FOURTEEN
1. IWM Sound Archive 02440.
2. Shean, op. cit., p. 170.
3. There were to be more frustrations for *Syrtis*. A little later she twice encountered the same unsuspecting U-boat but was forced to hold fire for fear of compromising the *Tirpitz* operation.
4. Quoted in Gallagher, op. cit., p. 79.
5. Quoted in Jacobsen, op. cit., p. 127.
6. Gallagher, op. cit., p. 81, authenticated by Eve Compton-Hall.
7. Peillard, op. cit., p. 217.
8. Interview with author.
9. Quoted in Gallagher, op. cit., p. 83.

CHAPTER FIFTEEN
1. Peillard, op. cit., p. 224.
2. PRO ADM 1/20026.
3. PRO ADM 1/20026.
4. IWM Sound Archive 2441.
5. *Tirpitz: Kriegstagebuch* [hereafter *KTB*], p. 233.
6. Peillard, op. cit., p. 251.
7. *KTB*, p. 204.
8. Gallagher, op. cit., p. 125.
9. Interview with author.

10. Quoted in Jacobsen, op. cit., p. 161.
11. Obituary, *The Times*, February 9, 2006.
12. Interview with author.
13. Gallagher, op. cit., p. 141.
14. Interview with author.
15. *KTB*, p. 205.
16. Interview with author.
17. Until long after the war Henty-Creer's family clung to the belief that he had suceeded in dropping *X-5*'s mines under *Tirpitz* and campaigned for the award of a VC. In 2011 a Royal Norwegian Navy ordnance disposal team working in Kaafjord destroyed a device which may have been one of *X-5*'s side charges.
18. Quoted in Peillard, op. cit., p. 255.
19. Interview with author.
20. *KTB*, p. 99.
21. Ibid., p. 237.
22. *Fuehrer Conferences on Naval Affairs, 1939–1945*, p. 381.

CHAPTER SIXTEEN

1. Churchill, op. cit., vol. V, p. 233.
2. There were alternative overland routes to the Soviet Union via Persia and Vladivostok but they took longer and the railways could not shift the same quantities as ships.
3. Quoted in Brodhurst, Robin, *Churchill's Anchor*, Leo Cooper, 2000, p. 1.
4. Quoted in Churchill, op cit., vol. V, p. 118.
5. Ibid., p. 237.
6. Loewenheim, Francis L., Langley Harold D., and Jonas, Manfred, eds, *Roosevelt and Churchill: Their Secret Wartime Correspondence*, Barrie & Jenkins, 1975, p. 380.
7. Churchill, op. cit., vol. V, p. 239.
8. Ibid., p. 244.
9. Jacobsen, op. cit., p. 182.
10. Golovko, Admiral Arseni, *With the Red Fleet*, trans. Peter Broomfield, Putnam, 1965, pp. 180–81.
11. Roskill, op. cit., vol. III, p. 78.
12. See: www.admirals.org.uk.

13. Interview with author.
14. Quoted in Woodman, op. cit., p. 256.
15. Interview with author.
16. Dönitz, op. cit., pp. 375–76.
17. PRO ADM 1/20026.
18. Dönitz, op. cit., pp. 381–85.
19. Woodman, op. cit., p. 372.
20. Interview with author.
21. Roskill, *The War at Sea*, vol. III, part 1, p. 88.
22. Dönitz, op. cit., pp. 383–84.

CHAPTER SEVENTEEN

1. Brünner, op. cit.
2. Interview with author.
3. Sweetman, op. cit., p. 83.
4. Woodman, op. cit., p. 385.
5. PRO PREM 3/191/1.
6. AIR 2/8394.
7. PRO ADM 205/56.
8. PRO ADM 205/43.
9. *Cunningham Papers*, vol. II, p. 234.
10. IWM Sound Archive 31043.
11. PRO ADM 199/941.
12. Ibid.
13. IWM Sound Recording 2507.
14. PRO ADM 199/941.
15. IWM Sound Recording 2508.
16. Quoted in Sweetman, op. cit., p. 92.
17. Interview with author.
18. All details drawn from reports in PRO ADM 199/941, the Admiralty report on the operation, unless otherwise stated.
19. Brünner, op. cit.
20. *Cunningham Papers*, vol. II, p. 233.
21. IWM Sound Recording 28775.
22. Quoted in Sweetman, op. cit., p. 122.
23. *KTB*, 25/08/44.

CHAPTER EIGHTEEN

1. Interview with author.
2. AIR 14/1971.
3. Quoted in Sweetman, op. cit., p. 128.
4. Ibid.
5. Dönitz, op. cit., pp. 385–86.
6. AIR 14/1971.
7. Harris, Sir Arthur, *Bomber Offensive*, Pen and Sword, 2005, p. 255.
8. Morpurgo, J. E., *Barnes Wallis*, Longman, 1972, p. xv.
9. Quoted in ibid., p. 283.
10. Interview, *Target Tirpitz*, 1973.
11. Address at memorial service, St Clement Danes, London, November 21, 2007.
12. Private Papers of J. B. Tait.
13. Interview with author.
14. IWM Sound Recording 9208.
15. Edith Stowe, quoted in Morris, Richard, *Cheshire: The Biography of Leonard Cheshire VC*, Viking, 2000.
16. Private Papers of J. B. Tait.
17. Ibid.
18. Quoted in Morris, op. cit., p. 99.
19. Interview with author.
20. Interview with author.
21. Iveson DFC, Squadron Leader Tony, and Milton, Brian, *Lancaster: The Biography*, André Deutsch, 2009, p. 189.
22. AIR 14/1971.
23. Ibid.
24. Iveson and Milton, op. cit., p. 187.
25. AIR 20/6187.
26. AIR 14/1971.
27. BBC Archives, Caversham.
28. AIR 20/617.
29. IWM Sound Recording 2509.
30. AIR 20/6187.
31. IWM Sound Recording 2509.
32. IWM Sound Recording 2510.
33. AIR 20/6187.

CHAPTER NINETEEN

1. Interview with Georg Schlegel, *Schlachtschiff Tirpitz*.
2. Brünner, op. cit.
3. Dönitz, op. cit., p 386.
4. Quoted in Sweetman, op. cit., p.181.
5. Brünner, op. cit.
6. Quoted in Jacobsen, op. cit., p. 228.
7. PRO ADM 223/87.
8. Ibid.
9. IWM Sound Recording 11592.
10. Harris, op. cit., p. 256.
11. PRO PREM 3/191/1.
12. Ibid.
13. Iveson heard later that Wyness and his wireless operator Flying Officer Bruce Hosie had been shot in cold blood after capture.
14. Iveson and Milton, op. cit., p. 193.
15. AIR 20/6187.
16. Interview with author.
17. Ibid.
18. AIR 14/1903.
19. Interview with author.
20. Ibid.
21. Ibid.
22. AIR 27/2129.
23. AIR 20/6187.
24. Interview with author.
25. IWM Sound Archive 2519.
26. Interview with author.
27. IWM Sound Archive 21029.
28. See www.liveleak.com, 'RAF Bombers sink the *Tirpitz*'.
29. AIR 27/2129.
30. AIR 27/128.
31. Ibid.
32. IWM Sound Archive 2518.
33. Quoted in Jacobsen, op. cit., p. 240.
34. Military Court Proceedings of 17, 18 and 20 December 1944 Arising out of the Loss of the Battleship *Tirpitz*.

35. Interview with author.

36. Brünner, op. cit.

37. Interview with author.

38. The Sinking of the Tirpitz, Report of an Eye Witness.

39. Interview with author.

40. PRO PREM 191/1.

41. Bruce Buckham obituary, *Sydney Morning Herald*, August 17, 2011.

42. AIR 27/2129.

43. Quoted in Cooper, Alan W., *Beyond the Dams to the Tirpitz*, Goodall Publications, 1991, p. 123.

EPILOGUE

1. Iveson and Milton, op. cit., pp. 198–202.

2. Roskill, *The War at Sea*, vol. III, part 1, p. 388.

3. Private Papers of J. B. Tait.

4. *Lincolnshire Echo*, 14 November 1944.

5. Private Papers of J. B. Tait.

6. Interview with author.

7. Private Papers of J. B. Tait.

INDEX

12th Submarine Flotilla, 235, 244
49th Parallel (film), 244

A

Aaland Islands, 47
Aasegg, Olaf, 312
Aasfjord, 66, 111, 113
Admiral Graf Spee (battleship), 15
Admiral Hipper (heavy cruiser), 14, 113, 204
Admiral Scheer (battleship), 15, 47, 52, 66, 70, 73, 113, 188, 356
Admiralty, 16–17, 20–21, 28, 32, 42, 45–46, 54, 58–59, 65–66, 69, 73–74, 78, 89, 91, 126, 130, 133–35, 142–43, 147–48, 152–53, 159–60, 164, 167, 172, 176–77, 217, 225, 227–29, 232, 234, 250, 252, 260, 262, 288–90, 292, 302, 314–15, 317, 331–32, 336, 338–39, 365–66, 388
  Operational Control Centre, 32
Admiralty Citadel 149, 153
Admiralty Fleet Order, 231
Agdenes, 64, 73, 178, 183, 186
Air Ministry, 54, 107, 387
Aitken, Bob, 257, 285–87
Akureyri, 298
Albacore "Applecore" biplane, 54, 74–77, 80–85, 316
Aldis lamp, 76
Alexander, Albert, 317
Alexander, Robbie, 264
Alexandria Harbor, 164
Allen, G. P., 27–28
Alta, 217, 249–50, 270, 312–13, 332, 365
Altafjord, 133, 140, 142, 148–50, 153–56, 204, 207, 217, 219–20, 225, 252, 262, 270–71,
273–74, 302, 312, 314, 321, 323, 332, 363–64
Alteidet, 249, 312
Altenfjord, 133, 149, 358
Andersen, Lale, 193
Anglo-German Naval Agreement (1935), 14, 16
Arado seaplanes, 77, 82, 201, 223, 279
Archangel, 51, 140, 295, 349, 352, 357
Archer, Ernest, 316
Arctic Ocean, 51, 67, 130, 149
Ardtaraig House (Loch Striven), 241
Armitage, J., 325
Arnhem, 394
Arøya Island, 273
Arthur, 61, 177–87, 190, 203
Arthur, Duggie, 222–24
Ashbourne, Lord, 172–73
Assman, Heinz, 199, 328
Auschwitz, 312
Auskarneset, 262, 270, 273–74
Australia, Australians, 118, 121, 229–30, 244, 248, 345–46, 351–52, 372, 380
Austria, 10–11, 13, 345
Avengers, 333
Azerbaijan (tanker), 145

B

Bader, Douglas, 343
Baker-Falkner, Roy, 323–25
Baltic, 22, 24, 47–48, 50, 52, 96, 215, 217, 277, 295, 314, 341
Bardney, 349, 351, 370, 394
Bardufoss, 364, 373, 381–82, 386, 392
Barentsburg, 221–24, 262
Barents Sea, 135–36, 140, 142–43, 153, 155–56, 158, 204–5, 207–8, 218–19, 299, 309

Barracudas, 316–20, 322–27, 330, 333, 336

Barry, Claud, 172, 190, 252–53, 255–56, 272, 274, 289

Basle, 367

Battle of the Atlantic, 20, 90, 219, 291–92

Battle of the Barents Sea (1942), 205, 208, 218, 299

Battle of Britain, 20, 90, 340

Battle of North Cape (1943), 300–9

Bay of Biscay, 89, 95

Bay of Seine, 65

Bazin, James, 340, 360, 365, 375, 387

BBC, 207, 351, 355–56, 365, 387–88, 394, 398

Bear Island, 50, 68, 79–80, 133, 135, 140–43, 150, 154, 219, 302

Beattie, Stephen "Sam," 93, 97, 99

Beaufort (aircraft), 107

Beaverbrook Newspapers, 141

Belgrano (cruiser), 165

Bell, Thomas, 326

Bell, T. I. S. "Tizzy," 241

Beniers, Leo, 381

Bennett, Donald, 109, 116–23, 343

Benson, 114

Berchtesgaden, 208

Bergen, 19–20, 111

Berlin, 24, 49, 72, 140, 154–55, 201, 213, 216, 220, 277, 288, 296, 338, 344, 358, 362, 392, 394

Bernadotte, Count, 122

Bey, Erich, 301–4, 308–9

Bidlingmaier, Gerhard, 82

Bielfeld, Kapitänleutnant, 156

Binney, Constance, 346

Bismarck, 15–16, 19–27, 29–35, 37–42, 44, 46–47, 49, 52, 65, 69, 71, 74–75, 80, 90, 134, 136, 321, 393

Bjørnøy, Palmer, 177, 180, 182–84, 186–87

Blenheims, 55

Bletchley Park, 22, 78, 80, 148, 153, 302

Blohm and Voss 138 seaplane (Flying Clog), 141

Blücher (heavy cruiser), 14, 49

Bodø, 87, 371, 381

Bofors anti-aircraft cannon, 222

Bogen, 87, 191, 195, 198, 202

Bogen Bay 87, 175–76, 201, 217

Bogstar (horse), 114

Bomber Command, 50, 54, 56, 90, 104, 108–9, 113, 118, 199, 227–28, 315, 336–39, 341, 344, 346, 366, 369, 387, 395

No. 5 Group, 110, 345, 348, 352, 366, 371, 374, 387

Bomber Command Squadrons,

9 Squadron, 340, 348–49, 351, 353, 357, 359–60, 365–67, 375–77, 380, 382, 386–88, 392, 394

10 Squadron, 109–10, 116, 123, 344

15 Squadron, 56

35 Squadron, 55, 109–10, 115, 119, 122–23, 344

44 Squadron, 115, 117, 122

76 Squadron, 53, 109, 115, 120, 122, 347

78 Squadron, 117, 344, 347

97 Squadron, 115, 117, 122

149 Squadron, 56

426 Squadron, 351

607 Squadron, 340

617 Squadron "Dambusters," 315, 335, 340, 342–43, 346, 348–49, 351–53, 355, 357, 366–68, 370, 372, 375–77, 380, 382, 388, 392, 394–95

bombs, 319–20

armor-piercing (AP), 55, 108, 319, 325, 327–29, 333–34, 336

Highball, 228, 315–16

JW "Johnny Walker," 351, 357, 360, 371

Mark XIV bomb sights, 357

Mark XIX mines, 108, 116, 120

semi-armor-piercing (SAP), 108, 320, 325, 328

Stabilized Automatic Bomb Sight (SABS), 342, 357, 359

Tallboy, 339–42, 348–51, 357, 360–62, 367, 371–72, 379–80, 388, 392

V1s and V2s, 341, 348

Bonaventure, 251–52, 255, 264

Bonham-Carter, Stuart, 127, 130

Bonnell, Chuck, 165, 167

Bottomley, Norman, 350

Bougainville (merchant cruiser), 317

Bovell, Henry, 81, 86

Bowles, Francis, 327

Boyd, D. W., 317

Boyd, Tom, 98

Brattholm, 270, 273–74

Brekstad, 73

Bremen, 104

Brest, 23, 32–33, 41, 50, 65, 342
Brewster, William "Jock," 179–81, 185–90
Briggs, Dennis, 33
Brinkmann, Helmuth, 25, 30
Bristol Taurus II radial engine, 75
British intelligence agencies 57, 65
British Mission, 190
Brittany, 29, 32–33, 95
Broome, Jack, 134–35, 141–42, 144–45, 148,
    151–52, 154
Brown, A. "Jock," 179, 185, 187
Browning, P. C. A., 170
Brünner, Adalbert, 52–53, 196–99, 203, 216–
    17, 221, 223, 225, 311, 329, 362–63, 384
Brunsbüttel, 52, 113, 340
Buckham, Bruce "Buck," 351, 359, 373, 375,
    380, 388
Buckham, Gwen, 388
Bud, 180
Burnett, Robert, 296, 300, 302–8
Burns, George "Paddy," 326
Byam-Corstiaens, Guy, 355–58, 394

C
Cameron, Donald, 233–34, 248, 252–53, 262,
    264–65, 269–78, 280–81, 283–84, 288, 394
Cameron, Eve (*née* Kilpatrick), 234, 241–42,
    252–53, 271, 288
Canaris, Admiral, 11
Cannon, Andrew, 327
Cape Wrath, 174, 255
Caplan, Conrad, 312–13
Cardiff, 92
Carey, Bill, 352, 372
Carls, Rolf, 72, 140, 210
Carlton (merchantman), 158
Carroll, Ernest, 327
"Cassidy." *See* Mark I Human Torpedo
Castagnola, James, 379
Catalina flying boat, 33, 126, 147
Causer, Malcolm, 179, 181, 185, 187–89
CBS, 388
Chamberlain, Bill, 100
Chamberlain, Neville, 11, 14
Channel Dash 66, 73, 263
Chant, Stuart, 100
Chequers, 21, 28, 32
Cherwell, Lord, 228
Cheshire, Leonard, 343, 346–48, 368, 395

Christiansen, Arne, 174, 176
Christopher Newport (merchantman), 143
Church House, 41
Churchill, Clementine, 21
Churchill, Sarah, 21
Churchill tanks, 156
Churchill, Winston, 17, 20–22, 28, 32–33, 36,
    41, 45–46, 51, 54, 56, 68–71, 87–88, 90–91,
    97, 109, 116–17, 126, 153, 159–60, 164,
    218–20, 227–28, 290–95, 314–15, 317, 323,
    330, 366, 387, 393
Ciliax, Otto, 65–66, 72–73, 77–80, 82, 84, 86
Clayton, Rear Admiral, 153
Coastal Command, 23, 32–33, 107, 114, 117,
    316
Coastal Command Squadrons,
    209 Squadron, 33
    217 Squadron, 107
    618 Squadron, 316
Cochrane, Sir Ralph, 348, 370, 374–75, 395
Coles, Vernon "Ginger" 233, 238, 248–49,
    251–52, 290, 298
Colgan, Flight Sergeant J., 119
Collett, Charles, 20, 25–27
Cologne, 199, 344
Colwill, Colin, 327
Combined Operations Headquarters, 91, 132
Commandos, 91–94, 99, 101–4
Condors, 33, 72–73, 76, 90
Coningsby, 368
convoys, 21, 23, 51–52, 66–68, 70–72, 77–80,
    86, 90–91, 109, 125–30, 132–45, 148–56,
    159–61, 174, 176, 204–5, 207–8, 211,
    215–20, 230–32, 251, 291–304, 306, 309,
    314–15, 320–21, 331, 333, 337, 365, 393
    Arctic, 51, 66, 68, 70, 80, 126–30, 133, 139,
    141, 204–5, 216, 218, 220, 291–92, 294–95,
    299, 365
    HX.229, 220
    JW.51, 218
    JW.51B, 204
    JW.52, 218
    JW.53, 218
    JW.54A/JW.54B, 295
    JW.55A/JW.55B, 296, 299–300, 304
    JW.58, 320–21
    JW.59, 333
    "Pedestal," 130

PQ.12, 71–73, 78–80, 86, 90, 111, 126, 208, 393
PQ.13, 126
PQ.14, 127
PQ.15, 127, 130
PQ.16, 128, 132
PQ.17, 130, 132–35, 137, 140–42, 145, 148, 160–61, 172, 174–75, 321, 393
PQ.18, 159, 176
QP.8, 71, 78
QP.10, 127
QP.11, 127
QP.12, 126, 128
QP.13, 130, 132, 142
RA.52, 218
RA.54A/RA.54B, 295
SC.122, 220
Coode, Tim, 36–37
Cooper, A. J., 324
Cooper, Alfred Duff, 131
Cooper, N. C., 35
Copland, Bill, 94
Corsairs, 317, 319–20, 322, 333
Courbet (battleship), 316
Craig, Don, 179, 185, 187
Crawford, Joan, 131
Crete, 21, 74
Cunningham, Andrew, 69, 292, 318, 330–31, 336, 366
Curteis, Alban, 71
Czechoslovakia, 10–11

D
Dabner, Esmond, 222–24
Daily Express, 131, 388
Daniel, Danny, 359, 379
Danzig, 11
Dark, Philip, 102
Davis, Robert, 167, 232
Defence Committee, 127
Denham, Henry, 22, 133–34, 140, 150, 332
Denmark Strait, 19, 22, 25–26, 32, 69
Denning, Norman, 149, 153, 159
Denny, Michael, 319–22, 326, 328, 330
Deutschland (battleship), 15
Dogger Bank, 13
Dönitz, Emil, 210
Dönitz, Karl, 96, 210–17, 219–21, 296, 298, 301–2, 304, 308, 337, 362–63, 366, 369

Dornier 24 hospital plane, 158
Dortmund-Ems canal, 346, 367
Dover Hill (cargo ship), 293
Dowding, John, 151–52
Dreadnoughts, 13
Drennan, Robert, 326
Duff, Arthur, 258
Dunkirk, 74, 230
Dunworth, A. G., 82
Durrant, Tom, 103–4
Düwel, Paul, 196, 199
Dyce, 364

E
Eastern Fleet, 332, 336, 338
Eastern Front, 5, 50–51, 191, 214–15, 263, 291, 321
Easy Elsie, 372
Eden, Anthony, 131, 218, 294
Eder dam, 316
Edøy, 180
Ehrenfriedhof cemetery, 391
Ehrler, Heinrich, 374, 392
Eichler, Fregattenkapitän, 328
Eisenhower, General, 336, 340
Eisteufel (Ice Devil) submarine group, 153
Ekonomiya, 293
Elbe River, 52, 65, 210
El Capitan (freighter), 145
Ellis, Robert, 20
Emerson, H. R., 325
Empire Byron (merchantman), 156–57
Enigma, 65–66, 77, 80, 314
Evans, Bob, 179, 181, 185–87, 189
Evill, Douglas, 338–39
Experimental Diving Unit, 167
Experimental Submarine Flotilla, 169

F
FAA. See Fleet Air Arm
Faettenfjord, 44, 53–54, 56, 63, 66, 73, 87, 105, 107, 109–10, 113–18, 173–74, 176, 179–80, 186, 191, 193, 195, 197, 203, 228, 276, 369
Fairbanks, Douglas, Jr., 131–32, 140, 152, 159
Fairey Albacore torpedo planes, 74
Fane, A. F. P., 43–44, 54, 110–14
Faroe Islands, 22, 255
Fassbender, Alfred, 381
Fegen, Edward, 356

Feie (cutter), 59–61
Fell, William "Tiny," 166–67
Finland, 62, 217, 352, 357, 362, 373
Finnmark, 217
Fireflies, 364
First World War, 47–48, 94, 126, 164–65
Firth of Forth, 70
Fleet Air Arm (FAA), 16, 34, 37, 42, 54, 65, 74,
     76, 88, 295, 314, 316–18, 323, 333–34, 336,
     338, 350, 364, 393–94
Fleet Air Squadrons,
     817 Squadron, 74, 81, 83–85
     818 Squadron, 34, 36
     827 Squadron (8 Wing), 318–19, 322–23
     828 Squadron, 333
     829 Squadron (52 Wing), 318–19, 326–27
     830 Squadron (8 Wing), 318–19, 322–23,
          325–26
     831 Squadron (52 Wing), 318–19, 326, 330
     832 Squadron, 74, 81–82, 85
Flensburg, 114
Flesch, Gerhard, 56, 61–63, 189
Flying Fortresses, 315
Focke-Wulf aircraft, 33, 72, 90, 128–29, 374
Forbes, C., 120–22
Force H, 31, 33
Force One, 300, 302, 304, 306–7, 320
Force Two, 300, 320–21
Foreign Office, 15
Foresight (destroyer escort), 127
Forester (destroyer escort), 127
Fort Blockhouse (Gosport), 169
Franklin, A. E., 40–41
Fraser, Alexander, 281
Fraser, Bruce, 296–99, 301–2, 304–6, 318,
     320–21, 331–32
Freikorps, 216
Friedrich Eckholt (destroyer), 205
Friedrich Ihn (destroyer), 66, 73, 78–79, 81, 85
Friend, Charles, 34, 74–76, 81, 83–84, 86
Frosta peninsula, 186
Frøya, 173–74, 176
Fulmar fighters, 30, 74

G
Gay, Len, 235, 237–38
Gdynia, 24, 47, 52
George VI, King, 131, 330, 388
German Destroyer Flotilla, 301

German destroyers,
     Z-25, 66, 73, 78
     Z29, 223, 263
     Z31, 263
     Z33, 223
German Embassy (London), 15
German Military Intelligence, 11, 138
German Naval Staff, 66
German navy, 10, 13, 21, 159, 186, 205, 208–9,
     216, 221, 339, 358
German Submarine Flotillas, 96
Gestapo, 56–59, 62, 189, 250, 312, 386, 396
Gibraltar, 31, 95, 166, 230
Gibson, Guy, 343, 346, 368, 395
Giersch, Eric, 380
Giffen, Robert C., 131, 134
Gingles, Paddy, 379
Gneisenau (battle cruiser), 14–15, 21, 23–24,
     50, 52, 65, 91
Goddard, Edmund, 248, 264–65, 277, 280, 284
Golovko, Arseni, 297–98, 316
Goodall, Stanley, 329
Goodman, Lawrence "Benny," 348, 371
Göring, Hermann, 209
Gosport, 76, 169, 394
Goss, George, 174
Gotenhafen (Gdynia), 24, 47, 52
Gousev, Fyodor, 294
Graf Zeppelin (aircraft carrier), 15, 136, 214
Grande, Ivan, 63
Gran, Joe, 360
Great Shelford (Cambridge), 114
Greenland, 19–20, 25
Grille (German state yacht), 13
Grogan, Jack, 175
Grønn, Arne, 61
Grønn, Birger, 63–64, 174, 178
Guglielmotti (U-boat), 234
Gulf of Bothnia, 47, 352
Gunga Din (film), 131
Gunn, Sandy, 111
Gdynia. *See* Gotenhafen

H
Haakøy, 364, 369, 378–79, 384, 386, 396
Haida (destroyer), 300
Halifax (aircraft), 55–56, 108–9, 112, 114–20,
     122–23, 173, 344
Halifax (Nova Scotia), 356

Hamburg, 13
Hamilton, Louis "Turtle," 134–35, 142–43, 145,
    148–49, 152, 159
Hammerfest, 382
Hampden (aircraft), 55
Hamschmidt, Ewald, 381–82
Härer, Walter, 373–74, 381–82
Harriman, Averell, 21, 28
Harris, Arthur "Bomber," 56, 109, 227–28, 315,
    338–40, 347, 350–51, 365, 387, 395
Harte, Harry, 260
Hassell, Ilse von, 10
Hassell, Ulrich von, 12
Hassel, Magne, 64–65
Hatston, 318
Hegendorf (seaman), 4
Heine, Heinrich, 313
Heinkels, 54, 76, 128, 144–45, 158
Hela (light cruiser), 165
Helgesen, Herbert, 174, 178
Heligoland, 165
Hellcats, 317, 319, 323, 327, 333
Hellendoorn, Hein, 202, 279, 370, 373–74,
    383–84, 397
Henderson, Ian, 103
Henty-Creer, Henry, 244–46, 249, 252, 262,
    273, 285
Herbert, Godfrey, 165
Hermann Schoemann (destroyer), 66, 73, 127
Herrold, John, 323–25
Hestvik, 182–83
Hewitt, Ian, 110, 119, 121–22
Heyford biplane, 344
Highland Light Infantry, 175
Hill, Tony, 44, 112, 143
Hintze, Fritz, 301, 303, 306, 308–9
Hirden, 189
Hitler, Adolf, 9–14, 23–24, 44, 49–51, 54,
    65, 70, 72, 90–91, 125, 132, 136, 139–40,
    154–55, 176, 195, 200, 202–5, 207–16, 246,
    290, 295–96, 298, 308, 311, 321, 362–63,
    387–88, 394
Hitra island, 182
HMS Achates (destroyer), 205
HMS Anson (battleship), 320, 328
HMS Ark Royal (aircraft carrier), 31, 33–36,
    39–40, 75
HMS Ashanti (destroyer), 128
HMS Belfast (cruiser), 70, 296, 302–4, 306

HMS Berwick (cruiser), 71
HMS Bluebell (anti-submarine corvette),
    230–31
HMS Bramble (minesweeper), 205
HMS Campbeltown (destroyer) (formerly USS
    Buchanan), 92–100, 104
HMS Conqueror (submarine), 165
HMS Cumberland (cruiser), 134
HMS Dolphin (shore establishment), 231, 394
HMS Dorsetshire (heavy cruiser), 31, 34, 40–41
HMS Duke of York (battleship), 71, 134, 296–
    97, 299–300, 302, 304–8, 320, 333
HMS E9 (submarine), 165
HMS Eclipse (destroyer), 127
HMS Edinburgh (cruiser), 127, 135
HMS Effingham (light cruiser), 299
HMS Emperor (escort carrier), 317, 320
HMS Faulknor (destroyer), 233
HMS Fencer (aircraft carrier), 317, 320
HMS Formidable (aircraft carrier), 333
HMS Furious (aircraft carrier), 317–20, 322,
    327, 330, 333
HMS Garland (destroyer), 128
HMS Glorious (aircraft carrier), 263
HMS Hood (battle cruiser), 22, 25–29, 42, 49,
    69
HMS Howe (battleship), 174–75
HMS Implacable (aircraft carrier), 364
HMS Impulsive (destroyer), 300
HMS Indefatigable (aircraft carrier), 333
HMS Jamaica (light cruiser), 204–5, 296, 300,
    302, 305, 307
HMS Kenya (cruiser), 71
HMS Keppel (destroyer), 134, 141, 151–52
HMS King George V (battleship), 16, 22, 28, 31,
    33, 40–41, 46, 71, 73, 92
HMS London (cruiser), 134
HMS Magpie (anti-submarine sloop), 68
HMS Maori (destroyer), 41
HMS Nabob (aircraft carrier), 333
HMS Nelson (battleship), 179
HMS Newcastle (cruiser), 234
HMS Nigeria (cruiser), 134
HMS Norfolk (cruiser), 19, 22, 26, 28, 30, 134,
    296, 302–3, 305–6
HMS Offa (destroyer), 71, 161
HMS Onslaught (destroyer), 300
HMS Onslow (destroyer), 205, 300
HMS Oribi (destroyer), 71

HMS *Orwell* (destroyer), 300

HMS *Prince of Wales* (battleship), 22, 26–27, 29–30, 32, 45–46, 69, 87

HMS *Pursuer* (escort carrier), 317, 320

HMS *Renown* (battle cruiser), 31, 34, 71

HMS *Repulse* (battle cruiser), 28, 46, 87

HMS *Rodney* (battleship), 33, 40

HMS *Saumarez* (destroyer), 296, 306–7

HMS *Savage* (destroyer), 296, 306–7

HMS *Sceptre* (towing submarine), 273

HMS *Scorpion* (destroyer), 296, 306

HMS *Scourge* (destroyer), 300

HMS *Sea Nymph* (towing submarine), 258, 261

HMS *Searcher* (escort carrier), 317, 320

HMS *Seawolf* (submarine), 73, 128

HMS *Sheffield* (light cruiser), 31, 34–35, 37, 40, 204–5, 296, 302–4

HMS *Stubborn* (towing submarine), 257–58, 266–67, 273, 289

HMS *Sturgeon* (submarine), 234

HMS *Suffolk* (heavy cruiser), 19, 22, 25–27, 30

HMS *Syrtis* (towing submarine), 256, 259–60

HMS *Titania* (depot ship), 172, 174–75, 252

HMS *Trident* (submarine), 66, 73, 166

HMS *Trinidad* (cruiser), 127, 135

HMS *Truculent* (towing submarine), 253, 264–65

HMS *Trumpeter* (aircraft carrier), 333

HMS *Tuna* (submarine), 247

HMS *Una* (submarine), 234

HMS *Unbeaten* (submarine), 234

HMS *Unshaken* (submarine), 155

HMS *Urge* (submarine), 234

HMS *Valiant* (battleship), 164

HMS *Varbel* (Kyles Hydro, Bute), 241, 243, 248

HMS *Victorious* (aircraft carrier), 22, 30–31, 39, 71, 74, 77, 79–81, 86–87, 134, 155, 317–21, 326–28

HMS *Victory*, 235

HMS *Zulu* (destroyer), 40

Holden, George, 346

Holland, Lancelot, 22, 25–26, 29, 69

Hollett, George, 260

Holt, Paul, 131

Holtenau, 52

Home Fleet, 17, 22–23, 25, 28, 30, 34, 45–46, 68–69, 71, 79–81, 87, 90–91, 130, 135, 137– 38, 154–55, 220, 225, 251, 292, 296–97, 299, 318, 331–33, 364, 392

Hommelvik, 113

Horsea Lake, 163, 165, 167

Horton, Max, 164–65, 169, 179–80

Howard, Christopher, 368

Howard, Leslie, 244

Howarth, David, 176–77, 179

Hudspeth, Ken, 249, 262, 273–74, 289

Huffmeier, Friedrich, 220

Hunter, Hugh de Graff, 35

Huron (destroyer), 300

Hurricanes, 340

Hvalfjord, 19, 140

I

Iceland, 19, 22, 25, 45, 51, 71–72, 80, 135, 137– 38, 176, 213, 218, 295–96, 298–99

Indian Ocean, 46, 52

Ingram, D. C., 244

Iroquois (destroyer), 300

Isafjordur, 19

Isle of Bute, 235, 238, 241, 247

Isle of Lewis, 169

Ismay, Hastings "Pug," 21, 28

Isnestoften, 312–13

Italy, Italians, 76, 164, 166, 234, 295, 314, 323, 344

Ivan Kalyaev (paddle steamer), 354

Iveson, Tony, 335, 343–44, 348, 351–53, 355, 368, 371, 375–77, 395

Izhora (cargo ship), 78–79

J

Jacob, Ian, 45

Jacobsen, Terje, 250, 312–14, 396–98

Jade Bay, 9, 12

Jagdeschwader 5 fighter wing, 373, 392

Jan Mayen Island, 72, 133–34, 142, 250, 396

Japan, 44–46, 76, 87–88, 213, 242

Jellicoe, Lord, 14

Jervis Bay (merchant cruiser), 356

Johansen, Einar, 250

Johansen, Torbjørn, 249–50

Johnson, Johnnie, 343

Johnson, Stan, 224

Joint Planning Staff, 337

Jones, Mervyn, 114

Joubert de la Ferté, Philip, 114

Junge, Wolf, 279, 328, 361, 363, 370, 373
Junkers aircraft, 210
  Ju87, 54
  Ju88, 54 127–28, 144, 299
Jupp, Martin, 256, 259
Jutland, 13–14

K
K-21 (Russian submarine), 155
Kaafjord, 191, 217, 220, 246, 249–50, 252, 262, 265, 267, 270–72, 274, 276, 281, 288, 290, 296, 298, 312–14, 316–18, 323, 325, 327, 332–33, 336, 339, 349, 351, 355–56, 360, 362, 364–65, 369, 377
Kalve, Johannes, 177, 180–81, 184, 187
Kearon, Edward, 260
Keitel, Field Marshal, 189, 209
Kendall, Richard, 248, 264–65, 270, 280–81, 284
Kent, Duke of, 131
Kenyon, William, 158
Kerr, Jock, 175
Kharkov, 295
Kiel, 45, 55, 72, 80–81, 87, 139–40, 148, 155, 203, 289, 302, 304, 344
Kiel Canal, 52, 340
Kiel mutiny (1918), 196
Kiel Naval College, 13
Kimmins, Anthony, 322
King, Ernest, 126, 169
King George V (KGV) class, 16, 46, 174
Kinloss, 109, 116, 369
Knights, Bobby, 346, 379–80
Knilans, Nick, 353
Kola Inlet, 218, 297
Köln (light cruiser), 215
Kon-Tiki expedition (1946), 396
Korean War, 394
Krancke, Vizeadmiral, 140
Kriegsmarine, 13, 16, 21, 49, 66, 72, 77, 89, 91, 95, 98, 132, 148–49, 176, 189, 196, 200, 204–5, 208–9, 213, 297–98, 365
Kristallnacht, 212
Kristiansund, 117, 180, 184
Kronstadt, 47
Kummetz, Oskar, 140, 204–5, 207, 215, 217, 221, 263–64, 271, 276–77, 284, 296, 301
Kursk, 295

Kyles Hydropathic Hotel (Bute), 235, 241

L
Laites, "Taffy," 235, 237–38
Lake Erisort, 169–70, 172
Lancaster (aircraft), 2, 108, 110, 113, 115, 117, 122, 335, 341–42, 345, 348, 350–54, 357–60, 367–68, 370–73, 375–77, 379–82, 386, 388, 394
Land Spider (agent), 137–38
Langefjord, 262, 301
La Pallice, 55, 342
Larsen, Leif, 59–61, 176–90, 228, 395
Lawford, E. D. W., 141
Leach, John, 26–27, 32, 69
Le Croisic, 97
Lee, Bunny, 379–80
Leeming (North Yorkshire), 109
Leine, Herbert, 279–80
Leipzig (light cruiser), 215
Lend-Lease agreement, 33
Lerwick, 59, 61
Leuchars, 190
Levanger, 56, 62
Levy, Frank, 357, 366
Liberators, 351–52
Lincolnshire Echo, 394
Lindemann, Ernst, 24–25, 32
Linton-on-Ouse (North Yorkshire), 109, 344
Liverpool, 230–31, 320
Loch Cairnbawn, 246, 252, 264, 285
Loch Eriboll, 318
Loch Erne, 33
Loch Ewe, 295–96, 299, 320
Loch Striven, 234–36, 241, 243, 259, 316
Locke, David, 244
Lofjord, 113, 116, 120, 188, 203
Lofoten Islands, 50, 81–82, 142
Loire River, 29, 89, 92, 95–96, 103
Lorient, 342
Lorimer, John, 232–38, 240, 244, 247–48, 251, 264–65, 270–71, 277, 280–81, 284–85
Lossiemouth, 56, 109, 350–51, 369
Lucas, Bill, 82–84, 86
Ludwig, Herbert, 197, 201–2
Luftwaffe, 22, 51, 65, 70, 72, 74, 76, 87, 130, 139, 141, 143, 154, 168, 208–9, 213, 219, 295, 299, 314, 373, 392

Lund, Tobias, 64
Lunna Voe, 61, 176, 179–80, 203
Lütjens, Günther, 24–25, 27, 29–31, 40, 65, 90, 212
Lützow (pocket battleship), 132, 139–40, 142, 148, 204–5, 215, 217, 249, 252, 262, 275, 277, 295, 314

M

MacArthur, John, 355–56, 360
MacIntyre, Don, 119, 121–22
Mackintosh, L. D., 364
Maisky, Ivan, 218
Malaya, 46
Malcolm, Alastair, 285
Maleme, 22
Malta, 130, 211, 344
Mark I Human Torpedo ("Cassidy" code name), 164, 166–68, 169
Marseilles, 48
Martin, Harold "Mick," 346, 395
Martin, Terry, 249
McCarthy, Joe, 348
McFarlane, Brian "Digger," 248, 258, 260–62
McGregor, John, 265
McMullen, Colin, 352–53, 355
Mecke, Karl-Conrad, 97–98
Medmenham, 388, 398
Melrose, James, 359, 375
Mers-el-Kebir, 21, 75
Messerschmidts, 111, 373
  Me 109s, 110–11, 117, 214
  Me 110s, 110
Mettegang, Ludwig, 2–3, 7
Meyer, Hans, 216, 263, 279, 284–85, 301, 324, 328, 361, 370
MGB. *See* motor gunboat
MI5, 137–38
Middleton St George (County Durham), 109
Miller, John "Dusty," 38–39
Miller, Tommy, 81–82
Milltown, 369, 371, 375
Mitchell, L. H., 177
Moffat, John "Jock," 36–41
Möhne dam, 316
Monte Rosa (troopship), 313
Moore, Henry, 150, 318–20, 328, 330–33, 364
Moravia, 62
Moray Firth, 375

Morpurgo, J. E., 340
Morse code, 64, 76, 98, 353
Mortiboys, Ralph, 252, 285
Moscow, 68, 291–92, 294, 355, 362
Mosjøen, 381
Moskenes Strait, 82
Mosquitoes, 316, 336, 338, 351, 355, 360, 364, 368, 374–75, 388
  Mark IV, 316
Motig 1 (fishing boat), 59
motor gunboat (MGB), 94, 96, 98–99
motor torpedo boat (MTB), 94, 98–99
Mountbatten, Louis, 91, 93, 132, 227
MTB. *See* motor torpedo boat
Müller, Willi, 373
Mullins, Patrick, 28
Munro, Les, 348
Münster, 367
Murmansk, 51, 71, 86, 127–28, 135, 140, 155, 204–5, 218, 251, 292, 295–97, 340, 349
Murrow, Ed, 388
Mutt (agent), 137–38

N

Narvik, 50, 79, 81–82, 87, 133, 140, 142, 148, 153, 174, 176, 179, 202, 249, 252, 295
Naval Group Command West, 31
Naval Group North, 72, 81, 139–40, 148–50, 153, 210, 304
Naval Intelligence, 59, 98, 123, 329
Navarino (merchantman), 145
Nazi Party, 62, 212
Nazis, 10, 48, 62, 131, 200, 211–12, 312–13, 374, 392
Nelson (battleship), 179
Nelson, Tom, 78, 160, 285
Neumark (repair ship), 313
Newman, Charles "Charlie," 92–94, 96, 101
Nielsen, E. S., 173–74
Niemöller, Martin, 48
Night of the Long Knives (1934), 212
Nordmark (supply ship), 276
Normandie dock, 90–92, 94, 96, 100–1, 104
Normandy landings, 332, 336, 345
North Africa, 214, 295
North Atlantic, 21, 30, 74, 91, 204, 219, 259, 314, 393
North Cape, 51, 140, 155, 217, 220, 304
Northern Ireland, 33

Northern Task Force, 217
North Sea, 52, 217, 238, 337, 367
Norway, 21, 43, 49–52, 54, 58–59, 61, 65–66,
     70, 74, 80, 110, 126, 128, 130, 132–33, 135,
     139–40, 142, 147–48, 173, 180, 190, 194–
     95, 197, 200, 207, 209, 213–17, 233, 241,
     255, 304, 362–63, 367, 374–75, 392, 397
Norwegian Military Academy, 58
Norwegian Naval Independent Unit, 59
Norwegian Nazi Party, 57
Norwegian resistance, 59, 173, 271
Norwegians, 57, 121, 176, 178–81, 183, 187,
     190, 195–96, 198, 223–24, 311, 388, 395
Norwegian Sea, 24, 72
Nuremberg, 11, 367

O
Oakley, John, 258, 261
O'Brien, Bill, 161
Oerlikon anti-aircraft cannon, 96, 222, 300
OIC. See Operational Intelligence Centre
Olav, Crown Prince, 388
Oliver, Vic, 21
Olivier, Laurence, 244
Onega, 353
Onslow, Dickie, 128
Operational Intelligence Centre (OIC), 78, 80
Operation Brawn, 332
Operation Catechism, 375
Operation Goodwood, 333, 336
Operation Mascot, 332
Operation Obviate, 368, 370, 374–75
Operation Oiled (1941), 55
Operation Paravane, 349, 375
Operation Servant, 316
Operation Source, 249, 252, 290
Operation Tiger Claw, 332
Operation Title, 174, 176, 180
Operation Tungsten, 317–18, 320–21, 331–32,
     361
Orkneys, 11, 318, 330, 375
Ormann, Leutnant, 184
Oslo, 58, 64, 189, 392
Oxley, Bill, 265

P
Pacific, 44, 52, 213, 338–39
Paint Research Station, Teddington
     (Middlesex), 74

Palomares (anti-aircraft ship), 141
Paris, 31, 387
Pas-de-Calais, 342, 348
Pathfinder Force, 118, 122
PBY Catalina (seaplane), 33
Pearl Harbor, 46
Perry, Dave, 121–22
Persian Gulf, 68
Peters, Rudolf, 363
Pettersen, Harry, 250
Petwood, 349, 368, 388
Philip, Peter "Uncle Peter," 241, 257, 266–67
Photographic Reconnaissance Unit (PRU),
     44, 56, 110, 112, 114, 117, 179, 203, 249,
     251–52, 262, 288–89, 351, 355, 360, 388
     B Flight, 114
     C Flight, 44, 110, 114
Pike, F. C., 98
Place, Godfrey, 234, 238, 248, 262, 266, 273–75,
     278, 281–83, 285, 394
Placentia Bay (Newfoundland), 45
Plan Tarantula, 137
Plan Z, 14
Plugge, Peter, 83
Pointe de Gildas, 97
Poland, 11, 62, 210, 212
Polarkoller (polar fever), 196
Portal, Charles, 338
Port Bannatyne (Bute), 235, 264
Portsmouth, 163, 169–70, 229, 231, 233–35,
     238, 242, 252, 264, 343
Posen (aka Pozna'n), 61
Pound, Dudley, 17, 21, 41, 45–46, 68–69, 87,
     91, 116, 126–27, 130, 134–36, 147–51,
     153–54, 159–60, 227–28, 292
Powell, Michael, 244
Pozarica (anti-aircraft ship), 141, 144, 152, 156
Pressburger, Emeric, 244
Price, Cyril, 333–34
Prinz Eugen (heavy cruiser), 14, 24–26, 30, 52,
     65–66, 73, 83, 113, 116, 120, 134, 166, 314
PRU. See Photographic Reconnaissance Unit
"P Tube," 75

Q
QUADRANT meeting (1943), 292
Queen Elizabeth, 164
Quisling, Vidkun, 57, 189, 195

R

Raaby, Torstein, 250–51, 332, 396

Rae, David, 224

Raeder, Erich, 10, 12–16, 23–24, 46, 49–51, 72, 74, 90, 132, 136, 139–40, 154–55, 176, 196, 200, 207–15, 217

RAF Coastal Command, 23, 32–33, 107, 114, 117, 316

RAF Waddington, 345, 359

Raikes, Dick, 73, 128–29

Rance, V., 327

Rasmussen, Karl, 250–51

Rastenburg, 208, 213

Red Army, 125, 295

Rendsburg, 52

Reykjavik, 140

Rheinübung (Rhine Exercise), 23–24

Rhine Exercise (1941). *See* Rheinübung

Richards, Julian, 299–300, 308

Richardson, Hubert, 327

Riis, Ib Arnason ("Cobweb"), 138

Rimington, John, 156–57

Rinnan, Henry, 62

River Afton (merchantman), 151

Robert Ley (cruise ship), 12

Robertson, I. G., 325

Roderick, Johnny, 99

Rohwedder, Karl, 326

Rohwedder, Klaus, 192, 370, 383, 385, 392, 397

Roosevelt, Franklin Delano, 21, 33, 45, 51, 126–27, 131, 219–20, 291–92, 294, 387

Rørholt, Bjørn "Rolf Christiansen," 58–61, 63–66, 177–78, 396

Rørholt network, 174

Roskill, Stephen, 130, 153–54, 160, 308

Rösselsprung (Knight's Move), 140

Royal Air Force (RAF), 16, 22–23, 32, 50, 55–56, 65, 74, 90, 107, 126, 147, 155, 168, 219, 227, 248, 251, 271, 311, 315–16, 334, 336, 343, 345–46, 351–56, 359, 369, 371, 387–88, 392–95, 398

Royal Australian Air Force, 380,

Royal Navy, 14–16, 23, 28, 44, 51, 72, 123, 149, 161, 165, 169, 174, 196, 209, 233, 242, 291, 300, 338–39

Royal Navy Reserve, 233

Roy, Donald, 100

Ruhr, 220, 228, 367

Rushbrook, Edmund, 329

Russell, Guy, 300

Russian Front, 191, 208

Ryder, Robert, 91, 96–98

S

Saltøya, 53, 198

Saunders, John, 379

Sayers, John, 380

Scapa Flow, 22, 44, 65, 71, 87, 130, 135, 137–38, 298, 330

Scharnhorst (battle cruiser), 12, 14–15, 21, 23–24, 50, 55, 65, 91, 116, 215, 217, 220–21, 246, 249, 262–63, 273–74, 277, 296–99, 301–8, 311, 393

Scheer (pocket battleship), 120, 132, 139–40, 142, 148, 314

Scheinwerfer, Der (*The Searchlight*), 48, 192

Schlegel, Georg, 49, 53, 361,

Schlesien (battleship), 47, 215

Schleswig-Holstein (battleship), 215

Schmundt, Admiral, 153

Schniewind, Otto, 132, 139–40, 155–56, 215, 304

Schulze, Kurt, 392

Scotland, 53, 55–56, 107, 109–10, 112, 114–15, 119, 122, 169, 172, 174, 190, 213, 221, 232, 277, 287, 290, 316, 318, 339, 350, 366, 369–70, 386

Seafires, 333

Secret Intelligence Service (SIS), 58

Shannon, Dave, 348

Shean, Maxwell, 229–31, 235, 240–47, 249, 259–60

Sherbrooke, Captain, 205

Shetland Islands, 22, 255, 290, 339, 374–75

Siebe, Gorman (diving equipment manufacturers), 167, 232

Singapore, 46

Skitten, 316

Skylark-A (Oslo), 58

Skylark-B (Trondheim), 58

Sladen, Geoffrey "Slasher," 166–67, 169, 172,

Slessor, Sir John, 316

Smalley, Chris, 100

Smart, Jack, 258

Smith, Bill, 68

Smith, Leonard B., 33

"Snoopy Joe," 141, 156

Sohler, Herbert, 96

Sokol (submarine), 234
Somerville, James "Slim," 31, 33–36
Sommer, Walter, 385
Sørli, Odd, 61
Sørøy, 270
Southampton, 92
   King George V Dry Dock, 92
Soviet Union, 23, 47, 51, 68, 91, 125, 134, 218,
Spartacist revolutionaries, 216
Special Operations Executive (SOE), 59,
   172–73, 176
   Technical Section, 228
Special Service Brigade, 91
Spitfire, 43, 110, 112, 114, 251–52, 262, 311
Spitsbergen 50, 220–22, 225, 227, 252, 262–63,
   393
SS *Lancastria*, 97
SS *Normandie*, 89–92, 94, 96, 100–1, 104
S-Sugar, 110, 119
Stalin, Joseph, 51, 68, 126, 159, 218, 291,
   293–95, 320, 387
Stavangerfjord (depot ship), 203
Stenning, John, 85
Stephens, Billie, 98, 101–2
Stewart-Moore, Lieutenant Commander,
   34–36
Stirling (aircraft), 55–56
Stjernøy, 273
Stjørdal, 187
St Nazaire, 29, 32, 89, 95–96, 104,
   Bassin de Penhoët, 92, 101
   Bassin de St Nazaire, 94, 96, 99
   Normandie dock, 90–92, 94, 96, 100–1, 104
Stockholm, 122, 133, 140, 173, 176, 178, 189,
   250, 332
Stord (Royal Norwegian Navy ship), 296
Storlien, 121
Stout, Geoff, 367
Strait of Dover, 65
Strand, Roald, 177, 182–83, 187
Strength through Joy cruises, 217
Stringbag, 75
Stringer, Pat, 37
Strøm, Nils, 182
Stubs, Gerhard "Lola," 62
submarines, 13–15, 41, 48, 51, 54, 57, 66, 68,
   71–73, 75, 77, 90, 94–96, 105, 115, 125, 128,
   132, 134–35, 138–42, 149, 152–53, 155,
   157, 160, 164–66, 169, 171–72, 176, 187,
   189–90, 208, 211–13, 215, 218–19, 227–28,

230–236, 238–42, 244, 246–50, 252–53,
   255, 258–262, 264, 266, 269, 271, 278–80,
   283–85, 288–90, 296, 314, 317, 320, 328,
   333, 337, 342, 366, 393. *See also* named
   submarines; Operation Source
   Davis Submarine Escape Apparatus, 231,
   236, 286
   S-class, 238, 246
   T-class, 238–39, 246
   Welman, 228
   X-Craft, 165, 229, 232, 234, 238–39, 241–
   42, 244–47, 249, 252–52, 256, 262, 270, 272,
   283, 289–90, 296, 312, 394
Sudentenland, 62
Sugden, Peter, 83, 85
Sumburgh, 374
Sunderland (flying boat), 173
Svalbard archipelago, 220
Sweden, 22, 50, 58, 107, 119–20, 122, 133, 178,
   188, 250, 314, 352, 371–72, 376, 381, 386,
   396
Swordfish, 30–31, 33–36, 38–40, 54, 74–76,
   136, 321
Syfret, Neville, 292, 331

T
Tain (Scotland), 109
Tait, Alexander, 343
Tait, James, 123
Tait, James Brian "Willie," 335, 342–49, 354–55,
   357–60, 367–69, 371–72, 374, 376–77,
   379–80, 387–89, 394–96
Tait, Peter, 123, 343–45, 347–48
Target Plan Four, 262
Tautra Island, 173, 185–86, 190
Tebb, Billy, 179, 181, 185, 187, 189
Thomas, Morgan, 238
Thompson, Alan, 318, 323, 325–26, 330
Thøring, Lars, 386
Tibbets, Nigel, 99
Tickler, Althea, 248
Tipito, 198
Tirpitz, 1–2, 5, 10, 15–16, 42, 48, 50–51, 59,
   70, 77, 107–8, 126, 134–36, 143, 147, 151,
   153–54, 174–75, 185, 195, 197, 201–203,
   208, 216–20, 225, 227, 242, 247, 263, 267,
   270, 275, 283, 301–2, 331, 337–38, 362–64,
   366, 370, 375
   aftermath, 391–96

Churchill and his plans for, 44–45, 54, 71, 88, 228, 290–92, 365, 387
  confirmation of sinking of, 386, 388–89, 393–94
  continued threat of, 72, 154, 156, 160, 349
  description of, 2, 16, 47–49, 116, 209, 288–89
  and destruction of the *Normandie* dock, 91–92, 94, 96, 100–1, 104
  destructive capabilities, 51, 80, 85, 91
  failure of second operation, 325–30
  at Faettenfjord, 44, 53, 56, 63–64, 105, 111, 113–15, 173, 179, 187, 191, 193
  final attack on, 377, 379–82, 384–89
  Harris's plan for, 228–29, 315, 338–40, 350–51, 365, 387
  journey to Faettenfjord, 52–53, 73
  launch and commissioning, 23, 49
  moved to Haakøy, 364, 369, 378–79, 384, 386, 396
  move to and time at Trondheim, 50–53, 57, 61, 66, 87, 110, 128, 132, 148–49, 166, 196, 227, 249
  and Operation Obviate, 368, 370, 374–75
  and Operation Paravane, 349, 375
  and Operation Title, 174, 176, 180
  and Operation Tungsten, 317–18, 320–21, 331–32, 361
  and Operation Source, 249, 252, 290
  out of action, 312, 314–17, 330
  plans to finish off, 133, 176, 283
  repairs to, 199, 203, 250–51, 264, 315, 332–33, 336–37, 361–63, 369–71, 373
  at sea, 23, 57, 64, 73, 77, 81, 155, 221, 324, 364
  success of, 45–46, 85, 87, 221, 223–24, 252, 279–82
  tests and trials, 82, 218, 321
  "Tirpitz Island," 198
  under Allied surveillance, 45, 64, 335–36
  unsuccessful missions against, 55–56, 73, 76, 78, 79, 81–87, 115–16, 118–20, 172, 246 123, 125, 186, 190, 262, 276–78, 282, 318–19, 321–24, 332, 357–58, 360
  visits and plans by Hitler, 90, 176, 200, 205, 215, 295–96, 311
Tirpitz, Alfred von, 10, 200
Tirpitz, Marie von, 10
Tomlinson, Tommy, 111

Tømmelholm, 270, 274, 288
Topp, Karl "Charlie," 24, 48–49, 53–54, 79, 82, 84, 86–87, 192–93, 196–200, 203–4, 209, 216, 370
Torneträsk Lake, 371, 376
Tovey, John, 22–23, 25, 28, 30–32, 34, 48, 69–71, 73–74, 77–81, 86, 130, 134–38, 143, 154–55, 159–60, 217–19, 296
Tragino, 344
Treaty of Versailles (1919), 11
Trehearne, Pat, 153
Trevethian, Leading Seaman, 175
"Tribal" ships (Canadian), 300
Tromsø, 79, 249–50, 288, 312–13, 363–66, 369–73, 375, 381–82, 385–86, 396
Trondheim, 50–51, 53, 56–66, 71, 79, 83, 87, 107–8, 110–14, 128, 132, 140, 142, 148, 166, 174, 177–78, 185–86, 189, 193–99, 203–4, 214, 217, 227, 249–50, 252, 371
  Hotel Phoenix, 62
  Institute of Technology, 58
Trondheimsfjord, 43, 53, 56–57, 63, 66, 73, 117, 173, 177–78, 180, 182–84, 193, 203
Tscholari, Freddie, 313
Turin, 344
Turner, John, 59
Turowsky, Bernhard, 201–2
Tuscaloosa (cruiser), 131, 134

U
U-boats, 14, 17, 21, 30, 33, 41, 48, 66, 70, 72, 75, 89–90, 95–96, 127, 129, 132–33, 135–36, 144, 147, 149–50, 154, 157–58, 176, 192, 204, 207, 210 , 212–15, 217–20, 222, 230, 234, 251, 258, 275, 295, 298–99, 301, 314, 320–21, 363–65, 393
  U-456, 142
  U-703, 156
  UB-68, 211
Ukraine, 215
Ultra, 77, 80–81, 87, 299
United States, 46, 91, 160, 202
US Army Air Force, 315, 353
US Navy, 33, 93, 126, 132
  Task Force, 45, 126, 130

V
Vaagsøy, 50
Vaenga, 251, 316, 371

Vaernes, 110, 114, 117
Varbel II (Loch Striven), 241
Varley, Cromwell, 241
Varley Marine, 233
Vaughan, Micky, 376
Verdal, 187
Vestfjord, 81–82, 87, 140, 148
Vickers-Armstrong, 22, 238
Vickers K guns, 76, 238
Vinnitsa, 215
Voigt, Erika "Klösel," 47–49
Voigt, Kurt, 47–49, 191, 193–96, 199–200
Völsing, Willi, 4
Vörde (Westphalia), 48

W
Wainwright (destroyer), 144
Wake-Walker, William, 32, 69
Walker, Geoffrey, 231
Wallis, Barnes, 228, 315–16, 340–41, 388
War Cabinet, 46, 160
War Cabinet Defence Committee, 71
Warren, Jim, 165, 167
Washington (battleship), 131, 134
Watkins, Harry, 380
Watson, George, 355–56, 360,
Watson, Lieutenant, 223–24
Watts, Freddie, 377, 388
Weber, Robert, 373, 382, 385
Wehrmacht, 10, 51, 197, 295
Weimar Republic, 13, 48
Welle-Strand, Erik, 58
Wellington (aircraft), 55, 97, 340
Western Approaches Command, 220
Wharton, John, 156–57
White, Leslie, 343–44

White Sea, 52, 293, 353
Whitley (aircraft), 55, 97, 344
Whitley, Willie, 238, 286–88
Whittaker, John, 327
Whittam, Bill, 285–88
Wichita (cruiser), 131, 134, 143, 152, 154
Wick, 44, 107, 110, 316
Wildcats, 317, 319, 323–24, 327, 329, 333
Wilhelmshaven, 10–14, 55, 65, 199, 204, 296
William Hooper (cargo ship), 145
Williams, Bill, 327
Williams, Dickie, 325
Wilson, John, 173, 176
Wilson, Ron, 119
Wilson, "Willie," 253, 265–66
Winn, Godfrey, 141, 144, 156
Wizernes, 348
Wolfschanze (East Prussia), 50, 208, 213, 298
Woodhall Spa, 113, 335, 349, 351, 370, 388–89, 394
Worthy, "Geordie," 175
Woytschekowski-Emden, Rolf, 283, 285
Wyness, Drew, 367–68

X
X-Craft, 165, 229, 232, 234, 238–39, 241–42, 244–47, 249, 252–52, 256, 262, 270, 272, 283, 289–90, 296, 312, 394. See also Operation Source

Y
Yagodnik, 349–51, 353–54, 360, 371
Yak fighters, 295

Z
Zuba, Alfred, 1–7, 386